TRAVEL AND DRAMA IN EARLY MODERN ENGLAND

The Journeying

CW01498867

EDITED BY

CLAIRE JOW

University of East Angua

DAVID McINNIS

University of Melbourne

CAMBRIDGE
UNIVERSITY PRESS

CAMBRIDGE
UNIVERSITY PRESS

University Printing House, Cambridge CB2 8BS, United Kingdom

One Liberty Plaza, 20th Floor, New York, NY 10006, USA

477 Williamstown Road, Port Melbourne, VIC 3207, Australia

314–321, 3rd Floor, Plot 3, Splendor Forum, Jasola District Centre, New Delhi – 110025, India

79 Anson Road, #06-04/06, Singapore 079906

Cambridge University Press is part of the University of Cambridge.

It furthers the University's mission by disseminating knowledge in the pursuit of education, learning, and research at the highest international levels of excellence.

www.cambridge.org

Information on this title: www.cambridge.org/9781108471183

DOI: 10.1017/9781108557771

© Cambridge University Press 2018

This publication is in copyright. Subject to statutory exception and to the provisions of relevant collective licensing agreements, no reproduction of any part may take place without the written permission of Cambridge University Press.

First published 2018

Printed and bound in Great Britain by Clays Ltd. Elcograph S.p.A.

A catalogue record for this publication is available from the British Library.

ISBN 978-1-108-47118-3 Hardback

Cambridge University Press has no responsibility for the persistence or accuracy of URLs for external or third-party internet websites referred to in this publication and does not guarantee that any content on such websites is, or will remain, accurate or appropriate.

TRAVEL AND DRAMA IN EARLY MODERN ENGLAND

This agenda-setting volume on travel and drama in early modern England provides new insights into Renaissance stage practice, performance history, and theatre's transnational exchanges. It advances our understanding of theatre history, drama's generic conventions, and what constitutes plays about travel at a time when the professional theatre was rapidly developing and England was attempting to announce its presence within a global economy. Recent critical studies have shown that the reach of early modern travel was global in scope, and its cultural consequences more important than narratives that are dominated by the Atlantic world suggest. This collection of essays by world-leading scholars redefines the field by expanding the canon of recognised plays concerned with travel. Reassessing the parameters of the genre, the chapters offer fresh perspectives on how these plays communicated with their audiences and readers.

CLAIRE JOWITT is Associate Dean for Research in Arts and Humanities and Professor of English and History at the University of East Anglia. She is the author of *Voyage Drama and Gender Politics, 1589–1642* (2003) and *The Culture of Piracy: English Literature and Seaborne Crime 1580–1630* (2010).

DAVID McINNIS is the Gerry Higgins Senior Lecturer in Shakespeare Studies at the University of Melbourne. He is author of *Mind-Travelling and Voyage Drama in Early Modern England* (2013) and co-editor (with Matthew Steggle) of *Lost Plays in Shakespeare's England* (2014).

Contents

Figure

Contributors

The Editors

Claire Jowitt is Associate Dean for Research in Arts and Humanities at the University of East Anglia, where she is also Professor of English and History. She is the author of *Voyage Drama and Gender Politics, 1589–1642* (2003) and *The Culture of Piracy: English Literature and Seaborne Crime 1580–1630* (2010). Her edited volumes include *Pirates? The Politics of Plunder, 1550–1650* (2006); with Daniel Carey, *Richard Hakluyt and Travel Writing in Early Modern Europe* (2012); with Estelle Paranque and Nate Probasco, *Colonization, Piracy and Trade in Early Modern Europe* (2017). She is General Editor, with Daniel Carey, of the forthcoming edition of Richard Hakluyt's *The Principal Navigations* (1598–1600). She is currently co-editing *The Routledge Handbook to Marine and Maritime Worlds 1400–1800* and *The New Handbook to Hakluyt*, and is writing a monograph on the figure of the early modern sea captain.

David McInnis is the Gerry Higgins Senior Lecturer in Shakespeare Studies at the University of Melbourne. He is author of *Mind-Travelling and Voyage Drama in Early Modern England* (2013) and co-editor (with Matthew Steggle) of *Lost Plays in Shakespeare's England* (2014). He is currently preparing a second co-edited collection and a monograph on lost plays, and is editing Thomas Dekker's *Old Fortunatus* for the Revels Plays series and Dekker's *If This Be Not a Good Play, the Devil Is in It* for Jeremy Lopez's new *Routledge Anthology of Early Modern Drama*. His essays have been published in journals including *Review of English Studies*; *Medieval and Renaissance Drama in England*; *Studies in English Literature, 1500–1900*; and *Notes & Queries*. With Roslyn L. Knutson and Matthew Steggle, he is founder and co-editor of the *Lost Plays Database*.

The Contributors

Richmond Barbour is Professor of English Literature at Oregon State University. His research engages the cultural economies of manuscript, print, and theatre in early modern drama, travel writing, and maritime and corporate history. He has published articles and chapters on Ben Jonson, William Shakespeare, and English travellers in the Levant, Yemen, Java, and India. His two books are Before *Orientalism: London's Theatre of the East, 1576–1626* (Cambridge University Press, 2003) and *The Third Voyage Journals: Writing and Performance in the London East India Company, 1607-10* (2009). He is preparing a scholarly edition of Capt. John Saris's 1611–14 East India Company journal and completing a book on the Company's founding generation.

Emily C. Bartels is Professor of English at Rutgers University and Director of the Middlebury Bread Loaf School of English. Her publications include *Speaking of the Moor: From Alcazar to Othello* (2008), and *Spectacles of Strangeness: Imperialism, Alienation, and Marlowe* (1993), which won the Roma Gill Prize for best work on Christopher Marlowe, 1993–94.

Andrew Gordon is Senior Lecturer in Renaissance Literature at the University of Aberdeen. His work on urban space, community, material textuality, and manuscript culture has appeared in such journals as *English Literary Renaissance, Journal of Medieval & Early Modern Studies,* and *Renaissance Quarterly* as well as in numerous collections. He is the author of *Writing Early Modern London: Memory, Text and Community* (2013) and has co-edited several collections including (with James Daybell) *Cultures of Correspondence in Early Modern Britain* (2016) and *Women and Epistolary Agency in Early Modern Culture* (2016), (with Thomas Rist) *The Arts of Remembrance in Early Modern England* (2013), and (with Bernhard Klein) *Literature, Mapping and the Politics of Space in Early Modern Britain* (Cambridge University Press, 2001, 2011). His current book project explores Renaissance culture of the foot.

Bernhard Klein is Professor of English at the University of Kent. He is the author of two monographs, *Maps and the Writing of Space in Early Modern England and Ireland* (2001) and *On the Uses of History in Recent Irish Writing* (2007). He has published many articles and book chapters, and edited or co-edited five essay collections. He has most recently written on early modern maritime culture in relation to the works of Shakespeare, 'Luis vaz de Camões, and Michael Drayton. He is a member of the Hakluyt Editorial Project (www.hakluyt.org), and was general coordinator of the EU-funded Erasmus Mundus Joint Doctoral programme TEEME – Text and Event in Early Modern Europe (2011–18; www.teemeurope.eu).

Clare McManus is Professor of Early Modern Literature and Theatre at the University of Roehampton, London. Her research challenges women's exclusion from early modern English theatre: her first book was *Women on the Renaissance Stage: Anna of Denmark and Female Masquing in the Stuart Court (1590–1619)* (2002). With the National Maritime Museum, Greenwich, she supervised an investigation into Inigo Jones's Queen's House and European queenship, and ran a major international conference at the Queen's House on Renaissance women's performance and the dramatic canon, essays from which appear in a special issue of *Shakespeare Bulletin*, 33.1 (2015), co-edited with Lucy Munro. She edited John Fletcher's *The Island Princess* (2013) and Shakespeare's *Othello* (2015) and is currently editing *The Fawn* for the John Marston project and James Shirley's *The Bird in a Cage* for the new *Routledge Anthology of Early Modern Drama*.

Steve Mentz is Professor of English at St John's University in New York City. His most recent book is *Shipwreck Modernity: Ecologies of Globalization, 1550–1719* (2015). He is the author of two earlier monographs, *At the Bottom of Shakespeare's Ocean* (2009) and *Romance for Sale in Early Modern England* (2006), and is also editor or co-editor of four collections: *The Sea in Nineteenth-Century Anglophone Literary Culture* (2017), *Oceanic New York* (2015), *The Age of Thomas Nashe* (2013), and *Rogues and Early Modern English Culture* (2004). He has written numerous articles on ecocriticism, Shakespeare, and maritime literature, and curated an exhibition at the Folger Shakespeare Library, 'Lost at Sea: The Ocean in the English Imagination, 1550–1750' (2010). He blogs at The Bookfish, www.stevementz.com.

Marianne Montgomery is Associate Professor of English at East Carolina University, where she teaches Shakespeare and early modern drama. Her research focuses on English travel and exchange in the early modern period. She is the author of *Europe's Languages on England's Stages, 1590–1620* (2012), which locates stage representations of European vernaculars within contemporary discourses about cross-cultural contact. Her work has appeared in *Studies in Travel Writing*, and she has contributed chapters to volumes such as *Emissaries in Early Modern Literature and Culture*

(2009) and *The Mysterious and the Foreign in Early Modern England* (2008).

Ladan Niayesh is Professor of English Studies at the University of Paris Diderot – Paris 7. She is the author of *Aux frontières de l'humain: figures du cannibalisme dans le theatre anglais de la Renaissance* (2009), and has edited a collection of essays on *Mandeville and Mandevillian Lore in Early Modern England* (2011). Her recent work focuses on the reception of the East, the Ottoman Empire and Persia more particularly, in early modern literature. Her edition of *Three Early Modern Romances of Eastern Conquest* will be published in 2018 in the Revels Plays Companion Library Series of Manchester University Press.

Anthony Parr is Professor Emeritus of English at the University of the Western Cape in South Africa, and a full-time reader at the Huntington Library in California. He has edited a wide range of dramatic texts from the Elizabethan and Jacobean periods, including *Three Renaissance Travel Plays* (1995), and is the author of a number of essays on early modern travel writing and cartography. His most recent book is *Renaissance Mad Voyages* (2015), a study of the ways in which the ancient trope of the fantastic voyage is activated in early modern English travel and related enterprises, as well as in literary uses of the voyage motif. He is currently editing plays by Shirley and Marston for the forthcoming collected editions of those authors.

Julie Sanders is Professor of English Literature and Drama and Deputy Vice-Chancellor of Newcastle University. She has published widely on early modern literature and has previously edited works by Jonson, Shirley, and Richard Brome. Her monograph *The Cultural Geography of Early Modern Drama, 1620–1650* (Cambridge University Press), won the British Academy's Rose Mary Crawshay Prize for international women's scholarship in 2012, and she also co-authored *Ben Jonson's Walk to Scotland* with James Loxley and Anna Groundwater (Cambridge University Press, 2014). Her current project is provisionally entitled 'Making Spaces in Early Modern Drama' and aims to think through material objects and their modes of production to understand the presence of lived practice and experience on the page and stage.

Daniel Vitkus holds the Rebeca Hickel Endowed Chair in Elizabethan and Early Modern Literature at the University of California, San Diego, where he has been teaching since 2013. He has edited *Three Turk Plays from Early Modern England* (2000) and *Piracy, Slavery and Redemption: Barbary Captivity Narratives from Early Modern England* (2001). He also is the author of *Turning Turk: English Theater and the Multicultural Mediterranean, 1570–1630* (2003) and numerous articles on early modern literature and culture. He serves as the Senior Editor of *The Journal for Early Modern Cultural Studies*. His current research is focused on 'The Global Renaissance', and particularly on the cultural implications of transnational capitalism, globalisation, and Eurasian imperialism in their emergent, early modern phase.

Acknowledgements

It is with great pleasure that we take this opportunity to thank the colleagues, family, and friends that have contributed so generously, and in more ways than they know, to this collection of essays. Our first debt is to Dr Emily Hockley and the Syndicate at Cambridge University Press for their faith in this project and commitment to it. We gratefully acknowledge the professionalism and support more broadly of the editorial, marketing, and production teams at that press. Anonymous press reviewers provided detailed and incisive feedback and suggestions that encouraged us to push beyond what had gone before in the field to attempt to redefine the relationship between travel and drama in this collection.

We also pay tribute to the contributors to *Travel and Drama in Early Modern England: The Journeying Play*, who enthusiastically embraced our aims for the collection. Uniformly, they have been responsive to editorial suggestions and generous in their engagement in defining the project's broader terms and what was at stake intellectually. In its boldness and ambition, this book has been a genuinely collaborative effort, with contributors responding and revising, and responding again, to us and each other as we have debated and refined our arguments. We particularly acknowledge the input of Tony Parr in helping us think through ways to define 'the journeying play' in our 'Introduction'. There are also a number of other scholars who have either commented on draft chapters or have discussed with us at conferences or seminars, or more informally, the arguments presented here, including Claire Bourne, Dan Carey, Andrew Hadfield, Alice Hunt, Rosamund Paice, Maria Shmygol, Garrett Sullivan, Will Rossiter, Stephen Watkins, and Rachel Willie. As editors, we of course take responsibility for all remaining errors and omissions in the book.

We also want to acknowledge the generosity of our respective academic institutions, and other organisations in supporting this project.

This book has been six years in the making, so Claire Jowitt has benefited from the insights and reflections of colleagues in the Departments of English and of History at the University of Southampton and, since 2015, in the Schools of History and of English, Drama, and Creative Writing at the University of East Anglia. Fellowships at the Folger Shakespeare Library, Washington, DC, in 2015, and the Huntington Library, California, in 2016 provided the archival resources and ring-fenced time to devote to the project, as well as convivial company and magnificent environments in which to work. David McInnis gratefully acknowledges the support offered by the University of Melbourne during this time, in particular the Faculty of Arts research grants for his work on Thomas Dekker's *Old Fortunatus* and for the group project, 'Character in Literature and Theatre', both of which have supported the present book. Both editors thank Emma Koch and Alex Thom for their assistance with the formatting and presentation of this volume.

Our respective families have been a source of inspiration and encouragement throughout.

Introduction: Understanding the Early Modern Journeying Play

Claire Jowitt

University of East Anglia

David McInnis

University of Melbourne

Our aims as editors of *Travel and Drama in Early Modern England: The Journeying Play* have been notably simple: to produce a collection of new and original essays by world-leading scholars at all stages of their careers, exploring the relationships between travel and drama in a period of English history (roughly late Elizabethan to early Restoration, *c.*1580–1670) when both activities were rapidly evolving; for the essays, taken together, to pose research questions that shape and stimulate future debates for new generations of researchers; and for the collection to redefine the limits of and, perhaps, expand the canon of recognised plays concerned with travel. Of course, however straightforward our aims, they are inevitably underpinned by a series of more complex research questions concerning the parameters and significance of the genre; in this Introduction, we outline the approaches we have taken to fulfil our ambitions for the collection. The Introduction also provides a concise survey of the critical terrain that constitutes our point of departure and a brief summation of how we think each essay takes forward the collection's research agenda, including, we hope, the areas of future scholarship it might serve to stimulate.

To facilitate intellectual coherence in an essay collection with these aims, it is important to define terms. Though critics often use the terms 'travel drama' and 'voyage drama' interchangeably, and in previous work we have each used both terms, we want to signal from the outset the collection's awareness of the ethical issues that have become associated with the term 'travel'. Although it was only in the mid-eighteenth century that the generic division between fiction and non-fiction became less permeable, once the boundary between fiction and non-fiction firmed up, each form of writing developed a different relationship with its readers

through explicit or implicit reading contracts. As Tim Youngs summa-
rises, 'travel writing consists of predominantly factual, first-person prose
accounts of travels that have been undertaken by the author-narrator.'[1]
Of course, since ancient times, books have always contained literary journeys (indeed Casey Blanton suggests 'the journey pattern is one of the
most persistent forms of all narratives'),[2] leading Peter Hulme to argue,
correctly in our view, for the need for exclusive definitions of literature
and travel writing. For texts to count as travel writing, Hulme believes
that their authors must have travelled to the places they describe, as there
is an ethical dimension to their claims to have made the journeys they
recount and, if an author's claim is later found to be false, the work is
'discredited' (says Hulme) and the text moves out of the category of travel
writing into another (such as the imaginary voyage).[3] However, ethical
concerns about the 'truth', or eye-witness authority, of travel accounts
are visibly evident among early moderns: for instance, in Richard
Hakluyt's decision to drop versions of *Mandeville's Travels* and David
Ingrams's account of a 2,000-mile walk he claimed to have been forced
to undertake for survival after shipwreck in the Gulf of Mexico in 1568,
from the second, much expanded edition of *The Principal Navigations*
(1598/99–1600), because he doubted their authenticity.[4] More generally,
the proverb 'travellers lie by authority' sums up the issue; those sceptical
of travellers' narratives argued that without witnesses to challenge their
stories, travellers' authority was unassailable.[5] Indeed this proverb was
evidently something of a recruiting sergeant for both those supportive
of *or* hostile to travel writing well before the eighteenth century: dozens
of writers weighed in on the argument, sometimes shedding more heat
than light, with, for instance, William Wood in *New England's Prospect*
(1634) exasperatedly railing against 'thick-witted readers' who quoted
the 'unjust aspersion' of the proverb: '[t]here is many a tub-brained cynic
[like Diogenes], who because anything stranger than ordinary is too large
for the strait-hoops of his apprehension, he peremptorily concludes that
it is a lie.'[6]

For clarity and coherence, and to make a defining intervention in the
debate, this collection has adopted what might be described as a flexed
version of Hulme's distinction. For us, if a play is based on a particular
documented voyage or focuses on the exploits of a historical traveller,
even though it is not necessarily the playwright's own experience being
dramatised, then it is described as travel drama. The plays about the
'rogue cosmopolitans' John Ward, Thomas Stukeley, and the Sherley
brothers, discussed by Daniel Vitkus in this volume (Chapter 7), are

examples of travel drama, for instance.[7] By contrast, Thomas Dekker's *Old Fortunatus* (discussed by David McInnis in Chapter 10) is better thought of as a voyage drama.[8] Dekker did not travel in the way that Fortunatus and his sons do, and even though he did apparently use Gerardus Mercator and Petrus Plancius's maps as partial inspirations, the main source of his characters' prolific journeying is German folklore. *Old Fortunatus* therefore accords with the status of later texts that Hulme might call 'literary' rather than 'travel writing'. For these reasons, William Shakespeare's *The Tempest* (*c*.1611), discussed by Emily C. Bartels in Chapter 9,[9] is also a voyage drama, plotted around a series of imaginary voyages and shipwrecks, notwithstanding its well-known engagement with William Strachey's account of a New World shipwreck on the *Sea-Venture*. It is perfectly possible for a play to be simultaneously both a travel and a voyage drama – Sir William Davenant's *The Cruelty of the Spaniards in Peru* (1658), for instance, incorporates 'Black Legend' accounts of Spanish conquistadors,[10] but ends with English forces liberating the Peruvians from Spanish oppression, despite the English being absent from Peru in the historical period depicted.[11]

As our title indicates, this collection has adopted a new umbrella term: the early modern 'journeying play', to cover both terms, 'voyage drama' and 'travel drama', because the relationship between travel and drama at this point is best understood by appealing to both. 'Voyage drama' is a more capacious term and arguably a more innovative category generically than 'travel drama'; conceptually, in that it referred to a range of enterprises and was not confined to sea journeys; and theatrically, since by the late sixteenth century the word 'voyage' was starting to be used to refer to a literary category.[12] Put another way, voyage drama is the more obviously inventive category since, as Mary Campbell puts it, fictional writing, including drama, 'provides the shoes of flight' where 'contemplation matters more than the acquisition of knowledge'.[13] However, even plays derived in some way from an authentic account or experience are *plays* – that is, fictionalisations, dramatisations. In other words they too are inventive, and are not travel narratives or diaries, though it should be recognised that some early modern journeying plays are, in Campbell's terms, more contemplative than others. The use of the new term 'the journeying play' enables this collection to open up more precise and nuanced understandings of the relationship between travel and processes of dramatic fictionalisation.

The flexibility of the term 'journeying play' also allows our collection to embrace stimulating ideas that superficially might seem to challenge its coherence – specifically that travel is not actually a requirement of the genre. For instance, the returned sea captain Young Franklin's failure to find maritime re-employment in Thomas Middleton and John Webster's *Anything for a Quiet Life* (*c.*1621), described by Marianne Montgomery (Chapter 6), results in him traversing the city of London instead – akin, in some ways, to the passage of imported luxury goods to the mercer's and barber's shops that provide the locations for much of the action. Foreign travel is never shown, yet the play restages it as domestic activity as well as repeatedly exhibiting the material products provided, and linguistic diversity enabled, by it.[14] Despite its apparent lack of travel, *Anything for a Quiet Life* is a voyage drama.

We have also used 'the journeying play' in the title of our collection to reference the origins of travel and voyage drama in the 'old' medieval journeying plays, such as the late fifteenth-century *Somonyng of Everyman*, where physical movement, such as Everyman's pilgrimage, mirrors both character development and the journey through life. But, even more importantly, and the reason why we chose it for the title in preference to either voyage or travel drama, is its self-reflexivity as both category and term. The journeying play usefully signals both the distance the genre has travelled over time and the collection's aim to steer its continued progression and future development, including our aim of redefining the canons of what constitutes both travel and voyage drama to show how productively the categories promiscuously mingle and overlap.

An appreciation of the true extent of the early modern journeying play, and of the intersection between voyage and travel drama (including an assessment of whether one category was more dominant than the other), is only possible if we consider both surviving plays *and* what we know about lost plays. In relation to travel drama, for instance, one way to approach the issue is by addressing what seem to be gaps in material, either about prominent historical events or figures that might reasonably be expected to be covered by the drama of the period. As Anthony Parr puts it, 'Where, it might be asked, are the plays about Drake and Hawkins and other heroes of maritime derring-do?',[15] referring to the way that no surviving plays focus on England's most famous 'sea dogs' or, indeed, explorers as their central protagonists.

Sir Francis Drake is an interesting and complex case. Drake, in fact, does appear on stage, just not always in ways we might expect. In the second part of *If You Know Not Me, You Know No Bodie* (probably written by Thomas Heywood, for the Queen Anne's Men, in 1604), a play that blends the genres of city comedy and history, the fact that Drake brings

Queen Elizabeth news of the Spanish Armada's defeat (in the B-Text, the news is borne jointly by Drake and Martin Frobisher) suggests that, generically, the play might also be categorised as travel drama.[16] Drake also features in mayoral pageants including John Webster's *Monuments of Honor* (1624),[17] and as the eponymous protagonist of an Interregnum entertainment by Davenant in 1659.[18] More intriguingly, a Sotheby's auction catalogue from 13 July 1887 listed a dramatic manuscript (now lost) in the hand of Mildmay Fane, Earl of Westmorland (1602–66), entitled 'Ladrones or the Robbers' Iland, an Opera in a Romansike Way'; the catalogue stipulates that 'amongst the Dramatis Personæ are Drake, Candish, Magellan, Lemaire, Vandernort, &c.', even though it was impossible for these five men to have been there at the same time, raising difficult-to-answer questions of whether this should be seen as voyage or travel drama, or both. Although Ferdinand Magellan's association with the islands was well established (he was said to have discovered and named them in 1521–22), Thomas Cavendish's and Drake's connections are less obvious, and the Dutch mariner Jacob Le Maire circumnavigated the world in 1615–16, approximately one hundred years after Magellan's voyage.[19] Tentatively dated to 1658 (and thus around the time of Davenant's piece about Drake), this operatic entertainment thus appears to recount a purely imaginary voyage, making the generic classification weighted towards voyage drama, with elements of travel drama also evident in the entertainment's use of historical explorers. Drake may also have appeared in his capacity as a 'leading figure in Plymouth politics' in a lost Admiral's Men play: the domestic tragedy 'Page of Plymouth' (1599) by Ben Jonson and Dekker, in which Ulalia Glandfield is forcibly married to Page of Plymouth but continues her romance with George Strangwidge after the wedding; she and George hire two men to kill Page, and when their crime is discovered, all four are tried by Drake, and executed.[20] Given that Drake executed his sometime friend and second-in-command Thomas Doughty for mutiny and treason on his circumnavigation, and the justice of the execution was widely debated and cast a shadow over Drake's subsequent career, it is possible that the execution in 'Page of Plymouth' revives the controversy, and thus might perhaps be seen as containing features of travel drama.[21] Famous travellers who saw the world imported their experience and judgement, for good or ill, back to domestic soils. Taken together, then, these examples of extant and lost plays show that Drake was not completely neglected by theatrical entertainments but none provide him with a centre stage part in a late Elizabethan or early Jacobean journeying play, when the genre was at its height. In other words, the small size of the role (in Heywood's play, the lost 'Page of Plymouth', and *Monuments of Honor*), the genre (of pageant and Interregnum entertainments), and the late date (Interregnum entertainments) work together to marginalise Drake in the early modern journeying play.

Captain John Smith, one-time governor of Virginia, is another famed English traveller whose presence on stage has also apparently disappeared from the record. In the dedicatory material prefacing his memoirs of 1630, Smith justified compiling 'this true discourse' on the grounds that 'they have acted my fatall Tragedies upon the Stage, and racked my Relations at their pleasure'.[22] Philip L. Barbour noticed a further allusion to a dramatisation of Smith's exploits in the commendation that Richard James wrote for Smith's *True Travels*:

> Can it be,
> That Men alone in Gonnels fortune see
> Thy worth advanc'd? no wonder since our age,
> Is now at large a Bedlam or a Stage.

One possible candidate for a travel drama featuring Smith would be 'The Hungarian Lion', written by Richard Gunnell and licensed for performance at his Fortune playhouse ('Gonnels fortune') in 1623.[23] Smith's epitaph in St Sepulchre's Church, London, notes that for 'great Service in that Climate done, / Brave Sigismundus, King of Hungarion, / Did give him as a Coat of Armes to wear', which lends credence to a play called 'The Hungarian Lion' featuring him.[24]

Detailed records exist for a handful of explicitly New World plays from the 1590s and early 1600s, including 'The New World's Tragedy' (Admiral's, 1595), 'The Conquest of the West Indies' (Admiral's, 1601), 'A Tragedy of the Plantation of Virginia' (unknown, 1623), and a play about the Amboyna massacre of 1623 (unknown, 1625).[25] The titles of these plays, which locate the action within specific geographies, indicate that each should probably be thought of as a travel drama, or perhaps as combining elements from travel and voyage drama, depending on the extent to which the location was a backdrop for imaginary characters and situations. Others may have disappeared altogether, for the theatrical subject (or subjects) of a vitriolic sermon preached by William Crashaw in 1609 remains untraced.[26] Crashaw criticised players for trifling 'with *Princes* and *Potentates*, *Magistrates* and *Ministers*, nay with *God* and *Religion*, and all *holy things*', claiming 'nothing that is good, excellent or holy can escape them' and specifically noting that 'they abuse *Virginea*'.[27]

He attempts to dismiss their abuses of the New World in what are most likely travel dramas by deridingly noting that 'they are but *Players*: they disgrace it: true, but they are but *Players*, and they have *played* with better things, and such as for which, if they speedily repent not, I dare say, vengeance waites for them.'[28] Crashaw proceeds to conjecture as to the players' motives:

> But why are the *Players* enemies to this Plantation and doe abuse it? I will tell you the causes: First, for that they are so multiplied here, that one cannot live by another, and they see that wee send of all trades to *Virginea*, but will send no *Players*, which if wee would doe, they that remaine would gaine the more at home. Secondly, as the *divell* hates us, because wee purpose not to suffer *Heathens*, and the *Pope* because we have vowed to tolerate no *Papists*: so doe the *Players*, because wee resolve to suffer no *Idle persons in Virginea*, which course if it were taken in *England*, they know they might turne to new occupations.[29]

Crashaw *may* have had the lost 'Conquest of the West Indies' in mind (as Wilhelm Creizenach implied),[30] but it is also possible he could have been recalling a satirical play such as George Chapman, Ben Jonson, and John Marston's voyage drama *Eastward Ho* (Children of the Queen's Revels, 1605).[31] But it sounds as though he may have had multiple journeying plays in mind: players seem to be repeat offenders who 'abuse' and 'disgrace' Virginia, and will continue to do so ('let them *play* on').

Travel, whether to the New World or closer to home, evidently loomed large in a number of lost plays from the London commercial playing companies' repertories. A couple of years before Shakespeare turned his attention to Elsinore, the Admiral's Men had a two-part play by Henry Chettle, Dekker, Michael Drayton, and Robert Wilson, 'Earl Godwin and His Three Sons' (1598).[32] The setting is eleventh-century England under, in turn, Canute, Harold, and Hardicanute (the last Danish king of England), and culminating in the accession of Edward the Confessor, despite Earl Godwin's best attempts to claim the crown for his offspring. The plays would have most likely included details of the earl's exile to Denmark and, after briefly returning to England, his exile to Flanders (and if so, should be seen as containing at least some element of travel drama). Exile (for protection rather than punishment) is also the premise of the surviving fragment of what appears to be a pseudo-historical voyage drama set in pre-Norman England, referred to as the 'Play of Oswald' after a prominent character.[33] Ethelbert's son Oswald is smuggled out of Mercia to Northumbria and, in a trope common in folklore, raised in ignorance of his true nobility, but he is reunited with and identified by his parents in the fragment of the play that survives. Some of these plays appear to incorporate scenarios related to documented travels of historical characters, but we can also see the influence of the 'old' journeying plays; the role of 'travail' is notable (meaning variously in the late sixteenth century hard work in general, the work required to travel from one place to another in particular, and the labour of childbirth),[34] as is the link between movement and identity (primarily political identity), and material from folklore. Put another way, these plays most likely combined elements of travel and voyage drama, in varying proportions.

    Heywood's *The Four Prentices of London* (1602) is one of the more famous early modern journeying plays concerned with pilgrimage and the Holy Land (another prominent theme in the medieval journeying play tradition), but it was preceded by a play called 'Jerusalem' (Strange's, 1591) and the possibly related 'Godfrey of Bouillon, Part 2' (Admiral's, 1594)[35], as well as the crusading plays 'The Funeral of Richard Coeur de Lion' (Admiral's, 1598) and 'William Longsword' (Admiral's, 1599) (also related to the tradition in the additional sense that 'journeying' could mean engagement in battle).[36] The pilgrimage-related metaphor of travel as life's journey – a recurrent motif of medieval and early modern writing – must have had a place in the lost two-part 'Fair Constance of Rome' plays by Dekker, Drayton, Richard Hathaway, Anthony Munday, and Wilson (1600). As Parr has noted elsewhere, 'the idea of the unpredictable journey that tests constancy and reveals God's purpose remained a potent one, as Chaucer's retelling of the tale of Constance shows, and it was a prime means of giving a Christian shape to the peripatetic motif in classical epic.'[37] The plays presumably followed Chaucer's *Man of Law's Tale*, in which the beautiful Constance narrowly escapes a massacre orchestrated by her future mother-in-law, and is set adrift on a rudderless boat off the coast of Syria (just as Prospero and the infant Miranda were cast adrift from Milan in an ungovernable vessel in *The Tempest*), ultimately landing in Northumberland where her rescue is followed by further trials and tribulations. After marrying the king of Northumberland, Constance is again the victim of an evil mother-in-law, this time being banished to sea through the device of a counterfeit letter. Constance is eventually reunited with her husband and her father in Rome.[38] These are only some of the more obviously journeying plays, as evidenced by their titles; the Levantine setting of 'Frederick and Basilea' (Admiral's, 1597) is suggested by the names of characters present in the surviving backstage plot,[39] while Stephen Gosson's account of 'the trechery of Turkes' in 'The

Blacksmith's Daughter' (Leicester's?, 1578) casts a rather different light on what might otherwise have been thought a crafts play of some kind.[40]

Despite the intuitive assumption that the early modern journeying play is one of the trickiest forms of drama to pull off, amateur playwrights also seem drawn to plays about travel. One of the most famous amateur dramatists of this period is Sir Edward Dering (1598–1644), whose conflation of Shakespeare's *Henry IV* plays for a 1623 performance at his residence in Surrenden, Kent, is discussed in this volume (Chapter 4) by Julie Sanders.[41] At a slightly later date (*c.*1627 or thereafter), Dering attempted to write a voyage drama about Philander, King of Thrace, set in Thrace (the first act) and Macedon (the remainder of the play).[42] A manuscript fragment at the Folger Shakespeare Library preserves Dering's 'plot' or outline of the projected drama; it provides detailed scene-by-scene summaries up to the end of the third act, then ceases abruptly (despite numerous subsequent blank leaves of paper). Tiffany Stern suggests that 'it may be that this is the plot for a collaborative play in which only Acts 1–3 were of interest to this particular author', or that Dering 'may have given up before completing the document'.[43] Though the outline may not be complete, the playwright, who amassed a great collection of books and manuscripts, undertook significant research from the most up-to-date cartographic and geographical sources available: folios 1^v–2^r of the draft provide extensive notes on the 'Mountaynes', 'Rivers', 'Cittyes and Townes and places' of Thrace and Macedon, as well as names of the 'provinces' and even '[t]he old names of Thrace'.[44] A marginal note on folio 1^v even reveals a source text: 'Speede in Greece', referring to the map included in the first world atlas to be compiled by an Englishman, John Speed's *A Prospect of the Most Famous Parts of the World*, published in 1627. This amateur dramatist, at least, seems to have thought that to write about particular regions he had not himself visited, it was necessary to research the imagined destinations, even if only in his own library.

A comparable example is the case of the philosopher John Locke, who at some point between late 1661 and late 1663 decided to try his hand at writing a voyage drama about 'Orozes, King of Albania', set in an unidentified Eastern country, in part at the court of a Mughal emperor, as Orozes battles the Persians.[45] Like Dering, Locke got as far as sketching a plot-scenario of the play, rotating one of his notebooks and using the blank portions of what can be described as folios 68^{v}rev.–64^{v}rev. Although Locke seems to have conceived the narrative himself, the names he gives his characters reveal indebtedness not just to classical sources

such as Cassius Dio or Plutarch (though more likely at second-hand, via
James Ussher's *The Annals of the World*, 1658), but also to contemporary
travellers' accounts – most notably Edward Terry's *A Voyage to East-India*
(1655), from which he drew the names for the Mughal and his two sons,
Khusrau and Khurram (the latter famous for commissioning the Taj
Mahal). Locke also relied on inspiration from prose romance and, akin
to the political allegory apparent in many other contemporary voyage
dramas,[46] his story about a disguised king who is saved from imminent
execution and restored to power may only have been set in the East to
distance it from historical events in England.

Curiously, the few cases of actual travellers who tried their hands at
writing plays do not appear to have been tempted to dramatise their
first-hand experiences of foreign lands.[47] Benjamin Greene, a factor with
the East India Company, travelled with Sir Henry Middleton on the
1610–13 voyage to Surat, and kept a journal from 15 November 1610
to 22 December 1612. The diary, preserved in the India Office Marine
Department Records, has been disbound and the individual leaves
remounted; the final leaf (which may be in a different hand) contains
a dramatic fragment consisting of dramatis personae, a stage direction,
and two lines of dialogue. As with Locke's plot, the character names
are drawn from prose romances including Marcos Martínez's *Espejo de
príncipes y caballeros* (1587; English translations of which appeared in *The
Mirror of Knighthood* between 1598 and 1601), *Parismus, the Renoumed
Prince of Bohemia* (1598), and *Parismenos* (1599).[48] Richard Norwood,
a seasick sailor-turned-navigation-tutor, returned to London from the
Mediterranean in 1612 and found himself frequenting playhouses (the
Fortune, specifically).[49] Being 'bewitched in affection and never satiated'
by the 'frivolous, false, and feigned things' depicted on stage, he 'began
to make a play and had written a good part of it' but, following a dispute
with the players, abandoned it.[50] For Norwood, playgoing was explicitly
a matter of turning away from 'anything that was serious, true, or good',
making it unlikely that the 'vanities' he subsequently regretted had anything to do with his real-life travelling.[51]

We can glimpse, then, in the fragmentary accounts of lost plays that
remain to us the same issues and concerns that shape the extant plays
discussed in *Travel and Drama in Early Modern England*. Of course, it
should not be forgotten that the practice of travel for early moderns (to
far-flung locations and domestic ones – the latter journeys just as important since most people only travelled short distances)[52] was undertaken
by only a small percentage of the population, because of both its expense

and the strict requirements governing the purpose of travel (it could be undertaken under licence *only* for education, pilgrimage, commerce). Yet, by the turn of the seventeenth century, people and goods *were* in motion across lands and seas to distances and on scales hardly imaginable just a century before. As a result, accounts of travel and voyaging at home and abroad, and dramas engaging with them, became the most popular and easily accessible sources of information about this newly envisageable wider world for a nation of armchair travellers. Indeed it is worth repeating the remark of Thomas Platter, a Swiss physician travelling in England in 1599, who commented on the importance of playgoing as an educative experience, enabling 'the English' to 'learn' about the rest of the world from attending the theatre:

> With these and many more amusements the English pass their time, learning at the play what is happening abroad ... since the English for the most part do not travel much, but prefer to learn foreign matters and take their pleasures at home.[53]

It is not known which production Platter attended in 1599; by that date a considerable number of plays had been performed which focused on travel abroad and encounters overseas, many of which are discussed by the essays in *Travel and Drama in Early Modern England*, including Christopher Marlowe's two *Tamburlaine* plays (1587) and *Dr Faustus* (*c.*1588), the anonymous drama about Stukeley, *The Famous Historye of the Life and Death of Captaine Thomas Stukeley* (1596), Dekker's 'journeying' play *Old Fortunatus* (1599), and the lost plays described above, as well as others with intriguingly travel-related titles such as 'Sir John Mandeville' (*c.*1592) or 'Muly Molloco' (*c.*1592).

In fact, the twin fields of theatre and travel in early modern England were changing at the fastest pace *ever* in the history of either domain. The professional theatre was rapidly developing with the establishment in London of a number of large, permanent, public, open-air playhouses and smaller, roofed theatres. The doubling of theatre capacity in just thirty years unambiguously reveals the increasing prominence of drama in early modern cultural life: around 1580, the total theatre capacity of London was about 5,000 spectators; by 1610, it exceeded 10,000,[54] with the playing companies performing both the hundreds of extant plays and, as we have seen, the many more that are now lost. Travel writing was able to provide new ideas and settings to furnish the appetites of the playgoers like those whom Platter observed in 1599, and to ensure the continued popularity and profitability of the playing companies. Indeed, the spectacular rise in popularity of the theatre closely reflects the heyday of the vogue for the early modern journeying play, which reached its peak at around the time when Shakespeare wrote *The Tempest*, and is reflected in the shape and scope of our collection, since the majority of essays focus on material dating from the early seventeenth century. McInnis's emphasis on the representation of travelling for pleasure in his reading here (Chapter 10) of *Old Fortunatus* connects thematically to the playhouses' increasingly dominant role in satisfying the popular imaginary: characters' on-stage pleasure offers a proxy for playgoers' desires.[55] However, the collection is mindful to provide coverage, and an account, of early modern journeying plays from across its chronological span. Parr's discussion (Chapter 1) of the journeying plays of the 1570s and his, Ladan Niayesh's (Chapter 2), and Steve Mentz's (Chapter 3) discussion of Marlowe's significance for the early history of the early modern voyage drama genre, particularly his theatrical juggernaut of the two-part *Tamburlaine*, gives prominence in the collection to the ways dramatists repurposed earlier theatrical traditions.[56] The collection is structured chronologically, enabling readers to understand the twists and turns, main routes and byways, undertaken by journeying plays. It ends with an essay by Claire Jowitt (Chapter 12) on the playwright Davenant, whose long interest in voyage drama spanned all regimes from the time of Charles I to Charles II, and her essay traces metonymically the ways the genre had developed by the latter part of the seventeenth century.[57]

In travel writing, the increasing size, scale, and ambition of the two editions of Hakluyt's collection *The Principal Navigations*, which expanded from one folio volume (*c.*600,000 words) to three (*c.*1.76 million words) between 1589 and 1598/99–1600, also shows the way that travel (and the colonial, imperial, and mercantile opportunities it engenders) was beginning to be decisive in shaping the English nation's fortunes and identity.[58] Travel writing in general, and particularly this collection of 'English' achievements, gestures to a newly sharpened national competitive determination to emulate the success of Spanish and Portuguese expansionist models. The size and reach of Hakluyt's collection (its popularity is registered by the number of contemporary references to it as well as the remarkable number of extant copies)[59] suggest both the ready, eager readership for, and extensive circulation of, travel accounts.

The cultural geographies that journeying plays engage, and the variety of readings that they support– ranging, for instance, from local concerns to do with metropolitan anxieties or court politics to larger geopolitical issues (whether European, transatlantic, or global) – have long been the subject of critical inquiry. *The Tempest*, for instance, 'has been located in every place and no place and enlisted in support of colonial, anticolonial and apolitical views'.[60] Bartels, in Chapter 9, takes this question in important new directions when she argues that in reading in one direction from Strachey's source to Shakespeare's play, critics have missed the latter's capacity to challenge the former. By focusing on the competing players and plots within what she terms both texts' 'ordinary undersides' – which themselves represent a dynamic negotiation of experience and expectation – we can see how theatre's processes of imagination and mediation have as much to bring to the historical text that theatre invokes as the historical text has to bring to drama.

More broadly, *Travel and Drama in Early Modern England* builds on, and takes account of, work on travel and drama undertaken since the publication in 1996 by Cambridge University Press of the landmark collection *Travel and Drama in Shakespeare's Time*, edited by Jean-Pierre Maquerlot and Michèle Willems. That collection was based on a conference at Rouen, where participants debated the 'interconnections between text and context' and especially between 'European cross currents and New World perspectives'.[61] Since then, however, the studies of both early modern travel writing and drama have changed considerably to become less centred on the Atlantic world in isolation and increasingly global in orientation.[62] For instance, geopolitical changes in the Middle East, alterations in, and debates about, the economic and political landscape of the European Union, as well as alterations in the global economic order, as Asia has started to regain the position it held in the Renaissance, have all added important new dimensions to studies of both travel writing and early modern drama.[63] Likewise, recent work on the ways drama represents the 'multicultural Mediterranean' – a space shared by Muslims, Jews, and Christians – and engages with ideas of transnationalism, has questioned what 'Europe' means, who counts as 'European', and has explored the complex power dynamics expressed in depictions of exotic alterity.[64] The ways early modern oceans operated as cultural spaces and contact zones, where connections and circulations could take place outside both established centres of control and the dictates of individual national histories, have also enriched both fields.[65] Mentz's essay in this collection (Chapter 3) focuses on Marlowe's depiction of the Eastern Mediterranean in *Dido, Queen of Carthage* (c.1588) and *Tamburlaine* in order to explore the idea of 'oceanic hybridity', where repurposed classical poetics takes on new geopolitical meanings reflecting England's increasing engagement with the maritime world.[66] Likewise, Richmond Barbour and Bernhard

Klein's essay (Chapter 8) seeks to make historical sense of 'drama at sea' by exploring the inherent theatricality of voyaging rather than merely focusing on whether two of Shakespeare's plays, *Richard II* and *Hamlet*, were actually staged in west and east African waters on the *Dragon*.[67]

A further branch of travel-writing scholarship, described in 2006 by Jonathan Sell as its 'self-reflexive turn', which uses descriptions in travel writing of the foreign and unfamiliar as a way of examining domestic issues, and explores how travel contributed to developments in conceptualising the English nation, has also been productive in generating new readings of early modern plays.[68] Several of the essays in this collection, including Montgomery's, McManus's, and Jowitt's, broadly sit against this tradition, but develop it in new ways. McManus's piece, for instance, with its tight focus on the theatrical season of 1621–22, which engaged issues associated with the Palatinate crisis, argues that the season should be seen as both a political *and* a related aesthetic, generic, experiment, as dramas (specifically Shakespeare's *Othello*, John Fletcher's *The Island Princess*, and Thomas Middleton and William Rowley's *The Changeling*) respond to each other in multiple ways.[69] This group, McManus suggests, circulates and recirculates particular theatrical techniques and specific scenarios to represent Europe to England and England to itself.

Further areas of recent critical interest in travel-writing studies – issues of 'internal colonisation' and related topics concerning domestic travel, a less culturally celebrated but much more regular activity for early moderns – underpin a cluster of essays in *Travel and Drama in Early Modern England*.[70] Geographical mobility, like social mobility, often provoked hostile sentiments from early modern commentators, and those who undertook it, wrote about it, or acted in plays about it had to work hard to counter the condemnation that apparent 'placelessness' provoked.[71] Sanders's essay on perambulation and chorography in Shakespeare's *Henry IV* plays emerges out of, and further develops, critics' discussions concerning how early moderns understood and experienced an environment to argue for these plays as generically experimental voyage drama which stage domestic and interior journeys. What is at stake in Hal's perambulations through his future kingdom is politically useful knowledge for a future monarch about the extent and diversity of the lands and peoples he will govern.[72] Motive drama is also the topic of Andrew Gordon's innovative reading (Chapter 5) of George Chapman, Jonson, and John Marston's *Eastward Ho* (1605), showing the forms and media of movement the play describes – on foot, or by boat, coach, or horse – to be vehicles of meaning.[73] Both Sanders' and Gordon's essays, as well as the collection's third essay in the cluster on domestic travel, that by Montgomery, make a series of links between the ways commodities (products and objects as well as ideas) were subject to trade, travel, and translation. These links, as well as the debate that Jean Howard and others have conducted concerning the level of early modern London's 'cosmopolitanism' (did London, like Antwerp, Venice, or Constantinople, show 'leadership in long-distance trade and new forms of commercial transactions' or was it a place of xenophobia, or simultaneously both?), are central to this group of essays.[74]

Indeed work on cosmopolitanism has been aiming to counteract what might be seen, in the wake of Stephen Greenblatt's *Marvellous Possessions: The Wonder of the New World* (1991), as too much focus on 'moments of encounter'.[75] While some critics are opening up the field to currents of 'world' and 'globalisation' histories, others are focusing ever more closely on 'microhistories' of encounter as a result. This wide variety of approaches is fully reflected in the present collection, as Jowitt, for instance, shows how Davenant redirected and turned in upon itself this most charged trope of expansionist colonial discourse, the 'moment of encounter' to question the very nature of English 'civility'. Indeed one way of continuing to define the genre of voyage drama is by thinking about specific memes or 'theatregrams' – to use the theatre historian and critic Louise George Clubb's influential term, which refers to the pervasive reuse and (importantly) recombination of types of characters, actions, and speeches, and theatre design which are traceable through plays, allowing us to identify resemblances obscured by conventional generic categorisations.[76] Derived from Italian drama, theatregrams are, importantly, transportable, marketable, and translatable: they operate through 'border' and 'contact' zones, and they can be transnational, but their mobility can also be resisted. In this volume, Chapters 11 and 12 by McManus and by Jowitt, respectively, make use of the theatregram concept in the context of voyage drama; other chapters focus instead on specific objects (Niayesh), characters (McInnis), or themes (venturing and language, for Parr and Montgomery respectively). Broader considerations informing voyage drama, such as performance conditions (Barbour and Klein; Sanders) or historical and intellectual contexts (Mentz, Gordon, Vitkus, and Bartels) are also explored. Taken together, then, the twelve essays in the collection address the question of what happened to 'voyage drama' and 'travel drama' over the course of the seventeenth century, pushing our conception of the journeying play in exciting and uncharted directions.

Notes

1 Tim Youngs, *Cambridge Introduction to Travel Writing* (Cambridge University Press, 2013), 4. For a concise overview of debates concerning how 'travel writing' has been defined, and issues of authority and reliability relating to it, see Carl Thompson, *Travel Writing* (London and New York: Routledge, 2011), in particular 9–33, 62–95.
2 Casey Blanton, *Travel Writing: The Self and the Word* (London: Routledge, 2002), 2.
3 Peter Hulme, 'Patagonian Cases: Travel Writing, Fiction, History', in *Seuils & Traverses: Enjeux de l'écriture du voyage*, vol. II, ed. Jan Borm (Brest: Centre de recherche bretonne et celtique, 2002), 223–37.
4 See Claire Jowitt, 'Hakluyt's Legacy: Armchair Travel in English Renaissance Drama', in *Richard Hakluyt and Travel Writing in Early Modern Europe*, ed. Daniel Carey and Claire Jowitt (Farnham: Ashgate, 2012), 304; Andrew Hadfield, 'Jonson and Shakespeare in an Age of Lying', *Ben Jonson Journal* 23.1 (2016), 52–74.
5 See Daniel Carey, 'Truth, Lies and Travel Writing', in *The Routledge Companion to Travel Writing*, ed. Carl Thompson (London and New York: Routledge, 2016), 3–14.
6 See Percy G. Adams, *Travel Literature and the Evolution of the Novel* (Lexington, KY: University Press of Kentucky, 1983), 95–96.
7 Daniel Vitkus, 'Rogue Cosmopolitans on the Early Modern Stage: John Ward, Thomas Stukeley, and the Sherley Brothers', Chapter 7 in this volume.
8 David McInnis, 'Travelling Characters in Early Modern Drama', Chapter 10 in this volume.
9 Emily C. Bartels, 'Strange Bedfellows: The Ordinary Undersides of "A True Reportory" and *The Tempest*', Chapter 9 in this volume.
10 See Eric J. Griffin, *English Renaissance Drama and the Specter of Spain: Ethnopoetics and Empire* (Philadelphia: University of Pennsylvania Press, 2009).
11 See Claire Jowitt, 'The Uses of Cultural Encounter in Sir William Davenant's Caroline-to-Restoration Voyage Drama', Chapter 12 in this volume.
12 See Anthony Parr, *Renaissance Mad Voyages: Experiments in Early Modern English Travel* (Farnham: Ashgate, 2015), 7. *OED*, 'voyage', n.7.
13 Mary B. Campbell, *The Witness and the Other World: Exotic European Travel Writing, 400–1600* (Ithaca, NY: Cornell University Press, 1988).
14 Marianne Montgomery, 'Language and Seafaring in Thomas Middleton and John Webster's *Anything for a Quiet Life*', Chapter 6 in this volume.
15 Anthony Parr, '"For his Travailes let the *Globe* witnesse": Venturing on the Stage in Early Modern England', Chapter 1 in this volume.
16 Thomas Heywood (ascribed), *The Second Part of, If You Know Not Me, You Know No Bodie* (London: 1606), sig. K; cf. *If You Know Not Me, You Know No Body. The Second Part* (London: 1633), sig. K3ᵛ.

17 For discussion, see Richmond Barbour, *Beyond Orientalism: London's Theatre of the East, 1576–1626* (Cambridge University Press, 2003), 97–101; Sarah Trevisan, 'The Golden Fleece of the London Drapers' Company: Politics and Iconography in Early Modern Lord Mayor's Shows', in *Ceremonial Entries in Early Modern Europe: The Iconography of Power*, ed. J. R. Mulryne et al. (Aldershot: Ashgate, 2015), 258–60.

18 William Davenant, *The History of Sir Francis Drake* (London: 1659).

19 See the entry for 'Ladrones, or The Robbers' Island', in the *Lost Plays Database*, ed., Roslyn L. Knutson, David McInnis, and Matthew Steggle [http://lostplays.folger.edu]. The convention is to reserve the use of italics for titles of extant plays, and to use quotation marks for the titles of lost plays.

20 Harry Kelsey, 'Drake, Sir Francis (1540–1596)', *Oxford Dictionary of National Biography* (Oxford University Press, 2004; online edn, Oct. 2009) [www.oxforddnb.com/view/article/8022, accessed 10 May 2016]; Roslyn L. Knutson, 'Toe to Toe Across Maid Lane: Repertorial Competition at the Rose and Globe, 1599–1600', in, *Acts of Criticism: Performance Matters in Shakespeare and His Contemporaries*, ed. June Schlueter and Paul Nelsen (Madison, NJ: Fairleigh Dickinson University Press, 2005), 21–37, at 27.

21 See David Beers Quinn, *Sir Francis Drake as Seen by His Contemporaries* (Providence, RI: John Carter Brown Library, 1996), 4–5.

22 John Smith, *The True Travels, Adventures, and Observations of Captaine John Smith, In Europe, Asia, Africa, and America, from Anno Domini 1593 to 1629* (London: 1630), sigs. A2^{r-v}.

23 N. W. Bawcutt, ed., *The Control and Censorship of Caroline Drama: The Records of Sir Henry Herbert, Master of the Revels* (Oxford: Clarendon Press, 1996), entry 71.

24 Philip L. Barbour, ed., *The Complete Works of Captain John Smith*, 3 vols. (Chapel Hill, NC: University of North Carolina Press, 1986), III, 390.

25 See David McInnis, 'Lost Plays from Early Modern England: Voyage Drama, A Case Study', *Literature Compass* 8/8 (2011), 534–42.

26 Alan H. Nelson began to address this question in his unpublished paper, 'William Crashawe, Players, and the Virginia Colony', presented at the Shakespeare Association of America's annual meeting in Atlanta, Georgia, in 2017.

27 William Crashaw, *A Sermon Preached in London before the Right Honorable the Lord Lawarre, Lord Governour and Captaine Generall of Virginea, and others of his Majesties Counsell for that Kingdome, and the rest of the Adventurers in that Plantation* (London: 1610), sigs. H3^v–[H4].

28 Ibid.

29 Ibid.

30 Wilhelm Creizenach, *The English Drama in the Age of Shakespeare* (New York: Haskell House, 1964), 183n.

31 For a discussion of this text, see Andrew Gordon, '*Eastward Ho* and the Traffic of the Stage', Chapter 5 in this volume.

32 See 'Earl Godwin and His Three Sons, Parts 1 and 2', in the *Lost Plays Database*.

33 British Library (BL) MS Egerton 2623, ff 37–38; see also the *Lost Plays Database* entry for 'Play of Oswald (BL MS Egerton 2623)'.

34 For discussion of the relationship between travel and travail, see Daniel Vitkus, 'Labour and Travel on the Early Modern Stage: Representing the Travail of Travel in Dekker's *Old Fortunatus* and Shakespeare's *Pericles*', in *Working Subjects in Early Modern Drama*, ed. Michelle M. Dowd and Natasha Korda (London and New York: Routledge, 2016), 225–42, especially 229–30.

35 See Martin Wiggins, *British Drama, 1533–1642: A Catalogue*, 5 vols. (Oxford University Press, 2011–15), V, entries 892 and 960.

36 *OED*, 'journeying', n.

37 Parr, *Renaissance Mad Voyages*, 104.

38 For details of this and the preceding discussion, see 'Fair Constance of Rome, Parts 1 and 2', in the *Lost Plays Database*.

39 See the digitisation of British Library Add. MS10449, f.2 in the *Lost Plays Database* entry for 'Frederick and Basilea'.

40 Stephen Gosson, *The School of Abuse* (Printed at London: for Thomas Woodcocke, 1579), 23.

41 Julie Sanders, 'Making the Land Known: *Henry IV*, *Parts 1 and 2*, and the Literature of Perambulation', Chapter 4 in this volume.

42 Folger MS X.d.206; see the *Lost Plays Database* entry, 'Scenario of a play set in Thrace and Macedon (Folger MS X.d.206)' for a digitisation of the fragment and accompanying scholarship.

43 Tiffany Stern, *Documents of Performance in Early Modern England* (Cambridge University Press, 2009), 13.

44 Edward Dering, 'Scenario of a play set in Thrace and Macedon', Folger MS X.d.206, fos.1ᵛ–2ʳ.

45 Bodleian Library, MS Locke e. 6; see David McInnis, '"Orozes, King of Albania": An Unpublished Plot for a Stage Romance, by John Locke', *Review of English Studies* 65 (2014), 266–80, and a more extensive discussion in the introduction to the critical edition of the plot as edited by J. R. Milton and David McInnis in *The Clarendon Edition of the Works of John Locke: Literary and Historical Writings* (Oxford: Clarendon Press, forthcoming).

46 See Claire Jowitt, *Voyage Drama and Gender Politics, 1589–1642: Real and Imagined Worlds* (Manchester University Press, 2003).

47 The relationship between travel and drama here contrasts with that between travel and prose writing, where, as exemplified in Thomas More's *Utopia* (1516), there is a much stronger tradition of autobiographical writing, or stories that engage their author's experiences in a more direct way.

48 'Fragment of a play in the Journal of Benjamin Greene', in the *Lost Plays Database*.

49 See the *Lost Plays Database* entry, 'Unfinished Play by Richard Norwood'.

50 Wesley Frank Craven and Walter B. Hayward, ed., *The Journal of Richard Norwood, Surveyor of Bermuda* (Ann Arbor, MI: Scholars Facsimiles & Reprints, 1945), 42.

51 Ibid.
52 See Hamish Scott, 'Travel and Communications', in *The Oxford Handbook of Early Modern European History, 1350–1750*, ed. Hamish Scott (Oxford University Press, 2015), 170–72.
53 *Thomas Platter's Travels in England 1599*, trans. Clare Williams (London: Jonathan Cape, 1937), 170.
54 Ann Jennalie Cook, *The Privileged Playgoers of Shakespeare's London, 1576–1642* (Princeton University Press, 1981), 176–77.
55 McInnis, 'Travelling Characters', Chapter 10 in this volume.
56 Parr, 'For his Travailes', Chapter 1 in this volume; Ladan Niayesh, 'Seeing and Overseeing the Stage as Map in Early Modern Drama', Chapter 2 in this volume; Steve Mentz, 'Marlowe's Mediterranean and Counter-Epic Forms of Oceanic Hybridity', Chapter 3 in this volume.
57 See Jowitt, 'The Uses of Cultural Encounter', Chapter 12 in this volume.
58 For discussion, see, most recently, the twenty-four essays in *Richard Hakluyt and Travel Writing in Early Modern Europe*.
59 See Anthony Payne, *Richard Hakluyt: A Guide to his Books and to Those Associated with Him 1580–1625* (London: Quaritch, 2008) [www.hakluyt.com/hakluyt_census.htm].
60 See Peter Hulme and William H. Sherman, *'The Tempest' and Its Travels* (London: Reaktion Books, 2000).
61 Jean-Pierre Maquerlot and Michèle Willems, ed., *Travel and Drama in Shakespeare's Time* (Cambridge University Press, 1996), 1.
62 For instance, the alteration of the title of the journal *Atlantic Studies* to *Atlantic Studies: Global Currents* in 2013 reflects this broadening of scholarly attention.
63 See, for instance, Nabil Matar, *Islam in Britain 1558–1685* (Cambridge University Press, 1998); *Turks, Moors and Englishmen in the Age of Discovery* (New York: Columbia University Press, 1999); *Britain and Barbary 1589–1689* (Gainesville, FL: University of Florida Press, 2005); Matthew Dimmock, *New Turkes: Dramatizing Islam and the Ottomans in Early Modern England* (Aldershot: Ashgate, 2005); Linda McJannet, *The Sultan Speaks: Dialogue in English Plays and Histories about the Ottoman Turks* (New York: Palgrave Macmillan, 2006); Robert Markley, *The Far East and the English Imagination, 1600–1730* (Cambridge University Press, 2006); Anna Suranyi, *The Genius of the English Nation. Travel Writing and National Identity in Early Modern England* (Newark, DE: University of Delaware Press, 2008); Barbara Sebek and Stephen Deng, ed., *Global Traffic: Discourses and Practices of Trade in English Literature and Culture from 1550 to 1700* (New York: Palgrave Macmillan, 2008); Jyotsna G. Singh, ed., A Companion to the Global Renaissance: *English Literature and Culture and Literature in the Era of Expansion* (Oxford: Wiley–Blackwell, 2009); Ofer Gal and Yi Zheng, ed., *Motion and Knowledge in the Changing Early Modern World: Orbits, Routes and Vessels* (Dordrecht: Springer, 2014); Jane Grogan, *The Persian Empire in English Renaissance Writing, 1549–1622* (Basingstoke: Palgrave, 2014).

64 See Daniel Vitkus, *Turning Turk: English Theater and the Multicultural Mediterranean, 1570–1630* (London and New York: Palgrave, 2003); Brian Lockey, *Early Modern Catholics, Royalists, and Cosmopolitans: English Transnationalism and the Christian Commonwealth* (Burlington, VT: Ashgate, 2015).

65 Steve Mentz, 'Toward a Blue Cultural Studies: The Sea, Maritime Culture, and Early Modern English Literature', *Literature Compass*, 6 (2009), 997–1013; Lauren Benton, *A Search for Sovereignty: Law and Geography in European Empires 1400–1900* (Cambridge University Press, 2010); David Armitage, 'The Elephant and the Whale: Empires and Oceans in World History', in Armitage, *Foundations of Modern International Thought* (Cambridge University Press, 2012), 46–56.

66 See Mentz, 'Marlowe's Mediterranean', Chapter 3 in this volume.

67 Richmond Barbour and Bernhard Klein, 'Drama at Sea: A New Look at Shakespeare on the *Dragon*, 1607–08', Chapter 8 in this volume.

68 Jonathan P. Sell, *Rhetoric and Wonder in English Travel Writing, 1560–1613* (Aldershot: Ashgate, 2006). See, for instance, Andrew Hadfield, *Literature, Travel and Colonial Writing in the English Renaissance 1545–1625* (Oxford University Press, 1998) and Helen Ostovich et al., ed., *The Mysterious and the Foreign in Early Modern England* (Newark, DE: University of Delaware Press, 2008).

69 See Clare McManus, '"Constant Changelings", Theatrical Form, and Migration: Stage Travel in the Early 1620s', Chapter 11 in this volume.

70 Mark Netzloff, *England's Internal Colonies: Class, Capital, and the Literature of Early Modern English Colonialism* (New York: Palgrave, 2003); Andrew McRae, *Literature and Domestic Travel in Early Modern England* (Cambridge University Press, 2009).

71 See, for instance, Julie Sanders, *The Cultural Geography of Early Modern Drama, 1620–1650* (Cambridge University Press, 2011); Garrett A. Sullivan, Jr., *The Drama of Landscape: Land, Property and Social Relations on the Early Modern Stage* (Stanford, CA: Stanford University Press, 1999).

72 Sanders, 'Making the Land Known', Chapter 4 in this volume.

73 Andrew Gordon, '*Eastward Ho* and the Traffic of the Stage', Chapter 5 in this volume.

74 For discussion, see Jean Howard, 'Introduction: English Cosmopolitanism and the Early Modern Moment', *Shakespeare Studies* 35 (2007), 19–23, at 19, as well as the essays in the issue.

75 Stephen Greenblatt, *Marvellous Possessions: The Wonder of the New World* (Oxford: Clarendon, 1991).

76 'Theatregrams' are the 'interchange and transformation of units, figures, relationships, actions, *topoi*, and framing patterns'; see Louise George Clubb, *Italian Drama in Shakespeare's Time* (New Haven, CT: Yale University Press, 1989), 6. For a recent discussion of their influence, see Jacques Lezra, 'Trade in Exile', in *Transnational Mobilities in Early Modern Theater*, ed. Robert Henke and Eric Nicholson (Farnham: Ashgate, 2014), 199–216; see also Henke and Nicholson's 'Introduction', 1–23.

CHAPTER I

'For his Travailes let the Globe witnesse': Venturing on the Stage in Early Modern England

Anthony Parr

University of the Western Cape

'How mightely Playes pull us backe from our travell', wrote Stephen Gosson in 1582, in *Playes Confuted*, the second of his anti-theatrical tracts.[1] Gosson was a former actor and dramatist who turned against the theatre and in a polemical skirmish with his ex-colleague Thomas Lodge (who continued to write plays for the rest of the century) laid the foundations of an argument about the morality and function of the public stage that would rage for the next sixty years. In that period, and particularly through the last twenty years of Elizabeth I's reign and the first Jacobean decade, as England's overseas activity steadily increased, Gosson's declaration was echoed and rephrased in different contexts, and with different shades of meaning – most notably by the supporters of the Virginia Company when the Jamestown colony was struggling to survive in 1609–10. In those years the company launched a propaganda campaign to save the venture, and a number of sermons and pamphlets objected strongly to 'the licentious vaine of stage Poets', demanding to know 'why are the *Players* enemies to this Plantation and doe abuse it?'[2] By then the theatre had other kinds of foreign venture in its sights as well: Sir Philip Sidney had correctly predicted in 1578 that before long 'wee Travellers shall bee made sport of in Comedies', presumably because he had seen enough of his fellow-countrymen's behaviour in Europe to realise that this was a ripe topic for criticism.[3] He may also have been apprehensive about the newly built Shoreditch playhouses (The Curtain and The Theatre) discrediting a practice that, as a good European, he thought was important, and was no doubt aware of the long literary tradition of satire on the pretensions and fabrications of the traveller that was about to be adapted and updated on the public stage, and which was probably already deployed in academic drama. Jerome Turler's declaration, in a 1575 English translation of his Latin manual *De Peregrinatione* (Strasbourg: 1574), that 'the Tragicall and Comicall Poets, when they bringe in any far traueiling Woman, for the most parte they feine her to be incontinent', is likely to refer mainly to pedagogic plays in Latin written by German humanists,[4] though as a traveller himself he could have seen their equivalents in England; and the so-called 'university wits' who created much of the first wave of drama in permanent theatrical venues were ready to adapt the cautionary tropes of academic plays to their own ends.[5]

However, Gosson was not admiring these satirical efforts when he declared 'How mightely Playes pull us backe from our travell', because he was not willing to grant the theatre even that much critical space. What he meant was that plays divert their spectators from the path of right-eousness: 'We are placed as Pilgrimes in the flesh', he says, 'by which as by a jorney we must come to our own home' and reach heaven through the travails of an earthly existence.[6] The well-worn but hallowed meta-phor of life as a journey, virtually inescapable in devotional writing of the period and central to the plot of morality drama, was one that Gosson found to be derelict in the kind of theatrical performance emanating from inn-yard stages and the earliest of the purpose-built public theatres. These plays, with plots plundered from old romances, were a popular sta-ple of London's new playhouses, and they were an important stage in the development of a fully secular drama. But Gosson was clearly exasperated by Lodge's Ciceronian claim, later to be repeated by Ben Jonson, that contemporary drama provided an image of truth, since the romance plots of the journeying plays popular in the 1570s were in his view certainly no pilgrim's progress:

> Sometime you shall see nothing but the adventures of an amorous knight, passing from countrie to countrie for the love of his lady, encountering many a terrible monster made of broune paper, & at his retorne, is so wonderfully changed, that he can not be knowne but by some posie in his tablet, or by a broken ring, or a handkircher, or a piece of cockle shell, what learne you by that?[7]

This recoil from escapist theatrical fare is closely related to the objec-tions that Roger Ascham and others made to the translations of Italian prose fiction that were appearing in England at much the same time, stories whose complicated plots and serpentine narratives were seen to lack the clean lines of a moral tale capable of guiding the life of the reader. Ascham believed that reading Italian *novelle* was almost as dangerous as visiting Italy itself, and Gosson argued that 'many wan-ton Italian bookes ... have poysoned the olde maners of our Country with forrein delights', so that 'severer writers are trode under foote', and 'This contempt of good bookes hath breede a desire of fancies & toyes.'[8] In this context Gosson sees the theatre as the Devil's backup plan for the illiterate: since many cannot read 'Italian baudery', he 'presenteth us Comedies cut by the same paterne, which drag such a monstrous taile after them, as is able to sweep whole Cities into his lap'.[9] Books and plays that do not foster an understanding of the Christian path are liable to transport their auditors into the wrong kind of experience; and the question Gosson levels at the drama, 'What learne you by that?' was also the constant cry of those, like Ascham, who were opposed to foreign travel or who sought to steer young men away from frivolous and risky behaviour while abroad.

The moralists thought Italian fiction and the plays that flowed from it were as bad as travel to Italy because they were *like* such travel; and in this period there is a persistent collocation of players and travellers: both itinerant, both traders in far-fetched tales, both dressed in borrowed robes. It was another lapsed playwright, Anthony Munday, who offered perhaps the most telling thrust against the dramatists of the journeying play:

> The writers of our time are led awaie with vainglorie... The notablest lier is become the best Poet; he that can make the most notorious lie, and disguise falshood in such sort, that he maie passe unperceaved, is held the best writer... Our nature is led awaie with vanitie, which the auctor perceiving frames himself with novelties and strange trifles to content the vaine humors of his rude auditors, faining countries he never heard of; monsters and prodigious creatures that are not: as of the Arimaspie, of the Grips, the Pigmeies, the Cranes, & other such notorious lies.[10]

Munday dresses the playwright in the garb of a familiar caricature – the lying traveller – and equates his literary efforts with John Mandeville's *Travels*, the medieval account of exotic adventure best known to Elizabethan readers from editions in 1568 and 1582.[11] Munday also exploits the common distrust of fiction that Sidney was trying to deal with in the *Apology for Poetry* (written c.1580, published 1595), and is able to pick up on the already common comparison between the player and the traveller as vagrants and mountebanks, one that was all the more available in the 1580s as itinerant English acting groups made their way to the Continent and were notorious for the clownish and bawdy elements in their performances.

The romantic journeying plays of the 1570s (few of which have survived)[12] were scorned not only by Gosson and Sidney, but also by the
theatrical *avant-garde*, though on aesthetic rather than moral grounds.
Those plays must have been mostly composed in the 'jigging vein of
rhyming mother wits' that Christopher Marlowe dismisses (and effectively makes obsolete) in the prologue to *Tamburlaine*[13] – the fourteeners
and Poulter's measure that his 'mighty line' replaced – and this can only
have highlighted the rambling and episodic tendency of their plots. At
the same time, these romantic comedies anticipated those of John Lyly
and William Shakespeare in important respects, and were the ancestors
of Thomas Heywood's popular voyage dramas. One reason for this, as
Kent Cartwright shows, is that they are partly shaped by a tradition of
humanist drama that they helped to popularise and bring into the commercial mainstream.[14] Gosson hated these secular plays because they
were not traditional moralities; but he refused to see that the themes of
love and honour and identity this drama deals with, however clumsily,
were generated by the meeting of humanism and romance in earlier
sixteenth-century interludes like John Redford's *The Play of Wit and
Science* (c.1544) and Nicholas Udall's *Ralph Roister Doister* (c.1566).
What humanism brings to romance is a set of moral and intellectual
interests, so that discovery – the moment of recognition after a long process of wandering – becomes invested with ideas of knowledge and self-
renewal.[15] The case for viewing secular drama in these terms, however,
commonly foundered on a particular sticking point for many critics of
the popular stage, namely the doctrine of the dramatic unities.

A key objection to the wandering or journeying play, or an explanation for its baggy shape, was that it failed to observe the unities of time
and space – an objection, of course, that by definition applied to virtually any play trying to represent a journey. It is usually said that English
drama at this date is too much the product of a native popular tradition
to be interested in neoclassical rules of construction. Yet the importance
of the unities for coherent playmaking is a chronic theme in the period:
Jonson used it as a stick with which to beat Shakespeare, explicitly in
his rejection of the dramaturgy in the *Henry VI* plays that can 'make
a child, now swaddled, to proceed / Man, and then shoot up... Past
threescore years', and less directly in his scorn for the expansive idiom of
Shakespeare's late voyage dramas, which he dismissed as '*Tales, Tempests*
and such-like drolleries'.[16] And in 1614 the writer Richard Brathwaite
complained that the stage has set the example for, or lent credence to, a
great deal of eclectic and confused writing, from natural history to travel

accounts to prose fiction, 'phanaticke Chymeras' or 'erroneous stories' that, he said,

> are like some Comoedies wee reade now a daies; The first Act whereof is in *Asia*, the next in *Affrica*, the third in *Europa*, the fourth in *America*: and if *Ptolomeus*, or *Marcus Paulus* had found out a fifth part of the world, no question but it had beene represented on their universall Stage.[17]

Twenty years later the fifth continent would duly make its appearance, in Richard Brome's *The Antipodes* (1638), albeit in a dramatic conceit that cunningly circumvents the problem of conforming to the unities of time and space. But in important respects the issue of shifting location and time frame had been resolved long before, and not just through a cavalier disregard for the rules. The classical precepts on the unities had been elaborated by Italian theorists into a highly prescriptive regime; yet when the Italian humanist Titus Livius Frulovisi was lured to England to work for Humphrey, Duke of Gloucester in the 1430s, having already written in Venice a number of neo-Latin comedies that were staged in England during his stay, he composed there (in 1437) another play called *Peregrinatio*, whose prologue announces that:

> we are about to show you what comforts travellers enjoy as well as how many hardships and great dangers their journeys lead them into... Our hero's journey will be rather extensive... And so the focus has shifted. Other writers merely describe actions at Thessalonica, Venice or Ravenna, Syria or Troy, but we present all locations in one place. The others use messengers or letters to tell of happenings in distant places. But now when things happen in Rhodes the tale is told at Rhodes, in Crete at Crete. The custom is the same in Britain. Everything happens right here: and when the action takes place, as it were, right in front of you, then you'll know how effective the author's inventiveness is.[18]

Whether or not the custom of dramatising multiple settings was firmly established in native playwriting at this date, as Frulovisi seems to suggest, his remarks attest to a humanist dramaturgy that was known and accepted in England, and arguably created a kind of blueprint for the play of voyaging and adventure. Frulovisi, whose own play is a Plautine comedy of loss and rediscovery that moves between Britain, Rhodes, and Crete and is considerably more peripatetic than, for instance, *The Comedy of Errors* (*c*.1592) (which it distantly resembles), prompts us to look anew at the tradition behind the general English flouting of the unities, and to ask how this may have prepared the stage to deal with an unprecedented number of exotic subjects just as it was achieving its greatest organisational strength.

Brathwaite's complaint about 'phanaticke Chymeras' and 'erroneous stories' invading English literary culture is a reminder of the formal and intellectual challenges posed by geographical discovery: how to assimilate and assess all this new information, and how to represent it? The English stage at a formative moment in its development was handed a treasure trove of new topics, ideas, and potential settings, and indeed, in traditional accounts of the Renaissance, national expansion and the flowering of English drama have long been felt to belong together, as twin manifestations of a new energy and confidence. And although a great deal of postcolonial cold water has been poured on this way of thinking, it partly survives in materialist analyses of the London playhouses – as joint-stock operations whose economic structure resembles that of the East India and Muscovy companies, and as organisations patronised by noblemen with investments in colonialism and trade. This kind of perspective yields, for instance, Richard Wilson's reading of Marlowe's *Tamburlaine* as an allegory of the Muscovy Company's designs on Eastern trade, 'open[ing] the golden road to Samarkand' following the establishment of ties with Ivan the Terrible's Russia.[19] There is also valuable work being done on the workings of the theatre companies that asks questions about the kinds of expertise required by these exercises in venture capitalism. In an important article, Evelyn Tribble brings ideas developed by social scientists about early modern navigation to bear on theatre of the period, suggesting that the kinds of group expertise and co-operative work required to conduct a voyage efficiently are akin to those operating in the complex repertory system of the London theatres, combining strict hierarchy and operational rules with a high degree of collaboration and the constant training of apprentices.[20] Social scientists call this 'distributed cognition', whereby the system is greater than the sum of its parts: it may enable and at times require individual genius, a Shakespeare, a Richard Burbage or a Will Kemp, or a Francis Drake, John Hawkins, or Richard Chancellor, but the sustained, incremental achievements of early modern English theatre and navigation alike depended on possibly unprecedented levels of mental and physical co-operation. Tribble uses this argument to think about how the theatre repertory system worked; we might also want to ask how distributed cognition helped to solve the demanding problems of representing journeys and exotic settings on a stage.

Such an approach might help to deal with the fact that the early modern stage paid scant attention to the achievements of England's most famous mariners – the navigators, freebooters, and sea dogs who were later mythologised as the architects of imperial greatness. Where, it might be asked, are the plays about Drake and Hawkins and other heroes of maritime derring-do? A logical explanation for their absence is that long sea voyages can scarcely be staged, and several early modern playwrights felt compelled to echo the Chorus in Heywood's *Fair Maid of the West* (*c.*1597)*:* 'Our stage so lamely can express a sea / That we are forced by Chorus to discourse / What should have been in action'.[21] Is this one of the reasons why, when dramatists considered how to use the momentous reports of England's first exploratory forays eastward beyond familiar European boundaries, the play that emerged was not the eventful tale of the search for a North-East Passage to Cathay in 1554, a harrowing maritime ordeal that led to Chancellor's celebrated introduction to the court of Ivan the Terrible, but (if Wilson is right) one in which 'Tamburlaine's transit into Persia and Turkey ["near 5000 leagues"] recapitulates the expeditions that regularly earned Muscovy Company shareholders dividends of 400 per cent in the terrible years of Ivan'?[22] The seminal events of the 1554 voyage were a study in tragic heroism, though we can see why Marlowe would be more interested in writing about tycoons than navigators, but the obvious advantage for theatrical purposes of the Tamburlaine story, and of merchant adventuring in the Middle East, was that they were land enterprises. *Tamburlaine* is a more old-fashioned play than it claims to be, dependent for much of its cumulative effect on processional spectacle as Tamburlaine pursues his journey of conquest, and it could draw on a long theatrical tradition of pageantry and courtly display.

On the other hand, should we take the apologia of Heywood's Chorus at face value? Likewise, does the presence of these choric figures in a number of early modern journeying plays indicate a real difficulty with staging journeys, especially sea voyages, and shifts of location? Or are they rhetorical devices to focus the drama's storytelling power? It is true that the early modern theatre seems to have left the great maritime ventures alone: Martin Frobisher and Henry Hudson, Drake and Thomas Cavendish, Richard Grenville and the last fight of the *Revenge*, and the early voyages of the East India Company are all absent from the dramatic record, though with so many plays lost (with titles like *Conquest of the West Indies* and *The New World's Tragedy*), we should probably reserve judgement about whether these stories were actively avoided.[23] And it is worth asking whether the playhouses were genuinely inhibited about staging this kind of action, despite their choruses' professions of difficulty or inadequacy. When Gosson's antagonist Lodge, together with Robert Greene, wrote an Old Testament play in which at one point 'Jonas the

Prophet [is] cast out of the Whales belly upon the Stage', it is as though Gosson's assertion that plays and spiritual travel, or travail, are incompatible has been answered by a piece of exemplary stagecraft.[24] Similarly, the opening scene of *The Tempest* is a *tour de force* of technical playmaking, and although it dramatises a shipwreck, it is a splendid illustration of Tribble's argument about the congruence of navigational and theatrical expertise. Taken together with the exciting scene in Heywood's *Fortune by Land and Sea* (*c.*1622) where one ship is boarded and taken over by another, and various devices to suggest a maritime context, like the lurching rhythm of the drinking scene aboard Pompey's galley in *Antony and Cleopatra* (*c.*1608), or the use of different levels and sight lines to evoke the archipelago setting of Fletcher and Massinger's *The Sea Voyage* (1622),[25] it seems clear that the playhouses were quite capable of turning much of what they could find in Richard Hakluyt's *The Principal Navigations* into vivid theatre.[26] Even the epic voyages of the Elizabethan navigators contain incidents and situations that are gifts to a dramatist, whether it be the struggle for power in the first stage of Drake's circumnavigation that led to the trial and execution of Thomas Doughty at Puerto San Julián (where Ferdinand Magellan had also executed mutineers in 1520), or the brooding intensity of Cavendish's tragic end.

We need also to remember, as Gosson perhaps did, that English drama was originally constituted by the enactment of ritual journeys and possessed a symbolic machinery to express motion and conveyance and give it specific meanings. In the liturgical rituals out of which church drama grew, this took the form of procession, or the marking of the Stations of the Cross, or the tracing of a symbolic labyrinth on the church floor. Later, the miracle plays were mounted on pageant wagons, and always included a representation of Noah's Ark, while large-scale model ships were a familiar sight in courtly entertainments and tournaments. Ship pageant cars also featured regularly in civic entertainments,[27] and it is likely that stage drama appropriated this device for its own purposes. In plays roughly at either end of the sixteenth century, one of the period's most influential nautical metaphors becomes briefly central to the action and may have been realised as a stage property. In the interlude *Hickscorner* (*c.*1514) the eponymous Vice-figure is a ship's master and is first heard shouting naval commands as he anchors his vessel, and then describes in detail the company of villains that he is shipping into England. The list of misfits and criminals who form his crew draws on the well-known trope of the Ship of Fools (two English versions of Sebastian Brant's *Narrenschiff* had appeared five years earlier),[28] and his vessel's safe arrival in England is ironically juxtaposed with a graphic recollection of recent maritime disasters and their innocent victims.[29] Riot and disorder duly invade the playing space as several characters come to blows and turn it into a simulacrum of the unruly ship itself. Ninety years later, John Marston reverses this dramatic sequence in his play *The Fawn* (1604), as the state is cleansed by an order to transport all offenders, who are sentenced in a final trial scene and put one by one on board the Ship of Fools. As Marston's editor David Blostein comments, a wheeled ship made partly visible would be the most effective way to stage this scene, and was well within the capacities of the Blackfriars theatre. It would also have been readily available to Charles Brandon, the courtly sponsor of *Hickscorner*, who, as Greg Walker shows, was concerned to highlight a threatened invasion of England.[30] But even if the public stages did not make much use of such vessels, their existence for various ceremonial purposes gave them a theatrical identity that must have helped to bridge the gap in people's minds between oceanic tales and the business of the stage. And because public culture was so imbued with concepts like the ship of state and the ship of fools, their metaphorical if not actual presence in the theatre also kept posing questions for the audience about the ethical structure of travel acts that Gosson believed, wrongly, could no longer be represented on a stage.

Nowhere was this humanist faith in drama's contract with venturing more evident than in the circumstances surrounding the production of what is often seen as the first English travel play, John Rastell's *Interlude of the Four Elements* (c.1518) – though, by the Introduction's terminology, it is categorised as both travel and voyage drama.[31] Rastell, the brother-in-law of Sir Thomas More, was committed to the new learning, studying geography, and practising mercantile law, and in 1517 he became involved in a trading expedition to the northern fisheries of the New World. The voyage was a fiasco, getting no further than Ireland, and ironically foreshadowed some of the difficulties that beset later expeditions to Virginia. There were attempts by some members to put into a French port so that the trade goods could be sold for a quick profit, and by others to divert the voyage to piracy. It ended in mutiny, with the captain locked in his cabin while the crew returned to England. At this very early moment in England's imperial effort, we have a tale of unfortunate travellers that seems to provide a script for later satires on misbegotten ventures and abortive voyages. Yet Rastell went on to write a rather different play, in which, while briefly censuring the 'maryners, / Fals of promys and dissemblers', who had wrecked the expedition, he develops a humanist

allegory in which Experience, a much-travelled figure rather like Raphael
Hythloday in More's *Utopia* (1516), brings on stage a chart or globe
that he explicates to Studious Desire before trying to get the attention
of Humanity, who has been temporarily seduced from his geographical
studies by Sensuall Appetite.[32] It is certainly arguable that the figure of
Humanity in this play anticipates the vain and misguided traveller of later
satire, and that a view of English overseas ventures as fragile and easily
sabotaged is what emerges from the allegory and Rastell's references to the
events that generated it. But these anxieties are part of the humanist project, not signs – at this point anyway – of a disengagement from national
expansion or corrosive doubts about its worth. Rastell built a theatre in
his house in Finsbury that showed his commitment to plays capable of
exploring the humanist fear of self-betrayal in pursuit of a greater grasp of
the material world, and also of testing new knowledge against the traditional assumptions enshrined in the form of the morality play.[33]

On the face of it, this faith in drama's constructive engagement with
travel had been considerably weakened by the closing decades of the sixteenth century. The critique of 1570s journeying plays by writers such as
Sidney and Gosson gave way to more influential satire within the theatre
milieu itself, with the rise of the boy players and their mockery of the
dramatic fare offered by some of the adult companies – patriotic dramas
with a crusading or swashbuckling theme, and sagas of romantic adventure or of earnest pilgrimage. These intertextual skirmishes sometimes
tell us more about rival theatrical tastes than actual attitudes to overseas
enterprise, yet the sceptical note sounded by parody of the 1570s journeying play inevitably infiltrated public debate about England's expanding horizons. The individual tourist, long a target of 'character' writing, is
repeatedly a figure of ridicule on the English stage, and his (or occasionally her) absurdities must often have been taken as supporting the case
against travel as frivolous and degrading. The traveller Fynes Moryson
complained in 1595 about the way in which 'Stage-players' had brought
into contempt the custom of making 'a long journy' on a wager – a practice that informed a good deal of tourism to Continental destinations in
the period, though it is not clear whether he was criticising theatrical representations or peripatetic actors intruding on a gentlemanly preserve.[34]
Above all, the promoters of the Virginia Company were convinced that
their cause had been hurt by the players, who, claimed Robert Johnson,
helped to ensure that 'the name of *Virginea*' is 'vildly depraved, traduced
and derided by ... unhallowed lips'.[35] Even allowing for exaggeration,
it seems clear that some of those writing for the stage saw no reason to

exempt the colony from a wide-ranging satire on foolish and dangerous ventures.

On the perils of much overseas enterprise, there was a surprising degree of congruence between preachers and players. Johnson, declaring 'experience teacheth us, what need we have to seeke some world of new employment', took aim at those who 'doe daily runne out to robberies at home, and piracies abroad, arming and serving with Turkes and Infidels against Christians', and at 'the wits of England, whereof so many of unsetled braines betake themselves to plots & stratagems at home, or else to wander from coast to coast, from *England* to *Spaine*, to *Italy*, to *Rome*, and to wheresoever they may learne and practise any thing else but goodnesse'.[36] Virginia, he counsels, as a virtuous exception to all this illicit roaming, will take the musty superfluity and reform it. But the playwrights were not impressed by the argument: in *Greenes Tu Quoque*, a play by John Cooke produced about 1611, a gallant called Stains, very much one of those tourists with unsettled brains that Johnson identifies, enters pursued by creditors and complains: 'I dare not walke abroad to see my friends, for feare the Serieants should take acquaintance of me: my refuge is *Ireland*, or *Virginia*; necessitie cries out.' Later he changes his mind and declares he will go to sea, where he will do, he says, 'as other Gallants doe that are spent, turne pyrate'.[37] These options clearly echo Johnson's charges against improvident venturers. It was the casual inclusion of Virginia among these vicious destinations that infuriated the promoters, as did jokes like the one in Middleton and Dekker's *The Roaring Girl* (1611), where Moll Cutpurse cautions Sebastian Wengrave against marrying simply to get out of debt: 'Take deliberation, sir, never choose a wife as if you were going to Virginia.'[38] A decade later, in 1622, as Virginia Company investors sat in the Blackfriars and watched *The Sea Voyage*, they were treated to an unflattering comic vision of stranded voyagers and colonists, one that seems to expand on an enigmatic exchange in the play that Shakespeare composed at a moment when the viability of the Jamestown colony was being widely debated. The scene in *The Tempest* (1611) where the court party take stock of their shipwrecked condition produces a tense exchange in which Sebastian and Antonio confound the positive observations of their companions about the island:

ADRIAN: The air breathes upon us here most sweetly.
SEBASTIAN: As if it had lungs, and rotten ones...
GONZALO: Here is everything advantageous to life.
ANTONIO: True, save means to live.
SEBASTIAN: Of that there's none, or little.[39]

Many in the audience must have been tempted to interpret this riff as a comment on the propaganda wars over Virginia of the previous two years.

As the last two examples suggest, however, satiric commentary on the world of travel was not confined to barbed analogies or vignettes of the self-regarding tourist, and – in the hands of its more thoughtful practitioners in the theatre – was capable of engaging with the complex motives and responses generated by increasing mobility. One way of illustrating this is to look at some treatments of the wager on travel that Moryson thought had been devalued by the players. This mechanism may hardly seem to be at the centre of the ethical challenges facing English adventurers, and in fact wagering was another of the practices that unsympathetic observers could conclude was common to footloose actors and travellers.[40] Yet it registers significantly in the more sustained attention that Shakespeare and Jonson give to travel experience.

I have discussed elsewhere Jonson's painstaking delineation in *Every Man Out of His Humour* (1599) of Puntarvolo's proposed wager journey to Constantinople, a highly entertaining sketch that throws light on the idiosyncratic aspirations and methods to which early modern travellers had recourse.[41] The serio-comic scrutiny that Jonson habitually brought to his dramatic material is even more suggestively deployed in Shakespeare's treatment of the travel wager. In *The Tempest*, the 'living drollery' of a banquet in the wilderness that Prospero creates for his shipwrecked enemies prompts the awestruck Gonzalo to declare:

> When we were boys,
> Who would believe that there were mountaineers
> Dew-lapped like bulls, whose throats had hanging at 'em
> Wallets of flesh? – or that there were such men
> Whose heads stood in their breasts? – which now we find
> Each putter-out of five for one will bring us
> Good warrant of. (3.3.43–49)[42]

In future, says Gonzalo (with his tongue firmly in his cheek), he will treat the tall tales of travellers with more respect. This is Shakespeare's most explicit reference to the vogue for wager-journeys (in which the traveller 'put out' a stake to be repaid at an agreed rate of multiplication if he completed the journey successfully), and it allows him to play a game of his own within the fiction he has created. At the very moment when the illusory banquet is delivering its clear moral lesson, Gonzalo declares that it is no less (and by implication no more) trustworthy than the exotic stories used to help win a traveller's bet. Can even the most ethical of

fictions be reliable as a guide to conduct, or do they traffic in and encour-
age the very follies they seem to condemn, as the Puritan critics of literary invention (especially stage plays and romances) argued? Gonzalo will
later applaud as providential the expedition that brought the court party
to the island, but here he reads it as a fantastic venture, one that produces
the kind of testimony associated with the travel wager. The question
posed by Shakespeare's design is this: which discourse engages more effectively with the moral complexities of the action, the radiant certainty of
Gonzalo's final speech about the purpose of the voyage (and Prospero's
own conviction that 'providence divine' brought him and Miranda to the
island), or the destabilising play of ideas that the dramatist deliberately
contrives with his provocative analogies?

A much more sober, even potentially tragic example of the travel wager
is offered in Shakespeare's *Cymbeline*, which was staged in 1610 at the
height of the Virginia promotional campaign. The wager that is con-
tracted in Rome between Posthumus and Giacomo, whereby the latter
will win Posthumus's ring if he goes to Britain and succeeds in seducing
his wife, is set up as a contemporary bet on travel: Rome in the play is a
Renaissance destination and Giacomo and Posthumus look like modern
tourists, despite the play's setting in ancient Britain. Giacomo, having
tricked his way into Innogen's bedroom, gathers the detailed evidence he
needs to prove his having been there, his 'testimonie of the performance',
as Jonson's Puntarvolo would have it;[43] but his actual attempts to corrupt her mind and body are more redolent of the immoderate violence
generated by other kinds of Renaissance venturing. When Giacomo first
meets Innogen he is dumbfounded by her beauty and virtue, and resorts
to a cheap trick to unsettle her, speaking *sotto voce* about Posthumus's
supposed betrayal of her but making sure he can be overheard: 'are men
mad? Hath nature given them eyes / To see this vaulted arch and the rich
crop of sea and land … and can we not / Partition make with spectacles
so precious / 'Twixt fair and foul?'[44] Giacomo's imagery ('the rich crop
of sea and land') extends the trope of the woman as geographical discovery that Posthumus initiated in setting up the wager: 'If you make your
voyage upon her and give me directly to understand you have prevailed'
(1.5.154–56). The fact that both men resort to this metaphor increases
our sense of a joint male venture – already suggested by the bond – in
which Innogen is the innocent victim. Giacomo's graphic language, while
purporting to describe Posthumus's perverse behaviour, is profoundly
revealing of his own compulsion to defile what he has found, and conjures an unreasoning, irresistible will to consume and exploit: 'The cloyèd

will, / That satiate yet unsatisfied desire, that tub / Both filled and running, ravening first the lamb, / Longs after for the garbage' (1.6.49–52). For anyone pondering the appalling state of affairs in Virginia when *Cymbeline* was first produced – ravenous venturers more interested in finding gold than growing food – and reading Johnson's warning about 'that bitter root of greedy gaine' that is in danger of being 'setled in our harts',[45] Shakespeare's dark parable of mercenary voyaging might well have struck a chord.

My point here is not to claim that *Cymbeline* is really 'about' Virginia in the same way that Sir Petronell Flash's venture in *Eastward Ho* is,[46] but that Shakespeare's treatment of a topical practice – the travel wager – is designed to delve into its psychology and possible implications, and in doing so exposes the connections with other kinds of adventure that Jonson merely hinted at in his collocation of *'Constantinople, Ireland,* or *Virginia'* as favoured destinations of the improvident traveller.[47] Shakespeare is interested in other kinds of 'putting out': what happens when characters place themselves in extreme and unfamiliar conditions, exposed to hardship or new temptation? In the same way, we might compare the comic trope of the aborted voyage that Clifford Leech traces in a sequence of plays[48] with what Shakespeare does with it in *King Lear*, where Edgar leads Gloucester in a parodic pilgrimage to a suicide that the old man thinks will deliver him from his troubles. What would Gosson have thought of this episode? Edgar stages a theatrical coup that flirts with the same comedy of disappointed expectation found in *Eastward Ho*, but its effect is to deliver Gloucester instead from despair. What the charade pulls him from is not his 'travell', his proper journey through life, but the pitfalls of spiritual blindness.

Jean-Christophe Agnew proposes that in the early modern theatre spectators are asked to *'discover* a relation to the play world that an earlier drama had merely directed them to recall'.[49] This may also be to say that they had to discover a relationship to the theatre itself. This was a playing space that sought to represent the world in a very different way from the medieval stage's imitation of a *theatrum mundi*, for it was not seeking to be a cosmic theatre in a universal sense. It is tempting to see it purely as a 'poor' theatre in Jerzy Grotowski's sense, a neutral space to put on plays; and in a way that is how Edgar treats it, as a space over which he can stretch his own fictional meaning. The flexibility of the public theatre stage was an important part of its capacity to represent so many different kinds of environment, and create a sense that those environments were or could be linked in some way, or could be compared with each other or talk to each other. This may put it too benignly: Stephen Greenblatt talks of the essential meaninglessness of the stage space in Marlowe's plays, an arena which Tamburlaine can reduce to a map of his own desires, so that the theatre seems to mimic the abstracting, erasing quality of the colonising act.[50] Thus the poor theatre of Renaissance London becomes an image, and perhaps an instrument, of England's colonial designs on a wider world. But Tamburlaine's designs are not the whole drama, and Edgar's charade is a play within a play; and all the more obviously so when theatres like the Globe sought to represent, and to embody in their very shape, the variety and richness of the terrestrial world. When critics argue about whether the early modern stage was marginal or central to society, a place of entertainment and pleasure or a space that retained a kind of sacramental function, the evidence they muster seems to demonstrate that it could be all these things, in varying proportions and depending on which playhouse you were in and when, over a period of about forty years. Representing travel and the wider world was an acute test of the theatre's capacity to educate, to entertain, to argue, and to warn, and to do all this without pulling a Christian audience from its 'travell'.

Notes

1 Stephen Gosson, *Playes Confuted in Five Actions* (London: T. Gosson, 1582), G2. The title quotation is taken from J. Stephens, *Essayes and Characters* (London: P. Knight, 1615), 270.

2 'Epistle Dedicatorie' to Robert Johnson, *The New Life of Virginea* (London: W. Welby, 1612), A3ᵛ; William Crashaw, *A Sermon Preached ... before the ... Lord Governor and Captaine Generall of Virginia* (London: W. Welby, 1610), H4.

3 Philip Sidney, *Profitable Instructions: Describing what Speciall Observations are to be Taken by Travellers* (London: B. Fisher, 1633), 81.

4 Jerome Turler, *The Traveiler* (London: Abraham Veale, 1575), 9. Turler specifically mentions Medea in this connection, and classical plays were an important shaping influence on humanist dramaturgy in Germany. See James A. Parente, *Religious Drama and the Humanist Tradition* (Leiden: E. J. Brill, 1987), 9–29.

5 Thomas Lodge was one of this group of university-educated writers that also included John Lyly, Christopher Marlowe, and Thomas Nashe. See Robert Logan, ed., *The University Wits* (Farnham: Ashgate, 2011).

6 Gosson, *Playes Confuted*, Gᵛ.

7 Ibid., C6.

8 Ibid., B6.

9 Ibid., B6ᵛ.

10 Anthony Munday, *A Second and Third Blast of Retrait from Plaies and Theaters* (London: W. Seres, 1580), 104–05.

11 *The Voiage and travayle of syr J. Maundeville* (T. East, 1568 and 1582).
12 Surviving examples of such plays are *Clyomon and Clamydes* (c.1570) and *The Rare Triumphs of Love and Fortune* (c.1580). For lost plays, see the *Lost Plays Database*, ed., Roslyn L. Knutson, David McInnis, and Matthew Steggle (Washington, DC: Folger Shakespeare Library, 2009+) [http://lostplays.folger.edu]; David McInnis and Matthew Steggle, ed., *Lost Plays in Shakespeare's England* (Basingstoke: Palgrave Macmillan, 2014); 'Introduction' to this volume.
13 Christopher Marlowe, *Tamburlaine the Great* [1590], ed. John D. Jump (London: Edward Arnold, 1967), *Part 1*, prologue, 1.
14 Kent Cartwright, *Theatre and Humanism: English Drama in the Sixteenth Century* (Cambridge University Press, 1999), 1–24.
15 See Cartwright's discussion of *Wit and Science* in ch. 2 (49–74) of *Theatre and Humanism*, and the analysis of plays dealing with female experience in ch. 5 (135–66).
16 Ben Jonson, *Every Man in his Humour* (Folio Version, 1616), Prologue, 7–9, in David Bevington, Martin Butler, and Ian Donaldson, ed., *The Cambridge Edition of the Works of Ben Jonson* (Cambridge University Press, 2012), IV, 631; *Bartholomew Fair*, Induction, 97–98, in *Cambridge Works of Ben Jonson*, IV, 281.
17 Richard Brathwaite, *The Schollers Medley* (London: G. Norton, 1614), 69.
18 Grady Smith, trans. and ed., *Travel Abroad: Frulovisi's 'Peregrinatio'* (Tempe, AZ: Arizona Centre for Medieval and Renaissance Studies, 2003), 49–51.
19 Richard Wilson, 'Visible Bullets: *Tamburlaine the Great* and Ivan the Terrible', in *Christopher Marlowe and English Renaissance Culture*, ed. D. Grantley and P. Roberts (Aldershot: Scolar, 1996), 57.
20 Evelyn Tribble, 'Distributing Cognition in the Globe', *Shakespeare Quarterly* 56, no. 2 (2005), 135–55.
21 Thomas Heywood, *The Fair Maid of the West, Part 1*, ed. R. K. Turner, Jr., (London: Edward Arnold, 1968), 4.5.1–3.
22 Wilson, 'Visible Bullets', 56.
23 G. M. Sibley, *The Lost Plays and Masques 1500–1642* (Ithaca, NY: Cornell University Press, 1933), 30–31, 110; and see note 8 above.
24 Thomas Lodge and Robert Greene, *A Looking Glass for London and England* (London: W. Barley, 1594), F4ᵛ. For an interesting discussion of possible staging of this scene, see Jenny Sager, *The Aesthetics of Spectacle in Early Modern Drama* (Houndmills: Palgrave Macmillan, 2013), 63–64.
25 *Fortune by Land and Sea*, Act 4, in *Dramatic Works of Thomas Heywood*, ed. R. H. Shepherd (London: Pearson, 1874), VI, 410–20; *Antony and Cleopatra*, Act 2, scene 7, ed. D. Bevington (Cambridge University Press, 2005), 154–61; *The Sea Voyage*, Act 1; Act 2, scene 1, in *Three Renaissance Travel Plays*, ed. Anthony Parr (Manchester University Press, 1995), 137–59. Shakespeare's scene may employ a familiar theatrical trope: C. R. Baskervill suggests that a 1618 allusion to a performance at the Fortune theatre of 'The Ship' refers to a jig whose subject was 'the ancient one, still popular in

the seventeenth century, of drunkards imagining themselves on a rolling ship'. See *The Elizabethan Jig* (University of Chicago Press, 1929), 300–01, and, on the realism of the opening shipwreck scene in *The Tempest*, Gwilym Jones, *Shakespeare's Storms* (Manchester University Press, 2015), 126–31.

26 Richard Hakluyt, *The Principall Navigations of the English Nation* (London: G. Bishop, 1589), enlarged in three volumes from the same publisher, 1598/99–1600. See the discussion by David McInnis in *Mind-Travelling and Voyage Drama in Early Modern England* (Houndmills: Palgrave Macmillan, 2013), 114–21, which came to my attention after this essay was completed.

27 See Glynne Wickham, *Early English Stages*, 3 vols. (London: Routledge, 1959), I, 54, 208–09, and the vivid contemporary account of a 1583 pageant in which 'a Ship ready rigged ... seemed as though it had newly come from *India*, and by great travel and danger had brought home her burden, laden with Gold and Silver', in William Wood, *The Bow-Man's Glory* (London: E. Gough, 1682), 53–54.

28 Alexander Barclay, *The Present Boke named the Shyp of folys of the Worlde* (London: R. Pynson, 1509), and Henry Watson, *The Shyppe of Fooles* (London: W. de Worde, 1509).

29 *Hickscorner*, in Ian Lancashire, ed., *Two Tudor Interludes* (Manchester University Press, 1980), ll. 331–74; Greg Walker, *Plays of Persuasion: Drama and Politics at the Court of Henry VIII* (Cambridge University Press, 1991), 45–47.

30 David Blostein, ed., *Parasitaster or The Fawn* (Manchester University Press, 1978), 29–30; Walker, *Plays of Persuasion*, 44–45. Walker argues that Hick's ludicrous account of his travels is a lampoon of the movements in exile of Reginald de la Pole, pretender to the throne and a political enemy of Charles Brandon. The play was first performed in Brandon's Southwark mansion: half a century before the first public theatres were erected in London's liberties, a play was mounted south of the Thames making edgy use of travel themes to score a political point.

31 See 'Introduction' to this volume.

32 John Rastell, *A New Interlude and a Mery of the Nature of the iiiij elements* (London: J. Rastell, *c.*1520), C1ᵛ.

33 See C. R. Baskervill, 'John Rastell's Dramatic Activities', *Modern Philology* 13 (1916), 557–58.

34 Fynes Moryson, *An Itinerary Containing His Ten Yeeres Travel* [1617] (Glasgow: James Maclehose, 1907), I, 428.

35 Johnson, *New Life of Virginea*, A3ᵛ.

36 Ibid., F4ᵛ.

37 John Cooke, *Greenes Tu Quoque* (London: J. Trundle, 1614), E.

38 Thomas Middleton and Thomas Dekker, *The Roaring Girl*, ed. P. Mulholland (Manchester University Press, 1987), 2.2.68–89.

39 William Shakespeare, *The Tempest*, ed. Stephen Orgel (Oxford: Clarendon Press, 1987), 2.1.47–52. All further quotations refer to this edition and will be cited by act, scene, and line numbers in the text.

40 See Murray Bromberg, 'Theatrical Wagers: A Sidelight on the Elizabethan Drama', *Notes & Queries* 196 (1951), 533–35. I discuss the travel wager at length in my *Renaissance Mad Voyages* (Farnham: Ashgate, 2015), 35–43, 99–138.

41 Ben Jonson, *Every Man Out of His Humour*, 4. 3. 31–41, in *Cambridge Works of Ben Jonson*, I, 364; Anthony Parr, '"Going to Constantinople": English Wager-Journeys to the Ottoman World in the Early-Modern Period', *Studies in Travel Writing* 16, no. 4 (2012), 1–13.

42 For a detailed discussion of this play, see Emily C. Bartels, 'Strange Bedfellows: The Ordinary Undersides of "A True Reportory" and *The Tempest*', Chapter 9 in this volume.

43 Ben Jonson, *Every Man Out of His Humour*, 4.3.31, in *Cambridge Works of Ben Jonson*, I, 364.

44 William Shakespeare, *Cymbeline*, 1.6.33–39, in Stanley Wells and Gary Taylor, ed., *Complete Works* (Oxford: Clarendon Press, 1986), 1282. All further quotations refer to this edition and will be cited with act, scene, and line numbers in the text.

45 Robert Johnson, *Nova Britannia* (London: S. Macham, 1609), sig. C.

46 But see Jean E. Feerick, '*Cymbeline* and Virginia's British Climate', in Feerick, *Strangers in Blood: Relocating Race in the Renaissance* (University of Toronto Press, 2010), 78–112.

47 Ben Jonson, *Epicene*, 2.5.97–98, in *Cambridge Works of Ben Jonson*, III, 428.

48 Clifford Leech, 'Three Times *Ho* and a Brace of Widows', in D. Galloway, ed., *The Elizabethan Theatre III* (Toronto: Macmillan, 1973), 14–32.

49 Jean-Christophe Agnew, *Worlds Apart: The Market and the Theater in Anglo-American Thought, 1550–1750* (Cambridge University Press, 1986), 123.

50 Stephen Greenblatt, *Renaissance Self-Fashioning* (University of Chicago Press, 1980), 195–56.

CHAPTER 2

Seeing and Overseeing the Stage as Map in Early Modern Drama

Ladan Niayesh

Paris Diderot University

'Mapmindedness' is a commonplace often used about early modern English drama.[1] The frequent dialogue between theatre and cartography has long been commented on through the famous examples of the name of the Globe theatre, the titles of such landmark atlases as Abraham Ortelius's *Theatrum orbis terrarum* (1570) and John Speed's *Theatre of the Empire of Great Britain* (1610/11), or the identification of the exact map – Ortelius's Africa – used by Christopher Marlowe to trace the itinerary of Techelles's conquering army in his epoch-making, heroic romance of *Tamburlaine* (part 2, 1588, 1.3).[2] The discourse of power attached to cartographic displays both off-stage and on-stage has also been much studied in recent criticism, from the recurrent inclusion of globes and maps in Elizabeth I's state portraits such as the Ditchley, Sieve, or Armada portraits,[3] to the key interventions of maps as props in plays staging political contention, most famously in Marlowe's *2 Tamburlaine* (5.3), and William Shakespeare's *1 Henry IV* (c.1596–99, 3.1) and *King Lear* (c.1606, 1.1). The discourse of power is particularly noticeable and frequently commented on in the geographical fantasies of Stuart court masques such as Ben Jonson's *Masque of Blackness* (1606) and George Chapman's *Masque of the Middle Temple* (1613), respectively bringing in the daughters of the river Niger sailing out of Africa and Virginian priests travelling on their island to Whitehall, to offer their persons and their riches to the all-seeing, all-reclaiming gaze of the British monarch. Here, it is the masques' carefully worked out focal perspective that symbolises omniscience and omnipotence.[4] But what has been less studied is the trickling down in the public theatre of the device of enabling perspective usually associated by critics primarily or solely with the masque. In fact, as this essay will show, it existed in the public theatre long before the process was exploited to the full by Jonson and Inigo

Jones in the geographical fantasies of their Jacobean court entertainments. In the public theatre of the late sixteenth and early seventeenth centuries, cartographic fictions were not just a way of displaying the *theatrum mundi*, but, more significantly, they also invited their spectators to engage in a power relation with it through a process of visual and imaginative appropriation of perspective. Accordingly, my focus will not only be on plays featuring maps as props, although I will include developments on the two plays most famously using this feature, *Tamburlaine the Great* (*c.*1587–88) and *King Lear*. In these and other plays of travel and/or conquest discussed here as important examples of the cartographic imaginary – including Thomas Heywood's *The Four Prentices of London* (*c.*1594), Thomas Dekker's *Old Fortunatus* (1599), and John Day, William Rowley, and George Wilkins's *The Travels of the Three English Brothers* (*c.*1607) – what interests me primarily is instances in which maps of kingdoms or world maps appear to overflow the boundaries of an on-stage, hand-held prop or a running metaphor to become the stage itself, putting the spectators in the empowered, overseeing perspective of the cartographer surveying and drawing a stage map.

Before focusing on the plays, it is useful to situate the discussion by providing a brief overview of the extent and implications of cartographic literacy among the English public in the last decades of the sixteenth century. My larger argument is that the phenomenon of cartographic literacy was not just an elitist one targeting the most educated members of a theatrical audience, but was identifiable by, and directed at, a larger public.

'At the beginning of the sixteenth century, England was a geographical backwater', notes D. K. Smith in his authoritative study, *The Cartographic Imagination in Early Modern England*, before going on to demonstrate how radically the situation changed over the next half-century, to the point that 'by 1579 England had taken its place at the forefront of geography, creating the first national atlas in the west'; that is to say, Christopher Saxton's *Atlas of the Counties of England and Wales*.[5] The spread of cartographic interest and production in England over the sixteenth century was (to sum up the stages detailed by Smith) prompted by the general context of the travels of discovery and trade undertaken by newly founded international trade companies, the first colonial attempts in Ireland and the New World, and an overall sense of national consciousness encouraged by Tudor political and religious propaganda, well beyond just the rich and educated spheres of early modern society. Audiences' mapmindedness was in turn facilitated by the appearance and circulation of portable printed maps and atlases, as well as by the commissioning of land surveys, especially as part of the process of enclosure. Indeed, as noted by Peter Barber, images derived from Saxton's county maps soon circulated widely in a variety of accessible forms, from cheap woodcuts hanging for decoration in non-elite houses or even taverns, to playing cards adorned with maps of the country's fifty-two counties.[6]

This circulation, and relative democratisation, of cartographic material in wider spheres of society than just the highest or most literate ones was accompanied, as Smith points out, by a shift in the canons of representation, increasingly making the map 'an implicitly physical volume that could be imaginatively inhabited'.[7] Among the technical innovations that enable this transformation, Smith lists the development of scale maps from the 1540s onward, the spread of the bird's-eye perspective, and the rise of panoramic representations of cities and coastlines. The imaginative insertion of viewers within the cartographic illusion is best exemplified by the two human figures taking measures on the foreground of the 1558 chorographic map of Norwich in William Cunningham's *The Cosmographical Glasse* (1559) (see Figure 2.1).[8] Both standing inside the image and taking part in its making with their instruments, the two figures look as if they had moved in from the opposite page, which features a dialogue on chorography between Spoudaeus (the scholar) and Philonicus (the teacher). Breaking down the barriers between the categories of text, map, painting, and even of the theatrical dialogue which their gesturing arms pursue, the two enabled groundlings of this cartographic show of Norwich at once to construct the fiction and are constructed by it through the identity and prominent function that the image confers on them. They are the inside relays by which the outside viewer's perspective is guided, the empowered agents and informants drawing and commenting on the cartographic spectacle for us by proxy.

Similarly empowered choric figures acting as the viewer's surrogates adorn the pages of various other volumes featuring chorographic views and narrative captions of cities in the period, both in England and in continental Europe. Prominent examples include the figures on all the finished maps in Georg Braun and Franz Hogenberg's *Civitates orbis terrarum* (1572). In a similar manner to Cuningham's *Cosmographical Glass*, the figures systematically come in pairs, the experienced one initiating and leading the novice decipherer of the cartographic alphabet. The two types and the attitudes they embody are summed up in the names *Thaumastes* (the one who marvels) and *Panoptes* (the one who sees all) in the preliminary material of *Civitates* commented on by Lucia Nuti.[9]

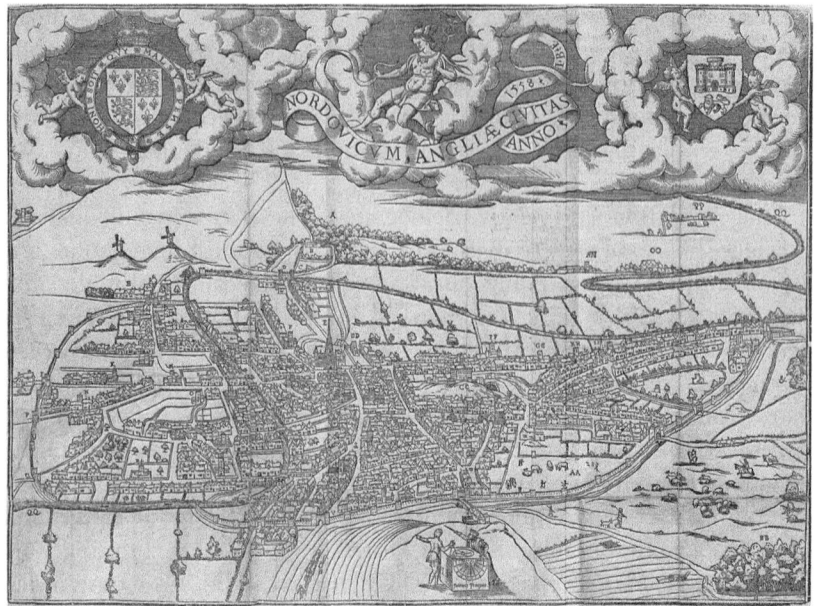

Figure 2.1   William Cuningham, *The Cosmographical Glasse, Conteinyng the Pleasant Principles of Cosmographie, Geographie, Hydrographie, or Navigation* (London: John Day, 1559), map facing fo. 8. Reproduced by permission of the Folger Shakespeare Library [http://luna.folger.edu/luna/servlet/s/f1y296].

Together they can be said to stand at the making and receiving ends of the cartographic illusion, holding hands and inseparable from each other in the process.

In *Making Space: Revisioning the World, 1475–1600*, John Rennie Short studies 'ocular fascination' as a major characteristic of the early modern period.[10] Examples such as the common playing cards adorned with maps of English counties clearly show that ocular fascination was by no means limited to the educated or noble elites, or even the targeted readership of *The Cosmographical Glasse* coming a notch lower on the social hierarchy, or the supporters of John Norden's *Speculum Britanniae* project of topographical and antiquarian mapping of the counties of Britain. The frequency of an empowering rhetoric of cartography and that of perspective – closely related to it – on the public stage is, I shall argue, further proof of the extent to which the phenomenon extended down the social scale.

In his study of the Marlovian models of voyage drama in the immensely popular and recurrently revived epic of power, *Tamburlaine*, David

McInnis marks a distinction between a protagonist model of roving over the map or grasping for dominion over it inside the plot, and a playwright model of making, watching, and controlling both the protagonist and the stage map on which the plot unravels. His distinction recalls Cuningham's Spoudaeus and Philonicus, or Braun and Hogenberg's Thaumastes and Panoptes, the one receiving authority and the other giving it. McInnis further suggests that the audience is by turns invited to imaginatively align with the one or the other model.[11] We can go further, however, since even the protagonist model itself at times intersects with the playwright model. This is exemplified in the famous passage in which Tamburlaine redefines his sword as a cartographer's pen about to draw a new, gridded Ptolemaic map to replace the old tripartite *mappamundi*:

> I will confute those blind geographers
> That make a triple region in the world,
> Excluding regions which I mean to trace,
> And with this pen reduce them to a map,
> Calling the provinces, cities, and towns
> After my name and thine, Zenocrate.
> Here at Damascus will I make the point
> That shall begin the perpendicular.[12]

This *mise-en-abyme* shows us Marlowe's protagonist both standing in Damascus and invoking a map on which he places the city and its meridian, while the speaking actor and the audience are at the same time in a real-life London and an embedded fictional Damascus. The polysemy of several words in the passage prolongs the effect, allowing the picture to be drawn and viewed from the inside, very much in the manner of the map of Norwich in Cuningham's treatise. Thus the 'pen' conflates the figures of the playwright composing the text, the cartographer drawing the map, and the hero wielding his sword and launching his battles over the text, the map, and the stage. To 'trace' regions in that context amounts both to travelling through them as a fictional character and to charting them as a surveying cartographer, while to 'reduce' places involves both subjecting them as a conqueror and drawing them to scale. The mainstay of the cartographer-cum-conqueror's power is his superior ability to see beyond the current appearance and limits of a world he plans to change, and this is what gives him the upper hand over the 'blind geographers' whom he purports to confute.

Repeatedly through the two parts of *Tamburlaine*, the ability to see is equated with the ability to conquer and appropriate. This is a privilege that the protagonists share with both the playwright creating the cartographic illusion line after line, and the audience receiving it in the

same way, both on-stage – as with Tamburlaine's addressee Zenocrate in
the above quotation – and off-stage in the playhouse. In so doing, the
protagonists relay our fantasies of overseeing and overpowering inside
the cartographic recreation taking shape before us, like so many relays
in a picture using multiple perspectives.[13] This is what happens, for
example, when Techelles, marching over Ortelius's map of Africa, which
he ekphrastically redraws in his report, takes possession of the items by
viewing them one by one: 'And with my power did march to Zanzibar,
/ The western part of Afric, where I viewed / The Ethiopian sea, rivers
and lakes' (2 *Tam*, 1.3.194–96). Again we note here the play on two
registers, with 'view' having both the sense of watching and that of drawing a survey of the land.[14] On-stage, Techelles and Tamburlaine's other
lieutenants further embed the process of surveying in their persons, by
becoming one with the lands they have viewed and conquered when
they receive the geographical titles of kings of Argier, Moroccus, and Fez.
Characterisation becomes here a function of space – both cartographic
space and performance space – as we watch these lands morphing into
characters on a stage that we in turn view and survey, as if our reception
of the play were yet a larger frame narrative of appropriation.

The stage in *Tamburlaine* remains a map of heroism inhabited and
drawn from the inside until the end, with Tamburlaine's famous map-
reading episode at the hour of his death, when an actual map is brought
on-stage as prop (2 *Tam*, 5.3.123–60). Conflating the parts of cartographer, conqueror, and stage manager, Tamburlaine goes back over his
military achievements by pointing at the map, using precise cartographic
references, such as 'Cutting the tropic line of Capricorn, / I conquered all
as far as Zanzibar', while metadramatically telescoping the map he points
at and the stage on which he performed his feats over the two parts of
the play (2 *Tam.*, 5.3.138–39). Thus his 'Here I began to march towards
Persia' can be understood as both a location that he identifies on the map
and a location that can be traced on the physical stage where he stood
at the start of his adventures (2 *Tam.*, 5.3.126). Likewise his 'here, not
far from Alexandria' is both a point on the map and Babylon (2 *Tam.*,
5.3.131) – an alternative name for Cairo in late medieval times, and
therefore close to Alexandria on a map of Africa – where the character is
supposed to be as he utters that line. We may add that this is also a locus
in heroism besides being a geographical location and a theatrical one, as
Babylon – the homonymous Mesopotamian one this time – was also the
place where Alexander, the greatest conqueror in the Western imaginary,
met his death. Again place name and character name come together with

the city named after Alexander, and create an intersection for the categories of place, character, and performance on Tamburlaine's map. Being 'not far from Alexandria' makes Tamburlaine not far from Alexander's achievements in our mental associations, and 'viewing' in his case remains to the end a synonym for mapping and conquering, on the stage and through our eyes and minds. Indeed, if from where we are in the playhouse we do not directly see the items he points to on his hand-held map, we do see the map in our mind's eye through him and his words, acting like a looking-glass or perspective for us.

How far would contemporary audiences have been aware of this effect of spatial and imaginary perspective achieved by means of a character? Judging by the example of another early modern dramatic standard of heroism highly popular on the public stage, *Henry V* (1599), we may venture to say that the audiences could have been well aware of the effect. Indeed, as the action of that play draws to its climactic conclusion, with territorial conquest becoming conflated with the enterprise of conquering the French princess, Henry exclaims that he no longer sees the cities of France as she stands in his way. This prompts her father to reply 'my lord, you see them perspectively', inviting him – and through his eyes, us – to envision the un-assailed beauty of the rich cities of France through the glass of his daughter's virginity.[15] The princess acts here both as an enabling 'perspective glass' magnifying the image of distant cities and making them visible to Henry and us, and as a magic 'prospective glass' – the two spellings being interchangeable in the early modern period – allowing the English king and the English audience for which he stands on stage to see into a future in which he becomes possessor of them by marrying Katherine.

As noted by Henry S. Turner, perspective in the early modern period 'consisted more of a loosely related series of practices and methods than a formal, codified, and unified theory'.[16] With little backdrop, few properties, and very limited lighting effects, perspective in the early modern public theatre necessarily had to rely heavily on spoken dialogue and the use of stage space by the actors. Two typical cartographically oriented examples in this respect are provided by Heywood's 'apprentice' play in every sense of the word – his first play, a play staging apprentices as heroes, and targeting that type of audience as well – *The Four Prentices of London*, and Dekker's *Old Fortunatus*.

The plot of *The Four Prentices*, downsizing its princely crusading heroes to the level of London apprentices in order to allow popular audiences to identify more closely with them, gets launched by a shipwreck, the consequences of which are described in dumbshow by a Presenter. Drawing us into this cartographic fantasy early in the play, the choric figure invites us to complete the illusion in our mind's eye by imagining the four brothers 'Disperst to severall corners of the world';[17] that is to say, Boulogne for Godfrey, France for Guy, Italy for Charles, and Ireland for Eustace. One by one, they come into our view for a show of their adventures commented on by the Presenter, and then recede so that we can turn our attention to the next brother. As with Techelles's African journey of conquest in *Tamburlaine*, the impression is one of moving around a map, that of Europe in this case, under the guidance of the Presenter-cum-mapmaker who shifts our perspective at every turn to make the rest of the picture visible. The picture keeps expanding beyond the visible stage, with the four brothers exiting severally as they are about to draw a new map, that of their conquests at the 'severall corners' where the Presenter sends them off at the end of each dumbshow. The effect of this scene could have been further enhanced on the rectangular stage of the Red Bull theatre where the play was revived around 1606, if the brothers receded to or exited through four corners of the stage becoming the equivalents of the four corners of a map.

Similar to the way the historical maps of Ortelius's ever expanding *Parergon* section make room for historical and legendary data in the later editions of his *Theatrum*, the action of *The Four Prentices* goes on to constantly reconfigure the stage map spatially and temporally from the inside, extending the domain of ownership for both the apprentice heroes and their audience of London apprentices vicariously enjoying the conquests achieved by their fictional doubles. Thus, on the brothers' map of triumphs, the Babylon/Cairo of such late medieval romances as *The Sowdone of Babylone* (mid-fifteenth century) is conflated with the sixteenth-century Persian empire of the Safavids, as both the Sultan and the Sophy are defeated as antagonists in a plot which is otherwise a re-enactment of the eleventh-century First Crusaders' assault on Jerusalem. Meanwhile the brothers' recurrent references to London locations peopled by apprentices – such as 'Oh that I had with mee / As many good lads, honest Prentises, / From *Eastcheape, Canwicke-streete,* and *London-stone*' and 'Oh for some *Cheap-side* boyes'[18] – resolutely pull the spectators into the illusion and make them participants in the fictional redrawing of this multilayered, palimpsestic map of heroism.

The connection between the stage as a map of conquest and success and the cosmographer-spectator's mind's eye is made even clearer by the two choric figures intervening at the start of Acts 1 and 2 in Dekker's *Old Fortunatus*. Having started with a reference to the spherical shape of the eye for each member of the audience – 'the circle of each eye / (Being like so many Suns in his round Sphere)' – the Prologue to the play embeds inside that shape the 'circumference' of the round-shaped stage, like an earthly globe within the armillary sphere of the sun and other celestial objects' courses: 'for this smal Circumference must stand, / For the imagind Sur-face of much land'.[19] Acting as a cosmographer's measuring instrument, it is the spectator's eye, or mind's eye, that holds together the dramatic illusion which it surrounds: 'Your thoughts to helpe poore Art', as the Prologue concludes. The polysemic 'circumference' – orbit of the eye, armillary sphere, round-shaped earth, circular stage – equally opens the Chorus's speech at the start of the second act. Here, the spectator's 'active thought' is invited to turn the stage or globe round to see Fortunatus transported to another part of the world.[20] Clearly, it is the spectator's empowered eye rather than the dramatist's art alone that serves as the optical instrument allowing the stage to exceed its naturalistic possibilities and to offer a world-encompassing triumphal action.

The optical enabling device was perfected and completed a few years later in yet another patriotic drama of brothers achieving international greatness, if only in fantasy. Whether or not Day, Rowley, and Wilkins had *The Four Prentices of London* in mind when composing *The Travels of the Three English Brothers* (1607) cannot be established with any degree of certainty. The closest connection which can be made between the two plays is the revival of Heywood's play taking place at the Red Bull theatre while Day, Rowley, and Wilkins's play was also performed there, though the latter play was originally written for the Curtain.[21] The Epilogue (10 SD) to the play features the three Sherley brothers introduced by Fame acting as Chorus and equipping each with 'a prospective glass' so that they can see each other and offer to embrace despite their standing in different locations of the world, England for Thomas, Spain for Anthony, and Persia for Robert. Meanwhile, Fame also equips the spectators' eyes with an imaginary instrument, not just for them to be a party in the show like the fourth brother in *The Four Prentices*, but to be the very drawers of the perspective map:

> But would your apprehensions help poor art,
> Into three parts dividing this our stage,
> They all at once shall take their leaves of you.
> Think this England, this Spain, this Persia.
> Your favours then, to your observant eyes
> We'll show their fortunes' present qualities. (Epilogue, 8–12)

Dividing the stage in their imaginations like a cartographer drawing a tripartite map, the spectators are then able to place countries on it and complete their map with figures and captions. Fame's speech here does not solely act as a perspective glass offering passive spectators an all-inclusive picture of the brothers' fortunes at different spots of the globe. It rather puts into their hands a much more enabling 'prospective glass' which transforms the stage point by point – 'Think this England, this Spain, this Persia' – and changes it into a make-it-yourself map rather than a ready-made map of the Sherley brothers' would-be forthcoming worldwide achievements.[22] Further into the Epilogue, Fame's reference to 'Some that fill up this round circumference' and who might know more about the brothers' present and future states makes the spectators oscillate between McInnis's above-mentioned 'protagonist model' and 'playwright model', as they both 'fill up' the round shape of the Curtain theatre by standing or sitting in it and 'fill up' the circumference of the play's world map by adding vignettes and captions to the picture (Epilogue, 25).

Quoting William E. Miller's research based on a marginal note in Abraham Fleming's 1598 translation of Virgil's *Georgics*, McInnis suggests that the *periaktoi* – revolving stage machinery painted with different backdrops on three sides – may have been in use as early as the first years of the seventeenth century at the Blackfriars theatre.[23] Whether or not this hypothesis holds, the examples of the plays studied above are proof of the extent to which audiences of popular heroic plays were invited to imaginatively draw or complete a perspective stage map and engage with it, even in the absence of any backdrop in the form of machinery or cloth hangings.

Examples of this phenomenon are numerous in the plays of the period, particularly but not exclusively in heroic romances and history plays. The purpose of this chapter is not to survey the many occurrences of this device, but to assess its contribution to meaning for the plays in which it appears. Accordingly, the last section of this chapter offers two contrasting readings of the most frequently quoted example of cartographic intervention on the early modern stage, from Shakespeare's *King Lear*.

There is a long critical tradition of considering Lear's map, along with the other two famous examples of maps used as props on the early modern stage – Tamburlaine's map of unfinished conquests in the last scene of 2 *Tamburlaine* and the rebels' indivisible map in 1 *Henry IV* (3.1) – as emblems of political failure and dispossession. Valerie Traub's reading is a prominent example of this perspective, concluding with an analysis of the failure of what she calls 'the logic of the grid'; that is to say, the logic of rationality and control expected from a mapping enterprise.[24] Dan Brayton reaches a similar conclusion, suggesting that the use of the map as an epistemological tool in the play leads to 'an epistemological impasse'.[25] In what follows, I summarise the main arguments that lead to this kind of interpretation, in order to show how it is perfectly consistent with the main plot of Lear and his kingdom, while it leaves out the corrections in perspective contributed by the secondary plot of Gloucester and Edgar. The latter plot, I will argue in a second statement, is precisely about experimenting with a different method for seeing, no longer through 'the logic of the grid', but 'feelingly', as Gloucester calls it.[26]

Right from the outset, it is possible to see Lear's division of the map as a metaphor for the drawing and quartering of the body politic which is soon to follow, or as a prefiguration of the sufferings in the king's own natural body and those of his family members. Indeed, the overlapping of the categories of prop, actor, and stage is encouraged by Lear's anthropomorphic description of the items on his map, such as 'the plentuous rivers and wide-skirted meads' offered to Goneril (1.1.65). The conflation of categories is added to with place names from the map spilling out of it to be made characters on the stage and stand for the different parts of the kingdom about to be disjointed. Thus the north is represented by Albany (a synonym for Scotland, named after Albanact, son of the mythical founder of Britain, Brutus), the south by Cornwall, with Gloucester for the west and Kent for the east completing this on-stage map turned alive around a centre formed by Lear on his throne. Consequently, prop, character, and stage are made one in suffering the violence inflicted by Lear as he divides the map and expels part of it by banishing Kent and rejecting Cordelia, whose very name suggests 'core' and thus the centre that should hold the kingdom together.

One immediate result is to produce what Kent in the quarto version of the play calls 'this scattered kingdom',[27] one in which geography soon turns as mad as the raving king himself, to the point that Cornwall – a place name conflated with a character's name – gets displaced to Gloucester, where both the duke and his territorial possessions are eliminated in the middle of the play. Meanwhile, having given away both his map and lands, Lear is left to roam the unchartered territory of what is customarily referred to in the play's later editions as 'the heath', but which in effect receives not even that minimal geographical qualification in either the 1608 quarto or the 1623 folio edition of the play.[28] As the king is gradually stripped of all the visible signs of his identity – his hundred knights, his heirs, his royal attire, and the scenery around him, and even his sense of orientation as he awakes from his madness and mistakes his own kingdom for France ('Am I in France?')

(4.7.76) – his plot turns out to stage what Brayton considers 'a cartography of dispossession'.[29] His last geographically associated follower is Tom 'of Bedlam', who metaphorically comes from the seat of madness itself.

The conflation of a geography made meaningless and an identity made ineffectual for the characters is pursued right to the end of the play, which takes us to Dover, technically situated in Kent, but where the character of the same name fails to be recognised in what should be the seat of his power, and proves unable to prevent even there the horror of the murder of Cordelia.

From Lear's original command 'Give me the map there' (1.1.36) to his final words, 'Look there, look there!' as he points to a non-existent entity (5.3.309), the play seems to have been haunted by the presence in filigree of a key prop, the map of something – Lear's entire kingdom – gradually turned into a map of nothing, 'an O without a figure', as the Fool calls it (1.5.183–84), like a medieval T–O map without a T, as Brayton interprets this passage.[30] A *trompe l'œil* device revealing emptiness at the very heart of profusion, Lear's map could therefore be said to have been by turns a prop, a set of characters, and a stage to ultimately denounce, not just the interchangeability, but also the vanity of these categories in his doomed world.

Yet, despite the play's bleak ending, I believe we would miss something of the full picture if we do not take into account an alternative cartographic option sketched by the play's secondary plot of Gloucester and his son Edgar. If Lear's already drawn geographical map at the start of the play provides one option, Edgar's chorographic mapping enterprise from the top of the cliffs of Dover (4.6) offers a fleeting glimpse of a radically different option, giving a further twist to the 'angling' quotation retained by Brayton in the title of his article.

Often governed by a bird's-eye perspective as is the case here, chorographic representations, especially but not exclusively of towns and cities, were among the major cartographic innovations of the period. Overcoming the limitations of the profile view (which only revealed foreground objects on a two-dimensional, shore-like strip, hiding whatever else lay behind), the plan view (locating objects from above, but without showing what they actually looked like on the ground), and the linear perspective (from one fixed vantage point, with foreground objects much larger and masking the rest), the bird's-eye view offered a revolutionary representational solution.[31] Using multiple focal points and combining different scales in an oblique view from above, the bird's-eye view allowed for what Hilary Ballon and David Friedman call 'an all-encompassing, elastic vision' of space, one in which the observer had the illusion of moving around objects and obstacles in a three-dimensional landscape.[32] A fascinatingly enabling device, the bird's-eye perspective allowed viewers to see more than they normally could by standing at any one given location, thereby gaining a nearly godlike, panoptic command over the scenery. Using that very kind of empowering perspective to describe the would-be view from the top of the cliffs of Dover to his blind father, Edgar's mapping in *King Lear* compensates for Gloucester's deficiency with a vengeance, by involving a complex interplay of different scales and angles all captured in one image.

Indeed, unrealistic though it is, Edgar's superimposition of perspectives enhances rather than confuses the apprehension of his imaginary objects. This is what happens, for example, with his description of the samphire gatherer first seen hanging from the cliff and then immediately reduced to his head seen from above ('Half-way down / Hangs one that gathers samphire, dreadful trade, / Methinks he seems no bigger that his head') (4.4.14–16) or the barque diminished to the size of her cock and then of her buoy over the short span of just two lines ('and yon tall anchoring barque / Diminished to her cock, her cock a buoy / Almost too small for sight') (4.4.18–19). The landscape Edgar describes to Gloucester on-stage and the spectators off-stage is therefore one that is not simply viewed, but imaginatively appropriated, inhabited, and transformed. For both categories of audiences, imagination's eye travels over Edgar's map, plunging from the cliff, past the samphire gatherer about to fall, then recedes to view him again from above, before getting close enough to notice the tallness of the barque, and again quickly moving back to see it undergo a dramatic reduction to the point of almost disappearing over less than two lines.

Although as short-lived as the cure Edgar offers to his father, his one-scene experimentation with cartography serves to show that an enabling alternative can and does exist alongside Lear's map of despair and dispossession. With its fragments of narrative involving 'crows and choughs that wing the midway air' (4.6.13) and 'fishermen that walk upon the beach' (4.6.17), Edgar's map even to some extent recalls the ships, animals, figures, or textual captions commonly inserted into early modern maps and making them dynamic theatres of action, discovery, and empowering imaginative possession, spaces in the making rather than predetermined places fixed once and for all, to use Michel de Certeau's terminology.[33]

How much of Edgar's alternative, enabling perspective we believe remains to counterbalance Lear's tragedy of loss of place and identity at the end of the play partly depends on the attribution or non-attribution to Edgar of a share in the conclusion and final lines of the play (the quarto and folio versions differ on this), as he may or may not be about to become a partner in redrawing and retrieving Lear's scattered kingdom. But what in all cases is beyond doubt is the original audiences' ability to discern the two cartographic options offered by the play and to get imaginatively involved with both. *King Lear* may be Shakespeare's 'quintessential play of placelessness', as Lloyd E. Kermode calls it,[34] but placelessness in this case, as often in early modern plays involving a wide geography, is not necessarily a synonym for annihilation of place. It rather amounts to opening up and pluralising the experience of being in space and in some cases the potential scope of power and action that goes with it.

Bruce R. Smith theorises that specific, early modern relation to theatrical space as 'phenomenal space', one that 'combines the physicality of performance with the imagination of reception'[35] and leaves room for combining character, geography, and power within the spectator's experience of living the play. The present chapter has been an attempt to retrieve some of that early modern theatrical experience, as inflected by a cartographic imagination commonly accessible to Shakespeare's contemporaries, while it is less readily part of today's audiences' engagement with and appropriation of stage space. At the start of *Mind-Travelling and Voyage Drama*, McInnis reminds his readers how the wooden structure of the Elizabethan theatre was recurrently used to evoke a ship allowing the audiences' minds to travel/travail (the two spellings were interchangeable at the time) with and through the plays.[36] The cartographic metamorphoses of the stage studied in this chapter offer similarly empowering opportunities to audiences for taking part in a creative travail in the specific context of dramas of travel and conquest composed for the early modern public theatre.

Notes

1 See P. D. A. Harvey, *Maps in Tudor England* (London: British Library, 1993), 15.

2 Ethel Seaton, 'Marlowe's Map', *Essays and Studies by Members of the English Association* 10 (1924), 13–35. On the theatrical incidences of the cartographic paradigm in the early modern period, see the landmark studies of John Gillies, *Shakespeare and the Geography of Difference* (Cambridge University Press, 1994); John Gillies and Virginia Mason Vaughan, *Playing the Globe: Genre and Geography in English Renaissance Drama* (Madison, NJ:

Fairleigh Dickinson University Press, 1998); D. K. Smith, *The Cartographic Imagination in Early Modern England* (Aldershot: Ashgate, 2008).

3 See David Buisseret, *Monarchs, Ministers and Maps: The Emergence of Cartography as a Tool of Government in Early Modern Europe* (University of Chicago Press, 1992), 77–78.

4 On the power symbolism of perspective in court masques, see the ground-breaking study by Stephen Orgel, *The Illusion of Power: Political Theatre in the English Renaissance* (Berkeley, CA: University of California Press, 1975). For a more recent consideration of the topic, see Martin Butler, *The Stuart Court Masque and Political Culture* (Cambridge University Press, 2008).

5 Smith, *The Cartographic Imagination*, 41.

6 Peter Barber, 'Mapmaking in England, *ca.* 1470–1650', in *The History of Cartography*, III, *Cartography in the European Renaissance*, part 2, ed. David Woodward (University of Chicago Press, 2007), 1665.

7 Smith, *The Cartographic Imagination*, 8.

8 William Cuningham, *The Cosmographical Glasse, Conteinyng the Pleasant Principles of Cosmographie, Geographie, Hydrographie, or Navigation* (London: John Day, 1559), map facing fo. 8.

9 Lucia Nuti, 'The Perspective Plan in the Sixteenth Century: The Invention of a Representational Language', *Art Bulletin* 76, no. 1 (March 1994), 105–28; see 127.

10 John Rennie Short, *Making Space: Revisioning the World, 1475–1600* (Syracuse, NY: University of Syracuse Press, 2004), 154.

11 David McInnis, *Mind-Travelling and Voyage Drama in Early Modern England* (Basingstoke: Palgrave Macmillan, 2013), 60–63.

12 Christopher Marlowe, *Doctor Faustus and Other Plays*, ed. David Bevington and Eric Rasmussen (Oxford University Press, 1995), *1 Tamburlaine*, 4.4.77–84. All subsequent references to *1 Tamburlaine* and *2 Tamburlaine* refer to this edition and will be cited by act, scene, and line numbers within the text.

13 On the relays inside a picture in perspective, see, for example, the discussion of Diego Velázquez's *Las Meninas* in the study by Hubert Damish, *L'Origine de la perspective* (Paris: Flammarion, 1987), 363.

14 *OED*, 1.c.

15 William Shakespeare, *King Henry V*, ed. T. W. Craik (London: Thomson Learning, 1995), 5.2.317.

16 Henry S. Turner, *The English Renaissance Stage: Geometry, Poetics, and the Practical Spatial Arts 1580–1630* (Oxford University Press, 2006), 167.

17 Thomas Heywood, *The Foure Prentises of London, With the Conquest of Jerusalem* (London: I. W., 1615), sig. C1ʳ.

18 Ibid., sig. D4ᵛ.

19 Thomas Dekker, *The Pleasant Comedie of Old Fortunatus* (London: William Aspley, 1600), sig. A2ᵛ. For a detailed discussion of this play, see David McInnis, 'Travelling Characters in Early Modern Drama', Chapter 10 in the present volume.

20 Dekker, *Old Fortunatus*, sigs. C4ᵛ–D1ʳ.

21 See editor Anthony Parr's note, quoting from the entry in the Stationer's Register – 'as yt was played at the Curten' – in *Three Renaissance Travel Plays* (Manchester University Press, 1995), 55. All further quotations from *The Travels of the Three English Brothers* refer to this edition and will be cited by act, scene, and line numbers in the text.

22 For the different meanings of 'prospective glass' in the early modern period, see Alan Shickman, 'The "Perspective Glass" in Shakespeare's *Richard II*', *Studies in English Literature 1500–1900* 18, no. 2 (April 1978), 217–28.

23 McInnis, *Mind-Travelling*, 156–57.

24 Valerie Traub, 'The Nature of Norms in Early Modern England: Anatomy, Cartography, *King Lear*', *South Central Review* 26, nos. 1–2 (2009), 42–81; quoted at 66.

25 Dan Brayton, 'Angling in the Lake of Darkness: Possession, Dispossession, and the Politics of Discovery in *King Lear*', *English Literary History* 70, no. 2 (Summer 2003), 399–426; quoted at 423.

26 William Shakespeare, *King Lear*, ed. R. A. Foakes (London: Thomson Learning, 1997), 4.6.145. All quotations from *King Lear* refer to this edition and will be cited by act, scene, and line numbers in the text.

27 That particular page of the quarto is reproduced as Appendix 1 in Foakes's edition, 3.1.31, p. 394.

28 For a fuller discussion, see Gavin Russell Hollis, 'Stage Directions: Shakespeare's Use of the Map', unpublished MPhil dissertation, Shakespeare Institute (2000), 92.

29 Brayton, 'Angling in the Lake of Darkness', 401.

30 Ibid., 411.

31 For more on the background of the bird's-eye view and other representational options in the sixteenth century, see Nuti, 'The Perspective Plan', 105–28.

32 Hilary Ballon and David Friedman, 'Portraying the City in Early Modern Europe: Measurement, Representation, and Planning', in, *The History of Cartography*, III, part 1, ed. Woodward, 680–704, at 688. Ballon and Friedman take the example of Cornelis Anthonisz's 1538 map of Amsterdam presented to Emperor Charles V, in which the angle of elevation shifts throughout the image, from profile to nearly overhead, while monuments are represented on a larger scale than the rest of the buildings. The overall effect is that of a 'space [which] fluctuates as if seen from different vantage points that imperceptibly slip and change' (690).

33 Michel de Certeau, *L'Invention du quotidien*, I: *Arts de faire* (Paris: Gallimard, 1990), 172–73.

34 Lloyd E. Kermode, 'Experiencing the Space and Place of Early Modern Theatre', *Journal of Medieval and Early Modern Studies* 43, no. 1 (Winter 2013), 1–24; quotation at 9.

35 Bruce R. Smith, 'Taking the Measure of Global Space', *Journal of Medieval and Early Modern Studies* 43, no. 1 (Winter 2013), 25–48; quotation at 35.

36 McInnis, *Mind-Travelling*, 3.

CHAPTER 3

Marlowe's Mediterranean and Counter-Epic Forms of Oceanic Hybridity

Steve Mentz

St John's University

Christopher Marlowe's fascination with the Mediterranean is well documented. Four of his earliest-known plays, *Dido, Queen of Carthage* (*c.*1588), the blockbuster successes *Tamburlaine, Parts 1 and 2* (1587), and *The Jew of Malta* (1589), locate themselves on exotic Eastern shores.[1] His interest in the side of the Mediterranean dominated by Ottoman Turkey during the sixteenth century becomes meaningful inside a dense confluence of early modern geopolitics and classical poetics. As scholars such as Richmond Barbour, Matthew Dimmock, Anders Ingram, and Daniel Vitkus have recently emphasised, the Ottoman presence in Elizabethan literary culture was pervasive.[2] The Eastern Mediterranean was Turkish territory, and Marlowe's maritime poetics evince a tangled mixture of envy, desire, and fear of Turkish cultural influence. Marlowe's theatrical Mediterranean also derived much of its literary flavour from the symbolic force of the sea in Latin poetry. The nature of Marlowe's use of classical poetic sources, including Musaeus, Virgil, Lucan, and Ovid, received an influential recent restatement in Patrick Cheney's *Marlowe's Counterfeit Profession*, which argues that Marlowe's career followed an Ovidian career model of 'counter-nationhood' that inverts the familiar Virgilian pattern followed by Edmund Spenser.[3] Extending Cheney's notion of a counter-epic Marlowe, I argue that, especially in his early plays but also throughout his career, Marlowe's drama and poetry draw together the exotic cultures of the Eastern Mediterranean, the classical models of Latin poetry, and recent travellers' accounts of the region to articulate a distinctly oceanic hybrid. By staging in these works the Ovidian model that rejects normative Virgilian epic, Marlowe engages with the early phase of England's transformative encounter with oceanic travel. His plays engage with and contribute to England's growing fascination with the maritime world.

Much recent critical work on Elizabethan understandings of the
Mediterranean emphasises palimpsestic elements of the Near East and
suggests that Marlowe engages classical poetics and sixteenth-century
geopolitics simultaneously.[4] Building on this rich scholarship, this essay
considers Marlowe's treatment of the East through multiple maritime
viewpoints, including the deck of a ship, a globe-spanning imperial
throne, and the immersive experience of a swimmer. Through these portraits of figures that sail and swim in and beyond the Mediterranean,
Marlowe reveals his artistic engagement with the alterity and hybridity of the maritime environment. Oceanic language and settings in
1 Tamburlaine and in *Doctor Faustus* (1588) extend maritime concerns
through metaphoric and literal images of trans-oceanic travel. Taking
Aeneas in *Dido, Queen of Carthage* as a model sailor, Tamburlaine as
an ocean-spanning ruler, and Leander in *Hero and Leander* as a model
swimmer, I suggest that Marlowe's Mediterranean can supplement
Cheney's counter-Virgilian reading of his literary career with salt-water
portrayals of emotional dependency and environmental enmeshment.[5]
A Mediterranean and oceanic perspective can restructure the poetics of
imperial expansion. Encountering salt water in Marlowe's works turns
heroic male bodies into unstable hybrids. For Marlowe, the dissolving
charm of the clear waters of the Turkish Mediterranean undergirds his
combative relationship with both Elizabethan politics and classical poetics.
As I shall argue, the dramatist-poet found in the Eastern Mediterranean
diverse sources from which he constructed counter-epic art.

Like most historicist scholars working on the early modern
Mediterranean, I labour in the shadow cast by Fernand Braudel's classic
study, *The Mediterranean and the Mediterranean World in the Age of Philip
II*.[6] For Braudel, the Mediterranean world provides an ideal case study
in the mutual engagement of environment and human history. More
recently, Peregrine Horden and Nicholas Purcell's *The Corrupting Sea* has
updated Braudel's synthetic approach with a reading of the region that
focuses on the *longue durée* and on the 'ready connectivity' between different parts of the inland sea.[7] Horden and Purcell's 'ecological history without catastrophes' makes a resonant case for the multiplicity of the region
that Braudel treated as a unified whole. In this essay, however, I will take
as my primary model Predrag Matvejevic's evocative memoir-history,
Mediterranean: A Cultural Landscape, which adds literary colouring to the
historical analyses of Braudel and Horden and Purcell.[8] Matvejevic's recur-
sive exploration of the distinctive quality of 'Mediterranity' offers a useful way to clarify the poetics of Marlowe's Mediterranean. As Matvejevic

shows, the historical and cultural density of the region produces a distinctive rhetorical effect, a gathering together of styles, languages, and poetic modes that generate complex cultural and linguistic hybridities.[9] This historical and literary recursivity contextualises Marlowe's engagement with the region. I will argue that Marlowe reads the Mediterranean as Matvejevic would much later write it, with an eye for hybridisations that form through encounters between ancient poetics and modern travelogues. More than Braudel, who presents a massive historical sweep, or Horden and Purcell, who revel in hyper-localism, Matvejevic emphasises the distinctive rhetorical mixing of Mediterranean cultures. His description of an environmental system built on trade routes and linguistic exchange makes his Mediterranean less imperial than Braudel's and less mercantile than Horden and Purcell's. Instead Matvejevic presents an incessantly hybrid cultural and rhetorical environment. Marlowe's shipwrecked heroes, travelling conquerors, and immersed lovers become legible, I will suggest, within this circulating and disorienting matrix.

According to Matvejevic, the history of the Mediterranean is 'less of waves than of winds', because in the inland sea waves, tides, and global currents are less powerful than seasonal winds.[10] In reading the Mediterranean as a place caught between sailing and swimming, I suggest that the more intimate experience of the swimmer, in particular the shipwrecked swimmer who has lost his ship before being plunged into the waves, represents the fundamentally disorienting experience of Mediterranean culture to which Marlowe responds. Josiah Blackmore, in a reading of the early modern sonnet tradition and especially the work of the Portuguese epic and lyric poet Luis vaz de Camões, argues that the swimmer who 'lives both the experience and the possibility of depth' became for many sixteenth-century European poets and dramatists an emblem of a new subjectivity: 'The voyage or movement downward is also the voyage in – sudden submersion, the imminence of the plunge, mobilizes the poet to write.'[11] In Shakespeare, famous swimmers such as Ferdinand in *The Tempest* and the lost twins in *The Comedy of Errors* display the potency of immersion as narrative and philosophical topos.[12] In Marlowe's drama and verse, sailors and swimmers juxtapose themselves as contrasting emblems of the human encounter with the sea. By bringing Aeneas the sailor in touch with Leander the swimmer and suggesting that both can supplement more familiar Marlovian figures such as Tamburlaine and Faustus, I emphasise that Marlowe's hybrid Mediterranean world operates through generic and political complexity. These figures and their works treat their maritime settings as symbols of

an exoticism that shocks and entices English audiences and readers with
the possibility of radical change. As we shall see, warm salt water facili-
tates a new combination of traditional classical forms with attractive but
disturbing non-European features.

The core fantasy of Marlowe's Mediterranean never quite appears in his
works, which turn aside to follow exhausted Aeneas to Italy, or in textual
terms conclude with George Chapman's morally doctrinaire conclusion to
Hero and Leander, written after Marlowe's death and published in 1598.
At the centre of Marlowe's Mediterranean engagements sits a fantasy about
the transformative relationship between poetry and politics, imagined
through interactions between human bodies and the sea. All of the oceanic
Marlowe texts that I consider, *Dido, 1 Tamburlaine, Faustus,* and *Hero and
Leander*, imagine hybrid fantasies in which human powers extend themselves onto oceanic scale. None of these newly created systems last; they
all collapse, as in a metaphorical sense Ovidian counter-epic falls beneath
the unstoppable forward march of Virgilian imperial epic. Marlowe's special interest in the Mediterranean, however, creates through this region a
briefly flourishing counter-space of erotic and environmental mutuality.
The politics of this fantasyland oppose Rome and European dominance
even if that opposition cannot be sustained. The possibilities appear clear-
est in *Dido*, where the imaginary kingdom that the two Asian refugees
Aeneas and Dido might have ruled over in African Carthage represents a
multicultural, multiethnic polity that spans the European, African, and
Asian shores of the Mediterranean basin. Marlowe cannot entirely ignore
Virgil's narrative, and he does not allow his hero to escape the burden
of history and the Rome that must come. As we shall see, in revising
Augustan empire – in other words, Rome's imperial foundations – into
Tamburlaine's conquests, or in presenting Faustus's magic as an alternative to Renaissance humanism, Marlowe's plays stake out exceptions
to Virgilian modes. His depictions of England's encounters with warm
Eastern waters present a still-potent fantasy about the allure of otherness
and difference that, perhaps, can continue to trim the sails of Empire even
in the present. My larger argument is that reading Marlowe in the context of maritime travel shows him presenting alternatives to the emerging
imperial ideology of British expansion.

Dido and the Sailor's Fantasy

Marlowe's *Dido, Queen of Carthage* presents a sailor's fantasy of rescue
after shipwreck in which the storm recedes to present political, sexual,

and material comfort. The still-dripping Aeneas emerges from the surf to catch the queen's fancy, with a little help from the god Eros. As the play's pointedly non-Virgilian title indicates, the male hero does not dominate the action but rather receives erotic and political attentions from the powerful queen. The drama represents an early effort, at least plausibly co-written with Thomas Nashe, whose name appears on the printed title-page in 1594.[13] The play's action slices the shipwreck aftermath out of *Aeneid* Books 1–2 and 4. My contention is that *Dido* represents a peculiarly oceanic fantasy that mingles the poetic and Ottoman currents of Marlowe's Eastern Mediterranean. In its overt gestures towards an Eastern cultural multiplicity that Elizabethan viewers would have associated with Ottoman Turkey, the play imagines a non-European version of the once-Roman sea. By building an Asiatic cultural fantasy on top of Virgilian materials, Marlowe implies that even the most Roman of all epics can, if reconsidered in a salt-water light, become something radically different.

To be more specific, I am arguing for a postcolonial and ambivalently anti-imperial conception of Marlowe's attitude to his classical sources and his Eastern political setting. As Emily C. Bartels has argued in *Spectacles of Strangeness*, Marlowe's play frames Aeneas's encounter with Dido's Carthage through the lens of early modern ideas about colonialism and cultural difference.[14] Bartels argues that Marlowe's play distinguishes itself from other Elizabethan portraits of Africa, especially those collected by Richard Hakluyt in *The Principal Navigations* (1589; 2nd rev. edn, 1598/99–1600), by the playwright's willingness to present both the perspective of Aeneas, who represents Rome though he is in fact from Asia Minor, and the alternative views of Dido and her African allies.[15] Extending Bartels's argument, the postcolonial scholar Sid Ray connects Marlowe's *Dido* to the critical portrayal of the colonialist project in Joseph Conrad's *Heart of Darkness* (1899) in a way that redeems the ethical perspicacity of both texts: 'once we consider *Dido, Queen of Carthage* as an intertext, *Heart of Darkness* manifests a postcoloniality heretofore unremarked upon, one which suggests that Conrad's response to the colonisation of Africa and its impact on women is more radical than has been thought.'[16] Ray's Conrad-centred analysis is useful for its emphasis on the centrality of Dido to Marlowe's play, which is imagined to contain 'an understanding and empathy for Dido's complex subject position as a Phoenician female ruler of an African city-state'.[17] Using this postcolonial lens to reconsider Marlowe's relationship to Virgil further implies that the cultural fantasies of Marlowe's play represent alternative visions of the Eastern Mediterranean, in which multicultural colonial politics swim happily alongside classical poetic models.

The possible union of Aeneas and Dido gives rise to a utopian vision that may have horrified some of its early modern English audiences but also emphasises a multiplicity and interconnectedness that recalls Horden and Purcell's vision of the Mediterranean basin as defined by 'ready connectivity'.[18] Marlowe's dramatic world also resonates with the dense linguistic and environmental hybridity of Matvejevic's 'Mediterreanity'. The fantasyland that Aeneas imagines he would build with Dido combines East and West in fluid dynamism:

> Triumph, my mates, our travels are at end.
> Here will Aeneas build a statelier Troy
> Than that which grim Atrides overthrew.
> Carthage shall vaunt her petty walls no more,
> For I will grace them with a fairer frame
> And clad her in a crystal livery
> Wherein the day may evermore delight;
> From golden India Ganges will I fetch,
> Whose wealthy streams may wait upon her towers,
> And triple-wise entrench her round about:
> The sun from Egypt shall rich odours bring,
> Wherewith his burning beams, like labouring bees,
> That load their thighs with Hybla's honey spoils,
> Shall here unburden their exhaled sweets,
> And plant our pleasantest suburbs with her fumes.[19]

The rejection of both Trojan past and Carthaginian present for a 'statelier' and 'fairer frame' underlines the hero's vision of possible new worlds. Marlowe's fantasy, however, does not range westward towards Virginia or Newfoundland, but gathers together the riches of the East: sun from Egypt, honey from the proverbial Hybla in Sicily, golden waters from the Ganges. Referring to the imagined city as feminine throughout the speech not only emphasises Dido's role as presumptive queen but also eroticizes the relationship between hero and kingdom; Aeneas will 'grace' his city, 'clad her' in gorgeous 'livery', 'entrench her round about'. Eroticised and feminised, this vision of the Mediterranean inverts Virgil's classically masculine Rome, towards which the hero must embark once his fling with the East ends.

The proposed names for this Trojan/Phoenician/African utopia remain problematic and plural, because Aeneas and his men cannot decide if the city they imagine represents their past, present, or future.

His followers ask that it be named 'Aenea, by your name' after the warrior who preserved them from both Troy and the waves (5.1.20). Another compatriot, thinking of the future, prefers the name 'Ascania, by your little son' (5.1.21). Aeneas himself indicates that he remains stuck in the past by preferring 'Anchisaeon / Of my old father's name' (5.1.22–23). Marlowe's triplicate name-game highlights the contrast between the imagined hybrid settlement that would expand horizontally in space – from Sicily to the Ganges – but refuses to fix itself in the vertical dimension of historical time. Only Rome and its conquering destiny, as Marlowe's Virgilian source insists, can promote a linear relationship with the progress of imperial time. When Marlowe's play provides Aeneas with a venue to express his presumably sincere desire to remake himself with Dido's love – 'This is the harbor that Aeneas seeks, / Let's see what tempests can annoy me now' (4.4.59–60) – it enacts a temporary protest against the Virgilian imperative. Rome must be founded, and it will be – but Marlowe's Aeneas first imagines other options.

At the heart of the sailor's fantasy stands the beautiful woman who beckons from shore, and Dido's offer to Aeneas in Marlowe's play combines erotic with political hospitality. When Aeneas temporarily promises to stay in Carthage, Dido repositions and recolours him as Phoenician rather than Trojan. In so doing she makes the refugee hero a monarch:

> Stout love, in mine arms make thy Italy,
> Whose crown and kingdom rests at thy command.
> 'Sichaeus', not 'Aeneas', be thou called,
> The 'King of Carthage', not 'Anchises' son'.
> Hold, take these jewels at thy lover's hand
> These golden bracelets and this wedding-ring
> Wherewith my husband wooed me yet a maid,
> And be thou King of Libya, by my gift. (3.4.56–63)

Dido's speech mixes the regal and erotic, but the twin monarchies she offers, of Carthage and Libya, mark her kingdom as alien to Marlowe's audience. Like the Ottoman sultan, Dido and her imagined consort rule a non-European land, occupying the heart of a Mediterranean world in which Roman power had been long displaced by Turkish rather than European navies.

My emphasis on the Mediterranean nature of this political fantasy emerges from its shipwrecked birth, to which the play often refers. Dido's offer of aid to the Asian refugees who wash up on her shores gives them back the tools of maritime mobility but asks them not to make full use

of them: 'Aeneas, I'll repair thy Trojan ships, / Conditionally that thou
wilt stay with me, / And let Achates sail to Italy' (2.1.112–15). A crucial
plot-twist that Marlowe adds to Virgil's story puts Iarbus, Dido's African
suitor, in a position to return to Aeneas his rigging and tackle, which
he happily does (5.1.71–74). Dido's Carthage functions as a kind of
imaginary island, escapable only by water, arrived at only by shipwreck.
It is much more culturally alien than Prospero's island in *The Tempest*
(*c.*1611), though Shakespeare's imaginary place is not too far offshore.
Aeneas enters Carthage as a disoriented refugee, not a famous Trojan
hero. He misidentifies the towers and environs of Carthage as Troy: 'yon
Ida's hill, / there Xanthus' stream ... / And when I know it is not, I die'
(2.1.7–9). He seems to have lost his identity in the waves: 'Sometime
I was a Trojan, mighty queen,' he says to Dido, 'But Troy is not. What
shall I say I am?' (2.1.75–76). Dido, dressing him in 'the garments which
Sichaeus ware', wishes to rescue this refugee (2.1.80). At the climax of
the hero's narrative of the burning of Troy, adapted from *Aeneid* Book 2,
Aeneas escapes by water as he sees Polyxena murdered by Greek soldiers:

> Moved with her voice, I leapt into the sea.
> Thinking to bear her on my back aboard,
> For all our ships were launched into the deep,
> And as I swam, she, standing on the shore,
> Was by the cruel Myrmidons surprised
> And after by that Pyrrhus sacrificed. (2.1.283–88)

The contrast between the death of Polyxena on land and Aeneas's escape
by sea demonstrates the need for the Trojan remnant to abandon firma-
ment for flux. Aeneas, a reluctant swimmer who later turns sailor, finds
in Dido's city a place of new possibilities, a polyglot and heterodox kingdom that only divine commands can force him to exchange for Rome.
While Marlowe's ideological position is always hard to discern, it is not
hard to imagine that he, like today's postcolonial scholars, cannot bear to
sympathise fully with imperial futurity. The distinctive space of *Dido* is,
as its title announces, the space of the queen, or more precisely the imagined place that Aeneas and Dido could perhaps invent together. Like the
Tamburlaine plays through which Marlowe made his public reputation,
Dido glistens with desire for the East.

Oceanic Visions in *Tamburlaine* and *Doctor Faustus*

Alongside *Dido*'s anti-imperial Mediterranean fantasy sits a vision of
global oceanic empire in *1 Tamburlaine*. Accepting Martin Wiggins's

argument that *Dido* may have been written after, rather than before, the break-out success of the *Tamburlaine* plays on the London stage need not overcomplicate the relationship between the two plays, which present complementary visions of empire and the sea. In *Dido*, Marlowe's counter-epic explores a multicultural Eastern Mediterranean world that responds critically to Virgilian norms. In *1 Tamburlaine*, the conquests of the Scythian shepherd encompass global oceanic expanses beyond the Mediterranean basin. After capturing Bajazeth, emperor of Turkey, Tamburlaine describes a route outward from the Mediterranean core of early modern global trade:

> The galleys and those pilling brigantines,
> That yearly sail to the Venetian gulf,
> And hover in the straits for Christians' wrack,
> Shall lie at anchor in the isle Asant
> Until the Persian fleet and men-of-war,
> Sailing along the oriental sea,
> Have fetched about the Indian continent,
> Even from Persepolis to Mexico,
> And thence until the Straits of Jubalter,
> Where they shall meet and join their forces in one,
> Keeping in awe the Bay of Portingale
> And all the ocean by the British shore.
> And by this means I'll win the world at last.[20]

The conquering vision expressed here expands outward from the Mediterranean to the world Ocean, culminating in its attention to the Atlantic shores of England and Portugal. The fleet of the Turkish empire that Tamburlaine has defeated will remain imprisoned by the inland sea, but his own Persian ships will circle the globe, sailing east across the 'oriental sea' to Mexico until at last they reach the European coast. If the Eastern Mediterranean represents a hybrid vision of political multiplicity in *Dido*, in *1 Tamburlaine*, the same waters become a launching pad.

Most readers and audiences recognise that Tamburlaine's global ambitions speak for those of Marlowe himself as he launches his public career as dramatist. Cheney, in emphasising the role of Ovid in defining the literary style of the *Tamburlaine* plays, shows in them that Marlowe 'presents himself as a serious rival to the New Poet', Spenser.[21] This emphasis on the turn away from the Virgilian path and 'laureate' career that Richard Helgerson finds in Spenser clarifies Marlowe's *Tamburlaine* as an announcement of a new model in Elizabethan stagecraft.[22] An oceanic perspective, however, suggests that Tamburlaine's proposed global encircling of England represents a movement beyond the merely classical or Mediterranean worlds. Notably, the conqueror inverts the standard depiction of the Straits of Gibraltar as a west-facing gate separating the Old World from the New World. Tamburlaine's fleet instead sails eastward to the Straits from the Pacific and Mexico, meeting and presumably defeating European ships en route. The classical world remains central, but instead of remaining local-ised, as in *Dido*, it wraps itself around the oceanic globe.

Marlowe refashions metaphors of oceanic vastness by contrasting Tamburlaine's global vision with portrayals of the sea articulated by the monarchs he vanquishes. When Mycetes of Persia laments the perfidy of his brother, he treats distant seas as indexes of things lost forever: 'O where is duty and allegiance now? / Fled to the Caspian or the ocean main?' (1.1.101–02). Bajazeth of Turkey names non-Mediterranean oceans as parts of his kingdom, but these watery domains operate as intensifiers that serve to expand his power. Bajazeth vaunts himself as not just 'Dread lord of Afric, Europe, and Asia, / Great king and con-queror of Graecia', but also ruler of 'The ocean Terrene, and the coal-black sea', which all together make him 'The high and highest monarch of the word' (3.1.22–26). The contrast between Tamburlaine and rulers who cannot hold the seas they claim accentuates the contrast between the conqueror's dynamism – his ships are always moving, sailing vast oceans and '[k]eeping in awe' European shores – and static proclama-tions. Mycetes and Bajazeth name seas, but Tamburlaine spans oceans.

The local Mediterranean hybridity of *Dido* combines with the cir-cumnavigating reach of *Tamburlaine* to suggest that Marlowe uses the sea to symbolise ambition, both poetic and dramatic. Tracing maritime language through his career suggests that the topos remains powerful. In *Faustus*, the hero treats the ocean as a reservoir for the protagonist's deep-est desires. With the power granted him by Mephistopheles, Faustus will send his spirit minions to 'Ransack the ocean for orient pearl'; command 'the ocean to overwhelm the world'; and walk upon the waves with 'a band of men'.[23] This cluster of ocean-imagery connects Faustus's magic with Tamburlaine's global sea power. In death, too, Faustus returns to oceanic vistas, which have now become a terrifying image of escaping the bounds of his condemned self:

> O soul, be changed into little waterdrops
> And fall into the ocean, ne'er to be found! (4.215–16)

The play's final lines treat the ocean as refuge and also dissolution, a place in which Faustus will not suffer because there will be no unitary Faustus.

The maritime environment comes to represent absolute alterity, a place in which neither bodies nor selves, nor vulnerable souls, can endure. From the relatively friendly if unsustainable waters of Dido's Eastern Mediterranean, the global visions of *Tamburlaine* and *Faustus* expand into infinitely alien space. As the great waters become more global, they also become less accessible. Marlowe would return to human-sized encounters, however, in one of his final non-dramatic works, *Hero and Leander*.

Hero and Leander and the Suffering Swimmer

The polyphonic and erotically fluid Mediterranean towards which Marlowe's *Dido* and *Tamburlaine* reach occupies a central place in Marlowe's poetic and dramatic career. If, as Cheney has argued, Marlowe's career-long endeavour pursued Ovidian *libertas* as a form of counter-nationhood, the erosive tang of sea water appears essential to that project.[24] The logical and individual end point of Mediterranean counter-epic, however, was not directly engaged until late in Marlowe's short writing life, when he takes up the swimming adventures of Leander crossing the Hellespont in an erotic poem, *Hero and Leander* (1592–93). Many critics explore this poem in the tradition of Renaissance epyllia (or 'mini-epics'), with Marlowe's project appearing notably sceptical or radically playful.[25] In a compelling recent reading that connects Marlowe's Hellespont to the cultural resonance of Ottoman objects in early modern English culture, Miriam Jacobson argues that in Marlowe's treatment Hero's body resembles 'orient pearls not as emblems of feminine purity but as indicative of a kind of sexual fluidity and freedom from Western mores'.[26] For Jacobson, Hero represents both sexuality and fluidity, which together create a freedom that mixes the erotic fantasies of *Dido* with a personal, if not quite political, freedom.

To shift from Jacobson's vision of transformed female sexuality at the poem's circulatory centre to a swimming-centred vision of Leander's encounter with Mediterranean waters does not require too great a leap – especially since pearls are brought to land by undersea divers. Swimming often assumes a sexualised meaning in early modern English culture, in part because of its associations with exotic warm-water locations from the Eastern Mediterranean to the Caribbean. For example, the description of Sebastian in *Twelfth Night* (*c.*1601) struggling in stormy seas has a distinctly erotic flavour: 'I saw your brother ... bind himself ... To a strong mast that lived upon the sea ... I saw him hold acquaintance with the waves.'[27] Phallic masts and vaginal acquaintance limns a semi-pornographic subtext that Shakespeare may well be adapting with a glance at Marlowe. The more overtly erotic *Hero and Leander* makes Shakespeare's allusions seem timid, as Marlowe's poem plunges more overtly into sexual fluids and fluidity. Like *Dido*, this poem proffers a vision of free multiplicity that it locates, in this case even more directly, in Mediterranean waters.

One crucial distinction among Marlowe's triplicate oceanic fantasies – multicultural utopian dreams in *Dido*, global domination and encirclement in *Tamburlaine* and *Faustus,* and his return to Mediterranean waters in *Hero and Leander* – shows itself in the more intimate scale of the poem. The key symbolic terms in the poem are individual bodies, not city-states or political collectives. Leander's body defines itself in relation to water: 'let it suffice', observes the poet, 'That my slack muse sings of Leander's eyes, / Those orient cheeks and lips, exceeding his / That leapt into the water for a kiss / of his own shadow'.[28] The poet's 'slack muse', an Ovidian affectation, shows his swimming protagonist exceeding Narcissus, another drowned classical boy. Hero, too, announces her beauty by connection to water creatures, 'For like sea-nymphs inveigling harmony, / So was her beauty to the standers by' (*H&L*, 1.105–06). Later, when Leander has crossed the straits to her shores, Hero's joy becomes even more explicitly aquatic, resembling a 'crooked dolphin when the sailor sings' (*H&L*, 2.234).[29] Their hypersexualised bodies are primed with water, and in Marlowe's poem their encounter combines individual eroticism with elemental symbolism, while skipping over the political forms so central to *Dido* and *Tamburlaine*.

My oceanic reading of *Hero and Leander* focuses on the sexualised description of Leander swimming the Hellespont and his encounter with the amorous and aggressive Neptune (*H&L*, 2.153–226). Neptune, the sea god who on some level represents the Mediterranean itself, becomes an erotic pursuer and mistakes Leander's body for that of Ganymede, newly fallen from his place at Jupiter's side. Notably, Marlowe's *Dido* begins not with Aeneas's shipwreck but with a petulant Jupiter asking for the Trojan Ganymede to 'play with me' (1.1.1), which scene soon gives way to the arrival of the Trojan hero on African shores (1.1.133). The boy Ganymede in both the play and the poem represents a queer erotics of inverted domination, with the boy's body luring a powerful god away from his duties. Through the eyes of Neptune, the vision of Leander as Ganymede brings the poem to crystalline depths:

> therefore on him he seized.
> Leander strived, the waves about him wound,

And pulled him to the bottom, where the ground
Was strewed with pearl, and in low coral groves
Sweet singing mermaids sported with their loves
On heaps of heavy gold, and took great pleasure
To spurn in careless sort the shipwreck treasure. (*H&L*, 2.158–64)

This undersea passage reprises and exceeds the opulence of Dido's imagined kingdom; more beautiful than 'heavy gold' and 'shipwreck treasure' are sporting mermaids and pearls. Neptune's kingdom refuses politics and the petty business of accumulating wealth, replacing the political obsessions of dry land with fluid sexuality and 'pleasure'. This bottom-of-the-sea land of perpetual dalliance exchanges the political fantasies that animated *Dido* and *Tamburlaine* for more physical bodily sensations.

By reimagining the dangerous act of swimming as erotic in its tactile dangers, Marlowe replaces the empire-building that in the Virgilian model is the central task of the poet. Realising that Leander is human and cannot live beneath the waves, Neptune returns him to the surface 'almost dead' (*H&L*, 2.170), where human and nonhuman bodies become nearly indistinguishable:

He watched his arms, and as they opened wide
At every stroke, betwixt them would he slide,
And steal a kiss, and then run out and dance,
And as he turned, cast many a lustful glance,
And threw him gaudy toys to please his eye,
And dive into the water, and there pry
Upon his breast, his thighs, and every limb,
And up again, and close beside him swim. (*H&L*, 2.183–90)

The god's sexual assault appears inseparable from what water does to the immersed body, interposing its fluid touch across every bit of the swimmer's vulnerable skin. The tactility of the verse highlights pleasure, though that pleasure locates itself in the leering god and voyeuristic reader more than in the assailed swimmer himself. Leander in this moment has dangerously entered into full immersion in the alien sea, and his senses and Marlowe's lines teem with momentary and threatening sensations that neither promise nor presume any political payoff. This underwater world overflows with momentary actions – stealing, kissing, running, dancing, glancing – with no imperative to build or last. In a homoerotic fantasy that anticipates the climax of Leander's visit to Hero, this passage presents a non-political sea-poetics of victimisation, aggression, and desire.

As in *Dido* and *Tamburlaine*, such perfect pleasures cannot endure. In 'Hero and Leander', normative sexuality undoes divine love, just as the imperial future undoes Dido and Aeneas's imagined kingdom. Leander asserts his masculinity – 'I am no woman, I' (*H&L*, 2.192) – and refuses the god's smiling invitation to subaquatic pastoral dalliance. Neptune's enraged blow at the boy, however, rebounds on itself, causing Leander to pity the love-wounded deity: 'When this fresh bleeding wound Leander viewed / His colour went and came, as if he rued / The grief which Neptune felt' (*H&L*, 2.113–15). Reaching the far shore is not exactly a triumph of epic heroism, since Neptune descends 'To the rich Ocean for gifts' in order to further tempt the swimmer, who escapes only by leaving the water (*H&L*, 2.225). Marlowe's Leander crosses the water as erotic subject and opportunist. The fleeting vision of a salt-water paradise rearticulates Marlowe's commitment to Matvejevic's hybrid Mediterranean ethos. For Marlowe, being underwater may be more deeply and painfully felt than arriving at the far shore – but submarine intensity cannot last.

Conclusion: The Counter-Epic Mediterranean

Marlowe's plays and his last-written poem bear traces of a nonhuman Mediterranean fantasy-space that suggests that the writer's counter-epic project relies upon the discourse of this sea. Considering Marlowe as a sea-loving or 'thalassophilic' writer can refashion elements of the counter-epic reading of his career that has come to structure recent criticism. Putting Marlowe's work in touch with oceanic strains of other Renaissance writers such as Shakespeare, Spenser, and Camões may connect this poet to an emerging story of global maritime poetics.[30] An ocean-centred reading of Marlowe can refine our established understandings of the poet's classical influences, awareness of sixteenth-century geopolitics, and glancing engagements with the European project of global maritime expansion then under way.

Marlowe's classicism becomes newly legible through an oceanic lens that clarifies how much of a critical reader this writer was of the received poetics of his age. That Marlowe was an Ovidian poet has become a standard reading in the wake of Cheney's influential study, but considering his interest in sea as opposed to land may give new detail to this familiar analytical approach. In particular, his emphasis in *Dido* on the maritime undercurrent of the *Aeneid* suggests that Marlowe was not simply an Ovidian but also a counter-Virgilian, reading beneath and against Virgil's own poem's outward ideology.

Perhaps even more significantly, Marlowe's ocean appears to be at least as Ottoman as it is global. While his imagination spans the world in *Doctor Faustus*, his closest encounters with sea water locate him in the Turkish-dominated Eastern Mediterranean. Readers of *Tamburlaine* have long argued for the importance of Marlowe's interest in Islam and the Ottoman world.[31] Considering Turkey as a maritime power and its domain as the Eastern Mediterranean suggests that Marlowe's works imagine a maritime frontier very different from Virginia, Peru, or Newfoundland. This distinctive maritime world is itself underwritten by Greek, Roman, and biblical history. The Mediterranean basin was a special case, as critics from Braudel to Horden and Purcell to Matvejevic have argued. Marlowe's oceanic vision might be usefully contrasted with the global expansion coming into view in the Atlantic.

Marlowe's image of Leander as fragile swimmer, threatened by the intensity of Neptune's watery desire, also points to the emerging fields of the 'blue' humanities and post-sustainability ecostudies as discourses to which Marlowe scholarship might make renewed contributions. Marlowe might join Shakespeare among the early modern writers whose conceptions of 'blue' or oceanic culture appear crucial in providing a meaningful cultural history for an age of hurricanes and floods.[32] The stillborn utopian kingdom of Aeneas and Dido on African shores might represent an ecological response to storms as well as a way to endure political crises. The threatened figure Blackmore terms the 'shipwrecked swimmer' represents a mismatch between human capacities and environmental hostility. This violent relationship, given striking representation in Marlowe's *Hero and Leander*, may be increasingly important as our own era of rising sea levels and catastrophic storms continues.

Notes

1 *Dido* was long considered an apprentice play, possibly written while Marlowe was still at Cambridge, but it is now dated around 1588, roughly a year after Marlowe finished his Cambridge MA and also a year after the stage debut of *Tamburlaine*. On the dating of this play, see Martin Wiggins, 'When Did Marlowe Write *Dido, Queen of Carthage?*', *Review of English Studies* 59 (2008), 521–41.

2 See Richmond Barbour, *Before Orientalism: London's Theatre of the East, 1576–1626* (Cambridge University Press, 2003); Daniel Vitkus, *Turning Turk: English Theater and the Multicultural Mediterranean* (New York: Palgrave, 2002); Matthew Dimmock, *New Turkes: Dramatizing Islam and the Ottomans in Early Modern England* (London: Routledge, 2005), and Anders Ingram, *Writing the Ottomans: Turkish History in Early Modern England* (London: Palgrave, 2015).

3 Patrick Cheney, *Marlowe's Counterfeit Profession: Ovid, Spenser, Counter-Nationhood* (University of Toronto Press, 1997), 19.

4 See, for example, the essays in Goran Stanivukovic, ed., *Remapping the Mediterranean World in Early Modern English Writings* (London: Palgrave Macmillan, 2007), as well as Stanivukovic's recent monograph, *Knights in Arms: Prose Romance, Masculinity, and Eastern Mediterranean Trade in Early Modern England, 1565–1655* (University of Toronto Press, 2016).

5 For reasons of space, I do not explore the oceanic resonances of *The Jew of Malta* in this chapter.

6 Fernand Braudel, *The Mediterranean and the Mediterranean World in the Age of Philip II*, 2 vols., trans. from the 2nd rev. edn, 1966, by Sian Reynolds (New York: HarperCollins, 1972–73).

7 Peregrine Horden and Nicholas Purcell, *The Corrupting Sea: A Study of Mediterranean History* (Oxford: Blackwell, 2000).

8 Predrag Matvejevic, *Mediterranean: A Cultural Landscape*, trans. Michael Henry Heim (Berkeley, CA: University of California Press, 1999).

9 Ibid., 93.

10 Ibid., 24.

11 Josiah Blackmore, 'The Shipwrecked Swimmer: Camões's Maritime Subject', *Modern Philology* 109 (2012), 312–25, at 325.

12 On these and other oceanic figures in Shakespeare, see Steve Mentz, *At the Bottom of Shakespeare's Ocean* (London: Bloomsbury, 2009).

13 The meaning of Nashe's name on the title-page is unclear; editors remain divided on whether any other evidence connects Nashe to the play, though Nashe was clearly well connected in Elizabethan publishing circles by 1594. On Nashe's speculative interest in oceanic literature, see Steve Mentz, 'Nashe's Fish: Misogyny, Romance, and the Ocean in *Lenten Stuffe*', in *The Age of Thomas Nashe: Texts, Bodies, and Trespasses of Authorship in Early Modern England*, ed. Stephen Guy-Bray, Joan Pong Linton, and Steve Mentz (Aldershot: Ashgate, 2013), 63–73.

14 Emily C. Bartels, *Spectacles of Strangeness: Imperialism, Alienation, and Marlowe* (Philadelphia: University of Pennsylvania Press, 1993), especially 29–52.

15 Ibid., 30.

16 Sid Ray, 'Marlow(e)'s Africa: Postcolonial Queenship in Conrad's *Heart of Darkness* and Marlowe's *Dido, Queen of Carthage*', *Conradiana* 38, no. 2 (2006), 143–61.

17 Ibid., 144.

18 Horden and Purcell, *The Corrupting Sea*, 123–71.

19 Christopher Marlowe, *Dido, Queen of Carthage*, in *The Complete Plays*, ed. Frank Romany and Robert Lindsey (New York: Penguin, 2003), 5.1.1–15. All further quotations from *Dido, Queen of Carthage* refer to this edition and will be cited by act, scene, and line numbers within the text.

20 Marlowe, *1 Tamburlaine*, in *The Complete Plays*, 3.3.248–60. All further quotations from *1 Tamburlaine* will be cited by act, scene, and line numbers within the text.

21 Cheney, *Marlowe's Counterfeit Profession*, 120.
22 See Richard Helgerson, *Self-Crowned Laureates: Spenser, Jonson, Milton, and the Literary System* (Berkeley, CA: University of California Press, 1993).
23 Marlowe, *Doctor Faustus*, in *The Complete Plays*, 1.85, 3.40, 4.108. All further quotations from *Doctor Faustus* will be cited by act, scene, and line numbers within the text.
24 Cheney, *Marlowe's Counterfeit Profession*, 22.
25 For a good summary of the critical literature, see L. E. Semler, 'Marlovian Therapy: The Chastisement of Ovid in *Hero and Leander*', *English Literary Renaissance* 35, no. 2 (2005), 159–86, 159n.
26 Miriam Jacobson, *Barbarous Antiquity: Reorienting the Past in the Poetry of Early Modern England* (Philadelphia: University of Pennsylvania Press, 2014), 166.
27 William Shakespeare, *Twelfth Night*, ed. Keir Elam (London: Arden 3, 2009) 1.2.14–17. On this passage, see Mentz, *At the Bottom*, 53–54.
28 Christopher Marlowe, *Hero and Leander*, in *The Collected Poems of Christopher Marlowe*, ed. Patrick Cheney and Brian J. Striar (Oxford University Press, 2006), 193–220, Book 1, lines 71–74. All further quotations from *Hero and Leander* will refer to this edition and will be cited by book and line numbers within the text.
29 On the cultural symbolism of dolphins and the eroticism of the dolphin–sailor relationship, see Steve Mentz, 'Half-fish, Half-flesh: Dolphins, Humans, and the Early Modern Ocean', in *The Indistinct Human in Renaissance Literature*, ed. Jean Feerick and Vin Nardizzi (London: Palgrave, 2012), 29–46.
30 On this global maritime poetics, see Blackmore's forthcoming monograph *The Inner Ship: Maritime Literary Culture in Early Modern Iberia* (University of Chicago Press).
31 See, for example, Dimmock, *New Turkes*, 135–61.
32 On Shakespeare, the 'blue' humanities, and ecological crisis, see Mentz, *At the Bottom*.

CHAPTER 4

Making the Land Known: Henry IV, Parts 1 and 2 and the Literature of Perambulation

Julie Sanders

Newcastle University

The latter half of the sixteenth century was a period of geographical, cultural, and social transition which transformed the ways in which people thought about and made sense of the world. Actual travel, foreign and domestic, and also imaginative travel – the kind inspired by the fictional and non-fictional publications that were increasingly available – made major contributions to this process. The ways in which drama played a role in both reflecting and shaping the attendant debates around place and identity, at national and local levels, as well as the ways those themes were made manifest through a particular form of the early modern journeying play focused on domestic mobility and notions of regional perambulation, will be the focus of this essay. The argument will place at its centre Shakespeare's two ground-breaking and generically experimental *Henry IV* plays (1596–99). From this vantage point, travel, as both practice and concept, will be seen to influence literary genre but also to be shaped by it in turn.[1]

Jean E. Howard and Phyllis Rackin have observed that the rambling structure of Shakespeare's *Henry IV* plays is directly comparable to the ways in which the genre of chorography was attempting to write the English landscape and its regions into being at this time:

> No longer confined to the elevated domain of court and battlefield, the world of *Henry IV* includes a variety of vividly detailed contemporary settings, ranging like a disordered chorographic 'perambulation' from Shallow's bucolic Gloucestershire, to an inn yard on the road to London, to Falstaff's bustling, urban Eastcheap.[2]

Chorography as a form and practice reached its zenith in the 1570s, 1580s, and 1590s, salient decades for any consideration of the composition and context for the *Henry IV* plays. Formally the art of describing a particular region, place, or space, this subgenre corresponded to and built upon the work of both cartographers and poets, bringing together in informative dialogue poetic and scientific attempts to describe place. It thus connected what might otherwise be viewed as distinct genres such as chronicles, historiography, and staged drama, in a highly productive matrix.

Shakespeare's history plays as a collective have long been understood through the lens of the chronicle tradition, but Richard Helgerson aligned the textual practices of chorography and chronicle specifically as ways of seeking to describe a nation.[3] What might it yield for us, then, to read the *Henry IV* plays alongside contemporary chorographical writing and against what Helgerson termed the 'perambulatory' mode?[4] As well as understanding the influence of this particular form of descriptive narrative, one that engaged with the nation and its regional and provincial geographical particularities through a form of walking the nation, can we trace lines of influence from the theatrical domain and from experimental texts like the *Henry IV* plays back into the practice and aesthetics of the perambulatory literature and performative events which followed?[5] These discussions bring into the frame the relationship between metropolitan and provincial cultures, not least theatrical cultures, and for that reason this essay will close with a microstudy of one particular provincial performance of the *Henry IV* plays in 1623 in Surrenden, Kent, which brings all these related issues into relief.[6]

New technologies that were made available in the field of mapping, as well as changes wrought by new practices of cartography and surveying, impacted on the early modern cultural and spatial imagination and, as John M. Adrian's comprehensive survey of the types of geographical writings produced at this time indicates, travel narratives, historical geographies, and, perhaps most significantly for the purposes of this discussion, the emergent genre of chorography, all played a significant role in what was a socially transformative process.[7]

Chorography's investment in different forms of travel, mobility, and description encouraged an interaction with literary modes that was particular to this time. William Camden's *Britannia* (first published in Latin in 1586) was, as indicated by its English title, attempting to work on a national scale by offering a 'chorographicall description of the most flourishing kingdoms, England, Scotland and Ireland'. Yet in many ways that text's commitment to localised description and engagement with place and community was parallel to more regional chorographies, such as Richard Carew's *Survey of Cornwall* (1602), or what has been termed the 'very first county chorography', William Lambarde's *Perambulation of*

Kent (1570).[8] Camden certainly undertook his own regional perambulations when constructing his 'verbal map' of the realm.[9]

Perambulation and walking in its many guises will be a defining feature of the analysis undertaken here. The 'literature of perambulation' as I
am describing it was part of a wider engagement with ideas of travel and
mobility as means of understanding place. The 'Water Poet' John Taylor's
pamphlet *The Pennyles Pilgrimage*, which records his 1618 journey from
London to Edinburgh relying on the hospitality to be found in the places
where he stopped, is a prime example of a small wave of perambulatory
events and publications in the late-sixteenth and early-seventeenth centuries, the most famous of which is surely playwright Ben Jonson's own
walk to Scotland, which predates Taylor's trip by just a matter of weeks.[10]
The extant record we have of Jonson's walk is decidedly non-literary; a
recently discovered manuscript daybook kept by a hitherto unknown
travelling companion has provided us with insight into the practical itinerary and daily occupations of this consciously performed perambulation
as well as the national and indeed highly localised issues with which it
interacted, both deliberately and by chance.[11] Placed alongside other real-
life depositions and records of journeys, texts and events such as Taylor's
and Jonson's walks serve to highlight the complex ways in which the
nation was described and understood by contemporaries and the ways in
which literature might intervene in this process.

In terms of 'perambulatory literature', central reference points here
will be the work of Will Kemp, a renowned comic actor in Shakespeare's
company, the Lord Chamberlain's Men, in the 1590s, who undertook
a carefully staged Morris dance from London to Norwich, which was
published under the title *Nine Daies Wonder* in 1600, and the two
later 'perambulations' already mentioned, undertaken from London to
Edinburgh, and performed by Jonson and Taylor in 1618. Jonson's journey was an entirely pedestrian affair from which the promised literary
outputs never materialised. In Taylor's case, his account of the journey
was published soon after its completion. The interest of these journeys
lies in their occurrence, their publication history, and the fact that they
were predetermined. An instructive line of connection can be drawn
between this kind of purposeful walking and journeying and Prince Hal's
'I know you all' soliloquy in the first act of *Henry IV, Part 1*. This lends
credence to the sense that audiences can make of the journey Hal under-
takes in that play and its sequel: his 'perambulation' to the tavern land-
scapes of Falstaff and Poins and his eventual 'return' to the court:

> I know you all, and will awhile uphold
> The unyoked humour of your idleness.
> Yet herein will I imitate the sun,
> Who doth permit the base contagious clouds
> To smother up his beauty from the world,
> That, when he please again to be himself,
> Being wanted he may be more wondered at
> By breaking through the foul and ugly mists
> Of vapours that did seem to strangle him.
> ...
> I'll so offend to make offence a skill,
> Redeeming time when men think least I will.[12]

It is worth noting that this notion of the perambulatory instinct in Hal is complementary to readings of his moral and physical wandering and straying as a prodigal son narrative. Critics have suggested that an education of sorts takes place in Hal's tavern sojourn and hard evidence for those claims might be traced in Hal's words later in the play when he suggests he is learning the discourse of the common people over whom he will rule:[13]

> Sirrah, I am sworn brother to a leash of drawers, and can call them all by their Christian names, as Tom, Dick, and Francis ... when I am king of England I shall command all the good lads in Eastcheap... I am so good a proficient in one quarter of an hour that I can drink with any tinker in his own language during my life. (*1H4*, 2.4.6–9, 13–14, 16–18)

At this point, Hal mimics tavern-drawer language proficiently – 'Anon, anon, sir! Score a pint of bastard in the Half-moon' – and he and Poins perform their second act of disguise by posing as drawers to trick Falstaff (*1H4*, 2.4.25–26).[14] Hal's linguistic skill has been hinted at earlier in his confident deployment of vernacular idiom in exchanges with a hung-over Falstaff:

> What a devil hast thou to do with the time of day? Unless hours were cups of sack, and minutes capons, and clocks the tongues of bawds, and dials the signs of leaping-houses... (*1H4*, 1.2.25–29)

This is not the vocabulary – nor are these the geographical settings – that is usually associated with a regal character in a history play, but it is evidence of Hal's willingness to learn about all corners of his nation, to undertake in a hands-on way the kinds of surveys and descriptive journeys that were a publishing vogue at the time when the play was first performed in *c.*1597–98.[15]

By creating Hal as chorographer, Shakespeare harnesses the ways in which cartography was actively changing popular understanding of the world.[16] Falstaff's mistake is to assume that this pedagogic exercise will fundamentally change the landscape of the state when Hal becomes King Henry V: 'shall there be gallows standing in England when thou art king?' (*1H4*, 1.2.56–57). Hal's trajectory, like that of the perambulatory authors discussed here, is characterised by mobility and movement – even in 1.2 he is all restlessness and forward impulse compared to the snoring, static Falstaff; his time in Falstaff's company is more than simply a sojourn and must be understood through a kinetic framework, as movement and experiential journey rather than temporary stay. The educational aspect of Hal's journey can perhaps be explained best by thinking of it as training in cultural geography. Shakespeare's particular mode of depiction for Hal's journey into the everyday places and spaces of the country over which he will eventually reign is a product of a time when writers and mapmakers were taking 'effective visual and conceptual possession of the physical kingdom in which they lived' for the first time.[17]

These plays can be seen afresh if read in the context of other early modern textual and geographical experiments, such as, for example, the county maps of Christopher Saxton, the regional maps of John Speed, Camden's *Britannia*, or William Harrison's *Description of England* (1577 – and, notably, first published alongside Raphael Holinshed's *Chronicles*), or indeed the wave of county surveys that were being authored and published at this time, many of which took the form of perambulations in print. Helgerson notes of this survey tradition:

> Particular description ... takes the place of chronicle history... Kings and their doings, when they are not simply eliminated, are marginalised, they move ... from the center to the periphery. What moves to the center in their place is not, however, the land as a whole, but rather the land in all its most particular divisions.[18]

Though kings do not exactly disappear in the two parts of *Henry IV*, they are increasingly understood within the context of a far wider and carefully differentiated panoramic societal landscape.

I want to make a case here for the potential impact that the experimental melding of the chorographic with the chronicle impulse in the two parts of *Henry IV* might have had on real-life perambulations, in particular Kemp's Morris dance undertaken from London to Norwich (in reality, he combined walking, riding, and dancing). This event took place within a few years of Kemp's likely performance of Falstaff on the

London commercial stage and was published in 1600 soon after the public and highly publicised journey had taken place:

> *Kemps nine daies wonder:* Performed in a *Morrice* from London to Norwich. Wherein euery dayes iourny is pleasantly set downe; to satisfie his friends the truth, against all lying Ballad-makers; What he did, how hee was welcome, and by whome entertained.[19]

Kemp makes much of the huge crowds that attended him on his way and often hindered his progress.[20] One particularly striking passage is when he finds himself in direct competition with the Lord Chief Justice for an audience, when he enters Bury at one set of town gates at much the same time as Kemp's well-attended cross-country dance pirouettes in:

> [the] wondring and regardless multitude making his honor cleere way, left the streets where he past to gape at me; the throng of them being so great, that poor Will Kemp was seauen times stayed ere hee could recouer his Inne.[21]

It is perhaps too neat a line of connection to draw between Kemp and his remembered performance as Falstaff and those scenes in *Part 2* of Shakespeare's plays where Falstaff and the Lord Chief Justice character compete for the role as surrogate patriarch to Hal. Nevertheless, since these scenes would have been consciously staged as a spatial contest in the theatre and as a direct competition for audience attention, this seems to be mirrored in interesting ways within Kemp's narrative. There was a broader practice of regional journeying in contemporary touring theatre that could also have influenced Kemp. The Queen's Men company both invented the chronicle history format and toured extensively to the provinces, so their repertoire provides a fascinating precursor to the particular collocation of chorographical history writing and perambulation in the *Henry IV* plays.[22] *The Famous Victories of Henry V* is often credited with being the first commercial chronicle drama in England and shares much of its content with Shakespeare's Henriad.[23] There are lines of influence and appropriation here worth accounting for as they tell us much about generic cross-fertilisation and inter-theatrical and intertextual knowledge exchange in the early modern period, not least around themes of national history and regional identity.

In Kemp's enterprise Daryl Palmer has identified both a knowing performance of and a parodic imitation of a royal progress. Editors of the *Henry IV* plays have also registered parodic inversions of emblems of state in specific scenes. Perambulatory texts such as Taylor's 1618 *Pennyles*

Pilgrimage appear to imitate such manoeuvres.[24] In one section there is a description of how Taylor and his packhorse are forced to make camp in a field and the moment is hedged round with the lexicon of monarchical ceremony: 'We made a breach, and entred horse and man, / There our pavillion, we to pitch began.'[25] Shakespeare's *Henry* plays are overtly shaped by one particular set of geographical and chorographical writing traditions, but they also demonstrate an aesthetic experimentation of their own, and this in turn appears to feed back into a later cluster of perambulatory texts and events. Perambulatory literature and the events that precede their writing were certainly highly theatrical in their mindset and approach. There is evidence that, as well as being undertaken by people like Jonson and Kemp with connections to the Bankside theatres, many of these journeys were sponsored by individuals from wider theatrical networks.[26]

Kemp's text demonstrates an emphasis on popular culture and on folk traditions and perspectives that in turn draws a connecting line back to Bankside cultural geography. At Romford, for example, a bear-baiting is staged for his delectation (Kemp was a self-confessed enthusiast for the sport). Because of the press of the crowds, he claims he 'could only heare the Beare roare, and the dogges howle'.[27] Bankside practices clearly travelled with him on his chorographical dance and became a lens through which he understood his experiences. A later encounter in the narrative confirms this. Two cutpurses are apprehended at Burntwood. They have been following Kemp from London, presumably benefiting from pickpocketing the ready-made crowds attending his dance. On being arrested, they claim to have taken a bet out on the dance (this would of course map onto earlier observations about the sponsored nature of many of these perambulations),[28] but when the local constabulary later visit Kemp at the inn where he is staying to verify their story he recognises one of them from the London network of cutpurses who worked the playhouses. This passage visibly shows the mixed economy of performance at play; in Kemp's anecdotal comparison, the 'performance' of public punishment is actually brought onto the stage of the commercial theatres: 'I remembered one of them to be a noted Cut-purse such a one as we tye to a poast on our Stage, for all people to wonder at, when at a play they are taken pilfering.'[29]

Henry IV, Part 1 has its own version of petty thievery and highway robbery (a common threat to those undertaking perambulatory performance events) in the Gadshill episode, which proves to be stage-managed by Poins. Gad's Hill, a site near Rochester, was a common stopping point on the pilgrimage route to Canterbury. The perambulatory religious, as well as the common tradesmen who plied the national roadways, are mentioned as possible targets for the robbery by Poins, though in reality Falstaff and his men set on the king's receivers:

> POINS: But my lads, my lads, tomorrow morning by four o'clock early at Gad's Hill there are pilgrims going to Canterbury with rich offerings, and traders riding to London with fat purses... Gadshill lies tonight in Rochester. I have bespoke supper tomorrow night in Eastcheap. (*1H4*, 1.2.118–23)

The Gadshill sections of the *Henry IV* plays are fascinating as they bring very visibly onto the stage an awareness of the particular circuits of knowledge and encounter that the public highways fostered.[30] This is the exact geography of the perambulatory writings of Kemp, Jonson, and Taylor, though there is considerable variation in the extent to which they engage with the details of the everyday community of the roads.[31] In the same way, though, that Jonson's companion describes the itinerant preachers or the bands of gypsies they meet on their way out of London, so Shakespeare brings onto the stage characters such as the carriers at the Rochester inn, who bemoan the poor workmanship of the local ostler and the state of the bedding in fantastically rich vernacular expressions:[32]

> FIRST CARRIER: I prithee, Tom, beat cut's saddle, put a few flocks in the point. Poor jade is wrung in the withers out of all cess.
> *Enter another Carrier.*
> SECOND CARRIER: Peas and beans are as dank here as a dog, and that is the next way to give poor jades the bots. (*1H4*, 2.1.5–10)

As David Bevington notes: '[t]he comic world of *1 Henry IV* also finds room for ordinary commoners, like the men who haul provisions on the Rochester–London road and gripe about their hard life in foul-smelling hostelries (2.1). Language is vividly colloquial in such an environment.'[33] The character of Gadshill (who acts as organiser of the robbery for the Eastcheap crew) is equally colloquial and suggestive when recounting the company he keeps in his life of organised crime:

> I am joined with no foot-land-rakers, no long-staff sixpenny strikers, none of these mad mustachio purple-hued malt-worms, but with nobility and tranquillity, burgomasters and great oneyers... (*1H4*, 2.1.70–74)

His mention of 'foot-rakers' – that is, footpads who cannot afford a horse and do their highway robbery on foot – also implies that the roadways of the nation are sites of activity.

The Rochester carrier scene in *Henry IV, Part 1* is often cut for expediency in contemporary productions but it is central to the radical experiment in history writing and the writing of a nation that these plays represent. That scene also brings into the frame the importance of inns on these road networks as stopping points and significant pauses on the itineraries of perambulations and horseback or coach journeys, both literary and every day. In a 1612 deposition, one Wiltshire vagrant recounted his journey via a catalogue of inns and stopping places:

> First night, the Saracen's Head in Farringdon;
> Second night, the Star in Abingdon,
> Third night, an unnamed alehouse in Wallingford;
> Fourth night, the Hand in Reading;
> Fifth night, the Shoemaker's Last in Newbury;
> Sixth night, the Black Boys in Andover;
> Seventh night, the Chequers in Winchester;
> Eighth night, an unnamed alehouse in Amesbury;
> Ninth night, a barn five miles from Amesbury;
> Tenth night, The White Horse in Fisherton Anger.[34]

At a local level, the Wiltshire deposition maps onto the performance of the life of the mobile poor that Taylor undertook in his *Pennyles Pilgrimage*. This redacted list can be compared to the descriptive style of Taylor's hybrid verse-prose pamphlet, with its carefully mapped itinerary of sleeping places:

> And went that night as farre as Islington
> There did I find ...
> A Mayden head of twenty five yeeres old,
> But surely it was painted, like a whore,
> And for a signe, or wonder, hand'd at dore,
> ...
> At High-gate hill to a strange house I went
> And saw the people were to eating bent
> ...
> The Sarazens head at Whetstone entring straight
> I found an Host, might lead an Host of men...[35]

More generally, the Wiltshire deposition and Taylor's poetic reworking of the mobile vagrant's itinerary constitute additional forms of regional description to place alongside the history play, chorographical writing, and the perambulatory journal of Jonson's as-yet-unidentified companion as texts performing identity through accounts of travel. Hal's journey to the Eastcheap tavern starts to look like a very different enterprise in understanding the nation when it is read through the lens of these other encounters with the cultural cartography of the country.

Actual landscape description in these texts is rare, but it does appear when the way is hard or the weather particularly brutal: Kemp mentions the 'great snow falling' at Bury and on the way out of Chelmsford he notes the difficult terrain: 'This foule way I could find no ease In, thicke woods being on eyther side the lane: the lane likewise being full of deep holes, sometimes I skipt up to the waste.'[36] Jonson's companion mentions getting wet but also the walkers losing each other, presumably in thick mist, and Taylor is apt to tell us when the surface has been unusually hard and therefore tough on his blistered feet. But for the most part there are other ways in which the land is described, primarily through people and place. Bevington's edition of *Henry IV, Part 1* includes a map of the places mentioned, and this performs a genuine cartographic link to the walking itineraries from London to the North that Jonson, Taylor and others undertook. In most instances, the route was London, St Albans, Daventry, Coventry, Burton, Doncaster, and York. In his companion edition of *Henry IV, Part 2*, Weis claims that the 'wider politics of the realm' are more marginalised here than in *Part 1* but I think that is a contestable claim.[37] As Weis himself later acknowledges, the Gloucestershire scenes act as a significant microcosm of that wider cultural and political geography, but there is a whole host of places alluded to usually by means of association with particular individuals. It is the fact that so many of these individuals are neither significant nor even *seen* characters on the stage that bears revisiting.

Stanley Wells observed that there is an enhanced presence of 'ordinary people' in the *Henry IV* plays, and Weis calculates that twenty out of forty-nine characters in *Part 2* fit in this category.[38] Many are people with names, professions, and real-life addresses: William Cook, the Nightworks, and off-stage Gloucestershire litigants are mentioned by Weis;[39] there is also Samson Stockfish, the fruiterer, with whom Shallow once fought behind Gray's Inn when he was a trainee lawyer in the Inns of Court alongside Falstaff (*2H4*, 3.2.29–30); Little John Doit of Staffordshire, George Barnes, Francis Pickbone, and Will Squeal from the Cotswolds, are all Inns of Court men (*2H4*, 3.2.17–20) – the cultural geography of these networks should not be underestimated in provincial circles at the time. This grouping (all remembered figures from Shallow's youth) presage in significant ways the ordinary villagers of the juxtaposed press-ganging scene: Mouldy, Wart, Bullcalf et al. are men with real biographies, however much Falstaff attempts to reduce them to cannon fodder or a financial transaction.

In performance, Bullcalf with the cough he has acquired as a local bell-ringer – 'A whoreson cold, sir; a cough, sir, which I got with ringing in the King's affairs upon his coronation day, sir' (2H4, 3.2.175–78) – is a touching element in the scene but the issues raised by this small moment are far-reaching. The impact on the realm (and by extension in the provinces) of Henry Bolingbroke's accession to the position of King Henry IV is quietly registered here in ways that mimic the impulse of chorographic and perambulatory literature to respond to and value the local and the particular.[40] But attention is also drawn, albeit fleetingly, to the role of bells and the action of bell-ringing as 'soundmarks' for particular communities and, as a result, as particular expressions of the relationship between the local and the national which Hal's journey is also negotiating.[41]

Bullcalf's line brings the 'physical space of the parish church' and in particular the masculine domain of the belfry into brief visibility at this point.[42] Christopher Marsh has noted the huge increase in the number of English bells installed in parish churches from the 1590s onwards, so that travellers to the country made trenchant observations about 'the ringing island'.[43] Orazio Busino, chaplain to the Venetian ambassador in 1617 and 1618, noted in particular that boys made bets 'who can make the parish bells be heard at the greatest distance'.[44] Bruce R. Smith reads this in terms of parish 'sound marks' but also as an active example of parish identity and practice transgressing beyond local boundaries: 'Such wagers sound like deliberate attempts to breach the parish's acoustic horizon, to transcend the boundaries marked out in rotation processions.'[45]

The Henry IV plays offer, then, subtle examples of the spatial and imaginative expansion and contraction of parish boundaries, through Hal's travelling activities with Falstaff and the Boar's Head communities and through the plays' travel to Gloucestershire. Bullcalf would most likely have been part of a community of young men in his country who might have rung the bells both for official parish occasions and for recreational pleasure, sometimes even drunkenly.[46] Bells were, in Marsh's terms, used for 'marking the hours, warning of danger, honouring the monarchy' as well as ringing people to service, and they carried messages both around and between parishes. These aural communications were sometimes moral in tone and sometimes straightforwardly governmental in nature, and in this way bells functioned in a manner akin to the role of foot and horse posts, those travelling messengers who also feature in the storyline of the *Henry IV* plays.[47] In its opening scene, *Henry IV, Part 1* includes a messenger of sorts in the form of Sir Walter Blount, who is, as the king notes, newly arrived from the Percy strongholds in Northumberland:

> new lighted from his horse,
> Stained with the variation of each soil
> Betwixt that Holmedon and this seat of ours. (*1H4*, 1.1.63–65)

The image is a potent one; Blount as well as being 'loaden with heavy news' (in a manner akin to the Welsh post mentioned earlier in the scene) seems to bear physical traces of the landscape he has travelled through: 'Stained with the variation of each soil' (*1H4*, 1.1.37, 64). It is that variation and diversity in the realm that I am arguing Prince Hal is seeking to understand and capture in his own journeying away from the confines of the court, and it is the same note of variation that is sounded in the sideline story of Bullcalf's bell-ringing. The ringing in of the coronation that has led inadvertently to Bullcalf's head cold provides a link to a world of civic and parish practice in which ringing would have happened during royal progresses (a rather more ceremonial version of Hal's journey around his nation), and which is in turn echoed in perambulatory texts like Jonson's 'Foot Voyage' where the writer-walker is greeted by various townsfolk and civic authorities via the act of bell-ringing. Both Taylor and Jonson undertook their walks to Scotland in the wake of King James VI and I's 'salmonlyke' return to his native country the year before, so once again royal progress can be seen to underscore perambulatory literature and chorography in significant ways, further strengthening the links between Hal's travelling and Shakespeare's representation of the same to contemporary travel writing and events.[48] Bullcalf's seemingly throwaway comment begins to verbally map or describe a host of parochial practices and identities that relate to and comment on the central administration in ways that provide a microcosm of the plays' larger concerns with the relationship of monarchy to its people. Space, place, and time intertwine and enfold beautifully in this one fleeting moment.

Case Study

HENRY IV ON THE MOVE: A MICRO-
NARRATIVE OF TRAVELLING THEATRE

What is witnessed in all the examples offered above is the making known of
the regions in metropolitan culture, and indeed vice versa, through a series
of performative and literary 'events' involving travel. Chorography, real-life
perambulations, and Hal's 'journey' beyond the court in the *Henry IV* plays
can be better understood as generic experiments in a form of voyage drama
through this critical lens.

A further element in this story, as already indicated in references to the
repertoire and practices of the Queen's Men, is the role of travelling theatre,
the world of the touring players and their own perambulations of the English
countryside. Travelling theatre contexts enhance our understanding of Hal's
trajectories in the *Henry IV* plays but also shed light on the trajectories and
travel of the plays themselves as they toured the nation.[49]

In the late-sixteenth and early-seventeenth centuries, people of a certain
rank and position in society were able to move between London as the
capital city and their 'home', between city and region, traversing urban and
rural spaces with considerable alacrity. With them travelled ideas, news, and
sometimes physical texts – manuscripts and purchased plays – as this case
study will indicate. An understanding of this kind of cultural and geographical flow is altering the perception of how writers like Jonson, Richard Brome,
or indeed Shakespeare – who all had overlapping and intersecting London
and provincial networks and communities – constructed their own sense of
place, of the geopolitical and performative environment.[50] Touring players
and the texts they chose to transport with them on their routes are one
obvious way in which London theatre networks knew and moved about the
provinces, enabling a more complex emerging and emergent set of national
and regional geographies and identities in the process. Pioneering research
by the likes of Scott McMillin and Sally-Beth MacLean on the Queen's Men
and the extensive findings of the Records of Early English Drama (REED)
project in Toronto have radically challenged neat binaries between notions of
centre and periphery, metropolis and province, and indeed between commercial and amateur or private theatrical.[51] In these touring circumstances,
texts themselves performed a kind of chorographical perambulation: regional
households and estates, at William Cavendish's Worksop or Bolsover in
Derbyshire, or like the Willoughbys at Wollaton Hall in Nottinghamshire,
received touring players, and often texts were specially authored or adapted
for performance, contributing their own particular local relevance and
resonance. The huge spectrum of activity that comes under the broad
heading of 'touring playing' at this time and its intersection with private
household theatricals transform a sense of how the knowledge and indeed

the cultural economy functioned. And many plays represented these happenings and events back to a commercial theatre audience in the capital: Jonson's *The Alchemist* (1610–11) can, for example, be reconfigured as a story of semi-amateur household theatricals; Sir Bounteous Progress hires players (albeit ill-fatedly) in Thomas Middleton's *A Mad World My Masters* (1605); and *Histriomastix* (Anon.(?), 1599),[52] Shakespeare's *The Taming of the Shrew* (1590–92), and Brome's *The Antipodes* (1638) all feature itinerant acting troupes performing in domestic households.

It is intriguing that the *Henry IV* plays are also interested in so-called private extempore theatricals, through the mechanism of the playacting that takes place, supposedly behind closed doors, between Hal and Falstaff and their Eastcheap cronies. As the Hostess declares in *Part 1*: 'O Jesu, he doth it as like one of these harlotry players as ever I see!' (*1H4*, 2.4.382–83). Michael Dobson has recently connected these moments with amateur dramatics, but has also argued for their self-conscious engagement with state politics:

> Mounted at the Boar's Head by Prince Harry's alternative Eastcheap household, the improvised playlet in which Falstaff and the Prince role-play as the Prince and his father offers at once an explicit burlesquing of the public theatre … and an explicit defiance of the Prince's public duties…[53]

As a small example of how such events might have worked to connect regional and provincial practices to the new emergent national geographies and debates, I want to close with a brief focus on a single 1623 performance of a conflated version of the two parts of *Henry IV*. At his country residence, Surrenden in Kent, the recently widowed Sir Edward Dering effectively commissioned and staged (as Dobson notes) 'the first recorded non-professional production of a Shakespeare play to take place on British soil'.[54] The production is also significant because it was specially devised by Dering. We know from his book of expenses[55] that he paid the local rector to copy out this version. This is different from his usual practice of purchasing multiple copies of plays for household readings and performances, and it suggests a different kind of approach to this particular production which is worthy of exploring.

Several critics have ruminated on Dering's motives for the *Henry IV* performance. Peter Holland and Dobson are keen to stress that Dering's was a performance wholly interested in statecraft and not in the more regional or domestically inflected aspects of the plays. They do so by detailing the cuts, changes, and subsequent bridging work that Dering did to the text to achieve the conflated version, and it is certainly salient to observe at this point in the argument that for the most part the scenes and moments in the plays that have been focused on in this essay are excised or moved decisively off stage: Gadshill, the carriers at Rochester, most of *Part 2* including the Gloucestershire scenes, for example. But I want to pause and reconsider these decisions and what they might have signified for a Kent performance in 1623 and in turn for what Shakespeare might have imagined was needed

on the London stage in terms of provincial representation some two
decades earlier.

If we apply evidence from other household performances that Dering was
staging at this time we can suppose that *Henry IV* involved not professional
players but performers taken from his wider household, family members and
servants, and perhaps significant members of his neighbourhood networks.
We know from detailed entries also in his expense book that Dering was
both an enthusiastic theatregoer – over the space of a few years he saw many
plays – and an avid reader: he purchased over 200 literary texts for his own
collection.[56] A more sustained study could consider the particularities of
these purchases and how they give us a point of entry to the political interest
and mind-set of the man at this particular moment in time and how that
might map onto the work that he does with, and indeed reads into, the two
play texts of *Henry IV*. In brief, though, they included Thomas Gainsford's
The Glory of England, Philip Sidney's *Arcadia*, and the texts of Niccolò
Machiavelli, and this marked interest in statecraft has led both Holland
and Dobson to view this production and the conflated text produced for it
(several months before the publication of the 1623 First Folio, which was the
first time the two parts of *Henry IV* were published together) as wholly political in their leaning.[57] Holland notes that '[w]hatever the popular importance
of Falstaff and Prince Hal in 1622, Dering's version was far less concerned
with the former's exploits and the latter's reformation and far more concerned
with the defeat of the rebels and the death of the monarch.'[58]

The cuts are partly pragmatic – the age-old suggestion of the economics
of touring theatre, a need for smaller casts, and limited props, may play a
part in this;[59] economy alone might explain why scenes like those of Gadshill
and the Rochester carriers are excised. But I am intrigued that for all that
goes from *Part 2* (and in the case of that play text it is over 75 per cent of
the lines) a scene between Falstaff and the Hostess is nevertheless retained,
suggesting that a wholesale excision of the Eastcheap/Boar's Head storylines
is not what is at stake. Is there something different to suggest here? Perhaps
it indicates that a provincial performance to an insider audience with rather
different regional knowledge and understanding from a London Bankside
audience might not require the suggestion of the rural road networks and
the cultural and spatial geographies of the provinces in quite the same way.
The play might instead be connected to the high politics of the capital,
otherwise transported to the provinces only through news and gossip. While
I agree with Holland that abbreviated or adapted Shakespeare plays can be
understood, even in 1623, as 'a deliberate intervention in a history of cultural
reception', the important questions are why Dering was drawn to these plays
in particular, and why he wished to see a conflated and personalised version
of them performed?[60] Certainly *Henry IV, Part 1* was and continued to be
popular in household theatricals at all levels – in 1600 Lord Hunsdon staged
a production at a dinner for the Flemish ambassador, and King James saw

at least two productions at court, one soon after Dering's Kent activities.[61] Could it be, though, that the kinds of emerging interests in regional and national geographies argued for at the beginning of this essay were being capitalised on by these plays? The *Henry IV* plays' experimental approach to genre fed back into the ways in which the play texts were themselves mobilised by the very provincial places and spaces the plays were so keen to represent on the public stage. Perhaps at Surrenden in 1623 there was less need to make the case for a regional and vernacular voice in the performance itself because that was present in the bodies and the voices of both the performers and the audience. What were now being redescribed and made known in new ways were the topical issues of the day.

A reading of the *Henry IV* plays through the prism of chorographic and perambulatory literature might, then, reveal something fresh about the way in which these plays map 'England's identity in space' and not least its provincial identities.[62] The plays are a version of 'voyage drama' in that they depict a literal domestic as well as an interior journey, but also 'travel drama' as they perform a version of that journey as textual events and performances, helping to make the land known in both respects. Understanding this affords new points of entry into the purpose and performance of household theatricals at the time and further locates events such as Kemp's morris dance of 1600 or Taylor's and Jonson's Scottish walks within a Jacobean knowledge economy. Reading the *Henry IV* plays as an experimental version of domestic voyage drama also sheds light on the actions of King Henry V in the history play that followed them. It is worth remembering that when this version of Prince Hal encounters the dialect-speaking soldiers from all corners of the nation on the eve of the Battle of Agincourt, and they in turn get a 'little touch of Harry in the night',[63] he is doing what he has perhaps been doing all along: walking in an effort to get to know his people.

Notes

1 See David McInnis, 'Travelling Characters in Early Modern Drama', Chapter 11 in this volume.
2 Jean E. Howard and Phyllis Rackin, *Engendering a Nation: A Feminist Account of Shakespeare's English Histories* (London: Routledge, 1997), 161.
3 Richard Helgerson, *Forms of Nationhood: The Elizabethan Writing of England* (Chicago University Press, 1992), 140.
4 Ibid., 143.
5 On the experimental quality of these plays, see Lawrence Danson, *Shakespeare's Dramatic Genres* (Oxford University Press, 2000), 98.

6 In November 2014, the identification of a Shakespearean First Folio in the library of Saint-Omer in France was verified by Eric Rasmussen. The performance-related annotations of the *Henry IV* plays in this copy are believed to be close to the date of first publication. The findings suggest a broader culture of performance of the plays in the seventeenth century; see, for example, www.theguardian.com/culture/2014/nov/25/shakespeare-first-folio-found-in-french-library. The folio has been fully digitised and is available here: http://bibliotheque-numerique.bibliotheque-agglo-stomer.fr/idurl/1/18140

7 John M. Adrian, *Local Negotiations of English Nationhood, 1570–1680* (Basingstoke: Palgrave Macmillan, 2011), 11. See also D. K. Smith, *The Cartographic Imagination in Early Modern England: Re-writing the World in Marlowe, Spenser, Raleigh, and Marvell* (Aldershot: Ashgate, 2008).

8 Ibid., 51.

9 Ibid., 18. See also John M. Adrian, 'Itineraries, Perambulations, and Surveys: The Intersections of Chorography and Cartography in the Sixteenth Century', in *Images of Matter: Essays on British Literature of the Medieval and Renaissance*, ed. Yvonne Bruce (Newark, DE: University of Delaware Press, 2005), 29–46, at 29.

10 See my 'The *Pennyles Pilgrimage* of John Taylor: Poverty, Mobility and Performance in Seventeenth-Century Literary Circles', *Rural History* 24, no. 1 (2013), 9–24; and Anthony Parr, *Renaissance Mad Voyages: Experiments in Early Modern English Travel* (Aldershot: Ashgate, 2015).

11 James Loxley, Anna Groundwater, and Julie Sanders, ed., *Ben Jonson's Walk to Scotland: An Annotated Edition of the 'Foot Voyage'* (Cambridge University Press, 2015).

12 *Henry IV, Part 1*, 1.2.183–91, 204–05. The editions used of the *Henry IV* plays throughout are *Henry IV Part One*, ed. David Bevington (Oxford University Press, 1987) and *Henry IV Part Two*, ed. René Weis (Oxford University Press, 1997). All further quotations refer to these editions and will be cited by act, scene, and line numbers within the text.

13 See, for example, Marjorie Garber, *Coming of Age in Shakespeare*, 2nd edn (London: Routledge, 1997), 30–51.

14 On the importance of language proficiency, see Marianne Montgomery, 'Language and Seafaring in Thomas Middleton and John Webster's *Anything for a Quiet Life*', Chapter 6 in this volume.

15 On the emergence of surveying practices, see Garrett A. Sullivan, Jr., *The Drama of Landscape: Land, Property, and Social Relations on the Early Modern Stage* (Stanford, CA: Stanford University Press, 1999), 38–46.

16 Smith, *Cartographic Imagination*, 6; Andrew Gordon and Bernhard Klein, 'Introduction' to their *Literature, Mapping and the Politics of Space in Early Modern Britain* (Cambridge University Press, 2001), 3.

17 Helgerson, *Forms of Nationhood*, 107.

18 Ibid., 133.

19 *Kemps Nine Daies Wonder* (London: Printed by E. A[llde] for Nicholas Ling, 1600), A3.

20 Ibid., C3^r.

21 Ibid., C1^r.

22 Scott McMillin and Sally-Beth MacLean, *The Queen's Men and Their Plays*, 2nd edn (Cambridge University Press, 2006), 184–48. On the English history play as the company's 'signature offering', see Roslyn L. Knutson, 'The Start of Something Big', in *Locating the Queen's Men, 1583–1603*, ed. Helen Ostovich, Holger Schott Syme, and Andrew Griffin (Aldershot: Ashgate, 2009), 99–107, at 102.

23 Richard Dutton, '*The Famous Victories* and the 1600 Quarto of *Henry V*', in Ostovich et al., *Locating the Queen's Men*, 135–44.

24 Daryl W. Palmer, *Hospitable Performances: Dramatic Genres and Cultural Practices in Early Modern England* (West Lafayette, IN: Purdue University Press, 1993), 128.

25 Taylor, *Pennyles Pilgrimage*, B4^r.

26 For example, Gervase Markham's 1622 walk from London to Berwick seems to have been linked to a group of Red Bull actors. See Sanders, 'The *Pennyles Pilgrimage*', 13.

27 *Nine Daies Wonder*, A4^r.

28 Jonson's walk was possibly based at least in part on a wager: 'Ben Jonson is going on foot to Edinburgh and back for his profit', George Garrard to Sir Dudley Carleton, 4 June 1617, *CSP Dom.*, 1611–18, 472. At one point in his journey Jonson goes out of his way to cross via a bridge rather than use a more convenient river ferry to ensure he does not invalidate the claim to have walked the whole way (Loxley et al., *Ben Jonson's Walk*, 123). See also Parr, *Renaissance Mad Voyages*, especially 99–125 and his 'Going to Constantinople: English Wager-Journeys to the Ottoman World in the Early Modern Period', *Studies in Travel Writing* 16, no. 4 (2012), 349–61.

29 *Nine Daies Wonder,* B1^r.

30 On inns and road networks, see Andrew McRae, *Literature and Domestic Travel in Early Modern England* (Cambridge University Press, 2009), 122–41. The Gadshill discussion raises further intriguing lines of connection to the Queen's Men production of *The Famous Victories*, which begins with the Gadshill episode but with Prince Hal far more directly implicated in the robbery. For a full text of that play edited by Karen Sawyer Marsalek and Mathew Martin, see the online *Queen's Men Editions* [http://qme.internetshakespeare .uvic.ca/Library/Texts/FV/Q1/default/].

31 See Sanders, 'The *Pennyless Pilgrimage*', 19.

32 CRO MS ZCR 469/550, fo. 5^r.

33 Bevington, 'Introduction', 67.

34 Deposition of a vagrant, 1612; Wiltshire CRO QSR h:1 1613/154.

35 Taylor, *Pennyles Pilgrimage*, sigs. A4–B1^r

36 *Nine Daies Wonder*, sigs. C1^r, B2^v.

37 Weis, 'Introduction', 3.

38 Stanley Wells, *Shakespeare: A Dramatic Life* (London: Sinclair-Stevenson, 1994), 142; Weis, 'Introduction', 57.

39 Weis, 'Introduction', 57
40 In a brilliant reading of extant copies of Camden's *Britannia*, Adrian uses marginal annotations and markings to indicate the ways in which these texts were also understood 'locally'; *Local Negotiations*, especially 1–2.
41 See Bruce R. Smith, *The Acoustic World of Early Modern England: Attending to the 'O' Factor* (University of Chicago Press, 1999), 53.
42 Christopher Marsh, '"At it ding dong": Recreation and Religion in the English Belfry, 1580–1640', in *Worship and the Parish Church in Early Modern Britain* (Aldershot: Ashgate, 2013), 152–71, at 155, 160. See also his *Music and Society in Early Modern England* (Cambridge University Press, 2013).
43 Marsh, 'At it ding dong', 152, 155. Smith, for example, mentions travellers' accounts produced by Philip Julius Duke of Stettin-Pomerain in 1602 and Paul Hentzner in 1598 which refer to extensive, sometimes rowdy bell-ringing, *Acoustic World*, 52–53.
44 The Busino reference appears in *The Journals of Two Travellers in Elizabethan and Stuart England*, ed. Peter Razzell (London: Caliban Books, 1995), 169. Cited in Smith, *Acoustic World*, 52.
45 Smith, *Acoustic World*, 53.
46 Drunken parish performances in belfries or performances as conscious acts of social resistance which were the subject of parish legislation may have been part of audience knowledge that would be brought to bear on fleeting references such as Bullcalf's. Cf. Marsh, 'At it ding dong', 160. For an evocative account of the sociocultural and phenomenological meaning of bells, see Alain Corbin, *Village Bells: The Culture of the Senses in the Nineteenth-Century French Countryside* (London, Macmillan, 1999).
47 Marsh, 'At it ding dong', 166.
48 John Nichols, *The Progresses, Processions and Magnificent Festivities of King James the First*, 4 vols. (London, 1871), IV, 309–10; see Loxley et al., *Ben Jonson's Walk*, 115.
49 For discussion, see this volume's 'Introduction'.
50 Julie Sanders, 'Geographies of Performance in the Early Modern Midlands', in *Performing Environments: Site-Specificity in Medieval and Early Modern English Drama*, ed. Susan Bennett and Mary Polito (Basingstoke: Palgrave Macmillan, 2014), 119–37.
51 McMillin and MacLean, *The Queen's Men*.
52 Roslyn Knutson, '*Histrio-Mastix*: Not by John Marston', *Studies in Philology* 98 (2001), 359–77.
53 Michael Dobson, *Shakespeare and Amateur Performance: A Cultural History* (Cambridge University Press, 2011), 23.
54 Dobson, *Shakespeare and Amateur Performance*, 23. Folger MS V.b. 34 is Dering's conflation of the plays; see also *The History of King Henry the Fourth / as revised by Sir Edward Dering, Bart.*, prepared by George Walton Williams and Gwynne Blakemore Evans (Charlottesville, VA: University of Virginia Press,

1974) and Laetitia Yeandle, 'The Dating of Sir Edward Dering's Copy of "The History of King Henry the Fourth"', *Shakespeare Quarterly* 37 (1986), 224–26. See also John Jowett's as yet unpublished talk, 'Private Iteration and Public Life: Dering's 1623 Adaptation of Shakespeare's *Henry IV*' (Birmingham Shakespeare Institute, 2015) and his 'The Thieves in *Henry IV*', *Review of English Studies* 38 (1987), 325–33 (especially 332, n. 15).

55 *Booke of Expenses, 1617–27*, Kent Archives Office U350 E4. A full transcription by Laetitia Yeandle is available: *Sir Edward Dering, 1st Bart., of Surrenden, Dering and His "Booke of Expences", 1617–1628* (Kent Archaeological Society, paper no. 20), 146–47 ([fo. 28ᵛ]) [www.kentarchaeology.ac/authors/020.pdf].

56 T. S. Lennam, 'Sir Edward Dering's Collection of Playbooks, 1619–1624', *Shakespeare Quarterly* 16 (1965), 145–53. Dering also started to write a play about travel: see the *Lost Plays Database* entry for 'Scenario of a play set in Thrace and Macedon (Folger MS X.d.206)'. My thanks to David McInnis for this reference and other input to this essay.

57 Dering purchased multiple quartos of *The Woman Hater* and *Band, Ruff, and Cuff*, which may signify performance intentions, and later that year he purchased two copies of the Shakespeare First Folio and a copy of Jonson's 1616 *Works*. The Padua copy of the First Folio may be Dering's marked-up-for-performance copy.

58 Peter Holland, 'Shakespeare Abbreviated', in *The Cambridge Companion to Shakespeare and Popular Culture*, ed. Robert Shaughnessy (Cambridge University Press, 2007), 26–45, at 28.

59 Lawrence Manley and Sally-Beth MacLean, *Lord Strange's Men and Their Plays* (New Haven, CT: Yale University Press, 2014), 273–74. The Saint-Omer copy of the First Folio apparently includes a gender swap in the aforementioned *Henry IV* annotations ('hostess' becomes 'host' and 'wench' becomes 'fellow'), most likely for pragmatic reasons to do with availability of players [www.nytimes.com/2014/11/26/arts/shakespeare-folio-discovered-in-france].

60 Holland, 'Shakespeare Abbreviated', 28

61 Dobson, *Shakespeare and Amateur Performance*, 27.

62 Helgerson, *Forms of Nationhood*, 5.

63 Shakespeare, *Henry V*, ed. Gary Taylor (Oxford University Press, 1982), 4.0.47.

CHAPTER 5

Eastward Ho *and the Traffic of the Stage*

Andrew Gordon

University of Aberdeen

Motive Drama

George Chapman, Ben Jonson, and John Marston's *Eastward Ho* (1605) has long been seen as a defining example of 'topographical comedy'. In an influential article Ralph A. Cohen explored the multiple meanings of place in the play and first mapped the co-ordinates of the verbal and performative action.[1] Key to Cohen's reading is 4.1 where Slitgut, a figure detached from the play's plotlines, describes to the audience the river action he observes from a vantage point at Cuckold's Haven. From this fantastical lookout – 'the farthest-seeing sea-mark of the world' as it is mockingly described – Slitgut narrates the fate of the shipwrecked cast as they are borne downstream and deposited at various significant sites.[2] In these events Cohen finds 'an exquisite poetic justice ... expressed in terms of the river's topography' and this topographic lead has been followed in a number of important recent studies that have stressed the significance of place in *Eastward Ho*, and in early modern drama more broadly.[3] What is missing in Cohen's approach, however, is any attention to the arts of *motion*, and while the readings of Jean E. Howard and Henry S. Turner do consider the trajectories of the play – and in common with much recent critical work, are informed by a richer, Michel de Certeau-influenced understanding of 'space as practised place' – the motive aspects of early modern drama remain relatively neglected.[4] In the present essay I tackle this under-investigated subject, arguing that *Eastward Ho* is closely engaged with forms and media of movement as a principal vehicle of meaning. Rather than being place specific, the play's title expresses a directional dynamic, appropriating the everyday cry of the Thames watermen to announce the prospect of motion: the intention to go. Both the prospect and the practice of movement are anatomised in the play along with the discursive construction of the body in and through space. In order to explore these concerns, I propose a new approach to the play which reads *Eastward Ho* in the context of early modern voyage drama.[5]

Drama about travel flourished on the London stage from the end of the sixteenth century, functioning, according to Anthony Parr, as a key medium for the transmission of geographical knowledge.[6] With the narrow geographical scope of its action *Eastward Ho* does not conform to a strictly topographical approach to either 'voyage drama' or 'travel drama' that sees the staging of foreign locations and the encounter with foreign peoples as a defining characteristic. While the city of London and a handful of Thameside sites as far downstream as Greenwich Reach mark the limit of the settings staged, the play's engagement with the idea of voyaging is more far-reaching, extending beyond the representation of geographical place to reflect upon the genres of travel and their meaning. Recent work has stressed the allegorical function of travel writing in the development of the colonial imagination, and the accommodation of dual perspectives that display the shaping interests of the home nation within accounts of the colonial scene.[7] In *Eastward Ho* the prospects of colonial travel loom large. The planned sea voyage to Virginia is a focal element of the drama, and in a Billingsgate tavern Captain Seagull conjures for his sea-bound companions a telling vision of this faraway land:

> I tell thee, gold is more plentiful there than copper is with us; and for as much red copper as I can bring, I'll have thrice the weight in gold... Why man, all their dripping pans and their chamber pots are pure gold; and all the chains, with which they chain up their streets, are massy gold; all the prisoners they take are fettered in gold; and for rubies and diamonds, they go forth on holidays and gather 'em by the seashore, to hang on their children's coats, and stick in their caps... (3.3.26–35)

As commentators habitually note, Seagull's Virginia is composed of multiple sources.[8] Onto a detail on the exchange value of copper and gold noted in the third volume of Richard Hakluyt's *The Principal Navigations* (1600), Seagull grafts a well-known episode from Thomas More's *Utopia* (1516), thus combining two of the key works informing the early modern geographical imagination. Hakluyt's texts played a key role in promoting trade and colonisation, not only discursively 'bring[ing] the merchant into the nation', in Richard Helgerson's notable formulation, but also more materially, as others have argued, seeking 'to mobilize the ships and expertise in navigation, the credit and liquid capital, as well as the energies and entrepreneurial skills of England's commercial elite for his grand project'.[9] Yet the play highlights the distance separating the consumption of geographical knowledge from the practice of

long-distance travel and expansion.[10] Where playgoers of the period were
often provided with 'an imaginary experience of magical or effortless
transportation from one distant scene to another, without considering
the labour of mariners or the discomfort of travel on the road or the seas',
Eastward Ho restores to view the technologies and textures of motion.[11]
Hence, although Seagull's fantasies of lucrative exchange are fuelled by
Hakluyt, it is precisely the *mobilisation* of these interests that prove so
spectacularly unsuccessful in the play.

Seagull's other source, *Utopia*, has long been recognised as 'a foundational text for early modern English travel and colonial writing'.[12] More's
work had itself drawn on early travellers' accounts, and Seagull's vision
sees Utopian practices transposed back onto the New World, framed as
the object of colonial fantasy. In so doing the play posits a critical identification of the Commonwealth of Virginia with that 'best state of a commonwealth' that is the stated object of enquiry in More's text.[13] More's
allegorical investigations in political philosophy were accompanied by a
playful reframing of the book's central question as one of transportation;
of how one might *arrive* at the perfect commonwealth – a theme memo-
rably played out in the various paratextual materials that accompanied
the text from the mock maps of the early Latin editions, to More's letter
to Peter Giles. In More's text, the repeated failure to identify how to get
there from *here* in the face of demands from would-be visitors reported
in the letter to Giles (the only part of the paratextual apparatus included
with each edition of Ralph Robinson's English translation in 1551, 1556,
and 1597) is part of that persistent frustration of geographical desire
inscribed in the ambivalence of the island's title, poised between *good*-
place and *no*-place.[14] The ludic obstruction of travel to Utopia reorients
the reader away from the pleasures of fiction and towards the challenges
of determining (and working towards) a best state for the commonwealth
inhabited by the reader. In a parallel fashion, *Eastward Ho* undercuts the
pretensions of its apprentice voyagers who project their fantasies of ease
onto an eroticised virgin land, and ultimately redirects the energies of
these failed colonisers back towards the imperfect civic commonwealth.
The play curbs the impulse of its constituents towards geographical
expansion, substituting a more localised concern with the medium of
travel and its metaphorics. For George Puttenham, metaphor is itself 'the
Figure of transporte' and in its construction *Eastward Ho* is concerned
throughout with travel as a vehicle of meaning.[15] The examination of
movement in the play centres upon the body and extends from *transport*,
or the arts of conveyance, through to *com-portment*, the carriage of the

self. Just as the title evokes the intention to go, so the play specifically invites consideration of *how* one goes or attempts to go. That interest in the manner of one's going is epitomised by Gertrude's lament for the decline of chivalry in the final act of the play:

> The knighthood nowadays are nothing like the knighthood of old time. They rid a-horseback; ours go afoot. They were attended by their squires; ours by their lackeys. They went buckled in their armour; ours muffled in their cloaks. They traveiled wildernesses and deserts; ours dare scarce walk the streets. They were still prest to engage their honour; ours still ready to pawn their clothes. They would gallop on at sight of a monster; ours run away at sight of a sergeant. (5.1.37–46)

Gertrude's anatomy of urban gentry is focused on temporal antitheses of motion, juxtaposing ten different manners of going. Contrasting the travels of chivalric romance with the conduct of their contemporary counterparts in urban street passage, she identifies a crisis in comportment: afraid of detection, these modern-day knights lack a forthright manner for movement within the urban environment. The passage illustrates the concern with the cultural politics of motion in *Eastward Ho*, and its central significance for the play's examination of urban habitus. The 'social nature of the *habitus*' in bodily actions was first explored by Marcel Mauss, who saw that bodily techniques such as swimming, digging, and marching represent actual *incorporations* of social values.[16] In the work of Pierre Bourdieu the term came to describe the totality of learned skills for living acquired by the individual subject from those governing the body and its comportment, to the constitution of taste and style. Bourdieu focused attention on the transmission of the habitus, noting that '[b]etween apprenticeship through simple familiarisation, in which the apprentice insensibly and unconsciously acquires the principles of the "art" and the art of living ... and, at the other extreme, explicit and express transmission by precept and prescription, every society provides for the structural exercises tending to transmit this or that form of practical mastery'.[17] The early modern period had its own means for understanding the acquisition and incorporation of value, and a paradigmatic example occurs in the very section of More's *Utopia* alluded to in *Eastward Ho*.

> of gold and silver they make commonlye chamber pottes and other like vesselles, that serve for moste vile uses, not only in there common halles, but in every mans private house. Furthermore of the same mettalles they make great cheynes with fetters and gives, wherin they tye their bondmen. Finally who so ever for any offence be infamed, by their eares hange

ringes of golde: upon their fingers they were ringes of golde, and about
their neckes chaynes of gold: and in conclusion their heades be tiede about
with golde.[18]

The treatment of gold represents a key operation in the production of a
Utopian habitus. More provides us with a critique of value in early modern society that details how the negative signification of gold is produced
as part of the formation of the malleable youth. For Stephen Greenblatt,
communal pressure is the instrument of transformation as 'the Utopians
reveal their full reliance on shame as a method of social control', yet this
celebrated reading has tended to overshadow the focus on the material
production of an artisanal trade.[19] Utopians are imagined collectively as a
commonweal of goldsmiths-for-the-common-good who work upon gold
to work upon Utopians. For More, gold functions as an alternative to the
geographical fiction, a master sign through which arrival at the perfect
commonweal can be imagined – as suggested in the nicely ambiguous
subtitle: 'a truly golden handbook'.[20]

More's subtitle does not appear in the English translation of the work,
but something of its allusive value registers in the instrumental figure of
the translator, Ralph Robinson, who was for many years Clerk to the
Goldsmiths' Company and resident of Goldsmiths' Hall, and advertised
this association on the title-page to his first edition, framing the text as
'translated into Englyshe by Raphe Robynson Cittizen and Goldsmythe
of London'.[21] The metaphorical metallurgy of More's *Utopia* may be referenced in Robinson's evocation of his own civic goldwork but it finds
a fuller application in *Eastward Ho*. Literalising More's metaphor, the
play dramatises the formative work of the master goldsmith as he seeks
to train up his two apprentices to be good members of the civic commonweal. Touchstone's proficiency in a plastic art, along with his instruc-
tional catchphrase 'work upon that now', emphasizes the physicality of
the incorporation of an urban habitus, drawing attention to the body as a
vehicle of custom.

The literary construction of *Utopia* provides a dual route into the
significance of bodily motion in the play through its undercutting of
the fantasy project of travel and its interest in goldwork as an image for
the physical production of habitus. In what follows I trace the motive
drama of *Eastward Ho*, exploring the play's analysis of embodied custom
to reveal how early modern modes of movement are used to both invest
and critique a civic habitus. The instruments of motion explored in the
play can broadly be divided into four orders: the foot, the hoof, the
oar, and the wheel, and it is through its treatment of these four classes

of movement that *Eastward Ho* performs its moral analysis of urban conduct.

The Foot

As his name suggests it is the figure of Touchstone who provides the point of reference for much of *Eastward Ho*'s investigation of a civic habitus. The valuation of motion in the play is rooted in the actions of Touchstone and specifically grounded in the fall of his foot. This interest is established in the opening scene when the page of the new-made knight Sir Petronel Flash appears on stage looking for Touchstone and his premises. The response of his apprentice, Golding, is to present his master in an image of harmony between environment and motion: 'It is his shop and here my master walks' (1.1.85–86). The verbal image frames Touchstone in his place of business – a fixed location that the page must seek out. On stage, however, the emphasis falls on movement and the walk that must enact Touchstone's proprietorship and express the stable confidence of his place within the social order. Golding thus introduces (and draws attention to) a culturally inscribed form of bodily motion; a kind of walking that is self-consciously representational of a civic habitus. Close scrutiny of walking is a feature of many of the conduct texts of the period exemplified by the monitory attentions to the walking body in Thomas Gainsford's *Rich Cabinet* (1616):

> We must not run, nor goe too fast in the streete, least it make one sweate and puffe, which is too unseemly for a Gentleman, nor yet are we to goe so soft and demurely as a maide: neither should we shake the armes, or writh the body, mince it: or walke with high gate, and lifting up the leg, nor stampe with the feete, nor goe as it were splay-footed, nor stroake up the stockins in going, nor stare in ones face, nor looke up too high nor muse too lumpishly, nore doe any thing unseemly when wee would bee professed Gentlemen.[22]

In Gainsford's account, largely borrowed from Giovanni Della Casa's *Galateo* (1558) and constructed not through precept but prohibition, the qualities that identify a gentleman in motion remain ineluctable, but styles in walking are a key feature in habitus recognition – it was observing the 'social idiosyncrasy' of walking from the gait of French nurses that triggered Marcel Mauss's theorisation of bodily techniques.[23] In early modern English culture with its heightened attention to custom and conduct, the socially representational meanings of bodily motion were readily available to view. Something of the representational effect of

Touchstone's walking is suggested by Thomas Nashe's objectification of a
citizen stepping out in his comparison of the narrative pace in *Terrors of
the Night* (1594) to 'walk[ing] soberly and demurely half-a-dozen turns,
like a grave citizen going about to take the air'.[24]

In *Eastward Ho* the meaning of walking is explicitly moralised. Just
as Touchstone's prudent practice in business – how he 'bought low,
took small gain' (1.1.55) – is inscribed in proverbs about his humble
shop, so his dutiful daughter Mildred presents steady walking as a figure for modest social progress: 'Nature hath given us legs to go to our
objects, not wings to fly to them' (2.1.75-77). The source of Mildred's
maxim is in fact the Calvinist divine Henry Holland, whose plague-
time sermons on Psalm 91 cautioned Londoners, 'we must not flie in
the ayre for God hath not given us wings to flye, but legges to walke.'[25]
Holland emphasises the need 'to walke wisely within our boundes',
evoking the association of walking with collective practices of spatial
inscription such as the Rogationtide perambulation or beating of the
bounds that figure the ambulant body as a vehicle for the reproduction
of civic memory across generations.[26] The spiritual value of Mildred's
pedestrianism is thus infused with the force of civic habitus as a bodily
practice for the transmission of communal knowledge. The stable walking established by Touchstone and followed by his daughter sets a collective pace for the play, against which the excesses of other characters
can be measured. When his wife comes eventually to lament the
errors of their other daughter, she expresses the wish 'that [Gertrude]
had walked a foot-pace with her sister' (4.1.121–24). But the daughters of Touchstone demonstrate contrasting attitudes to the habitus
that is their father's bodily legacy. Gertrude's marriage to the knight Sir
Petronel is marked by a scene in which she learns from her tailor (or
body-maker) the new form of bodily movement required to make her
way at court.

Ger.   Most edifying tailor! I protest you tailors are most sanctified members,
         and make many crooked things go upright. How must I bear my hands?
         light? light?
Pol.   O AY, now you are in the lady-fashion, you must do all things light. Tread
         light, light. Ay and fall so: that's the court AMBLE.
                    She trips about the stage.   (1.2.66–72)

Gertrude's tripping about the stage, seeking to master this new comportment, illustrates how the text makes a place for the drama of embodiment as Touchstone's daughter emphatically rejects the incorporation of

a modest civic habitus. The sexualised 'court amble' she apprehends in its place is unstable, associated with both idleness and moral lassitude; it is a disposition training her to fall. The stage presence of a pet ape throughout the scene serves to further subvert Gertrude's delusions of social distinction by identifying her performance with apish imitation.[27] Equally, the lightness of tread to which she is exhorted by the tailor runs directly counter to the mechanics of memorial imprinting through the foot and hence to that manner of perambulatory walking associated with the transmission of collective knowledge with which both her father and sister are identified.

Like his daughters, Touchstone's two apprentices play out a parallel drama of bodily opposition. Their choreographed juxtaposition in movement is the opening action of the play:

> *Enter* MASTER TOUCHSTONE *and* QUICKSILVER *at several doors,* QUICKSILVER *with his hat, pumps, short sword and dagger and a racket trussed up under his cloak. At the middle door enter* GOLDING *discovering a goldsmith's shop and walking short turns before it.* (1.1.0.1–5)

While Golding, like a good apprentice in citizen habitus, rehearses the walking turns of his citizen master, Quicksilver enters at a run, pursued across the stage by Touchstone who harangues him, 'I am thy master ... and thou my prentice ... and I will see whither you are running' (1.1.12–15). Running in the play is a form of excess; a recklessness of pace set against the steady proceeding of the civic merchant that always threatens a loss of control. The risks of running echo discursively through the play: in bringing forth impetuous adulterous schemes that fall back on himself, the usurer Security's 'mind runs' (3.4.191), his plans 'run in my head' until his fertile imagination 'runs over' (3.3.340, 3.4.192), and when he realises his folly he resolves 'to run back and drown myself' (4.1.45). Quicksilver's particular speciality is running *away* (as he eventually acknowledges in his Repentance), and Touchstone's pursuit of him extends from these first steps, to his eventual imprisonment when his former master brands him 'my runagate', the term which associates his errant behaviour and rebellious desertion of a civic path with its expression in the body's manner of movement (4.2.6–7, 5.5.74). Quicksilver's characteristic excess in motion is linked to a verbal excess through his predilection for the bodily oath "sfoot' (by God's foot), and Golding draws attention to the transgression of this profanity ('Fie, how you swear') (1.1.122).[28] More than a mere failure to respect pious decorum in speech, the oath plays upon Quicksilver's name by signalling his association with the god Mercury. Like the light tread of Gertrude, the identification with the wing-footed deity embodies Quicksilver's refusal to subject himself to Touchstone's pace-setting and that grounded morality borrowed from Holland. Golding pointedly takes direct action against the hubristic, aspirational feet of Quicksilver when in mid-argument he 'trips up his heels' (1.1.153 SD).

The pairing of daughters and of apprentices foregrounds the process of instruction in the incorporation of civic habitus, but also its limitations. Quicksilver's failure to apprehend is further inscribed in the metallurgic properties of his name; the elemental instability emphasises the futility of the goldsmith's labour in seeking to shape his apprentice into a valuable and reliable form. In turn Quicksilver's resistance throws into relief an oppressive aspect to the will of civic incorporation. By his own reckoning Quicksilver's rejection of the tyranny of custom marks out the inherent nobility of his nature. Seeking distinction from the citizen flock, he mocks the pliability of his rival apprentice by converting the collective practice of following in footsteps into a critique of the ignobility of being led: 'how like a sheep thou look'st; o' my conscience, some cowherd begot thee, thou Golding of Golding Hall!' (1.1.147–49). The play on Golding's name underlines his rival's exchange of a gentry lineage, invested in a family seat, for a corporate identity invested in the trade hall.

Disruptive of Touchstone's working practices, Quicksilver's wit finds out flaws in the discursive production of civic habitus. His restless, performative energy and aspirational resistance to incorporation are among the driving forces of the play, as he seeks to make his own way in the world. The question of whether that energy can be accommodated in the early modern city is one that the play pursues.[29] His quest for an alternative to the incorporation of civic habitus produces an investigation of motive instruments that is informed by contemporary cultural debates as animated by the work of Michel de Montaigne, the reception of whose writings in early modern England was characterised by a focus on custom and the habits of contemporary life.[30] Given the strong association of Eastward Ho's authors with Montaigne's work and the literary topicality of the Essayes at the time, Montaigne's reflections upon social distinction and custom have a particular relevance for the understanding of Eastward Ho, especially book III of The Essayes, where this key interest of contemporary English readers is approached through the prism of movement and traffic.[31]

On the Hoof

'Our life is nothing but motion', writes Montaigne in his final essay 'Of Experience', where he provides a last reflection on the subject matter of knowledge, investigating the limits of reasoning (and of communication) in a wide-ranging enquiry that moves from a critique of legal and contemporary medical authority, towards a revalidation of the everyday.[32] In Jean Starobinski's memorable phrase the essay heralds 'the body's moment', exploring the knowledge of experience above all through the vehicle of the body and its motions, from internal operations (encompassing the pleasurable, the painful, and the unavoidable), to the temporal passage of life, and the spatial dimensions of embodied experience.[33] Contemplating the vulnerability of the body to change Montaigne remarks:

> Appoint a *Bretton* of threescore yeeres of age to drinke water; put a Seaman or Mariner into a Stove; forbid a lackey of *Baske* to walke: you bring them out of their element, you deprive them of all motion, and in the end of aire, of light and life.[34]

Cultural diversity is here examined through the acculturation of the human body viewed in its habits of consumption, of habitation (or environment), and of movement. Where Montaigne highlights the embodiment of cultural difference in the environmental embeddedness of the Breton, the Mariner, and the Basque lackey, however, this exists in a productive tension with attitudes towards modes of social and cultural distinction, a subject of continued investigation throughout the *Essayes*. That tension is exemplified later in the essay when Montaigne chooses to identify himself corporeally with the troubling element of mercury: 'It might likewise have beene saide of mee, that even from mine infancy, I had either folly or quicke-silver in my feete, so much stirring and naturall inconstancy have I in them, where ever I place them.'[35] Like *Eastward Ho*'s Quicksilver, Montaigne's feet signify instability, the restless energy they evoke puts him out of step with a pedestrian world. Instead, as he explains, 'since my first age, I ever loved rather to ride then walke upon paved streetes. Going a foote, I shall durtie my selfe up to the waste: and little men, going alongst our streetes, are subject (for want of presentiall apparence) to be justled or elbowed.'[36] With his lack of physical stature, Montaigne is not built for the hazards of pedestrian traffic and finds himself vulnerable to the competition for space and place on the street. The horse rescues him from this mêlée. But the celebration of horseback travel is not exclusively a matter of ease. The preference for travel by horse is well attested to throughout the *Essayes*, and in his travel journal where he makes several detours in order to continue by horse and avoid travel by water. For Montaigne, the horse provides an important vehicle of distinction through which he embodies his elevated status as the *Chevalier de Montaigne*.[37]

The overdetermined relationship between customary bodily habitus and the production of social distinction that marks Montaigne's final essay is also characteristic of the analysis of motion in *Eastward Ho*. Montaigne's personal resolution of these tensions entails a naturalisation of his social superiority through a kind of motive individuation that separates him from others. In the city streets of *Eastward Ho*, however, equestrianism is an aspiration denied to those most eager to enact their claims of knightly status. There is a distinct lack of horsemanship on display throughout – as Gertrude's earlier-cited complaint against urban knighthood suggests. In another of the performative turns which play on manners of going, Sir Petronel enters with his riding wand to announce 'I'll out of this wicked town as fast as my horse can trot', but this intention to travel, like his other motive projects in the play, is stalled (2.2.237–42). Security refuses stabling for Sir Petronel, while the 'running gelding' of Quicksilver is kept hidden from view (2.2.172–74), so that we find the horse as the knight's instrument of status expression cannot be accommodated in the London of *Eastward Ho*. The frustrated horsemanship of Sir Petronel and Quicksilver is instead displaced into travel by water, and the substitution comically played on throughout. In this most intertextual of plays, Security is ironically made to channel Shakespeare's Richard III, crying 'A boat, a boat, a boat, a full hundred marks for a boat!' (3.4.5–6). The Thames, and the projected voyage to Virginia, becomes the avenue for Sir Petronel and Quicksilver to fashion a male gentle distinction that cannot find a way in the city. But their pretension to the sail is itself prevented as they fall short in their bid for the open sea. In manners of maritime (or rather fluvial) motion, they never progress beyond the local lighterman's instrument of the oar. Even here the would-be voyagers prove utterly inept in their new art: unable to read the weather, unwilling to take on board advice, and ultimately incapable of navigation by either topographical or celestial signs. In the trial of their seaworthiness they are found wanting. The failed translation of frustrated knightly habitus into mastery of a liquid realm of adventure is spelled out in Sir Petronel's deluded belief that on the Isle of Dogs this 'chevalier d'Angleterre' has arrived in the land of Montaigne (4.1.181).

The Wheel

'The world runs on wheels' was a proverb of long standing, expressive of the pace of change: it was John Stow who applied it topically to the coach in 1603, adding 'with many, whose parents were glad to goe on foote'.[38] As Stow the urban perambulator understood, the adoption of the coach marked a temporal rupture across generations in habits of both going and knowing.[39] Following its arrival in Marian England, the popularity of the coach had expanded among courtiers and the nobility from the 1580s, becoming a feature of urban life and in 1601 generating calls in Parliament for 'the restraint of the excessive and superfluous use of Coaches'.[40] *Eastward Ho* is the play that announces on stage this revolution in urban spatial practices and the confusions it engenders, making the coach into a central plot vehicle.[41] The embarkation scene at the mid-point of the play is a civic event witnessed by a group of watching citizen wives for whom it outdoes the recent launch of a great ship. Their expectation that 'here will be double as many people to see her take coach as there were to see it take water' (3.1.19–21) emphasises the competitive aspect of the play's comparative treatment of transportation in which the sail again loses out. Travel by coach represents a double displacement, both concealing the body of the coach passenger and disrupting the enactment of civic habitus. When Gertrude insists 'my coach horses must take the Wall of your coach horses', she imagines a transposition of pedestrian status rites that threatens to override those she has left behind on the street (1.2.128–29). The coach brings with it a confusion of status signification as the chaotic preparations make clear. Gertrude's gentlewoman thrusts a bluecoat onto a water bearer to repurpose him as an attendant in her lady's service. The running footman is an appropriation to coach travel of the earlier figure who went before a horseback master, but one strange enough to Gertrude's mother that she has to verify his duties: 'But must this young man ... run by your coach all the way afoot?' (3.2.48–49). Named Hamlet and in the service of his mistress Gertrude, this breathless figure is contrasted with his notable namesake as emphatically a man of action. The scenic spectacle of his mode of movement is distinguished from the restless energies of Quicksilver, by his association with an emerging body of theatrical conventions that stress the footman's low status, dishevelled appearance, and panting exhaustion.[42] The curiosity of these observers illustrates not the novelty of the coach per se, but the moment of its dramatic arrival and sudden accessibility to the citizenry. As the coachman called from his breakfast by the palaver notes, 'Here's a stir when citizens ride out of town' (3.2.1).

Withholding the body from view, the coach presented new possibilities for female agency and mobility among the urban elite.[43] As a consequence, in *Eastward Ho* it is explicitly sexualised. Jonson's *Poetaster* (1601) had earlier given voice to coach-desire ('I do long to ride in a coach most vehemently', exclaims the citizen-wife Chloe),[44] but *Eastward Ho* presents its consummation in the extended sexual wordplay that attends its climactic arrival (3.2.28–47). While her husband invests his displaced desires in Virginia, and the chaste wife of Security, the active sexuality of Gertrude already trained in the light tripping and falling of the court amble, now seeks satisfaction via the coach. Although Gertrude's readiness to believe herself to be pregnant from the anticipated ride is another sign of eagerness over experience, the sexualisation of the coach as a form of female riding is nevertheless a powerful figure for familiar male anxiety over the insatiability of female desire, equating social and sexual agency (3.2.34–36). As Quicksilver tells Sir Petronel to his utter consternation, 'there is not turnspit dog bound to his wheel more servilely than you shall be to her wheel' (2.2.315–17). The image of the sexual labour of the husband at his lady's 'wheel' evokes the sweaty corporeality of Hamlet, the running footman, who finds himself the sexualised object of Mistress Touchstone's attentions as she urges, 'let the poor youth have something twixt his legs to ease 'em' (3.2.51–53). In this light, Gertrude's ultimate lament over the decline of nobility and the absence of riding can be seen to associate the displacement of knightly habitus with sexual impotence and a marked lack of movement within gentry manhood.

As a sign of the gendered politics of transport in the play, the coach is an instrument with which to anatomise a crisis in aspirational urban conduct. It is also, of course, the titular subject of one of Montaigne's most celebrated late essays (III.vi) where the author caustically revisits the relationship of the Old World with the New.[45] In that essay the coach is a failed vehicle of social distinction in the Old World, a wasteful sign of expenditure in direct contrast to the dedication to the common good exemplified by the best achievements of civilisation that find their highest expression in the 'cawcie or high-way which is yet to be seene in *Peru*'; a roadway built by Kings and measuring 'three hundred leagues in length, straight, even, and fine, and twentie paces in breadth'.[46] Thrown into relief against the achievements of a New World civilisation brought down within a mere fifty years, Montaigne's coach becomes a figure for that loss of moral compass epitomised in the barbarous cruelty and banal greed of the colonial project. With bitter irony he asks 'Who ever raysed the service of marchandise and benefite of traffike to so highe a rate?'[47]

The failed coach ride to a new life in *Eastward Ho* distils anxieties over female social and sexual agency into a comic vehicle: in keeping with the motive concerns of the play, there is no destination in this journey but only the manner of travelling. Yet the play also invites us to understand the coach's significance in the context of the great sea voyages to which, in the embarkation scene, it is compared (3.2.16). To do so we might note how the traffic of the stage departs here from the course described in Montaigne's essay. *Eastward Ho*, like the author of *The Essayes* himself, never reaches the New World. This failure we may read after Montaigne as some small mercy. Where Montaigne's own distaste for travel by water ensures he does not participate in that traffic with the Americas which 'Of Coaches' indicts, *Eastward Ho* takes the displaced projectors and scuttles their venture, before they can escape London's river mouth. Rather than setting foot on foreign ground, they are conveyed to the Counter until they walk in public penance through the city's streets.

Conclusion

There is then a careful logic to the management of movement in *Eastward Ho*. While much recent work has highlighted the newly emergent sites being produced in the outskirts of early modern London and the cultural practices that accompany them, *Eastward Ho* overlays competing modes of motion in the concentrated spaces of the early modern city in a richly imaginative way.[48] Beyond mapping the places and routes of early modern drama, *Eastward Ho*, with its fourfold counterpoint in modes of movement, suggests the value of attending to motion, and examining the ways in which drama can construct the movements of the body and the body being moved, both discursively and through the choreography of stage traffic. I have pointed to the way in which More's *Utopia* and Montaigne's final essays in particular illuminate this dynamic. In conclusion we might review how the play forges a final ambivalent accommodation of its errant energies. To represent the moment of his delivery to repentance, Quicksilver returns to the proverbial resources of the body in motion:

> At last the black ox trod o' my foot
> And I saw then what longed unto 't

> Now cry I, 'Touchstone, touch me still,
> And make me current by thy skill'. (5.5.85–89)

Feet firmly returned to earth, Quicksilver's accommodation is explicitly imagined in terms of submission to the hands of the goldsmith Touchstone, the guarantor of civic habitus whose hallmark approves his new-found worth. Quicksilver's lively energies have been redirected (away from the pursuit of colonial fantasy and an ideal elsewhere) towards *negotium* and the improvement of the civic commonweal. It is Quicksilver who choreographs the final act of accommodation, urging his suit 'that I may go home through the streets in these [his prison clothes], as a spectacle, or rather an example to the children of Cheapside' (5.5.214–17). The penitent prisoners step out alongside the stately Touchstone and Alderman Golding, 'the careful father [and] thrifty son' in a procession analogised to a mayoral pageant (5.5.220). The play's conclusion thus expressly performs the reincorporation of Quicksilver into the civic community through his humble enactment of a civic habitus, following at last in the footsteps of his master and elders. Yet, as many commentators have observed, *Eastward Ho* cannot be read as a simple validation of civic order. Lest we too readily equate London with a perfected commonweal, there is a note of ambivalence here for just as Quicksilver's metallic properties strain the credibility of any conversion into gold, so we might detect a defamiliarising Utopian aspect to the concluding tableau. From this perspective, as Alderman Golding and the proud Master Goldsmith step forward in their civic stateliness ready to process before a comic audience, they resemble nothing so much as the Anemolian ambassadors who in the Utopians' inverted order of signification were mistaken for prisoners or the ambassadors' fools, while those of humblest condition attracted most respect. Throwing into critical relief the city's corporate elite, and reviving Utopian contempt for Western uses of the goldsmith's art, the play's ending invites a comic scrutiny to be applied to these representational urban bodies as they set forth to reproduce the civic habitus in walking the city's streets.

Notes

1 Ralph A. Cohen, 'The Function of Setting in *Eastward Ho*', *Renaissance Papers* (1973), 85–96.
2 George Chapman, Ben Jonson, and John Marston, *Eastward Ho*, ed. R. W. Van Fossen (Manchester University Press, 1979), 4.1.315–16. All further quotations from *Eastward Ho* refer to this edition and will be cited by act, scene, and line numbers within the text.
3 Cohen, 'The Function of Setting', 89; Jean E. Howard, *Theater of a City: The Places of London Comedy, 1598–1642* (Philadelphia: University of

Pennsylvania Press, 2008), 100–02; Henry S. Turner, *The English Renaissance Stage: Geometry, Poetics, and the Practical Spatial Arts, 1580–1630* (Oxford University Press, 2006), 211–13; Darryll Grantley, *London in Early Modern English Drama: Representing the Built Environment* (Basingstoke: Palgrave Macmillan, 2008); Adam Zucker, *The Place of Wit in Early Modern English Comedy* (Cambridge University Press, 2010).

4 Michel de Certeau, *The Practice of Everyday Life*, trans. Steven Rendall (Berkeley, CA: University of California Press, 1984), 117. James D. Mardock, *'Our Scene is London': Ben Jonson's City and the Space of the Author* (London: Routledge, 2008).

5 For definitions of voyage and travel drama, see the 'Introduction' to this volume.

6 Anthony Parr, 'Introduction', in *Three Renaissance Travel Plays*, ed. Parr (Manchester University Press, 1995), 3.

7 See, in particular, Thomas Scanlan, *Colonial Writing and the New World, 1583–1671: Allegories of Desire* (Cambridge University Press, 1999); Claire Jowitt, *Voyage Drama and Gender Politics, 1589–1642: Real and Imagined Worlds* (Manchester University Press, 2003); Andrew Hadfield, *Literature, Travel, and Colonial Writing in the English Renaissance, 1545–1625* (Oxford University Press, 1998).

8 Seagull's sources were first identified by A. H. Gilbert, 'Virginia in *Eastward Ho*', *Modern Language Notes* 33, no. 3 (1918), 183–84.

9 Richard Helgerson, *Forms of Nationhood: The Elizabethan Writing of England* (University of Chicago Press, 1992), 176; David Harris Sacks, 'Richard Hakluyt and His Publics, *c.*1580–1620', in *Making Publics in Early Modern Europe: People, Things, Forms of Knowledge*, ed. Bronwen Wilson and Paul Yachnin (New York: Routledge, 2010), 159–76, at 167.

10 Claire Jowitt, 'Hakluyt's Legacy: Armchair Travel in English Renaissance Drama', in *Richard Hakluyt and Travel Writing in Early Modern Europe*, ed. Daniel Carey and Claire Jowitt (Farnham: Ashgate, 2012), 295–306, at 296.

11 Monica Matei-Chesnoiu, *Re-imagining Western European Geography in English Renaissance Drama* (Basingstoke: Palgrave Macmillan, 2012), 12.

12 Hadfield, *Literature, Travel, and Colonial Writing*, 11. See also Chloë Houston, ed., *New Worlds Reflected: Travel and Utopia in the Early Modern Period* (Farnham: Ashgate, 2010).

13 Thomas More, *Utopia*, in *The Complete Works of Thomas More*, vol. IV, ed. Edward Surtz and J. H. Hexter (New Haven, CT: Yale University Press, 1965), 1.

14 On the confounding of geographical knowledge in *Utopia*, see Louis Marin, *Utopics: Spatial Play*, trans. Robert A. Vollrath (London: Macmillan, 1984), 42–59, 201–07.

15 George Puttenham, *The Arte of English Poesie* (London: Richard Field, 1589), 148.

16 Marcel Mauss, 'Techniques of the Body', *Economy and Society* 2 (1973), 70–88, at 73.

17 Pierre Bourdieu, *Outline of a Theory of Practice*, trans. Richard Nice (Cambridge University Press, 1977), 88.
18 Thomas More, *A Frutefull, and Pleasaunt Worke of the Beste State of a Publyque Weale, and of the New Yle called Utopia*, trans. Raphe Robinson (London: Abraham Vele, 1551), sig. Kviii.
19 Stephen Greenblatt, *Renaissance Self-Fashioning from More to Shakespeare* (University of Chicago Press, 1980), 48–49.
20 More, *Utopia*, 1.
21 John Bennell, 'Robinson, Ralph (1520–1577)', *Oxford Dictionary of National Biography* (Oxford University Press, 2004; online edn, May 2006) [www.oxforddnb.com/view/article/23863, accessed 4 Nov 2014]. More's English translator and his text can be linked to an active circle among the civic elite who debated the implications of More's work for the reform of London's commonweal. See Jennifer Bishop, 'Utopia and Civic Politics in Mid-Sixteenth-Century London', *Historical Journal* 54 (2011), 933–53; Terence Cave, 'The English Translation: Thinking about the Commonwealth' in *Thomas More's Utopia in Early Modern Europe: Paratexts and Contexts*, ed. Cave (Manchester University Press, 2008), 87–103.
22 T[homas] G[ainsford], *A Rich Cabinet ... whereto is Annexed the Epitome of Good Manners extracted from Mr John della Casa* (London: I. B. for Roger Jackson, 1616), sig. Aa3^v.
23 Mauss, 'Techniques of the Body', 72. Although Mauss was less concerned with the social *legibility* of bodily techniques as an object of representation than with challenging modern preconceptions of the individuality of walking, what he diagnosed from his hospital bed was the influence of cinema in disseminating 'American walking fashions'.
24 Thomas Nashe, *The Terrors of the Night*, in *The Unfortunate Traveller and Other Works*, ed. J. B. Steane (Harmondsworth: Penguin, 1972), 231.
25 Henry Holland, *Spirituall Preservatives against the Pestilence. Or Seven Lectures on the 91. Psalme* (London: T. C. for John Browne and Robert Jackson, 1603), 126–27.
26 Ibid., 126. On perambulation and civic memory, see Andrew Gordon, *Writing Early Modern London: Memory, Text and Community* (Basingstoke: Palgrave Macmillan, 2013), 147–54.
27 On the role of the ape in the scene, see Janet Clare, 'Marston: Censure, Censorship and Free Speech', in *The Drama of John Marston*, ed. Wharton, 194–211, at 207–08; James Knowles, '"Can ye not tell a man from a Marmoset?": Apes and Others on the Early Modern Stage', in *Renaissance Beasts: Of Animals, Humans, and Other Wonderful Creatures*, ed. Erica Fudge (Champaign, IL: University of Illinois Press, 2004), 138–63.
28 See also 1.1.118, 1.1.123, 2.1.120, 4.1.222–23. A wide range of corporeal oaths were in use, but the minced 'oath's foot' appears in only a handful of plays prior to *Eastward Ho*, among them works by Marston and Chapman. Hugh Gazzard, 'An Act to Restrain Abuses of Players (1606)', *Review of English Studies* 61, no. 251 (2010), 495–528, at 499–500.

29 See Jill Ingram, 'Economies of Obligation in *Eastward Ho*', *Ben Jonson Journal* 11 (2004), 21–40.

30 Warren Boutcher has shown that English engagements with the *Essays* in the early seventeenth century need to be seen in the context of contemporary anxiety over 'elite social and cultural reproduction ... rather than more abstracted notions of scepticism, individualism or self-consciousness'. 'Marginal Commentaries: The Cultural Transmission of Montaigne's *Essais* in Shakespeare's England', in *Shakespeare et Montaigne: vers un nouvel humanisme*, ed. Pierre Kapitaniak (Paris: Société Française Shakespeare, 2003), 13–27, at 22. William Hamlin has demonstrated a topical concern with custom in a large number of contemporary annotations to Florio's translation. William Hamlin, 'Florio's Montaigne and the Tyranny of "Custome": Appropriation, Ideology, and Early English Readership of the *Essayes*', *Renaissance Quarterly* 63, no. 2 (2010), 491–544.

31 Marston's *The Dutch Courtesan* (1605) makes sustained direct use of III.v. ('Upon Some Verses of Virgil'). Ben Jonson's copy of Montaigne is extant. A friend of Florio, his *Volpone* (1606) provides one of the earliest comments on the fashion for appropriating the *Essays*, mocking the tendency among 'All our English writers ... to steal out of ... Montaignié'. George Chapman's links are less direct, but his dramatic work engages closely with recent French history, and he shared with John Florio the interests of the translator and with Montaigne a deep classical learning. Peter Mack, 'Marston and Webster's Use of Florio's Montaigne', *Montaigne Studies* 24 (2012), 67–82; William M. Hamlin, 'Common Customer in Marston's *Dutch Courtesan* and Florio's Montaigne', *Studies in English Literature 1500–1900* 52, no. 2 (2012), 407–424; Jonson, *Volpone, or, The Fox*, ed. R. B. Parker (Manchester University Press, 1983), 3.4 87–90.

32 *The Essayes, Or, Morall, Politike and Militarie Discourses: of Lo: Michaell de Montaigne, Knight*, trans. John Florio (London: Val. Sims for Edward Blount, 1603), III.xiii, 652.

33 Jean Starobinski, *Montaigne in Motion*, trans. Arthur Goldhammer (University of Chicago Press, 1985), 138.

34 Montaigne, *The Essayes*, III.xiii, 646.

35 Ibid., III.xiii, 658.

36 Ibid., 652.

37 Georges Van Den Abbeele, *Travel As Metaphor from Montaigne to Rousseau* (Minneapolis, MN: University of Minnesota Press, 1991), 10–12. See also Felicity Green, *Montaigne and the Life of Freedom* (Cambridge University Press, 2012), at 99–105.

38 M. P. Tilley, *Dictionary of the Proverbs in England in the Sixteenth and Seventeenth Centuries* (Ann Arbor, MI: University of Michigan Press, 1950), W893; John Stow, *Survey of London* (London: John Windet, 1603), 85. The 1598 edition contains a description of coaches without this detail. Tantalisingly, the proverb was also the title of a lost (1599) play by Chapman. *Henslowe's Diary*, ed. R. A. Foakes (Cambridge University Press, 2002), 103, 105, 122.

39 Cultural historians have concentrated on the impact of the coach in the mid-to-late seventeenth century, and the advent of hired hackney coaches. See Mark Jenner, 'Circulation and Disorder: London Streets and Hackney Coaches, *c.*1640–*c.*1740', in *The Streets of London from the Great Fire to the Great Stink*, ed. Tim Hitchcock and Heather Shore (London: Rivers Oram Press, 2003), 40–53; Julia F. Merritt, *The Social World of Early Modern Westminster: Abbey, Court, and Community 1525–1640* (Manchester University Press, 2005), 169–73. See also Karen Newman, *Cultural Capitals: Early Modern London and Paris* (Princeton University Press, 2007), 73–75; Julie Sanders, *The Cultural Geography of Early Modern Drama, 1620–1650* (Cambridge University Press, 2011), 157–63.

40 Mark Brayshay, *Land Travel and Communications in Tudor and Stuart England: Achieving a Joined-up Realm* (Liverpool University Press, 2014), 109–11; Stuart Piggott, *Wagon, Chariot and Carriage: Symbol and Status in the History of Transport* (London: Thames and Hudson, 1992), 151; Simonds d'Ewes, 'Journal of the House of Lords: November 1601', in *The Journals of All the Parliaments During the Reign of Queen Elizabeth* (London: John Starkey, 1682), 602.

41 Leaving aside more figurative references, notable examples of coach talk occur in *Every Man Out of His Humour* (1599), *A Warning for Fair Women* (*c.*1599), *The London Prodigal* (*c.*1602), and *A Woman Killed with Kindness* (1603), as well as *Westward Ho* (1605).

42 David Carnegie, 'Running Over the Stage: Webster and the Running Footman', *Early Theatre*, 13, no. 1 (2010), 121–36. For a contemporary example, see Thomas Middleton, *A Mad World, My Masters* (1604/05), 2.1.5–95.

43 Merritt, *The Social World of Early Modern Westminster*, 171–73.

44 Ben Jonson, *Poetaster*, ed. Tom Cain (Manchester University Press, 1995), 4.2.17–18.

45 Edwin M. Duval, 'Lessons of the New World: Design and Meaning in Montaigne's "Des Cannibales" (I:31) and "Des Coches" (III:6)', *Yale French Studies* 64 (1983), 95–112; Tom Conley, 'The Essays and the New World', in *The Cambridge Companion to Montaigne*, ed. Ulrich Langer (Cambridge University Press, 2005), 74–95; Timothy Hampton, 'The Subject of America: History and Alterity in Montaigne's "Des Coches"', in *The Project of Prose in Early Modern Europe and the New World*, ed. Elizabeth Fowler and Roland Greene (Cambridge University Press, 1997), 80–103.

46 Montaigne, *The Essayes*, III.vi ('Of Coaches'), 549.

47 Ibid., 546.

48 See, among others, Howard, *Theater of a City*; Turner, *English Renaissance Stage*; Zucker, *The Place of Wit*.

CHAPTER 6

Language and Seafaring in Thomas Middleton and John Webster's Anything for a Quiet Life

Marianne Montgomery

East Carolina University

Middleton and Webster's comedy *Anything for a Quiet Life* (composed *c.*1621) belongs to the group of seventeenth-century London plays dealing with commerce, foreign imports, gender, and urban spaces described by Jean E. Howard in *Theater of a City*. London comedies like this one are much concerned with foreign exchange and its influence on the cosmopolitan city.[1] Leslie Thomson, introducing the play, points to the centrality of foreign and domestic fabrics – the mercer's shop is an important location, and the main plot features a wife obsessed with new fashions – to the play's treatment of commerce, social hierarchy, and theatricality. Given the decline of the English wool trade, concerns about cloth would have been familiar to the play's first audiences at the Blackfriars.[2] But *Anything for a Quiet Life*, even as it is interested in cloth as an object of exchange and a guarantor of identity, stages foreign imports and London commerce largely without anxiety. It also includes an unsatisfying about-face, in which the fashionable wife reveals she has merely been testing her husband and then puts on sober new English wool clothes. The combination of unproblematic commerce and problematic plot reversal has ensured that the play has received little critical attention in recent decades.[3]

The play, however, does not feature only material from abroad. It also draws attention to the ships that bring to England the imported luxuries in the mercer's shop. Among its characters is a sea captain, Young Franklin, who, when the play opens, is languishing in London, trying to figure out how to support himself after returning from Sir Walter Ralegh's Guiana voyage. Young Franklin is the most linguistically adept

I would like to thank the participants in the 'Neighboring Languages' seminar at the 2014 Shakespeare Association of America conference for comments on an earlier version of this essay.

character in the play. He speaks French and easily navigates the diverse spaces of the city, each marked by its own distinct way of talking.[4] Following him through the city, the audience is invited to share his mastery of the languages and codes of these various urban locations.[5] Though the only foreign language Young Franklin is heard to speak in the play is French, his ability to move through London's linguistically defined spaces seems shaped by his maritime experiences. Staging Young Franklin's travels through the city as an extension of his oceanic travels, the play offers what we might call a seafaring perspective on early modern London. The sea captain is a uniquely mobile figure – geographically, culturally, and economically. Young Franklin's language skills are part of his seafaring identity, and the play imagines voyaging as an activity that helps to produce the cosmopolitan London of Jacobean city comedy.[6]

This essay examines *Anything for a Quiet Life*'s use of stage languages in light of its repeated references to voyaging. The play's title introduces its languages by introducing sound. The prologue announces that, though men have different 'intents and appetites', they will all do 'anything for a quiet life'. A quiet life in the play is a peaceful life, but it is also a life without noise, as the prologue makes clear in describing a lawyer who 'talks himself into a sweat' for fees that will buy him a quiet life at home (Pro. 1, 4, 8). In the play's representation of London as noisy, languages are central. Indeed Middleton, in particular, consistently tends to be interested in how Londoners hear and understand strange languages. In *No Wit, No Help Like a Woman's* (1611), a visiting Dutch merchant serves as a credible witness who can report on shenanigans abroad; his two languages and wide travels make him a privileged intermediary. *A Chaste Maid in Cheapside* (1613) makes Latin into a foreign tongue, rendering school Latin comic when it is spoken in a goldsmith's house.[7] Like these other plays, *Anything for a Quiet Life* features a speaker of an alien tongue, but he is a mariner. Though *Anything for a Quiet Life* never explains where Young Franklin learned French (he could, for instance, have studied it in one of London's French language schools), the play emphasises his identity as a seafarer, suggesting that he most likely learned it in his travels: aboard ships or in foreign ports.[8]

Young Franklin as a Seafarer

The sea captain brings maritime attitudes into noisy London. Young Franklin is introduced as a man only reluctantly on land, unemployed and seeking a new post on a ship. When the play begins, he is in London waiting for a promised voyage. The play explains his past and hoped-for voyages in considerable detail, and it is worth dwelling on these details as they help to locate Young Franklin in late Jacobean maritime enterprise and culture. He is most likely among aristocrats drawn to the sea by opportunities for privateering and profit, not someone apprenticed as a mariner.⁹ Cheryl Fury explains that captains 'were normally persons of import in the land community and were given command of men-of-war – either naval or privateering vessels'.¹⁰ While the play does not specify precisely where he was born, Young Franklin is not a Londoner, as his father 'come[s] up' at the end of the play, seeks in the city 'a fellow ... born near' him, and is welcomed to London from 'th' country' (5.1.46–54). Young Franklin explains that, as a younger brother, he was compelled to go to sea to make his fortune and has recently returned from Ralegh's disastrous 1617–18 Guiana voyage: 'my fate / Throwing me upon the late ill-starred voyage / To Guiana, failing of our golden hopes' (1.1.166–68). Having failed to find gold in Guiana, he looks east, explaining that he intended to join the Duke of Florence to fight against the Turk. Though the title 'Duke of Florence' was outdated, Young Franklin likely refers to the small raids of Aegean and Mediterranean coastal towns by the navy of the Tuscan Order of St Stephen. This would be a timely reference for Middleton and Webster's audience given the death in February 1621 of Cosimo II de Medici, Grand Duke of Tuscany, and the succession of his son Ferdinando II.¹¹ Before he could join the crew of a Tuscan galley, though, Young Franklin was called to London by the corrupt aristocrat Lord Beaufort for another venture, probably with the English East India Company: 'Your lordship, minding to rig forth a ship / To trade for the East Indies sent for me', Young Franklin tells Beaufort (1.1.174–75, 1.1.175n). Yet, just as Ralegh's voyage failed (and led to Ralegh's execution), the Indies voyage did not materialise, as Young Franklin complains: 'I have stayed here two months / And find your intended voyage but a dream' (1.1.181–82). Young Franklin finds himself running out of the extensive funds required to maintain an urban lifestyle befitting his maritime command: 'Men that have command, my lord, at sea, cannot live / Ashore without money' (1.1.185–86). Having sought gold in the Americas and hoping to sail east for the East India Company, which in 1621 had just concluded payment on its first joint-stock, Young Franklin is squarely identified with long-range English overseas projects of the period.¹²

Young Franklin's seafaring past with Ralegh also implies involvement in piracy. The crown accused Ralegh of intending to turn pirate and of

engaging in piratical attacks against the Spanish in Guiana, though as
Claire Jowitt has shown, piracy itself was a politically contested term;
James, unlike Elizabeth, made no distinction between commissioned
and unauthorised prize-taking, condemning all violence at sea.[13] In any
case, Young Franklin's voyage with Ralegh has tainted his prospects. After
hearing Young Franklin's complaints about the Indies voyage, Beaufort
holds out another possibility: 'I had thought / To prefer you to have been
captain of a ship / That's bound for the Red Sea' (1.1.196–98). East India
Company trade to the Red Sea port of Mokha commenced in 1618 with
a single voyage but was then obstructed for several years due to a dispute
with the merchants of Surat; it resumed in 1621. The Red Sea trade
was particularly attractive to the English because it helped to maintain
English silver reserves; factors at Mokha 'paid for Indian and East Indian
products largely in specie' and English commodities could be exchanged
there for products to be traded in India.[14] But the merchants sponsoring
the Red Sea voyage do not want Young Franklin's command: 'the merchants are possessed / You have been a pirate' (1.1.198–99). East India
Company merchants preferred not to employ as captains gentlemen
who would prioritise prize-taking and warfare to trade.[15] Young Franklin
does not deny the allegation of piracy ('Say I were one still?') but claims
that any past piracy makes him a superior captain: 'If I were past the line
once, why, methinks / I should do them better service' (1.1.200–01).
With this boast, Young Franklin emphasises the long distance of his travels and his participation in Ralegh's attacks on the Spanish in Guiana.
The 'line' refers to the meridian in the 1494 Treaty of Tordesillas that
divided ownership of unknown lands beyond Europe between Spain
and Portugal. English activities 'beyond the line' referred to piracy in
Iberian-owned regions, though, of course, there was considerable overlap
between legitimate trade, colonial adventure, war at sea, and piracy in the
early modern period.[16] For Young Franklin, the range of his travels – in
both geography and activity – means that he can provide 'better service'
to the merchants, but they do not agree.

     Young Franklin, then, participates in the full and often overlapping
range of early modern adventures: voyages of discovery, merchant shipping, naval exploits, and piracy. His attitude towards voyaging, shaped
by shipboard life and its labour practices and customs, is also typical
of early modern seafarers. He acts largely as an independent free agent,
seeking the best possible employment. Seamen were conscious of the
value of their labour and in choosing posts, sought the best package
of wages, status, and perquisites;[17] he does not limit his service to only

English vessels;[18] and he is anxious about unemployment. Seafaring was seasonal and cyclical, and sailors ashore often faced financial hardship.[19] Demobilisation after peace with Spain was concluded in 1604 exacerbated widespread maritime unemployment and underemployment, with increases in both piracy at sea and vagrancy on land.[20] While Young Franklin's version of financial hardship is his lack of means to sustain a gallant lifestyle, his situation still expresses the difficulty of living on land between voyages, and, in his case, of maintaining, during peacetime, a life on land befitting his standing. By 1621, there were both court and parliamentary factions weary of James's attempts at mediation between Catholic and Protestant powers and eager to intervene in the Palatinate to restore his son-in-law, Frederick V.[21] Beyond issues of maritime unemployment, Young Franklin's idleness, especially given his association with Ralegh, may also reflect nostalgia for an idealised Elizabethan militarism and heroism – including activities that James labelled piracy – on the high seas.[22] A former pirate hero has become an unemployed rogue.

The financial hardships faced by seamen ashore helped to produce their reputation as lewd and lawless, and Young Franklin embodies this aspect of seafaring as well.[23] Unable to live within his means or find a new voyage, he turns to knavery. His friend Young Cressingham wants to go to the Low Countries (1.1.245), presumably to join English volunteers in the Palatinate, but Young Franklin dissuades him, promising they can 'live here i' th' city' if they turn to gulling, 'as other gallants do' (1.1.246, 249–50).[24] Anne-Julia Zwierlein describes the conventional 'plot of roguery' in early modern city comedy as an alternative to both 'adventure' – risk-taking in overseas trade – and 'increase' – the slow accumulation of wealth through hard work.[25] Adventure has failed Young Franklin and patient increase is not his style. But his seafaring has prepared him well for roguery, 'money-making through subterfuge'.[26]

Young Franklin's turn to gulling is enabled by his language skills. While *Anything for a Quiet Life* does not specify where Young Franklin learned French, given the national and ethnic diversity of ships' crews and the play's general emphasis on his voyages, it seems likely that his language skills were learned or reinforced aboard ship.[27] In the transnational maritime world of the seventeenth century, sailors encountered foreign languages spoken by their fellow crewmen. English ships sometimes had foreign masters (the master was responsible for maintaining order and discipline among the crew).[28] Crews were often made up of men with diverse origins, especially given the high rates of mortality at sea; empty posts could be filled by hiring in foreign ports.[29] For example, one Guinea voyage carried a mostly English crew that also included two Portuguese, including an interpreter, a French surgeon, another Frenchman, and a Fleming.[30] Pirate crews were especially ethnically and nationally diverse.[31]

One well-documented example of a seventeenth-century English mariner who learned multiple languages is Edward Coxere (1633–1694). Though his life postdates *Anything for a Quiet Life*, Coxere's case shows how seafaring produces transnational tongues. Born in Kent, Coxere narrates his linguistically wide-ranging maritime experiences in his *Adventures at Sea* (written in the decade before his death). After being sent abroad as a teenager to learn French, Coxere chooses a life of voyaging. Hired on a Dutch ship with an Irish captain, he 'soon' acquires Dutch from his shipmates.[32] His ship is hired to fight for Spain, and he learns Spanish 'very fluently' as well.[33] With his four languages – English, French, Dutch, and Spanish – Coxere was ideally positioned to prosper in the transnational and polyglot world of seventeenth-century shipping.[34] He encounters French, Dutch, Spanish, English, Italian, Portuguese, Moorish, and Irish sailors. He learns languages quickly and uses them to acquire new positions, earn better wages, escape imprisonment, plunder, and trade. He learns languages in his travels at sea, and he prospers because of them.

As a gentleman, a captain, and a sometimes-pirate, Young Franklin displays more limited language skills than the sailor Coxere, and he returns home rather than prospering abroad. But insofar as he knows French and adapts to and adopts jargons, Young Franklin functions in *Anything for a Quiet Life* as a similarly linguistically skilled seafarer. Beyond knowing French, he is also generally adept at navigating urban spaces defined by cants and jargons, such as the mercer's shop and the barber's surgery. Here too seafaring provides some precedent for Young Franklin's linguistic mobility. Seamen used colloquial language and a distinct idiom incorporating the terminology of seafaring life. John Smith's *A Sea Grammar* (1627) promises 'the exposition of all the most difficult words seldom used but among seamen [...] that any willing capacity may easily understand them'.[35] Mariners also communicated with other ships via a coded language of nonverbal communication including signals and flags.[36] So in addition to learning foreign languages in his travels by ship, Young Franklin would also have been immersed in a maritime subculture with its own forms of communication. We do not hear him deploy maritime jargon in London, but we do hear him adapt quickly and easily to the linguistically various city.

Travels in London Languages

Howard has argued that city comedies frequently link urban and oceanic navigation, equating skills in navigating the city with skills in navigating the New World.[37] This dynamic is prominent in *Anything for a Quiet Life*. Young Franklin's language skills give him a kind of urban fluency that allows him to talk his way through several linguistically defined social and commercial spaces of the city. The play represents London as noisily full of diverse ways of speaking, from the cries of shopkeepers to the anatomical cant of the barber to the French of a prostitute. Young Franklin's progression through the city and its tongues is a version of the perambulation described by Jonathan Horng Hsy in medieval texts, in which commerce 'provides the vehicle for the urban subject's motion through diverse sociolinguistic environments', so that 'travel through the city is inexorably tied to the traversal of its tongues' and invites 'improvisation and invention'.[38] Like the medieval subjects in the pamphlets Hsy reads, as Young Franklin moves through commercial locations – the mercer's shop, the barber's surgery, and the prostitute's street – he encounters and negotiates the languages spoken in each. By positioning Young Franklin as an interpreter of these languages, the play invites playgoers to imagine themselves, like Young Franklin, as fluent navigators of the city's linguistic regions.

Young Franklin travels through a city in which linguistic variety is linked to foreign imports. He begins by visiting the mercer Camlet's shop, in disguise as a lord with Young Cressingham as his tailor. With these disguises, they aim to convince Camlet that Young Franklin is rich and creditworthy. Camlet's apprentice, George, calling out in the familiar shopkeeper's refrain, 'What is't you lack?', markets the silks as 'the best in Europe' (2.2.80–82). One silk, he claims, was worn by the King of Naples, another is better than fabric worn by the Great Turk, and a piece of cloth-of-gold is as good as any worn by the Sophy (2.2.83–84, 106, 159). As a consumer, Young Franklin benefits from the availability of fabrics imported from the East Indies in a London shop and also reinforces his identity as a gentleman of the world. Playing the extravagant lord, he selects cloth very freely, but then (falsely) claims that his money is with his cousin, the barber, and asks Camlet to send a second apprentice, Ralph, to deliver the goods and collect the payment. The shift in setting from the mercer's shop to the barber's is accompanied by a shift in languages from the specialised language of the silk trade, with its conspicuous and duplicitous marketing of the luxurious, exotic, and royal, to the cant of the barber, which emphasises vulnerable male anatomy and the threatening tools of the trade.[39]

Young Franklin's plot at the barber's depends on the apprentice Ralph's inability to understand the barber's cant. Ralph expects money from the barber, but the barber thinks Ralph requires treatment for venereal disease. After Young Franklin sends Young Cressingham, still disguised as a tailor, away with the silks Ralph has brought, the barber takes Ralph into his back room. Following Young Franklin's instructions, the barber begins to prepare to operate on Ralph, calling for his 'rollers, bolsters, and pledgets armed' (2.4.6). While Camlet imports silks, Ralph, the barber claims, suffers from another supposed import, 'morbis gallicus or neapolitanus': syphilis, here claimed to be French or Italian (2.4.20–21). It becomes clear to the audience that the barber is preparing to castrate Ralph, but the apprentice remains uncomprehending, leading to an exchange that pivots on the barber's and Ralph's different understandings of 'ware' and 'tissue':

RALPH.   'Sdeath! Where's my ware?
BARBER.   Ware! That was well, the word is cleanly, though not artful. Your
              ware it is that I must see.
RALPH.   My tobine and cloth of tissue?
BARBER.   You will neither have tissue nor issue if you linger in your malady.
              Better a member cut off than endanger the whole microcosm.
              (2.4.27–33)

This exchange hinges on the fact that, though they both speak English, Ralph and the barber speak different languages; 'tissue' means one thing at a mercer's and another at the barber's. This bawdily explicit exchange continues as Ralph offers to measure his 'yard' and the barber prepares his instruments (2.4.40).

Though this might seem simply like low comedy, as Ralph's 'member' is endangered, the threat of circumcision or castration was regularly represented on the London stage in plays dealing with Ottoman trade and travel and 'turning Turk' (2.4.32).[40] While there is no explicit 'Turk' here, this scene might well have reminded audiences of the threat to bodies and souls posed by Ottoman traffic, especially given *Anything for a Quiet Life*'s references to trade and travel. As Daniel Vitkus points out, turning Turk could hold real appeal for early modern English sailors, offering both money and a lifestyle with more freedom.[41] Indeed, 'ware' is also used in a Turk play, Massinger's *The Renegado* (1624), with the same double sense of commodity and anatomy, by Gazet, the Italian servant who jokes about becoming a eunuch, promising to sell his 'wares' and 'part with all [his] stones'.[42] Ralph, though, is saved from emasculation when the barber realises that he too has been gulled; while the barber prepared to operate, Young Franklin stole his new brush. He expresses his position with a double entendre that, like Ralph's 'yard', links the materials of his trade to his vulnerable body: 'My razor's at my heart. These storms will make / my sweetballs stink' (2.4.69–70).

Young Franklin, after adeptly navigating the trade languages of the mercer and barber, proves able to speak an alien tongue as well: French. When caught by the constables sent by the barber, Young Franklin assumes a French speech disguise, feigning confusion at his arrest: 'Ha qui va la, que penses vous faire Messieurs, me voles vous derober, je nay point d'argent: Je suis un pouvre Gentilhomme Francois'.[43] The barber is not fooled, and demands that Young Franklin speak English, as he did when he bought fancy fabrics and tricked poor Ralph. Young Franklin continues to speak only in French, in long but fairly repetitive passages that would make clear – even to audience members with little or no French – that he is pretending not to know anything about the barber or his accusations and acting like the barber and the constables are trying to rob him. Camlet then enters and recognises Young Franklin as the 'lord' who stole his cloth, but Young Franklin continues to protest in French:

> Vous sembles estre in home courtois, Je vous pre entendes mes affaires: il y a ici deuz ou erois Quenailles qui m'ont assiege un pouvre estranger, qui ne leur ay fait nul mal, ny donner mauvaisse parrolle, ny tirer mon espet; l'un me prend par une espaule, et me frape deux Liure peisant; L'autre me tire par le bras, il par le je ne seay quoy: Je leur ay donne ma bource, et si ne me veulent point Laiser aller, que feray je Monsieur.[44]

This long appeal seems to overwhelm Camlet, who is convinced by the flood of French that the man in front of him cannot be Young Franklin: 'This is a Frenchman it seems, sirs' (3.2.70). Young Franklin is able to deploy French strategically and convincingly, to the point where Camlet recognises that the Frenchman looks exactly like the fugitive but concludes that he must not be the fugitive. He believes his ears over his eyes. The barber and Ralph, though, continue to insist that the Frenchman is indeed Young Franklin.

The impasse is resolved by the appearance of a 'real' French person, Margarita, a prostitute (or, more precisely, an English boy actor wearing, like Young Franklin, French as a costume, but within the fiction appearing as a real French person). In her person, she unites all the imports at play in the Young Franklin plot: cloth (she is metonymically called a 'French hood'), syphilis, and the French language (4.1.341).[45] Her entrance leads to a brief exchange entirely in French, as Young Franklin asks her to attest that he is French and reveals to her his improvisation – in French, so his pursuers cannot understand:

MARGARITA: Estes vous de France Monsieur?
YOUNG FRANKLIN: Madame vay est, que ie les ay trompes, et suis areste, et n'ay
                    nul moein de chaper quan chansant mon Language, aides
                    moy en cest affaire: Je vous cognois bien, or vous tenes un
                    Bordeau, vouset les vostre n seres de mieulx.
MARGARITA: Laises faire a moy; Este vous de Lyon dites vous.[46]

Young Franklin shares with Margarita details of his predicament and his need to 'chansant ... Language' as a last resort for escape, and she comprehends his situation and promises help ('Laises faire a moy'), despite the fact that he is not actually her countryman. His language enables their alliance. For the playhouse audience, the aside establishes the situation; they know the Frenchman is Young Franklin and so know his French is a conveniently donned speech disguise. Even if playgoers do not understand every word, the context and the central phrase 'chansant mon Language' make clear Margarita's understanding of the plot and willingness to play along. The playhouse audience is allowed access to Young Franklin's plot and to his French, becoming part of the French alliance between English rogue and French prostitute.

By contrast, the on-stage auditors hear this exchange very differently. For them, there is no differentiation between the initial greetings and Young Franklin's confession of his plot. They hear a conversation between a Frenchwoman and a Frenchman that smoothly establishes their shared origin – France, then narrowed to Lyon – and ultimately culminates in what the playhouse audience understands as a comically implausible recognition. Margarita 'recognises' Young Franklin as a long-lost cousin: 'Ma Cozin! Je suis bien aise de vous voire en bonne disposition.'[47] Her recognition fools the gullible Camlet: 'This is a Frenchman sure' (3.2.99). The barber, though, is more sceptical, insisting that Young Franklin looks like an Englishman, and so they decide to question Margarita.

The questioning takes the form of a brief comic translation scene in which the English mishear French words as English words. Margarita serves as the interpreter. In addition to her French (understood by Young Franklin), she speaks a broken English that registers as half-French and is much more comprehensible to Camlet and the barber. After some confusion over 'poisson' (*fish* versus *poison*), Camlet declares himself convinced:

'The error was in our eyes and now we find it in his tongue' (3.2.123–24). Camlet found that his eyes lied (in telling him that a Frenchman was English). But this comment also acknowledges more broadly Young Franklin's errant, improvisational tongue. Cultivated by seafaring, his tongues can be put on and taken off at will, so that he not only can approximate a Frenchman but also can ally himself with a Frenchwoman. In the last moments of their French dialogue, Margarita promises Young Franklin further French exchange: 'J'ay un fillie qui parle un peu Francois, elle conversera avec vois a la Fleur de Lice en Turnbull-Street.'[48] This French 'conversation' will occur at a tavern whose name offers an infestation pun, 'lice' for 'lis', located in a famously disreputable street in the Fleet, Turnmill Street.[49] She invites Young Franklin to travel within London to find further French exchanges, and he plans to visit her bawdy 'school' ('vostre Escole').[50] A. J. Hoenselaars notes that while the idea of a foreigner assisting an Englishman is not unusual, it is striking that this play 'introduces stereotyped features that paradoxically do not discredit the bearer'.[51] So Margarita appears as a licentious Frenchwoman, but one whose language skills are shared by Young Franklin, to both their credits. Young Franklin thus succeeds in living by his wits and his tongue (with some help from his father, who pays his debts), as he moves through a cosmopolitan, linguistically various London. He makes sense of and employs its tongues and invites the audience to identify with his urban fluency.

Travel Fantasy and Noisy London

The play also articulates an alternative view of the city, one that helps to highlight Young Franklin's seafaring as an alternative to London citizenship. This view belongs to the mercer Camlet, who fantasises about travelling away from London. Camlet announces his intention to 'seek out a quiet life' on a 'fine peaceable island'. Reminded that he already lives on a peaceable island – 'Why 'tis the same you live in' – he replies that islands, including England's, do not always match their reputations:

> No, 'tis so famed,
> But we th'inhabitants find it not so.
> The place I speak of has been kept with thunder,
> With frightful lightnings, amazing noises,
> But now – th'enchantment broke – 'tis the land of peace,
> Where hogs and tobacco yield fair increase.
> ...
> Gentlemen, fare you well, I am for the Bermudas.
> (5.2.88–95, 97–98)

Camlet's speech alludes to *The Tempest*, with its 'isle full of noises' disordered by the thunder and lightning of Prospero's enchantments.[52] But his own island and Caliban's have changed places. Britain, 'famed' as peaceable, proves distressingly noisy to its 'inhabitants', while the formerly wild island in 'the Bermudas' is idealised as a peaceful, domesticated space for agriculture. The reference to hogs suggests the dramatists' familiarity with William's Strachey's letter on the 1609 shipwreck of the *Sea Venture*, 'A True Reportory', itself a source for *The Tempest*, which reports on hogs corralled and fed by the English.[53] Most playgoers in 1621, though, would likely not have read the Strachey manuscript, which was not printed until 1625, and so would know Strachey by way of *The Tempest*. Camlet stands as a proxy for those playgoers, and he imagines voyaging to faraway islands using that play's language of noise and enchantment.[54] His travel fantasy is hyperbolic and vicarious; he travels only in the theatre.[55] In effect, he wants to convert playhouse travel into actual voyaging, and if he could not travel to Bermuda, he could travel to the London neighbourhood, between the Strand and Covent Garden, known as the Bermudas.[56] So just as Young Franklin's sea voyages are convertible into urban navigation, so too are Camlet's travel fantasies.

Unlike Young Franklin, whose sojourn in London seems as temporary as the play itself, Camlet has no intention of actually leaving the metropolis he finds so wildly loud. In the climactic scene of Camlet's plot, the noisy variety of languages of early modern London is again amplified. Camlet's wife, Rachel, confronts Margarita, the French prostitute, in the mercer's shop. Rachel's railing meets Margarita's heavily accented English. As she rejects the prostitute she thinks is her husband's new wife, Rachel rejects imported fashions: 'Is he to be married to a French-hood? I'll dress it the English fashion' (4.1.341-42). Rachel's threat plays on the double senses of 'French-hood' as garment and prostitute and of 'dress' as clothes and thrash.[57] Middleton and Webster also play with the city comedy convention of the reformed Londoner rejecting foreign frippery. In the main plot, the profligate woman, Lady Cressingham, becomes an English wife dressed not in imported silk but in domestic wool. Though her shift is sudden, this plot unfolds as we would expect: the Englishwoman obsessed with foreign fashions learns to be a more thrifty and modest wife, refashioning herself as a proper Englishwoman.

But Rachel Camlet's resolution is more complicated. Though she plans to beat Margarita in 'the English fashion', she does not have to get new clothes to emerge as a proper Englishwoman. When she finally meets Margarita, Rachel threatens to stomp on Margarita's 'French-hood' in a pair of 'pantofles' (4.2.50), also called 'chopines', Italian or Spanish slippers with cork soles, which were not widely worn in England but were common on the stage as a foreign costume.[58] Rachel therefore threatens to destroy Margarita's French garment using exotic imported shoes, all while acting in 'the English fashion'. In this play, a wife can behave in the English fashion without doffing her foreign fashions. *Anything for a Quiet Life* reconstitutes social stability without rejecting the influence of imports on Londoners and their urban spaces.

Though the comic resolution realigns quietness and domesticity and no one leaves London, travel is ever present. Seafaring has prepared Young Franklin to be linguistically flexible and improvisatory as he negotiates the noisy city. Camlet fantasises about travel for opposite ends, to find in a foreign isle not a variety of languages but an elusive quiet. Voyaging returns in the play's epilogue, which echoes *The Tempest*'s ('Gentle breath of yours my sails') and shows the players themselves metaphorically adopting a seafaring perspective as they hope for a successful voyage.[59] The epilogue figures the King's Men as a ship ready to sail on the winds of the audience's favour:

> Whether we do owe
> Our service to your favours, or must strike
> Our sails – though full of hope – to your dislike.
> ...
> Instruct us but in what we went astray,
> And to redeem it, we'll take any way. (Epilogue, 1–4, 7–8)

This epilogue features the conventional appeal to the audience's judgement and offer to 'redeem' the players' faults, and its appeal draws on metaphors of voyaging. Like Young Franklin, the players are uncertain about their future voyage; they will either be celebrated for their service or strike their sails, depending on the audience's favour. The company's sails, 'full of hope,' must be struck if the audience fails to applaud, and, continuing the metaphor, the audience's experience of the play is a kind of course from which the company could go 'astray'. The last line promises more and redemptive travel: 'we'll take any way'. Even a playing company firmly anchored in London can hope to set sail.

Notes

1 Jean E. Howard, *Theater of a City: The Places of London Comedy, 1598–1642* (Philadelphia: University of Pennsylvania Press, 2007), 2–4. On London's cosmopolitanism, see Crystal Bartolovich, '"Baseless Fabric": London as a "World City"', in *The Tempest and Its Travels*, ed. Peter Hulme and

William H. Sherman (Philadelphia: University of Pennsylvania Press, 2000), 16–17, and on early modern cosmopolitanism, see Daniel Vitkus, 'Rogue Cosmopolitans on the Early Modern Stage: John Ward, Thomas Stukeley, and the Sherley Brothers', Chapter 7 in this volume. In this essay, for convenience, I use the word 'foreign' in its modern sense to point to what the early modern English would call 'strange' or 'alien': people, languages, and things from abroad.

2 Leslie Thomson, 'Introduction', Thomas Middleton and John Webster, *Anything for a Quiet Life*, in *Thomas Middleton: The Collected Works*, ed. Gary Taylor and John Lavagnino (Oxford University Press, 2007), 1593–94. All further quotations from *Anything for a Quiet Life* will be cited by act, scene, and line numbers within the text. All further citations are to this edition except where otherwise noted. On cloth and identity, see Roze Hentschell, *The Culture of Cloth in Early Modern England* (Aldershot: Ashgate, 2008), 104–10; Ann Rosalind Jones and Peter Stallybrass, *Renaissance Clothing and the Materials of Memory* (Cambridge University Press, 2000), 1–5; Joan Pong Linton, 'Jack of Newberry and Drake in California: Domestic and Colonial Narratives of English Cloth and Manhood', *English Literary History* 59 (1992), 33–36.

3 A notable exception is David Coleman, 'Purchasing Purgatory: Economic Theology, Archipelagic Colonialism, and *Anything for a Quiet Life* (1621)', in *Region, Religion, and English Renaissance Literature* (Burlington, VT: Ashgate, 2014), 87–103.

4 On how sound defines the overlapping spaces of early modern London, see Bruce R. Smith, *The Acoustic World of Early Modern England: Attending to the O-Factor* (University of Chicago Press, 1999), 46–47.

5 Marianne Montgomery, *Europe's Languages on England's Stages: 1590–1620* (Farnham: Ashgate, 2012), 4.

6 The early seventeenth century saw major growth in the English shipping industry; see Kenneth Andrews, *Ships, Money, and Politics: Seafaring and Naval Enterprise in the Reign of Charles I* (Cambridge University Press, 1991), 16–24. For the importance of imports in the growth of English overseas trade, see Robert Brenner, *Merchants and Revolution: Commercial Change, Political Conflict, and London's Overseas Traders, 1550–1653* (Princeton University Press, 2003), 4–5, 25–33.

7 Montgomery, *Europe's Languages*, 61–67, 117–27.

8 For French language schools, see Montgomery, *Europe's Languages*, 7–8.

9 G. V. Scammell, 'Manning the English Merchant Service in the Sixteenth Century', *Mariner's Mirror* 56, no. 2 (1970), 140.

10 Cheryl A. Fury, 'The Work of G.V. Scammell', in *The Social History of English Seamen*, 37. See also Cheryl A. Fury, *Tides in the Affairs of Men: The Social History of Elizabethan Seamen, 1580–1603* (Westport, CT: Greenwood Press, 2002), 21.

11 Marco Gemignani, 'The Navies of the Medici: The Florentine Navy and Navy of the Sacred Military Order of St. Stephen, 1547–1648', in *War at Sea in the Middle Ages and the Renaissance*, ed. John B. Hattendorf and Richard W. Under (Woodbridge: Boydell Press, 2003), 182.

12 Kenneth R. Andrews, *Trade, Plunder, and Settlement: Maritime Enterprise and the Genesis of the British Empire, 1480–1630* (Cambridge University Press, 1984), 262.

13 Claire Jowitt, 'Scaffold Performances: The Politics of Pirate Execution', in *Pirates?: The Politics of Plunder, 1550–1650*, ed. Claire Jowitt (Basingstoke: Palgrave Macmillan, 2007), 165–68.

14 Andrews, *Trade, Plunder, and Settlement*, 274; Brenner, *Merchants and Revolution*, 49.

15 Andrews, *Trade, Plunder, and Settlement*, 262.

16 Claire Jowitt, *The Culture of Piracy, 1580–1630: English Literature and Seaborne Crime* (Farnham: Ashgate, 2010), 3; John C. Appleby, 'Jacobean Piracy', in *The Social History of English Seamen: 1485–1649*, ed. Cheryl A. Fury (Woodbridge: Boydell Press, 2012), 278–79.

17 Fury, *Tides*, 3, 17.

18 Ibid., 18.

19 Ibid., 19.

20 Appleby, 'Jacobean Piracy', 278–79; Roger Lockyer, *The Early Stuarts: A Political History of England 1603–1642* (London: Longman, 1999), 183–85.

21 Lockyer, *The Early Stuarts*, 157–60.

22 On this nostalgia, see Jowitt, 'Scaffold Performances', 163–64, 168; S. J. Houston, *James I* (London: Longman, 1973), 67–68.

23 Andrews, *Ships, Money, and Politics*, 62.

24 On the volunteer force, see Lockyer, *The Early Stuarts*, 158.

25 Anne-Julia Zwierlein, 'Shipwrecks in the City: Commercial Risk as Romance in Early Modern City Comedy', in *Plotting Early Modern London: New Essays on Jacobean City Comedy*, ed. Dieter Mehl, Angela Stock, and Anne-Julia Zwierlein (Aldershot: Ashgate, 2004), 77–79.

26 Ibid., 78.

27 Scammell, 'Manning the English Merchant Service', 134.

28 Ibid., 146–47; Fury, *Tides*, 18.

29 Fury, 'The Work of G. V. Scammell', 30.

30 J. D. Alsop, 'Tudor Merchant Seafarers in the Early Guinea Trade', in Fury, *The Social History of English Seamen*, 37, 92.

31 Appleby, 'Jacobean Piracy', 292.

32 Edward Coxere, *Adventures by Sea of Edward Coxere, a Relation of the Several Adventures by Sea with the Dangers, Difficulties and Hardships met for Several Years* (London: Oxford University Press, 1946), 11.

33 Ibid., 17.

34 Scammell, 'Manning the English Merchant Service', 134.

35 John Smith, *A Sea Grammar* (London, 1627), A6[r].

36 Fury, *Tides*, 86–88.

37 Howard, *Theater of a City*, 11.

38 Jonathan Horng Hsy, *Trading Tongues: Merchants, Multilingualism, and Medieval Literature* (Columbus, OH: Ohio State University Press, 2013), 4, 9, 22.

39 For an overview of the functions of cants and jargons, see Peter Burke and Roy Porter, *Languages and Jargons: Contributions to a Social History of Language* (Cambridge: Polity Press, 1995), 13–15.

40 Daniel Vitkus, *Turking Turk: English Theater and the Multicultural Mediterranean, 1570–1630* (New York: Palgrave, 2003), 104, 125–26.

41 Ibid., 110.

42 Philip Massinger, *The Renegado*, in *Three Turk Plays from Early Modern England*, ed. Daniel Vitkus (New York: Columbia University Press, 2000), 3.4.51, 53; Daniel Vitkus, 'Poisoned Figs, or "The Traveller's Religion": Travel, Trade and Conversion in Early Modern English Culture', in *Remapping the Mediterranean World in Early Modern English Writings*, ed. Goran V. Stanivukovic (New York: Palgrave, 2007), 55.

43 Thomas Middleton, *Anything for a Quiet Life* (London: Printed by Tho. Johnson for Francis Kirkman, and Henry Marsh, 1662), E1ʳ. For the French passages, I quote from the 1662 quarto (*Q*) rather than from the *Oxford Middleton*, as the Oxford editors regularise and correct the play's French. Translations are from the *Oxford Middleton*. 'Ha! Who's there? What do you think you're doing, sirs? Do you want to rob me? I have no money. I'm a poor French gentleman' (3.2.45–47n).

44 Middleton, *Q* E1ᵛ; 'You seem to be a courteous man. I beg you to listen to my troubles. Here are two or three ruffians who have besieged me, a poor stranger who has done them no harm at all, not spoken an ill word, nor draw my sword. One takes me by one shoulder and strikes me two heavy blows. The other pulls me by the arm. He says I don't know what. I have given them my purse, and if they don't want to let me go, what should I do, sir?' (3.2.62–69n).

45 On prostitutes as cosmopolitan figures, see Howard, *Theater of a City*, 144–57.

46 Middleton, *Q* E1ᵛ; Margarita: 'Are you from France, sir?' YF: Madame, the truth is I have cozened them and am detained, and have no means of escaping except by changing my language. Help me in this business. I know you well, where you have a brothel. You and yours will benefit.' Margarita: 'Leave it to me. You are from Lyon, you say?' (3.2.88–94n).

47 Middleton, *Q* E1ᵛ; 'My cousin! I'm so pleased to see you in good health' (3.2.96–97n).

48 Middleton, *Q* E2ʳ; 'I have a girl who speaks some French. She'll talk with you at the Fleur-de-lice in Turnbull Street' (3.2.125–31n).

49 E. H. Sugden, *A Topographical Dictionary to the Works of Shakespeare and his Fellow Dramatists* (Manchester University Press, 1925), s.v. 'Turnbull Street'.

50 On the association of French language learning with prostitution, see Juliet Fleming, 'The French Garden: An Introduction to Women's French', *English Literary History* 56, no. 1 (1989), 32–34.

51 A. J. Hoenselaars, *Images of Englishmen and Foreigners in the Drama of Shakespeare and His Contemporaries* (Rutherford, NJ: Fairleigh Dickinson University Press, 1992), 141.

52 William Shakespeare, *The Tempest*, ed. Virginia Mason Vaughan and Alden T. Vaughan, The Arden Shakespeare (London: Thomson Learning, 1997), 3.2.135. See also Charles Forker, 'Shakespearean Imitation in Act 5 of *Anything for a Quiet Life*', *Papers On Language and Literature* 7 (1971), 75–80.

53 William Strachey, 'A True Reportory', in *The Tempest*, ed. Vaughan and Vaughan, 295, 297.

54 On the manuscript circulation of 'A True Reportory', see Alden T. Vaughan, 'William Strachey's "'True Reportory'" and Shakespeare: A Closer Look at the Evidence', *Shakespeare Quarterly* 59, no. 3 (Fall 2008), 256, 261. For discussion, see Emily C. Bartels, 'Strange Bedfellows: The Ordinary Undersides of "A True Reportory" and *The Tempest*', Chapter 9 in this volume.

55 On playgoing as 'vicarious tourism', see Joseph Roach, 'The Enchanted Island: Vicarious Tourism in Restoration Adaptations of *The Tempest*', in *The Tempest and Its Travels*, ed. Hulme and Sherman, 60–70. See also David McInnis, *Mind-Travelling and Voyage Drama in Early Modern England* (Basingstoke: Palgrave Macmillan, 2013), 2.

56 Vaughan, 'Strachey's "True Reportory"', 260; Sugden, *Topographical Dictionary*, s.v. 'Bermoothes'.

57 'dress, v.' *OED Online* (Oxford University Press: June 2014) [www.oed.com/view/Entry/57672].

58 'pantofle, n.' *OED Online* [www.oed.com/view/Entry/137024]; 'chopine, n.', *OED Online* [www.oed.com/view/Entry/32260].

59 Shakespeare, *Tempest*, Epilogue, 11.

CHAPTER 7

Rogue Cosmopolitans on the Early Modern Stage: John Ward, Thomas Stukeley, and the Sherley Brothers

Daniel Vitkus

University of California, San Diego

During the sixteenth and seventeenth centuries, new commercial networks, cross-cultural encounters, and socio-spatial relations were making possible a kind of 'early modern' cosmopolitanism, one that resisted the bonds and boundaries set by local and national authorities, by ecclesiastical institutions, and by aristocratic or civic authority, even if the new cosmopolitans rarely defeated or escaped those traditional authorities completely.[1] Early modern cosmopolitanism has its own particular configuration and ideological structure, one that does not simply prolong a waning medieval worldview or prefigure modern forms of cosmopolitanism. Nor is it simply an extension of European empire into new 'worlds'. The dromological possibilities of the time – that is, the long-distance mobilities made possible by innovative maritime technologies – opened up new physical and mental territories that could be genuinely and fully cosmopolitan. New diasporic communities came into being and new hybrid cultures, languages, and literatures emerged. Developing trade networks produced a growing sense of interdependency linking Europe to other parts of the world. The early modern world system produced dynamical transformation, ripple effects, and cultural mixture across the globe – not only in Europe. Although I will focus here on English texts and perspectives, early modern cosmopolitanism was by no means limited to Europe. It took place along a chain of empires linked by trade routes, wars, and overlapping patronage networks. The theatre in London was sensitive to these changes and registered them by representing long-distance travel, and the cross-cultural encounters that ensued, in a variety of travel plays. In fact, the theatre helped to inform English playgoers about the emerging possibilities of global travel and the negotiation of new cosmopolitan identities in the spaces between empires. Travel plays, such as those discussed here, dramatised the exploits of specific historical figures who undertook long journeys and by doing so became models (either positive or negative) for interaction and exchange with foreign cultures, creeds, and powers. As a result, theatrical representations of travel whipped up excitement and enflamed both hopes and fears about the possibilities offered by commercial investments and military 'adventures' in far-flung lands.

So who were these travelling cosmopolitans? What kind of social, political, or economic circumstances enabled them to act like citizens of the world, not of a nation, tribe, or village? They were diplomats, courtiers, humanist scholars, artists, writers, merchants, mercenaries, spies, religious refugees, exiles, and a few eccentric wanderers. None could disentangle themselves completely from local or national connections and loyalties, for the dialectical tension between the utopian dream of universalism and the inevitable particularity of culture can never be completely eased. For my purposes here, I want to think in terms of certain historical conditions that enabled and defined early modern cosmopolitanism: first, the post-1492 globalisation empowered by maritime and military technologies; and, second, a relatively fluid geopolitical situation that predated the stabilisation of a post-Westphalian world system of nation states and empires and preceded the onset of the bureaucratic and juridical nation state in the eighteenth century.

In *Web of Empire: English Cosmopolitans in an Age of Expansion*, Alison Games describes the emergence of an early modern imperial cosmopolitanism that existed before the modern nation state: it was 'a world spanned by private enterprise and defined by cosmopolitanism before [that kind of global] sensibility waned and was replaced and eclipsed by the state's commitment to centralized authority and to coercive strategies'.[2] For Games, early modern cosmopolitanism, as it was exercised by European elites and imperialists, was a proto-liberal moment of freedom and understanding, made possible by the emergence of a globalising capitalist system that was still unrestrained by the laws of the state. This captures something of the historical specificity of early modern cosmopolitanism, but it also ignores an important part of the picture as Games fails to acknowledge the foundations of this 'private enterprise', an imperial endeavour which was not motivated by a disinterested curiosity about non-European cultures. In fact, imperial cosmopolitanism was, in its material practice, a brutal economic system that accumulated capital by exploiting and destroying lives from London to Virginia to Calcutta.

The most heterogeneous ideas are yoked together by the violence of global capitalism: 'cosmopolitanism' is a slippery and unstable term because it contains opposing forces representative of both hegemonic and anti-orthodox outlooks. It must, therefore, be understood as a dialectical phenomenon: in some instances, cosmopolitanism is the mark of a harmful and exploitative transnational elite that, with the support of its kindred classes abroad, swam rings around the world and felt at home everywhere because privileged everywhere by commercial connections. Corporations can serve as the bearers of a managerial cosmopolitan, but they are not formed in order to benefit all humankind. In some cases, however, cosmopolitanism takes the form of a subversive attitude or behaviour that manifests global citizenship as a resistance to both the local and transnational forms of upper-class power.

During the sixteenth and seventeenth centuries, rogue cosmopolitans were able to evade control, not by escaping completely from the restraints and limits of national identities and laws (in both their native settings and beyond), but by gaming those elite systems of trade, patron-client relations, war, diplomacy, and so on. This was the career path for the rogue cosmopolitans who will serve as my examples here – the Sherley brothers (Anthony, Robert, and Thomas), the renegade corsair John Ward, and the adventurer Thomas Stukeley. But I have also chosen them because they appear on the London stage in a group of travel plays performed during the Elizabethan and Jacobean periods. Once they are given imaginative form on stage, these mercenaries are celebrated as border-crossing anti-heroes but then restrained, exiled, or destroyed so that their freedom does not threaten the authority of the emerging nation state. Rogue cosmopolitanism delighted audiences who enjoyed the thrillingly transgressive ambition of such adventurers, but these plays stop short of endorsing the most extreme forms of transgression exhibited by characters like Stukeley, Ward, and the Sherley brothers.

I

With the outward growth and development of English culture between 1575 and 1625, and with the intensification of a wide-ranging trade diaspora that exhibited increased mobility and density of connection to the global system, more English subjects travelled abroad, and many of them began to inhabit new improvisational and hybrid identities. Post-Reformation tensions between Christian sects (and the concomitant potential for religious conversion) took place at the same time as new, modern identities were being constructed and enacted by the English merchants and soldiers of fortune who had technological knowledge of the latest and most effective maritime technologies, especially the tall ships and mobile cast-iron guns that were developed by the English, the Dutch, and others.[3] The old feudal armies and feudal warfare began to change as new kinds of mobility and technology came into play. The traditional military system, based on the notion of a feudal-aristocratic military class, was a system that 'raised' armies made up of levied or impressed soldiers who served on a temporary basis, supplemented by paid mercenary forces that were hired and then disbanded. With the emergence of merchant capitalism in the early modern period, there was a shift from temporary to permanent war. Gun-bearing ships now carried the threat of bombardment with them wherever they went. These ships were harbingers of modernity, which has been defined, in part, by the fear of bombardment.[4]

Modernity began during the sixteenth century, and as the collective known as Retort has put it recently, 'War, in a word, is modernity incarnate.'[5] I would suggest that the beginnings of modernity, globalisation, neo-liberalism, capitalism, 'permanent war' (Retort), and 'empire' (Michael Hardt and Antonio Negri) all emerge from the early modern phenomenon of maritime commerce or, even more specifically, from the development of gun-carrying warships. According to Paul Virilio, 'history progresses at the speed of its weapons systems'.[6] Before the sixteenth century 'the European way of war at sea did not fundamentally differ from that of the civilisations in the Indian Ocean area and the Eastern seaboard of Asia', and 'permanent navies controlled by states were rare'.[7] By the mid-seventeenth century, though, '[t]he navies had become permanent and complex organisations: they were the policy instruments of centralised states and the ships, guns and dockyards represented huge investments in capital.'[8] Thus, in Europe, this period saw the origins of an unending trans-imperial conflict that has been fulfilled today by the neo-liberal empire that presides over postmodern globalisation and permanent war. But during early modernity, this was only beginning, and the transition from traditional notions of chivalric warfare, waged by a military caste, was gradual. It was in the maritime sphere that the older notion of aristocratic, temporary war was being challenged most vigorously by the new violent commerce, carried out on the high seas and in coastal areas by both state-authorised corporations (like the English and Dutch East India Companies) and by plundering soldiers of fortune. The older, traditional categories of the aristocratic warrior and the peaceful merchant were changing: the merchants who engaged in overseas commerce sailed in convoys of heavily armed vessels while aristocrats

invested or participated in voyages carried out by adventuring freebooters like Francis Drake. In 1492, Christopher Columbus sailed with the
titles of admiral and viceroy, directly licensed and sponsored by the king
and queen of Spain, in order to establish a shorter and more profitable
trade route to China and India. Though his purpose was essentially an
economic one, his official identity and self-image were traditional: his
enterprise was charged with an unwavering Roman Catholic religiosity,
and his fealty to the Spanish dynasty was almost absolute. Mercantile
mercenaries like Drake and Columbus remained loyal to a particular
monarch once they had established a profitable and mutually beneficial
function under royal patronage, but others were quite willing to switch
patrons – and even change their religion – in order to pursue plunder
and profit through maritime violence.

II

When compared to England's class-bound, hierarchical society, the
Ottoman Empire and its Islamicate neighbours in North Africa could
seem like meritocracies. The Ottoman Empire, the Barbary regencies,
and the Moroccan sultanate all welcomed new converts to Islam and
tolerated Christians and Jews. These Islamicate societies differed radically
from what England had been before the commercial, seaborne expansion
of the late sixteenth century, but the new classes of mobile merchants
were becoming modern in similar ways. The tense post-Reformation
struggles (including the burning of heretics, peasant uprisings, mas-
sacres, civil strife, and open warfare) that plagued Western Europe created a religious, economic, and political environment that compared
unfavourably with the social circumstances of converts residing in the
Ottoman Empire or the North African regencies. The violent conflicts
between competing European polities (including England, France,
Spain, Portugal, and the Dutch Republic) spread to the New World and
beyond as long-distance trade and plunder developed rapidly under an
emergent capitalism. These costly geopolitical quarrels, including the
long war between England and Spain, encouraged the development
of maritime technomilitary power, spurring the construction of gun-
bearing ships that were highly mobile and effective. An international
class of mercenaries, gunners, and experts in navigation arose and gained
new mobility as a result of these conflicts and the technologies they
inspired. Those who chose to offer their skills to foreign patrons formed

a new mercenary class.[9] Among these freelance military advisers were those who moved across borders and sailed far away to pursue their careers. The five men discussed here were members of this new class of soldiers and ship captains who were trained in amphibious warfare near their English homeland but went on to seek employment abroad. In what follows, I concentrate on the tension between English identity and the new hybrid or unstable identities forged by these mercenaries and pirates.

As Barbara Fuchs has shown, nationalistic propaganda sought to enlist unruly pirates and adventurers to support the cause of the English Protestant nation against Roman Catholic adversaries – in war and plunder, and in early attempts at 'plantation'. According to Fuchs, the 'unstable continuum of privateer, pirate, and renegado disrupts the legitimacy of a view of the English nation based in commerce'.[10] English monarchs made strenuous efforts to control and profit from the piracy, plunder, and violent commerce that were carried out by English ship captains. When it suited their interest, they attempted to incorporate that energy within their state network so that these rogue elements could be harnessed to serve their economic or imperial agenda. When they could not do that, they attempted to limit that activity through proclamations, imprisonment, confiscation of goods and property, and other means, but they were never able to successfully control extra-legal commerce and its violence. Brian Lockey argues that 'an existing tradition going back to medieval times of warfare by non-state actors, of which Drake was a recent participant, was translated by [early modern] writers ... into an ideology of incipient nationhood. This incorporation was largely pro-duced by means of writings after the fact that attempted to situate the voyages of privateers within the larger national narrative.'[11] According to Lockey, this tradition sustained 'an older but still persistent transnational or "cosmopolitan" identity' that harks back to the pre-Reformation cos-mopolitanism shared by literate and aristocratic elites across the various feudal polities that made up Western Christendom, and Lockey insists that this form of cosmopolitanism transcends local chauvinisms to survive the emergence of the early modern nation state as an identity-structuring, ideological framework.[12] It thus retains 'a code of chivalry that was at once a system of values belonging to an earlier era and one that was experiencing a resurgence during the Elizabethan period. Such chivalric codes are bound up with English identity while also extending beyond such an identity.'[13] This survival of a transnational chivalric order was accompanied by the enduring notion of an anti-Islamic crusade, and the ambitious Portuguese expedition to Morocco in 1578 stands as an example of the persistence of the crusade into the early modern era – but that effort failed, and its transnational anti-Muslimism also failed because intra-Christian conflicts, as well as Christian alliances with Muslims, undermined any such nostalgic fantasy that 'the common corps of Christendom' could still combine forces in a large-scale military effort to push back Islamic empire.[14] After the raising of the Ottoman siege of Malta in 1565 and the defeat of the Ottoman fleet at Lepanto in 1570, there were far fewer actualisations of the pan-Christian, anti-Muslim crusade fantasy.

But a mercenary cosmopolitanism persisted within the decentred network of permanent, global conflict and plunder waged by various commercial, national, and imperial interests. Lockey cites and acknowledges Walter Mignolo's distinction between a hegemonic 'managerial cosmopolitanism' and a dissident tradition of 'critical cosmopolitanism', but he does not pursue the implications of alternative cosmopolitanism. If various ruler-patrons become interchangeable in the eyes of pirates and transgressive mercenaries like Stukeley, Ward, and the Sherley brothers, for whom religious difference no longer mattered as much as getting paid, then we might see a third variety of cosmopolitanism – a mercenary cosmopolitanism. Though its participants may serve hegemonic power, they are also a danger to it – loose cannons, so to speak. Nor are these cosmopolitan mercenaries resistant to imperial power in any collective or coherent manner. Rather, this class of martial border-crossers draws upon and feeds off the complexity of interlocking and competing empires in order to reproduce itself. These mercenary cosmopolitans are a variation of the 'trans-imperial subjects' described by Natalie Rothman, early modern agents who were able to move across borders and by doing so helped to articulate geopolitical and ethnolinguistic categories.[15]

Stukeley, Ward, and the Sherley brothers are 'famous' exemplars of this mercenary cosmopolitanism, but there were many others.[16] Their fame was partly a product of the new modes of cultural production – including the permanent playhouses, ballads, broadsides, news pamphlets, and cheap print – which played an important role in disseminating information, stimulating fantasies about other cultures, and shaping the ideological environment of early modern England. Let me turn now to a discussion of the actual deeds of these men, and then of the travel plays that represented them to English readers and audiences.

III

In life and as theatrical characters, the five English soldiers of fortune under consideration here were all willing and able to move beyond their homeland into a trans-imperial space where they took on new roles under new patrons. They began their careers as English Protestants but travelled to the Mediterranean where, for the sake of personal gain, they adopted new identities. Four of the five were converts to either Catholicism or Islam (only Thomas Sherley remained, as far as we know, a Protestant); each one gained the personal attention of English monarchs and powerful courtiers; they all pursued profit and glory in the Mediterranean border zones where Christians, Jews, and Muslims traded and fought each other; their exploits were represented in various texts printed in London; and they were all portrayed on the London stage. Although they were considered untrustworthy by their monarchs, they were remembered in England for many years after their deaths for their audacity and ambition. Each of these men capitalised on the opportunities that were made available by England's position in the newly expanded maritime system. They all developed skills as leaders who could manage sailors and soldiers as well as the material means to effect fear of bombardment and plunder through the use of the ships, guns, and other weapon technologies.

Thomas Stukeley was born about 1525 in Devonshire, the third son of a knight who served at the court of Henry VIII. He offered his services to a variety of patrons in England, France, Ireland, Spain, and the Low Countries, beginning with Edward Seymour, Duke of Somerset, and ending with Pope Gregory XIII and the Portuguese king, Sebastian I. In between, he was involved in military action on the Continent and in Ireland. In 1563 he received Elizabeth I's support in a scheme to establish an Anglo-French colony in Florida, but instead he took the ships he was given for that purpose and went to Ireland. There, he proceeded to use them to attack and plunder foreign vessels. His unauthorised piracies, spendthrift ways, and loud-mouthed arrogance earned him the queen's distrust, and she refused to allow him to serve in the local offices he had purchased in Ireland. This led him to leave Ireland for Spain, where he offered Philip I his aid in a proposed invasion of Ireland. Stukeley's scheme was seriously considered but never undertaken, but eventually the pope did sponsor a voyage from Italy to Ireland. On his way to Ireland, Stukeley's ship and crew of 600 soldiers stopped in Lisbon where he decided to join the forces preparing there for an invasion of Morocco.

Stukeley subsequently perished in 1578 at the Battle of Al-Kasr Al-Kebir along with the Portuguese king, Sebastian I, and two of the Moroccan claimants to the throne.[17]

John Ward was a fisherman from Faversham in Kent, who deserted after having been pressed into service as a common sailor in one of the Channel fleet ships maintained by the Royal Navy. In 1604 he turned to piracy and eventually made his way to Tunis, where he pursued a career as a corsair sponsored by the local Muslim rulers. Though he tried to negotiate a pardon from James I, the king refused his terms; Ward remained in Tunis, where he converted to Islam and took the name Yusuf Reis, married an Italian woman, and built himself a handsome mansion. He enjoyed a long and prosperous career in North Africa, dying there in 1622.

The Sherley brothers were the scions of an old Sussex family, and their father had served Elizabeth I in high office, but the family fell on hard times under James I.[18] The eldest, Thomas (1564–1634), was a soldier of fortune and pirate who served Queen Elizabeth in the Low Countries and Ireland. Thomas's unsuccessful privateering voyages culminated in a botched attempt to plunder the Greek island of Kea, where he was abandoned by his mutinous crew and captured by Ottoman forces. Thomas was held in an Ottoman jail for three years, until James I petitioned for his release. He returned to England where he was thrown in prison in 1607 for plotting against the Levant Company's interests. The rest of his career was undistinguished and marked by struggle with debt.

Thomas's younger brother Anthony (1565–1636) distinguished himself early in life on the field of battle in Brittany against Spanish troops, but later efforts to enrich himself through privateering in the Atlantic (he attacked the Portuguese in Africa and the Spanish in the Caribbean) proved unsuccessful. A mission to defend Ferrara against Pope Clement VIII, which had been sponsored by his patron the Earl of Essex, was abandoned. He continued instead to Venice, where he met his brother Robert (c.1581–1628). Together, and using the Earl's authority to obtain credit with English merchants in Constantinople and Aleppo, they travelled to Persia to seek their fortune, though they had no official sanction for visiting the Safavid court. Nonetheless, Anthony and Robert were well received by the Shah, Abbas I, and in 1599 Anthony was sent by Abbas on a diplomatic mission to visit the courts of Europe in an attempt to build a grand alliance against the Persians' perennial enemies, the Ottomans. His brother Robert was left as a hostage in Persia. Anthony never had much success in this mission: he quarrelled with the

Persian courtier who accompanied him, and despite the assistance of Emperor Rudolph II, he never achieved much, except to accumulate vast debts. He failed to return to Persia, ending his days in Madrid in poverty.

Meanwhile Robert remained in Persia where he aided Abbas I in training and organising the Persian army. Seven years after his departure, Anthony had still sent no word back to the Persian court, but at that point the Shah decided to allow Robert to attempt another diplomatic mission to the Christian courts of Europe. Robert travelled to Krakow, Prague, Rome, Madrid, and then England. James I was sympathetic to the idea of a Persian alliance and trade pact, but the Levant Company prevented any agreement from being negotiated. Robert eventually made his way back to Persia, via India, reaching Isfahan in 1615. Abbas sent him to Spain again, where he resided until 1622, engaging in fruitless negotiations to convince Philip III to aid the Persians against the Portuguese in the Gulf of Hormuz. After further Continental travels, Robert returned to England and stayed there for four years, during which time he attempted to forge a trade agreement between England and Persia that would give the English a monopoly over the Persian silk trade. This effort was opposed and thwarted, however, by the East India and Levant Companies. Robert then returned to Persia where he died.

Each of these men literally and figuratively transgressed the boundaries of religion and nation, but those transgressions did not result in blanket condemnation. If they were seen by some as failures or traitors, they were regarded by others as adventuring heroes and models of audacious mobility. Each of them pursued a personal strategy that they hoped would release them from the old bonds and commitments of native social hierarchies. Their skills as soldiers and as negotiators enabled them to acquire new identities and new sources of patronage and authority for their projects and ambitions.

An additional commonality is that they all experienced a second life as symbolic figures: they were the objects of tremendous interest, admiration, and even celebration, in cheap print and on the London stage. Why were they celebrated, and not reviled, in these popular forms? If early modern English culture constructed English identity by simply contrasting a properly virtuous English Protestant 'self' with a variety of demonised 'others' (Spanish Catholics, Jews, Muslims, 'pagans' in the New World, and so on), then people like Stukeley, Ward, and the Sherley brothers should have been roundly and universally condemned in Protestant England for venturing beyond the Protestant pale. They would have been the bad guys against whom good English Protestants defined themselves. But this was not the case: on the contrary, as cultural figures, these men came to function as avatars of the adventuring spirit in an expansionist age. As such, they were representations of a new type for a new era – the enterprising, adaptive 'adventurer' or 'traveller' whose exploits in foreign lands brought fame and renown to England – at a time when England was merely an ambitious but marginal sea-going nation at the edge of Europe, threatened by powerful foes but empowered by the advanced technology of its ships and guns. These men travelled within the interstices of a trans-imperial network that enabled the subjects of various nations to offer their skills and knowledge to a variety of powerful patrons – popes, monarchs, sultans, and the high-ranked officials that served under those rulers in the diasporic network of early modern polities (the Dutch Republic), proto-empires (Britain, France), and established empires (Spanish-Habsburg, Portuguese, Ottoman). An epochal shift in world economic history was taking place, giving rise to the early modern world system, creating a space for a new type of ambitious historical agency that would take part in an 'oceanic turn' that produced new linkages, new markets in the Atlantic world, the Mediterranean, and beyond.

If we look at the commercial, military, and diplomatic activities that connected the British Isles to the early modern Mediterranean and beyond, as well as the cultural context of early modern London and its theatre, we will be able to see how their far-ranging engagements with other cultures and religions produced English identities that functioned, not in accordance with a binary logic of English Protestant Self and non-Protestant Other, but rather in terms of a more complex and unstable hybridity that included Englishness but went far beyond. The theatrical representation of these hybrid figures helped to produce a semiotic 'third space' between the strict enforcement of religious difference and national identity, on the one hand, and, on the other, the sense of a wider world that was often open to improvisational identity, to religious toleration and cooperation, and to cross-cultural alliances and exchanges. In fact, adaptation to, and performance of, these flexible interactivities could be rewarded with success in the form of patronage, status, and income, and even when these men failed in their overreaching (and sometimes ill-considered) enterprises, they were rewarded with a symbolic status as heroic adventurers of magnanimous ambition and courageous spirit.

My first case in point is Stukeley, who was described by both Lord Burghley and Elizabeth I as a 'rakehell'.[19] Long after his death, William

Camden described him in these terms: 'Thomas Stukely, An Englishman, a Ruffian, and a ryetous spender, and a notable boaster of himself'.[20] He was a 'shifter' who would change sides, and change religion if need be, for personal gain; and though his patrons recognised this quality, they still found him a useful military commander, expeditionary, and go-between.[21] In popular literature, he was represented as heroic if unruly. For instance, Richard Johnson's ballad 'The Life and Death of the Famous Thomas Stukely', which was printed in 1612, declares in its opening lines that he was 'A famous gallant in his dayes', and 'Deeds of wonder he hath done, / To purchase him a long and lasting praise.'[22] 'If I should tell his story', goes the next verse, 'Pride was all his glory, / And lusty Stukely he was call'd in court.'[23] Though the ballad goes on to depict him as a spendthrift and describes him as cruel to his wife, it concludes with Stukeley's declaration that 'This me greatest comfort brings, / I lived and died in love of kings.' According to the closing lines, he was given a hero's burial, and 'a stately temple, builded brave / With golden turrets piercing in the skye' was erected to mark his grave.'[24]

Two Elizabethan plays feature Stukeley as an irrepressible, blustering soldier of fortune: first he appears in a supporting role in George Peele's *The Battle of Alcazar* (composed c.1588), and then he stars in *The Famous History of the Life and Death of Captaine Thomas Stukeley* (composed 1596).[25] In *The Famous History*, Stukeley has 'a fiery spirit' (23.24), and his rival Vernon says he is 'of a boundless mind, / Undaunted spirit, and uncontrolled spleen, / Lavish as is the liquid ocean / That drops his crowns e'en as the clouds drop rain' (10.71–74). In the earlier play, Stukeley arrives in Lisbon just as the Portuguese king, Sebastian I, is mounting his ill-fated expedition to Morocco. The governor of Lisbon asks Stukeley why an Englishman would be planning to lead an attack on Ireland and receives this reply:

> Lord Governor of Lisbon, understand
> As we are Englishmen, so are we men,
> And I am Stukeley so resolved in all
> To follow rule, honour and empery,
> Not to be bent so strictly to the place
> Wherein at first I blew the fire of life,
> But that I may at liberty make choice
> Of all the continents that bounds the world.
> For why, I make it not so great desert
> To be begot or born in any place,
> Sith that's a thing of pleasure and of ease,
> That might have been performed elsewhere as well. (2.2.26–37)

The scene ends with Stukeley alone on the stage, telling the audience,

> King of a mole-hill had I rather be
> Than the richest subject of a monarchy.
> Huff it, brave mind, and never cease t'aspire,
> Before thou reign sole king of thy desire. (2.2.81–84)

But later Stukeley is persuaded to put off his ambition to become king of Ireland when Sebastian tells him that Stukeley's force is 'far too weak / To violate the Queen of Ireland's right' (2.4.100–01). According to the logic of the play, it is the containment of this aspiring spirit under Sebastian's cause that leads to Stukeley's death at the battle of Alcazar. And it was Sebastian's impracticality, including his misguided faith in the notion that God will give his army victory, that proves the neo-medieval crusade concept to be inoperable in a post-Reformation context when competing Christian powers are deeply disunited as they vie for economic power in a wider zone of cooperation, competition, and conflict made possible by the new nautical technologies. In *The Famous History*, Philip II of Spain is depicted as a duplicitous player in the geopolitical game when he encourages Sebastian's crusade but then withholds the aid he had promised in order to weaken and doom Sebastian's chivalric, pan-Christian cause. According to Lockey, 'the dramatic portrayals of Stukeley's cosmopolitan perspective tend [to constitute] a critique of early modern ideologies that saw individual identity as exclusively connected to the emerging sense of English nationhood'.[26] Lockey goes on to argue,

> The subject thus gains his identity not in the static relationship with one sovereign, but in the movement among competing authority figures, a result of Stukeley's traveling from court to court and verifying again and again his own independent self-worth. Each separate sovereign recognises in Stukeley a sovereignty over the self that gives Stukeley an independence and self-determination that seem to exist outside of one binding relationship to a centralising authority. Their recognition of his innate nobility has the effect of transforming Stukeley into something like an independent sovereign who reigns over his own person.[27]

Lockey astutely acknowledges that in both plays Stukeley's Englishness is recovered and reasserted at the moment of his death, while at the same time his downfall is 'a punishment for his transgression of the national sphere'.[28] But Lockey also argues that 'Stukeley's cosmopolitan perspective is possibly more conservative than the national perspective that we are used to seeing celebrated in contemporary history plays', because it allegedly harks back to a transnational order that predates the emergence of the nation state during the early modern period.²⁹ Nonetheless, Lockey concludes that the Stukeley plays 'challenged emerging national ideologies'.³⁰ Perhaps Lockey is only seeing part of the picture here: Stukeley's cosmopolitanism is both nostalgically conservative *and* radically, transnationally modern. In both *The Battle of Alcazar* and *The Famous History*, Stukeley expresses the desire for an autonomous will-to-power through self-sovereignty, but he also demonstrates an affiliation with the new class of mobile mercenaries who aim to game the modern commercial-maritime system.³¹

For Stukeley to forsake Protestant England and turn Catholic in the age of the Armada might be compared to the conversion of another English renegade, John Ward, who turned Turk and joined the corsair community in Tunis during a period of intensified English conflict with the Barbary corsairs. *A Christian Turned Turk* (1612) stages Ward's conversion to Islam as the central act that damns and dooms him.³² Once he converts, he follows a tragic trajectory to his death. The play concludes with Ward's suicide, a fabrication added by the playwright (since Ward lived until 1622). The 1609 sources consulted by Daborne end, not with the report of a suicide, but with a hopeful prediction that Ward would be captured and executed. While Lockey concludes that Stukeley's cosmopolitanism works to undermine his Englishness, Gerald MacLean sees Daborne's play as one that 'insists on the irreducibility and undeniability of national being'.³³ MacLean argues that in its final scene the play insistently revives Ward's Englishness when he faces death at the hands of his Muslim co-religionists, but in the pamphlet sources used by Daborne, in the ballads that mention Ward, and in the rest of the play, Ward is repeatedly represented as an aspiring spirit whose identity is not limited by English culture. For example, one pamphlet describes Ward capturing a rich prize in these terms: 'Ward having thus taken this great Argosie, and (with her and others) so inestimable riches, his minde was so inflated with pride, and puft up with vaine-glorie, that he now thought, nay did not spare to speake, he was sole and only Commander of the Seas.'³⁴ A ballad, 'The Seaman's Song of Captain Ward, the Famous Pirate of the World', condemns him because 'He feareth neither God nor Devil', and declares 'His deeds are bad, his thoughts are evil, / His only trust is still upon his sword', but at the same time celebrates the fact that Ward 'grows famous in the world now every day', and expresses awe at the great things he has achieved by force and by venturing outside Christendom into a transnational maritime environment where all nations allow him 'the title of a Lord'.[35] Another ballad, 'The Famous Sea-Fight Between Captain Ward and the *Rainbow*', claims that 'There has not been such a rover found out this thousand year', and reports that Ward sent word to the king of England, 'go tell him thus from me, / If he reign King of all the land, I will reign King at sea.'[36] In the early scenes of Daborne's play, Ward establishes his identity as unbounded when he announces, 'That men call home / Which gives them means equal unto their minds, / Puts them in action' (1.37–38). Later, while in command of a piratical attack he asserts,

> The sway of things
> Belongs to him dares most. Such should be kings,
> And such am I. What Nature in my birth
> Denied me, Fortune supplies. This maxim I hold:
> He lives a slave that lives to be controlled. (3.83–87)

These are examples of how Ward's popular image and identity were not defined within English bounds, and even if Daborne created a false death and defeat for Ward at the end of the play, that was a sop to the censors. Many audience members would have known that Ward was still prospering in Tunis even as his death was enacted on stage in London.[37] As Fuchs puts it, 'pirate plays thematise the representation of national allegiance, they serve to chart social anxieties about the fidelity of piratical subjects, and their potential for destabilising the consolidation of an English nation.'[38] MacLean is obviously correct in saying that *A Christian Turned Turk* 'demonises the desire to convert to Islam', but perhaps he is reductive in his interpretation when he suggests that Daborne's play teaches 'that it is impossible for a native-born Englishman to forswear his national identity'.[39] Rather, Daborne's drama provides a highly ambivalent picture of Ward as a noble anti-hero who succeeds in escaping from his lot as a common sailor to reinvent himself as a rogue cosmopolitan and the 'sole and only Commander of the Seas'.[40]

MacLean argues that nationality is performative in the same way that (according to Judith Butler) gender and sex are performative, and he describes English travellers in the Ottoman Empire in this manner: 'to be English among the Ottomans was not only to be from somewhere else, but also to embark upon representing oneself, in historical actions and written accounts, as an imperial agent helping to run a global empire'.[41] This may be true for some of the travellers who represented themselves in autobiographical writings, but mobile renegades like Stukeley, Ward, and the Sherley brothers were not 'disoriented' or 'Othered' by their experiences in 'the East'. Rather, they were empowered by the opportunities that the global system provided to 'trans-imperial subjects'. In his suicide speech, Ward claims that he has shown his Muslim patrons 'the way to conquer Europe' (16.301), an allusion to the way that mercenaries like Stukeley and Ward placed their knowledge of the latest military and nautical technologies at the disposal of their patrons. The same may be said of the Sherley brothers, who also plied the trade of mobile mercenary in transformative ways that left any stable or essentialised English identity far behind.

As Anthony Parr has shown, a 'Sherley myth was built up by a series of publications in the early seventeenth century, ranging from firsthand accounts of the brothers' later travels (including autobiography) to a stage play about their adventures'.[42] Their exploits were described in Samuel Purchas's collection of travel narratives, and Purchas himself praised them with these words:

> Amongst our English Travellers, I know not whether any have merited more respect than the Honorable, I had almost said Heroike Gentlemen, Sir Anthony & Sir Robert Sherleys. And if the Argonauts of old, and Graecian Worthies, were worthily reputed Heroicall for Europaean exploits in Asia: what may we thinke of the Sherley-Brethren, which not from the nearer Graecian shoares, but from beyond the Europaean World ... have not coasted a little way (as did those) but pierced the very bowels of the Asian Seas and Lands, unto the Persian centre.[43]

The Travels of the Three English Brothers, a 1607 play by John Day, William Rowley, and George Wilkins, dramatises the careers of these three mercenaries and turncoats, not as a tragic cautionary tale, but as an episodic adventure play that serves to promote their reputation for bold action and heroic mobility.[44] Though Anthony and Robert turn Catholic and serve Catholic and Muslim princes, the play does not condemn this in any way.[45] Instead the play ends more or less happily with a celebration of their achievements. Fame appears and presents a tableau that magically brings together the three brothers after they have been separated for so many years (Robert in Persia, Anthony in Spain, and Thomas in England). The stage directions read, 'Fame *gives to each a prospective glass: they seem to see one another and offer to embrace, at which* Fame *parts them, and so exeunt all except* Fame.'[46] The price of Fame here is a physical separation of the family, but their mobility is then lauded as the means to achieve 'honors,' 'worth', and 'merit' (Epilogue, 19–21).

Much of the play's action takes place in Persia, where Anthony and Robert impress the Sophy with their demonstration of the latest artillery. Before showing him what their guns can do, Anthony tells the Sophy,

> Yet have we engines of more force than these.
> When our o'er-heated bloods would massacre
> We can lay cities level with the pavement,
> Bandy up towers and turrets in the air
> And on the seas o'erwhelm an argosy. (1.111–15)

The Sophy's response indicates, in an exaggerated manner, the power of English military technology to impress and awe even the ruler of the Persian Empire:

> Those tongues do imitate the voice of heaven
> When the gods speak in thunder; your honours
> And your qualities of war more than human.
> If thou hast godhead, and disguised art come
> To teach us unknown rudiments of war,
> Tell us they precepts and we'll adore thee. (1.122–27)

After the artillery demonstration, Anthony and Robert go on to aid the Sophy in his war against the Ottomans, and later they assist him in a diplomatic mission to create an alliance with Christendom against the Turks. Meanwhile, Thomas is taken prisoner by the Turks and shows great courage under torture, refusing to convert to Islam even though he is told that his conversion would mean release from prison. The last few scenes of the play, including one in which the Sophy stands godfather at the christening of Robert's child, emphasise the Christian identity of the brothers, in contrast to the Turkish Muslims and 'pagan' Persians. This appeal to a Christian cosmopolitanism elides the differences between Protestants and Catholics and represses the issue of conflict between Christians while promoting the careers of 'English brothers', whose English identity is not necessarily a Protestant one, and who would sell their military skills to Spain or Persia.[47]

The way that the exploits of these five transgressive anti-heroes were brought from life to stage demonstrates the viability of an identity that was not constrained by the borders of the nation, or determined by a binary self-other dynamic. Rather, they express a shockingly flexible kind of English identity abroad that was predicated on mobility and on a transferable knowledge of maritime and military technology. In the plays that feature them as protagonists, Ward and Stukeley both die tragically, and in their final speeches the value of their deaths is measured by their reversion to an English identity, but it is one that has been altered by their unruly cosmopolitanism. They both endorse a crusading Christianity and a recovered Englishness as they deliver their dying speeches to audiences in London. *The Travels of the Three English Brothers* also gestures towards home and family in its abrupt conclusion, one in which the brothers, still separated by vast spaces, are able to view each other. Anthony is shown in Spain, Thomas in England, and Robert in Persia: they are divided from each other but share in the favour of Fame. Fame's final words to the audience serve to dismiss concerns about the Sherleys' mercenary ties to foreign princes: 'Since they in all places have found favourites, / We make no doubt of you: 'twere too hard doom / To let them want your liking here at home' (Epilogue, 32–34).

What these plays offered to their London audiences was a new and exciting sense that English subjects could (and had) left their homes behind to become globe-trotting anti-heroes who could, paradoxically, both exceed their English identities and affirm them. At a time when many people still required a passport to leave their home parish, the mobility of these cosmopolitan champions who journeyed so far beyond the pale of their homeland was presented as a model for both admiration and trepidation. The transgressive accomplishments and vaulting ambition of these figures elicited, in the theatre at least, a profoundly ambivalent response to those who went beyond national attachments and domestic prejudices to become mercenary citizens of the world. What these rogue travel plays demonstrate is the construction and celebration of a versatile English identity that resists erasure; and yet, at the same time, a potentially unruly English identity that was delineated within a complex and shifting cultural mixture brought on by capital and empire and their fundamental need for violence. These mobile English agents took up new roles and new identities as exporters of English techno-violence. In general, early modern English travel plays attempt to have it both ways when they offer the exciting spectacle of cultural difference while also protecting and defining a certain English spirit or essence. Like other examples of early modern travel drama, the three plays discussed here performed important cultural work by displaying the place of English and Christian identities in the world beyond England. That 'world' had recently changed in ways that were transforming English society, and especially London. Offering the thrilling spectacle of a violence that moved across land and sea, between empires and religions, rogue travel plays test the limits of Englishness and its affiliation with foreign and non-Christian powers. In the case of the Sherley brothers, these mercenary cosmopolitans are represented as admirable travellers who shift loyalties and consequently endure various ordeals but in the end remain acceptable and laudable models. By contrast, in the cases

of Ward and Stukeley, religious conversions to Islam or alliances with
foreign Catholicism are depicted as problematic – as a bridge too far.
These choices lead to tragedy and death. But there is some consolation:
Ward and Stukeley are both shown to experience tragic anagnorisis, in
which they come to know that – for the sake of love, lucre, and personal
glory – they have strayed too far from English identity and so must pay
with their lives. It was the function of early modern English travel drama
to perform this kind of cultural work: testing and modeling for London
audiences a variety of behaviours and interactions with foreign peoples
and powers. These included cosmopolitan roles that would enjoy a long
history in the interstices of the British Empire, but were only just beginning during the Elizabethan and Jacobean periods.

What began as rogue cosmopolitanism would open the way for an
imperial, managerial cosmopolitanism to come. These five mercenary
anti-heroes are 'cosmopolitan' in a way that gestures towards a global
future, but that future is not one of perpetual peace. After all, they were
unruly rogues and mercenaries, not men of peace. The imperial desire
that brought spectators to cheer on their exploits on the world stage
would be fulfilled as English colonial and commercial power spread.
Today, we are still contending with the fulfilment of that imperial expansion in its current form, late capitalism, which manifests itself today
under the auspices of a truly global empire of mass exploitation, warfare,
and suffering. But still, hope, in the form of a critical cosmopolitanism,
lies in the corner of that Pandora's box first opened by early modern capitalism. Our hope lies in a resistance to managerial cosmopolitanism, and
in a peaceful revolution led by global citizens and anti-capitalist rogues
who oppose both the local and transnational forms of corrupt neoliberal
power. For today it is neoliberal power, wielded by the managerial cosmopolitans of the 1%, that carries on the permanent war begun in early
modernity.

Notes

1 For a discussion of the history of cosmopolitanism, see Eduardo Mendieta,
   'From Imperial to Dialogical Cosmopolitanism', *Ethics & Global Politics* 2,
   no. 3 (2009), 241–58.
2 Alison Games, *The Web of Empire: English Cosmopolitans in an Age of
   Expansion, 1560–1660* (Oxford University Press, 2009), 14.
3 See Jan Glete, *Warfare at Sea, 1500–1650: Maritime Conflicts and the
   Transformation of Europe* (New York: Routledge, 1999); and Nicholas A. M.
   Rodger, 'The Development of Broadside Gunnery, 1450–1650', *Mariner's
   Mirror* 82, no. 3 (1996), 301–24.

4 See 'Permanent War' in Retort, *Afflicted Powers: Capital and Spectacle in a New Age of War* (London: Verso, 2006), 78–107.

5 Ibid., 79.

6 Paul Virilio, *Speed and Politics*, trans. Mark Polizzotti (Los Angeles: Semiotext(e), 2006), 78.

7 Glete, *Warfare*, 2.

8 Ibid.

9 For a detailed study of the increasing importance of mercenaries (and their ties to the new capitalist economy) in land-based wars, see David Parrott, *The Business of War: Military Enterprise and Military Revolution in Early Modern Europe* (Cambridge University Press, 2012).

10 Barbara Fuchs, *Mimesis and Empire: The New World, Islam, and European Identities* (Cambridge University Press, 2001), 51.

11 Brian Lockey, *Early Modern Catholics, Royalists, and Cosmopolitans: English Transnationalism and the Christian Commonwealth* (Burlington, VT: Ashgate, 2015), 3.

12 Ibid., 7.

13 Ibid., 15.

14 See Franklin L. Baumer, 'England, the Turk, and the Common Corps of Christendom', *American Historical Review* 50, no. 1 (Oct. 1944), 26–48.

15 See E. Natalie Rothman, *Brokering Empire: Trans-Imperial Subjects Between Venice and Istanbul* (Ithaca, NY: Cornell University Press, 2014).

16 For a thorough description of this class of people, their interactions with rulers, and their role in the emergence of the modern nation state, see Janice E. Thomson, *Mercenaries, Pirates, and Sovereigns: State-Building and Extraterritorial Violence in Early Modern Europe* (Princeton University Press, 1994).

17 For more detailed biographical information on Stukeley, see Charles Edelman's introduction to his edition of *The Stukeley Plays* (Manchester University Press, 2005); and Juan E. Tazon, *The Life and Times of Thomas Stukeley, 1525–1578* (Burlington, VT: Ashgate, 2003).

18 For an account of the Sherley brothers and their adventures, see Anthony Parr's introduction to *Three Renaissance Travel Plays* (Manchester University Press, 1995), 7–19; see also the longer but less reliable study by D. W. Davies, *Elizabethans Errant: The Strange Fortunes of Sir Thomas Sherley and His Three Sons* (Ithaca, NY: Cornell University Press, 1967).

19 See Tazon, *The Life and Times*, 14–15.

20 Camden, *The Historie of the Life and Reigne of the most Renowmed and Victorious Princesse Elizabeth* (London: 1630), Book 1, 61–62.

21 See Tazon, *The Life and Times*, 140–41.

22 This ballad was published in Richard Johnson, *A Crowne-Garland of Golden Roses: Gathered Out of England's Royall Garden* (London: 1612). It was reprinted in *The Crown Garden of Golden Roses*, ed. W. Chappell (London: Percy Society, 1842), 33–38.

23 Chappell, ed. *The Crown Garden*, 33.

24 Ibid., 38.

25 All further quotations are taken from the Edelman edition of *The Stukeley Plays* and will be cited by act, scene, and line numbers within the text.

26 Lockey, *Early Modern Catholics*, 10. According to Lockey, 'identities that were not moored stably to some national identity posed a serious challenge to sovereigns of the period. The fictional Stukeley can navigate the transnational sphere precisely because his national identity is never in question. Thus his cosmopolitan identity is intimately tied to his national identity' (27).

27 Ibid., 29.

28 Ibid.

29 Ibid., 30.

30 Ibid., 32.

31 For additional discussion of Stukeley's career and his political significance on the stage, see Claire Jowitt, *The Culture of Piracy, 1580–1630: English Literature and Seaborne Crime* (Farnham, Surrey: Ashgate, 2010), 111–36, and her *Voyage Drama and Gender Politics, 1589–1642: Real and Imagined Worlds* (Manchester University Press, 2003), 61–103.

32 All quotations from Daborne's *A Christian Turned Turk* are taken from *Three Turk Plays from Early Modern England*, ed. Daniel Vitkus, and will be cited by act, scene, and line numbers in the text.

33 Gerald MacLean, *Looking East: English Writing and the Ottoman Empire Before 1800* (New York: Palgrave Macmillan, 2007), 144.

34 Andrew Barker, *A True and Certaine Report of ... the Estate of Captaine Ward and Danseker* (London: 1609), 82.

35 Vitkus, *Three Turk Plays*, 345–47.

36 Ibid., 351–52.

37 The sense of this ending, including its perception by the audience, is usefully discussed by Greg Bak in *Barbary Pirate: The Life and Crimes of John Ward, the Most Infamous Privateer of His Time* (Stroud, Gloucestershire: History Press, 2013).

38 Fuchs, *Mimesis and Empire*, 49.

39 MacLean, *Looking East*, 123.

40 Barker, *A True and Certaine Report*, 82.

41 MacLean, *Looking East*, 102.

42 Anthony Parr, 'Foreign Relations in Jacobean England: The Sherley Brothers and the "the voyage of Persia"', in *Travel and Drama in Shakespeare's Time*, ed. Jean-Pierre Maquerlot and Michèle Willems (Cambridge University Press, 1996), 15.

43 Purchas, *Purchas His Pilgrimes*, vol. I, 374.

44 See Thomas Middleton's pamphlet written to promote Robert Sherley's mission to the Jacobean court: *Sir Robert Sherley ... His Entertainment in Cracovia*, in *The Collected Works of Thomas Middleton*, ed. Gary Taylor and John Lavagnino (Oxford University Press, 2007), 670–78.

45 On the Sherley brothers' intervention in the Shiite–Sunni tensions in Safavid Persia, see Chloë Houston, '"Thou glorious kingdome, thou chiefe of Empires": Persia in Early Seventeenth-Century Travel Literature', *Studies*

in Travel Writing 13, no. 2 (2009), 141–52. On the conspicuous lack of condemnation of travelling characters on the early modern stage, see David McInnis, 'Travelling Characters in Early Modern Drama', Chapter 10 in this volume.

46 John Day, William Rowley, and George Wilkins, *The Travels of the Three English Brothers*, in *Three Renaissance Travel Plays*, ed. Parr, Epilogue, 13–14. All further quotations will be from this edition and cited by act, scene, and line numbers within the text.

47 Thus the play is compatible with the ecumenical, pacifist policies of James I, and his hostile attitude to the Ottoman Turks. See W. B. Patterson, *King James VI and I and the Reunion of Christendom* (Cambridge University Press, 2000).

CHAPTER 8

Drama at Sea: A New Look at Shakespeare on the Dragon, 1607-08

Richmond Barbour

Oregon State University

Bernhard Klein

University of Kent

The third voyage of the East India Company (EIC), 1607–10, has long claimed the attention of critics – not, however, for its historic status as the first English sea voyage to reach India, but for the possibility that its crewmen made the first stagings of Shakespeare outside Europe. References to three shipboard performances of Shakespeare plays in west and east African waters – twice of *Hamlet*, once of *Richard II* – appeared in the nineteenth century, in two separate locations, each time offered as verbatim extracts from the long-lost logbook of the expedition's flagship, the *Dragon* (aka *Red Dragon*). This unusual conjunction of theatre, travel, and maritime initiative has sparked critical debates over the authenticity of the nineteenth-century references and over the status of these putative stagings in relation to London's theatres and Britain's early imperial endeavours. Scholars who have commented on these passages fall roughly into three camps: the first arguing that the references are forgeries; the second assuming that they are genuine; and the third claiming that they can be neither verified as authentic nor discredited as a hoax. Critics in the first camp tend to discuss only the credibility of the references; critics in the other two camps often speculate at length about the potential cultural and historical meanings of the stagings.

Our purpose in revisiting these sources, the contexts in which they occur, and the debate which they have initiated, is twofold. First, we wish to suggest that in the absence of any conclusive proof that the nineteenth-century transcriptions are either forged or genuine, any historical effort invested in recreating their likely significance is so conjectural as to border on the irresponsible. Second, we wish to draw attention to what we see as the real and far more important element of theatricality embedded in these sources: the performative aspect of the voyage itself, especially as regards the performativity of the cultural encounter – a central aspect of the *Dragon* stagings as discussed in current scholarship. The debate over '*Hamlet* at Sea', as we see it, has so far been largely driven by the apparently indelible need of critics to affirm the cultural centrality of Shakespeare, not by the attempt to make historical sense of 'drama at sea'. The result has been that a few disputed lines from obscure nineteenth-century sources have taken on a force of their own that is distractive rather than helpful. In attempting to take this debate in a new direction sensitive to the full range of dramatic energies integral to voyaging, we will first summarise briefly the key arguments that have been advanced by critics in the three camps outlined above, then sketch out the various forms and meanings of early modern shipboard theatricality, and finally consider the third voyage as a historic example of an inherently performative practice.

The Critical Debate

The two nineteenth-century transcriptions from the *Dragon*'s logbook were published in 1825 by one 'Ambrose Gunthio', known as the author of three short prose pieces in contemporary magazines and anthologies but a complete mystery otherwise,[1] and in 1849 by Thomas Rundall, an EIC archivist and council member of the Hakluyt Society.[2] Gunthio's references first came to the attention of Shakespeare scholars in 1951,[3] those of Rundall probably in 1865.[4] The logbook ostensibly cited on both occasions was that of William Keeling, commander of the third EIC voyage and captain of the *Dragon*, whose journal was catalogued as missing in 1822, except for its first page, which is still preserved in the British Library.[5] Neither Gunthio nor Rundall gives an exact source for the quotations or states whether he had access to the original logbook or perhaps to a contemporary transcript.

The two sources have often been quoted but we provide their pertinent wording here for ease of reference. In the 1825 extracts published by Gunthio, Keeling notes that on 5 September 1607, while at anchor in Sierra Leone, 'we had ['gave' in 1849] the TRAGEDY OF HAMLET'; that on 29 September 1607 ['30 September' in 1849], while on the open sea in the south Atlantic, 'my company ["companions" in 1849] acted KING RICHARD THE SECOND'; and that on 31 March 1608 ['31 September 1607 [*sic*]' in 1849],[6] just before crossing the equator in the Indian Ocean, 'I ... had HAMLET acted

aboord me, which I permit, to keepe my people from idleness and unlaw-
ful games, or sleep.'⁷ All performances are described as occurring on the
Dragon, and none on the second English ship present in Sierra Leone in
1607, the *Hector*, captained by William Hawkins.

The hypothesis that these entries were forged was first formulated in
1898 by Sidney Lee,⁸ who followed Clements R. Markham in identifying
(erroneously) an anonymous *Hector* journal held at the India Office as
Keeling's original logbook and Rundall's probable source.⁹ That the journal was missing several leaves, including those that should have contained
the Shakespeare references, fuelled suspicions of foul play in both men
(Markham assuming a 'robbery'¹⁰ must have taken place after Rundall
had consulted the journal, Lee seeing a forger at work). The accusation
of forgery was revived in 1950, when Sydney Race proposed John Payne
Collier as the culprit, claiming, mistakenly, that Lee had already made
that connection.¹¹ When G. Blakemore Evans produced the Gunthio
extracts shortly afterwards in 1951, the discovery of a second transcript
invited the possibility that both Gunthio and Rundall had independently
copied a common source.¹² But then Race noted that Collier had access
to the Duke of Devonshire's library, where Gunthio says he found a copy
of the first quarto (Q1) of *Hamlet*, and that Collier and Rundall over-
lapped as members of the Hakluyt Society.¹³ These links could suggest
that Collier was Gunthio and that he handed an altered version of the
references to Rundall, a transmission that offers a possible explanation for
the discrepancies between the two sources, which include differences in
dates, spelling, the form of contractions, and lexical choice.¹⁴

The most recent advocate of the forgery hypothesis, the late Bernice
Kliman,¹⁵ again offers Collier as the culprit, even though Collier scholars now largely agree that the notorious forger cannot be blamed for
duping Rundall: in their definitive 2004 study, Arthur and Janet Ing
Freeman cite the Keeling entries in an appendix on 'Red Herrings'.¹⁶ Key
to Kliman's argument is the comparison between Gunthio and Collier
as Shakespeare scholars. In his 1952 essay, Evans had pointed out clear
differences between the two in their remarks on Q1 *Hamlet*,¹⁷ which
Kliman now disputes, claiming that Gunthio's views anticipate rather
than contradict Collier's.¹⁸ Such internal evidence may be persuasive or
not but cannot ultimately prove a forgery, and Kliman concedes that her
argument relies on 'reasoned conjecture', not demonstrable proof.¹⁹

The first elaborate defence of the Keeling passages as authentic records
came in 1923 from Frederick Boas, who based his case on linguistic
similarities between the Rundall extracts and the abridged Keeling

logbook published by Samuel Purchas, on the contextualisation of the Sierra Leone entries with passages from other journals kept on the same voyage, and on the general familiarity of English mariners with the tradition of stage plays.[20] Nailing his imperial colours to the mast, Boas praises the merchant navy for 'carrying Shakespearean drama into the uttermost parts of the earth',[21] and his work was cited approvingly by E. K. Chambers, who also accepted the Keeling entries as genuine and included them in his standard reference work on surviving records related to Shakespeare, published in 1930.[22] From then on, with the exception of Race and Kliman, most scholars have considered the stagings as historical fact, without always taking note of the detail. A historian of the EIC, for example, described in 1991 how the crew of the *Dragon* 'perversely rehearsed for *Richard II*'[23] while at anchor off Socotra in April 1608, ignoring that the relevant play mentioned in the entries is *Hamlet*, the date March 1608, and the location the open sea.

In 2001, in the first major research article on the Keeling entries by a Shakespearean scholar since 1923, Gary Taylor follows Boas's lead, though he distances himself from the latter's pro-imperial sentiment, arguing instead that the *Hamlet* staging off the African coast represents a 'moment of civilized multicultural exchange'.[24] Taylor no longer spends any time defending the entries as genuine. Instead, he inserts them silently into the extracts from Purchas that preface his chapter before imagining the on-board staging of *Hamlet* as a full blown performance in every manner similar to a show at the Globe, to the point at which 'Keeling's men' come to rival the 'King's Men'.[25] No evidence is cited that would make such a comparison plausible, apart from some perceptive analogies between theatres and ships.[26] More worryingly, perhaps, in speculating about the local reception of *Hamlet*, Taylor treats sixteenth-century ethnographic writings about Sierra Leone by Portuguese Jesuits as robust sources yielding accurate and reliable insights into African audience responses in 1607.[27]

Taylor's account of the local circumstances in Sierra Leone is largely based on research by the eminent historian of West Africa, Paul Hair. In a 1978 essay on the English visit to Sierra Leone in 1607, Hair is perhaps the first scholar involved in the debate about the Keeling entries who abstains from expressing a direct view on their authenticity, choosing instead to 'show that the African physical and social circumstances were such that *Hamlet* might reasonably have been presented in them'.[28] Hair's work, in this essay and many others,[29] remains unsurpassed in setting out the historical context of the Keeling expedition in Sierra Leone.

His position not to pronounce on the veracity of the entries is in keeping with the aims of his essay, since his historical reconstruction does not depend on the stagings having actually taken place. In this, his work differs from that of several other critics who also opt out of expressing a view on the sources. For example, in a 1997 essay on Indian adaptations of Shakespeare, Ania Loomba initially frames the stagings as 'the moment when Shakespeare first travelled to India', thus giving them the appearance of fact, only to contradict that claim immediately by stating that she is not concerned with 'the "truth" status of Keeling's journal entries'.[30] Loomba then focuses on the debate itself, not its subject matter, by showing how both sceptics and advocates of the stagings have colluded in class prejudice by denying the common English mariner a proper role in Shakespearean performance history (a 'crew of rude sailors', Race asserted in 1950, *pace* Boas, would surely not have been able to put on 'two of Shakespeare's most difficult plays',[31] and Foster concurred in the same year, while still defending the entries as genuine).[32]

In a 2014 study, Graham Holderness agrees with Loomba in arguing that the debate about the entries has by now become part of their history, irrespective of whether they are based in fact or not.[33] His alternative contribution is a critical-creative response to the archival record that takes the form of a further journal, written by a fictional young factor on the *Dragon*, in which Keeling strategically deploys Shakespeare to unsettle the political constellation in Sierra Leone and turn a 'regime' once hostile to the English into a friendly trading partner.[34] Holderness deliberately conflates the Sierra Leone visit with the Essex rebellion by showing that the crew staged *Richard II* rather than *Hamlet* in front of their African audience – an event which certainly did not happen, even if the entries are genuine, since *Richard II* would have been performed on the open sea without any locals in attendance. The ploy makes the Keeling entries foundational to the historical fiction, despite the initial declaration that the nineteenth-century sources cannot be authenticated, and imposes a bracingly Anglo-centric fantasy on Sierra Leone, where Shakespeare's drama of deposition initiates the *coup d'état* it failed to catalyse at home.

This brief survey of the debate over 'Shakespeare at sea' demonstrates that if critics do not reject the Keeling entries outright, as Kliman does, they tend to use the episode to advance weighty arguments about class, race, nation, or empire, all of which require as a first critical move the acceptance of the entries as genuine or at least probable sources. Yet the same critics (with the exception of Taylor, who thinks the veracity of the stagings is beyond doubt)[35] agree that in the absence of Keeling's original manuscript, or at least a reliable transcript, there is no way of knowing whether or not the entries are authentic. The paradox is obvious: how can the stagings be simultaneously accepted as unverified *and* discussed as having significant cultural impact? A 2009 essay by Patricia Akhimie is a case in point: while she calls the 1607 *Hamlet* performance 'largely unsubstantiated' and 'possibly apocryphal', she still proceeds to treat the references as reliable historical sources and compares the stagings to other moments of cross-cultural entertainment recorded by Purchas.[36]

In this essay we align ourselves with those critics who agree that it is currently impossible either to accept or reject the entries, yet we also wish to ensure that this indeterminacy is fully reflected in our treatment of the existing evidence. We prefer, that is, to focus not on what is most doubtful, but on what we actually know about the voyage to which these stagings have been linked. In the next section the essay offers a short survey of references to shipboard theatricals in other sources (English and Iberian) as a way of contextualising the subject matter of the Keeling entries, before approaching the topic of 'drama at sea' on the basis of the extant record of the third voyage as it has survived in the archive.

Forms of Shipboard Theatricality

The case for scepticism about the Shakespeare stagings on the *Dragon* rests not on their implausibility but on their improbability, given the historical specifics of the episode. The most eloquent recent defender of the performances, Gary Taylor, cites as perhaps his strongest argument in favour of the entries that the English visitors needed to honour local dignitaries with appropriate forms of entertainment.[37] If the shipboard performance of *Hamlet* on 5 September 1607 served that function, as it may well have done (though this would only explain the first, not the second and third stagings), the absence of any references to the on-board playacting in all of the extant merchants' journals – two of which have very full entries for the days around the Sierra Leone *Hamlet*[38] – cannot simply be glossed over.

Explanations of this silence include Boas's (not very plausible) suggestion that merchants were interested in transacting business, not in acting plays;[39] and Barbour's point that the company would probably have frowned on staging plays at sea in the same way that they prohibited 'diceing and other unlawfull games'.[40] Keeling may have been the only member of the expedition with the necessary authority – and the track record of facing up to the company's directors – to defend playacting in an official journal, which had to be submitted to principal shareholders at the close of the voyage. The counter case would rest on the argument that a theatrical performance put on in order to improve relations between locals and visitors – a crucial precondition for successful trade – should have been a noteworthy event especially for merchants, given their otherwise well-documented curiosity about potential new trading partners. Another third voyage journalist, for instance, sailing on the fleet's third ship, the *Consent*, with whom contact was lost shortly after the beginning of the voyage, duly documented a successful cross-cultural performance in the Moluccas: after dinner and 'great cheare' with the king of Buttone, crewmen of the *Consent* 'danced before him, who was well pleased, both at their dauncing and musique: at night the Kings Vnckle sent our Captaine foure fat Hogges'.[41] As this example suggests, it was part of the merchants' brief to report on aspects of the local culture that might be helpful to later English visitors (such as, perhaps, the favourable disposition towards scripted stage plays on the West African coast).

Allusions to dramatic activity were certainly not absent from journals or logs kept on English ships.[42] For example, there are two undisputed references to a 'play' on the sixth voyage of the EIC, 18 June 1610, outbound off West Africa: 'My generall invited me to dinner and to [a] play,' writes the *Peppercorn*'s captain Nicholas Downton, and the reference is corroborated by another mariner, Thomas Love, transferring onto the *Peppercorn* from the *Trades Increase*: 'we had a great feast and a play playd.'[43] The comments are intriguing and echo the Keeling entries by placing the 'play' in the context of a 'feast' or 'dinner'. Yet in both cases the 'play' in question has neither title nor author and could reference a variety of ludic practices ranging from background entertainment to mimed shows, staged readings, extempore retellings, even card-playing or perhaps dancing.[44]

A fragment from what looks like a more conventional theatrical script does make an appearance in the context of the sixth EIC voyage (1610–13): the last page of the journal by the merchant Benjamin Greene holds the dramatis personae and opening lines of a play.[45] But again the evidence is inconclusive, for the page may have been added to the journal at a later stage.[46] Certainly, if there was dramatic activity on both the *Dragon* and the *Trades Increase*, the continuity of personnel would strengthen the case: when the *Dragon* reached Plymouth in September 1609, its navigator home from Bantam, Matthew Mollineux, shipped out on the *Trades Increase* as the 'Pilot Major' of the sixth voyage, and he was not the only *Dragon* mariner to do so.[47] Supposing the Keeling entries to be genuine, crewmen could have reintroduced pastimes they had pursued at sea before.

In 1632, Walter Mountfort actually wrote a whole play, *The Launching of the Mary*,[48] on board a company ship, and an even more striking instance of drama at sea was reported by the English Dominican Thomas Gage, while travelling to Veracruz on a Spanish ship in 1625. On 4 August that year, the Dominicans aboard the *S. Anthony* 'had prepared a Comedy out of famous *Lope de Vega*, to be acted by some Souldiers, Passengers and some of the younger sort of Fryers; which I confesse was as stately acted and set forth both in shewes and good apparell, in that narrow compasse of our ship, as might have been upon the best stage in the Court of *Madrid*'.[49] Henrique Dias made a similar comparison in his account of the shipwreck of the Portuguese vessel *S. Paulo*. On the evening of 25 December 1560, off Cape Comorin, at the southernmost point of the subcontinent, a short nativity play was given 'on the deck, with torches, so well acted and with such good characters and props, as it might have been in the middle of Lisbon' ['de noite houve um auto na tolda, com tochas, tão bem representado e de tão boas figuras e aparatos, como o pudera ser dentro em Lisboa'].[50] There are further references in the Portuguese records to religious plays or ceremonies acted out around Easter time and on Corpus Christi Day on the *S. Bárbara* in 1574, the *S. Francisco* in 1583, and the *Santiago* in 1585.[51] One source also mentions an actor or comedian aboard the *S. Filipe* in 1563, whose irreverent activities caused some enraged Jesuits to intervene.[52]

These Iberian examples offer a useful contrast to the English case. While references to music, storytelling, and elaborate mockery as common pastimes on the *Carreira da India* have been noted as early as the Pedro Álvares Cabral expedition in 1500, scripted drama on Portuguese ships appears to have been purely religious in purpose. As in the Spanish performance reported by Gage, such plays were also usually staged by travelling missionaries or other passengers, often soldiers, not by crewmen. Performances of scripted drama, in other words, were calendar rites that served didactic and religious purposes, reminding common sailors of their moral and spiritual responsibilities on foreign shores. Such top-down discipline differed sharply from what Keeling may have had in mind in permitting his men (if he did so) to stage plays as a counter-measure against idleness, games of chance, and sleep.

With their references to individually titled, secular plays, the Keeling entries are thus tantalising in their suggestiveness, yet it is precisely this specificity which raises doubts over the likelihood of such comments being noted in an early company logbook, at a time when Shakespeare's plays had not yet become the widely recognisable literary works they are today. They certainly have no parallel elsewhere, as far as we know. It is also worth noting in this context that in Keeling's other logbook, written during his subsequent voyage to the East, 1615–17, which survives in full and contains many detailed observations on the social dynamics of shipboard life (unusually for company logbooks from that period),[53] no mention is made of any scripted stage plays, and no playacting occurs other than ritual celebrations in the widest sense.

Maritime ethnologists have argued that sailors still today possess a fundamentally oral culture.[54] Books were rarely (if ever) absent from ships even in the sixteenth and seventeenth centuries, and we know from Purchas that the *Dragon* was carrying an on-board library which contained at least the three volumes comprising 'M. *Hackluits* books of Voyages'.[55] But such records as survive about the contents of similar libraries suggest that their main purpose was spiritual edification, not the appreciation of secular writing: devotional literature almost always came top of the list (as on the EIC's eighth voyage, for instance),[56] followed by nautical, technical, and historical writing, while romantic tales, drama, and poetry were much rarer items.[57]

For sailors, the experience of 'reading' would have most likely constituted a collective experience on board, with a single reader surrounded by a still largely illiterate audience.[58] The act of communal reading or the telling of stories may indeed be the closest we get to any 'literary' theatre happening on English ships. As for shipboard theatricality in the wider sense, our most appropriate conceptual framework is probably the function of drama in the routine execution of maritime labour and the many theatrical aspects of shipboard life, not fully scripted plays acted out in the well of a ship. Maritime theatrical practices include, for example, such rituals as equatorial baptism or the choreographing of manual labour in rhythm, dance, song, and instrumental music, and they shape life and social interaction on board in countless other ways. Indeed, the performative character of voyaging by sea could be considered a constitutive aspect of the maritime experience – especially, as we shall now explore, in the instance of the cultural encounter.

Performing the Cultural Encounter

The published testimony of the EIC's historic third voyage now equips scholars to examine its distinctive cultures of showmanship more holistically than those fastening on Shakespeare's possible part in it have attempted. In 1625, Purchas redacted journals by Keeling, the merchant William Finch, and Captain David Middleton of the *Consent*. Markham edited Hawkins's logbook in 1878. The other extant manuscripts, by the merchants Anthony Marlowe, Francis Bucke, an anonymous writer, and both John Hearne and Finch, and an early digest of Keeling's vanished journal, formerly available only in excerpts or abstracts, were recently edited by Barbour as *The Third Voyage Journals* (2009). Initially drawn to them as plausible lenses on an incipiently transnational Shakespeare, Barbour suggested that the journals deserve publication for articulating wider concerns of great consequence: 'the defining predicaments of proto-imperial capitalism as it went global from England'.[59] This essay maintains that the Keeling expedition rewards attention with or without *Hamlet* and *Richard II*, and turns now to three representative scenes of intercultural theatre verifiably documented on the expedition. The EIC's commissions enjoined mariners, when seeking water and other supplies ashore, to behave civilly and 'procure ... ffreindshipp'[60] if they could. Showmanship – as Anthony Parr puts it, 'turning diplomacy into a theatrical rite'[61] – was vital to the process.

One instance of high drama in the service of intercultural exchange is made prominent by all the English merchants whose journals contain entries for the final days of August in 1607. On the morning of 30 August, six days before the alleged first performance of *Hamlet*, while still at anchor in Sierra Leone, captains Keeling and Hawkins were alerted by 'a tumult raysed ashoare' and went on land together, finding there 'manney negers come downe wth dartes, bowes & arrowes, whoe had brought downe *eleaven stickes* wth intent theirby to express their meaning'. Considerable confusion ensued, for 'wee being ignorante of theire Langeage, wch all the morning could not be understod'. Later in the day, the matter was cleared up: several English sailors had stolen a number of household items from a nearby African village (six brass basins and some cotton cloth), and the eleven sticks signified the number of missing items. Why the theft occurred is not recorded in the journals, but obviously the Africans had some goods worth stealing in the eyes of the sailors, despite the negative opinion of the professional tradesmen, who thought Sierra Leone afforded only moderate amounts of gold and ivory but 'nothing elles good', apart from the essentials required for victualling.[62]

After an informal inquest, which included torture, Keeling enforced rigid discipline: the stolen goods were recovered and restored to their

rightful owners, more goods (some knives) were added in compensa-
tion, and the offenders duly punished. One English sailor was ducked
at the yardarm, and two others tied to the capstan with weights hanging
from their necks, in front of the Africans they had robbed, whereupon
'one of the negeres ... fell one his knees and beate his elbowes to the
Decke in tocken of thankfullnes this done'. Here is an instance of real
shipboard theatre: the general's disciplinary power visited in a public
display on the first victims of his power, the common seamen; a cruel
spectacle of English justice performed for an African audience, preceded
by a ritualised African form of communication through material signs
(eleven sticks). The value of such public rituals to the commercial success
of the voyage was noted by Hearne and Finch: 'I doubt not but all of our
nation that shall heereafter come hither wilbee the better used and may
the more bouldly goe aboute their busines on shoare.'[63]

As a mobile piece of England anchored off Sierra Leone, the *Hector*,
where the punishment probably took place, constituted an apt venue for
a spectacle of (in Marlowe's phrase) 'our nationes Justice',[64] performed
for the mariners and African guests. The hazards of passage to the shore-
line elicited different protocols of English showmanship. On the beach,
mutually exposed in liminal space, groups met and appraised each other
in full reciprocity, as both performers and inquisitive spectators. In
Madagascar ('St. Augustine'), where the two ships sought refreshment
in mid-February 1608, Keeling's shore parties took up 'first-encounter'
methods of exploratory ostentation. Three journals describe the moment.
An initial party with Captain Hawkins and twenty armed men in two
pinnaces proceeded a mile upriver, walked inland where they saw two
men in a canoe go ashore, but found only footprints and a few abandoned items ('luggog[e]'). These things 'wee left as wee ffound them,
hanging some ffew beads by them' along with other eye-catching tokens
of good will, 'toyes to entice them to come downe to us'.[65]

Having respected and adorned the native possessions, they earned
a tentative welcome. The next day, four men appeared 'upon the sand
within the baye', and Keeling dispatched both pinnaces again, del-
egating the chief merchants Marlowe and Hearne 'to speake wth them,
Comaunding us to use them with all kindenesse'. As the boats neared
shore, 'they made signes to us that they had Kyne and sheepe, then they
layd away their weapones' and 'mad[e] signes that our men should leave
their weapones in the boate ... and soe they came together', unarmed.
The indigenous group initiated and directed the meeting. Without a
shared tongue, the conference resembled a dumbshow: the English 'by

signes demaunded ffor beefes and muttones', and the natives gestured to the sun to promise their return with livestock in the morning.[66]

Hawkins and Keeling joined the third landing party, which met 'about twenty men of this Iland', 'as lustey men as I thinke anney man Lyvinge hath seene for savage nacked people', declared one witness, 'and every one of them had his bundle of dartes [javelins], which ... were very artificially wrought, the heades wheirof wear boarded not far unlike some kindes of arrowe heades I have seene in Englande'. The weapons were set aside as before. The admiring, somewhat fearful English gaze, taking in shape and detail, recognising workmanship, is decidedly precolonial, not imperial. Marlowe likewise admired the lance-heads, 'very sharpe and neate, as bright as silver, the men strong and active and of a manly Countynance'. The transaction advanced by gestures and material displays. After a taste of sack, the local men refused it and likewise declined the invitation to visit the ships. They took no interest in the beads, rings, and bits of iron the English produced in hopeful payment for their animals – an exchange hitherto successful in Sierra Leone and Saldania (southern Africa). 'But they seemed a people of a very great understanding', Marlowe observed, for 'the[y] esteemed of nothing we had but silver'. While the mariners haggled and bought a sheep and lamb for 18 pence sterling, the natives abruptly departed with the steer they had brought, cutting off the exchange. The frustrating incident offered an important lesson in the limits of English persuasion in Eastern waters.[67]

A more felicitous spectacle of encounter, in which music and mutually understood speech (Keeling spoke Arabic and Spanish, he and several shipmates Portuguese) figured importantly, took place on the Yemeni island of Socotra, where no English ship had landed before. As in Sierra Leone, with significant numbers of seamen suffering from scurvy, the fleet, having failed of refreshment at Zanzibar, urgently needed water and fresh victuals as it neared the island. To establish supportive relations here was an existential imperative that required tactful negotiation of shared idioms of littoral spectacle. The English were confident in their artillery yet at risk ashore, the Socotrans cautious and elusive. Having vacated a small town on 22 April when the English fired rounds of ordnance and landed in large numbers, the islanders mustered troops before Tamrida, their capital on the northern coast, whose bay the fleet entered late on 25 April.

The communities afloat and ashore made calibrated gestures of threat and invitation to appraise and conciliate each other. The fleet's initial shore party met a group of two hundred men, 'all armed with gonns

[guns] swords and dartes, speaking ffriendly', who presented them with goats and a sample of local water but insisted the English land very few men. They were not welcome in the town. Slaves would fill their water casks, and livestock could be bought; yet this island, the inhabitants declared, was Abd-el-Kuri, not Socotra. On receiving this report, Keeling sailed deeper into the bay and discharged four rounds of ordnance. 'Then they of the towne in gratiffication gave our gennerall 6 peeces of ordnance and a volley of small shoot, soundinge their drums and gevinge a greate shoute'. The magnitude of this response, remarked Marlowe, 'was more then wee expected in this place'. Each group thus declared its capacity to compel, and disposition to confer, respect. They exchanged presents: five goats from the king to Keeling, who gifted him 'a pece of *Callico*'.[68]

Advised by the captain of an arriving Gujarati ship that the island was in fact Socotra, Keeling obtained further 'backstage' information from an escaped slave who told him, 'wee had seene all their force and the people were afrayde of us'. Intriguingly, the slave also told Hearne that a soldier whose dignified demeanour had attracted the merchant's gaze ashore was the island's ruler, disguised, inspecting them: both parties to the encounter took theatrical self-presentation as an investigative opportunity. The resupplied ships departed for the Red Sea on 29 April but were driven back to Tamrida on 14 May. Possessed of more information than before, and recognising that they might need to stay for several weeks awaiting the monsoon, Keeling performed a more assertive posture. He sent word ashore that he meant to land '100 men stronge' and speak with the king. As he and Hawkins put off, the ships fired eight rounds, and two Gujarati vessels at anchor, likewise frustrated of their hopes for Aden, '[c]ame in theyre boate ... to salute him'. Awaiting the English ashore were two hundred men 'verry well appointed [equipped, armed]'. Having ordered his men to 'keepe together and stand upon their guarde', Keeling 'demanded to speake wth their governour *Sedj Hamour Bensaid*'. A tussle over protocol ensued: each party was resolved to receive the other. The Socotrans invited him to enter the town 'wth some ffewe men' to meet the king. Keeling, 'not ffor any ffeare ... but ... ffor the honor of our Counterye', insisted that the latter, preinformed of his arrival, visit him where he stood.[69]

> Att last yt was one bothe sydes agreed, our men to stand all in rancke on one syde, and the Mores one the other, and our Generall wth about 6 men and the Kinge wth as many should theare meete, wch accordingly they did, and saluted and embraced one the other. Then they wthdrewe

themselves about 80 paces off under date trees fFrom the heate of the sonne, where our Generall upon a Carpett and the Kinge upon a Callico sate after the Turkey manner and Confferred together. Our Generalls trumpettes and the Kinges drums and one Trumpett ffor Joye sounded at theyre meetinge.[70]

Symmetrical displays of hierarchical power, armed phalanxes fronted by core elites, framed the rulers' embrace. Thus theatre – the shared viewing of symbolically charged persons and properties in orchestrated constellations – enabled and legitimated transcultural rapprochement. Iconic and musical reciprocities solemnised the meeting. After the embrace, in hybrid postures encoding chiastic ratios of figure to background, each man reposed on fabric honorific of the other: Keeling sat on a carpet in 'the Turkey manner', Bensaid on calico evocative of Keeling's earlier gift, perhaps the very piece, while mingled fanfares resounded.

Their welcome in Socotra was critical to the success of the voyage. The crews, who helped Bensaid's men launch a frigate on 17 May, recuperated here for several weeks. Then the ships parted ways. The *Dragon* sailed for Sumatra and Java on 22 June, the *Hector* for India on 4 August, after its carpenters assembled a companion vessel for the passage to India, the *Hopewell*, whose lesser draft enabled it to sound dangerous shoal-waters and cross the bar into Surat.[71]

Throughout the conduct of the voyage, as crewmen laboured in rhythm or entertained themselves at sea, and wherever the ships landed – in Sierra Leone, southern Africa, Madagascar, Socotra, and beyond – theatrical rituals remained vital to their progress. Two plays by Shakespeare may or may not have contributed to the fleet's versatile language of maritime spectacle. If they did, their inclusion was fortuitous and incidental, not essential to the episodic drama of voyaging at this early stage in Britain's bid for global access. The writing formulated on the *Dragon* and the *Hector* is not as eloquently suggestive as Shakespeare's, but it is alive to the moment, empirically attentive, simultaneously timid and arrogant, often nervous, self-questioning, and markedly precolonial in conception. As rich testaments of maritime experience and cross-cultural encounter at a pivotal moment in the emergence of England's transmarine empire, the journals of the voyage command critical attention in their own right, far beyond the three episodes discussed here. In particular, these corporate writings demonstrate that drama, which regularly transported audiences in London's theatres, was itself integral to voyaging and trade: that travel and drama constituted varieties of performance that articulated and confirmed each other in early modern England and beyond.

Notes

1 For Ambrose Gunthio's transcriptions of the Shakespeare references, see 'A Running Commentary on the Hamlet of 1603', *European Magazine*, New Series, 1, no. 4 (Dec. 1825), 339–47, at 347. Gunthio's other publications that have so far been identified can be found in *The Theatrical Inquisitor; or, Monthly Mirror* 8 (Jan.–June 1816), 189–93; 255–56; 414–16; 9 (July–Dec. 1816), 8–11; and William Oxberry, *The Flowers of Literature, or: Encyclopedia of Anecdote*, vol. I (London: W. Simpkin and R. Marshall, 1822), 265–72. In all three instances Gunthio published extracts from what he claims is 'a treatise [he has] written', entitled *The Dictionary of Love*, while admitting that some of these passages have been taken from an 'obscure publication of the same nature, translated from the French'. He adds that 'having candidly acknowledged this, I trust I shall not after this be charged with plagiarism' (*Theatrical Inquisitor* 8, 189–91; *Flowers of Literature*, 266–67). *The Dictionary of Love* is actually a work by John Cleland, first published anonymously in 1753, and itself partly the translation of a French original of 1741 by Jean François Dreux du Radier (*Dictionnaire d'amour*). Gunthio's borrowings from Cleland are unchanged from the original except for occasional words, despite his claims to the contrary. It may be seen as an argument in support of the forgery thesis regarding the Keeling entries that Gunthio's name (in the only other instances known to us in which this name has appeared in print) is clearly associated with a form of textual malpractice. The name *Gunthio*, which is not recorded elsewhere as a surname in use in England in the nineteenth century, is presumably a pseudonym or penname, possibly based on the minor character Gunthiof (or Gunthiovus) from Nordic legend.

2 Thomas Rundall's name is officially listed among the council members in an 1849 publication; for a facsimile, see www.hakluyt.com/PDF/Council_lists .pdf (accessed 13 April 2015).

3 See G. Blakemore Evans, 'The Authenticity of Keeling's Journal Entries on "Hamlet" and "Richard II"', *Notes & Queries* 196 (1951), 313–15.

4 See William Brenchley Rye, *England as Seen by Foreigners in the Days of Elizabeth and James the First* (London: John Russell Smith, 1865), cxi–cxii.

5 This assumption is based on the entry in the 'Catalogue of Letters Patent from the Crown Kept in a Trunk', dated '25 April 1822', third list, which states: 'Bundle 5, Paper 108, First leaf of Capt Keeling's Journal. (Much decayed and mutilated)'. But see Richmond Barbour's comment that 'the entry appears in a bundle of lists in the Register Office, not in a summa of all extant East India Company (EIC) papers', and that because of this, '[t]here is a strong possibility that the manuscript was lost between 1858 and 1867', not before 1822 (*The Third Voyage Journals. Writing and Performance in the London East India Company, 1607–1610* [New York: Palgrave Macmillan, 2009], 243).

6 On the non-calendrical date of 31 September, note the comment by Ann Thompson and Neil Taylor, who point out that 'Henslowe's diary contains two entries for 31 September 1601 which have never been challenged as forgeries' ('Introduction', *Hamlet*, ed. Thompson and Taylor, The Arden

Shakespeare [London: Thomson Learning, 2006], 55). Likewise Downton's launch diary of the *Trades Increase* lists dates in January 1609/10 extending to '36' (BL Egerton MS 2100, f39).

7 Gunthio, 'A Running Commentary', 347. Rundall's version of the references can be found in Thomas Rundall, *Narrative of Voyages towards the North-West, in Search of a Passage to Cathay and India, 1496–1631*, Hakluyt Society, 1st series, 5 (London: Hakluyt Society, 1849), 231.

8 See Sir Sidney Lee, *A Life of William Shakespeare* (London: Smith, Elder, 1898), 369.

9 See Clements R. Markham, ed., *The Voyages of Sir James Lancaster, Kt., to the East Indies* (London: Hakluyt Society, 1877), ix–x. Sir William Foster, the leading twentieth-century editor of EIC papers, was the first to note Markham and Lee's error in 'Forged Shakespeariana', *Notes & Queries* 145 (1900), 41–42, at 41. See also Barbour, *The Third Voyage Journals*, 244–45.

10 Markham, ed., *The Voyages of Sir James Lancaster*, x.

11 Sydney Race, 'J. P. Collier's Fabrications', *Notes & Queries* 195 (1950), 345–46, at 345. On Race and his 'irresponsible hit-and-run tactics', see Arthur Freeman and Janet Ing Freeman, *John Payne Collier: Scholarship and Forgery in the Nineteenth Century*, 2 vols. (New Haven, CT: Yale University Press, 2004), 211 (vol. I), 1026 (vol. II).

12 See Evans, 'The Authenticity of Keeling's Journal Entries'.

13 See Sydney Race, 'The Authenticity of Keeling's Journal Entries on "Hamlet" and "Richard II"', *Notes & Queries* 196 (1951), 513–15, at 513, 514. For a facsimile of the official list of Hakluyt Society members in 1850, containing the names of both Collier and Rundall, see www.hakluyt.com/PDF/Membership_list_1850.pdf (accessed 14 April 2015).

14 These discrepancies are described in detail in Barbour, *The Third Voyage Journals*, 243–45. Barbour concludes that independent transcription from a common source is the most likely explanation for these discrepancies.

15 See Bernice Kliman, 'At Sea About *Hamlet* at Sea: A Detective Story', *Shakespeare Quarterly* 62, no. 2 (2011), 180–204.

16 Freeman and Freeman, *John Payne Collier*, vol. II, 1039–40.

17 G. Blakemore Evans, 'The Authenticity of the Keeling Journal Entries Reasserted', *Notes & Queries* 197 (1952), 127–28.

18 Kliman, 'At Sea', 192–97.

19 Ibid., 187, n29. In terms of the seventeenth-century material Kliman cites, her case suffers from several ill-informed conjectures: for example, she claims Keeling's is the EIC's 'oldest surviving journal' (181), though several share the vintage; she believes Markham abstracted Keeling's journal, yet maintains that all but the first leaf vanished by 1822 (190); and, asking why Keeling produced no plays after 31 March 1608 if he believed theatre enhanced discipline, she imputes to Keeling in April 1608 an anxious remark on 'our wicked actiones' penned by the unnamed *Hector* journalist on 9 May 1607, months before the arrival in Sierra Leone ('At Sea', 184; see also Markham, *The Voyages of Sir James Lancaster*, 111; Barbour, *Third Voyage Journals*, 45–46).

20 Frederick S. Boas, *Shakespeare and the Universities, and Other Studies in Elizabethan Drama* (Oxford: Basil Blackwell, 1923), 84–95.

21 Ibid., 95.

22 E. K. Chambers, *William Shakespeare: A Study of Facts and Problems*, 2 vols. (Oxford: Clarendon Press, 1930), vol. II, 334–35.

23 John Keay, *The Honourable Company. A History of the English East India Company* (London: HarperCollins, 1991), 75.

24 Gary Taylor, 'Hamlet in Africa, 1607', in *Travel Knowledge: European 'Discoveries' in the Early Modern Period*, ed. Ivo Kamps and Jyotsna Singh (New York: Palgrave, 2001), 223–48, at 242.

25 Ibid., 235.

26 Ibid., 234–35. In arguing that the *Dragon* would have 'provided a playing space comparable in size to those of early modern theatres' (235), Taylor relies on Charles Boxer's account of Iberian vessels in *From Lisbon to Goa, 1500–1700* (London: Variorum Press, 1984), item I, 246, n89. As Boxer demonstrates, Iberian ships could easily be around 2,000 tonnes, about three times the size of the *Dragon*.

27 Taylor, 'Hamlet in Africa, 1607', 239–40.

28 P. E. H. Hair, 'Hamlet in an Afro-Portuguese Setting: New Perspectives on Sierra Leone in 1607', *History in Africa* 5 (1978), 21–42, at 23.

29 See especially P. E. H. Hair, *Sierra Leone and the English in 1607. Extracts from the Unpublished Journals of the Keeling Voyage to the East Indies*, Occasional Papers 4 (University of Sierra Leone: Institute of African Studies, 1981); and Hair, *Africa Encountered: European Contacts and Evidence 1450–1700*, Variorum Collected Studies Series (Aldershot: Ashgate, 1997).

30 Ania Loomba, 'Shakespearean Transformations', in *Shakespeare and National Culture*, ed. John Joughin (Manchester University Press, 1997), 109–41, at 111, 113. It should be noted, in the light of Loomba's claim that Shakespeare 'first travelled to India' on this voyage, that the *Dragon* never reached India (though the *Hector* did), and that the nearest any of the disputed performances came to the subcontinent was off the East African coast near Malindi, several thousand miles away from India.

31 Race, 'J. P. Collier's Fabrications', 345.

32 William Foster, 'J. P. Collier's Fabrications', *Notes & Queries* 195 (1950), 414–15. This piece is a direct response to the assertions of Race. Foster had first defended the authenticity of the Keeling entries against Lee 50 years earlier in 'Forged Shakespeariana'.

33 See Graham Holderness, *Tales from Shakespeare: Creative Collisions* (Cambridge University Press, 2014), 23–58.

34 Holderness uses the term 'regime change' deliberately. *Tales from Shakespeare*, 36 and throughout.

35 See Taylor, 'Hamlet in Africa', 246, n81.

36 Patricia Akhimie, 'Strange Episode: Race in Stage History', *Shakespeare Bulletin* 27, no. 3 (2009), 363–76, at 364.

37 Taylor, 'Hamlet in Africa', 232–33.

38 See Barbour, *Third Voyage Journals*, 87, 176.

39 See Boas, *Shakespeare and the Universities*, 92–93.

40 Sir George Birdwood, ed., *The First Letter Book of the East India Company, 1600–1619* (London: Bernard Quaritch, 1893), 116; quoted in Barbour, *Third Voyage Journals*, 26–27.

41 Samuel Purchas, *Hakluytus Posthumus, or Purchas His Pilgrimes*, 4 books (London: Henry Fetherstone, 1625), book 3, 227.

42 Some of the references in this paragraph have been noted before by Barbour (*Third Voyage Journals*, 25–28) but are given here a more sceptical interpretive slant, reflecting the joint authorship of this chapter.

43 Nicholas Downton's Journal, British Library, L/MAR/A/11; Thomas Love's Journal, L/MAR/A/10; elisions expanded with italics. Entries abstracted in Markham, *The Voyages of Sir James Lancaster*, 153, 147.

44 See also Kliman, 'At Sea', 183, n7.

45 Benjamin Greene's journal, British Library, L/MAR/A/12; page transcribed by Foster, 'Forged Shakespeariana', 42. See also the entry, 'Fragment of a play in the Journal of Benjamin Greene' in the *Lost Plays Database*, ed. Roslyn L. Knutson, David McInnis, and Matthew Steggle (Washington, DC: Folger Shakespeare Library, 2009+) [http://lostplays.folger.edu]).

46 See Boas, *Shakespeare and the Universities*, 88, n1. The fragment is in a different (seventeenth-century) hand from the rest of the journal. Race attributes the fragment to Collier in 'J. P. Collier's Fabrications', 346.

47 See Birdwood, *The First Letter Book*, 308, 329. On 8 January 1610, the *Court Book of the East India Company* (British Library B/3, IOR 573) indicates that the *Dragon's* purser, John Lancellott, was reassigned to the new flagship (fo. 165ᵛ). Other mariners are likely to have shared the trajectory.

48 See Walter Mountfort, *The Launching of the Mary, or The Seaman's Honest Wife*, ed. J. H. Walter (London: Malone Society Reprints, 1933).

49 Thomas Gage, *The English-American his Travail by Sea and Land: or, A New Survey of the West-India's* (London: R. Cotes, 1648), 16.

50 *História Trágico-Marítima*, compiled by Bernardo Gomes de Brito [1735], 6 vols., ed. Damião Peres (Porto: Universidade do Coimbra, 1943), vol. III, 84 (our translation). An earlier and much shorter version of Henrique Dias's narrative, which appeared in 1565, did not contain this passage. According to Charles Boxer, who included a translation of the 1565 account in *Further Selections from the Tragic History of the Sea*, ed. Boxer (Cambridge: Hakluyt Society, 1968), 57–107, the 1735 edition is likely to be 'the original manuscript or a copy of the same' (7), written by Henrique Dias at Malacca in 1561, from which an abridged version was published in 1565. The theory is supported by Carlos Francisco Moura in *Teatro a bordo de naus portuguesas nos séculos XV, XVI, XVII, XVIII* (Rio de Janeiro: Instituto Luso-Brasileiro de História Liceu Literário Português, 2000), 33–34.

51 See Moura, *Teatro a bordo*, 39–45; also Mário Martins, *Teatro quinhentista nas naus da Índia* (Lisbon: Brotéria, 1973).

52 Moura, *Teatro a bordo*, 36–38.

53 See *The East India Company Journals of Captain William Keeling and Master Thomas Bonner, 1615–1617*, ed. Michael Strachan and Boies Penrose (Minneapolis, MN: University of Minneapolis Press, 1971), 3.

54 See Knut Weibust, *Deep Sea Sailors: A Study in Maritime Ethnology* (Stockholm: Nordiska Museet, 1969), 115.

55 Purchas, *Hakluytus Posthumus*, book 3, 188 (marginal note). The plural ('books') suggests that the *Dragon* was carrying the second, three-volume edition (1598/99–1600) of Hakluyt's *The Principal Navigations*, not the earlier, single-volume edition (1589).

56 See Birdwood, *The First Letter Book*, 419.

57 See E. Pérez-Mallaína, *Spain's Men of the Sea: Daily Life on the Indies Fleets in the Sixteenth Century* [1992], trans. Carla Rahn Phillips (Baltimore, MD: Johns Hopkins University Press, 1998), 158–59. Data derived from the sixteenth-century Spanish Indies fleet applies, of course, only partially to English ships.

58 See Pérez-Mallaína, *Spain's Men of the Sea*, 158; and Harry R. Skallerup, *Books Afloat and Ashore: A History of Books, Libraries, and Reading Among Seamen During the Age of Sail* (Hamden, CT: Archon, 1974).

59 Barbour, *Third Voyage Journals*, 3.

60 Birdwood, *The First Letter Book*, 117.

61 Anthony Parr, 'Foreign Relations in Jacobean England: The Sherley Brothers and the "Voyage of Persia"', in *Travel and Drama in Shakespeare's Time*, ed. Jean-Pierre Maquerlot and Michèle Willems (Cambridge University Press, 1996), 14–31, at 25.

62 Barbour, *Third Voyage Journals*, 67, 81, 84, 174 (our italics).

63 Ibid., 68, 85–86, 175.

64 Ibid., 86.

65 Ibid., 69, 110, 200.

66 Ibid., 69–70, 110–11.

67 Ibid., 70, 111.

68 Ibid., 125, 217.

69 Ibid., 133, 221–22, 226.

70 Ibid., 134.

71 Ibid., 136, 144, 151.

CHAPTER 9

Strange Bedfellows: The Ordinary Undersides of 'A True Reportory' and The Tempest

Emily C. Bartels

Rutgers University

At the beginning of William Shakespeare's *The Tempest* (*c.*1611), Prospero seizes the moment of a shipwreck, which he claims to have induced, to tell his amazed and 'piteous' daughter Miranda 'how thou cam'st here'.[1] After twelve years on the island, he cues her to expect a finally relevant unfolding of knowledge: "'Tis time / I should inform thee' (1.2.23–24); 'Thou must now know farther' (1.2.34). What Prospero presents is a heated diatribe against his 'false' and 'perfidious' brother Antonio, who allied himself with the Neapolitan King Alonso and usurped Prospero's position as Duke of Milan (1.2.78, 68). Even so, as the play inaugurates its dramatisation of a travel event, indeed a series of travel events, it sets Prospero up not only as a European castaway but also as the controlling narrator of his own 'travailous history'.[2]

In that, Prospero is like William Strachey, whose letter to an unidentified 'Excellent Lady' (1610) – which circulated in manuscript and was published as 'A True Reportory of the Wreck, and Redemption of Sir Thomas Gates, Knight' by Samuel Purchas in 1625 – details a contemporaneous event: the 1609 shipwreck of English subjects, including Strachey and Virginia's interim governor, Gates, who were headed to Jamestown, caught in a 'dreadfull storme', and marooned for ten months in the Bermuda islands.[3] Although critics have long debated whether *The Tempest* is set in the New World, the Mediterranean, a utopian no place, or somewhere else, they tend to agree that the play's initial emphasis on a punishing storm and the resulting 'direful spectacle of the wreck' (1.2.26), and its reference to the 'still vex'd Bermoothes' explicitly link the two texts (1.2.229), which emerged roughly within a year of each other.[4] Strachey was eventually appointed secretary and recorder for the Virginia colony, and his letter clearly has a political agenda: to 'rays[e] ... from infamy' Jamestown's and Gates's reputations, both damaged by famine, disorder, and dissent among the colonists.[5] The text concludes with Gates's testimony to the Council of Virginia, arguing against 'abandon[ing] the action' at Jamestown by 'avouching' the colony's value and the implicitly remediable causes of its decline.[6] Yet, like Prospero, Strachey begins with the suggestion that his history will provide full knowledge about the expedition: 'Excellent Lady, Know'.[7]

In putting Prospero in the same position as Strachey, as both actor and narrator of a travel account, the play draws attention to the acts of dramatisation and narration, and to the relation between travel, narrative, and drama – prompting us, as readers and spectators, to think about how we come to know what we know about the 'brave new worlds' produced before us (5.1.183). If we enter those worlds through travel narratives, a form popularised in the early modern period especially by Richard Hakluyt's *The Principal Navigations* (1589; second, expanded edition 1598/99–1600), we expect to put ourselves in the hands of authoritative narrators whose accounts may have offered useful instruction for subsequent venturers, pressed or challenged colonialist projects and politics, grounded a scientific 'knowledge practice', provided a suggestive template for what would become the novel, or served some other practical, political, or aesthetic purpose.[8] Yet, in a play, a form comprised primarily by dialogue, that kind of narrative control and single-mindedness is rare. However much Prospero attempts to claim control over the unfolding history with his magic, spectacles, and rhetorical arts, he surely is not Shakespeare: nor is Prospero's interpretation and manipulation of people and events the only island story we see. Instead *The Tempest* builds its travel history on a series of voices and visions. These, we see, take shape as much from what – extraordinary strangenesses – the characters expect to find in this unfamiliar terrain as from the more ordinary conditions we see them experience. In the end, the play works to break apart the illusion of strangeness that it identifies as the stock and trade of travel, exposing its own extraordinary story of shipwreck and encounter as surprisingly ordinary.

The Tempest: Strangeness Recast

In 'observations' adjoined to his edition of *The Tempest* (1773), Samuel Johnson writes:

> Whatever might be Shakespeare's intention in forming or adopting the plot, he has made it instrumental to the production of many characters diversified with boundless invention... In a single drama are here exhibited

princes, courtiers, and sailors, all speaking in their real characters. There is the agency of airy spirits, and of an earthly goblin; the operations of magick, the tumults of a storm, the adventures of a desert island, the native effusion of untaught affection, the punishment of guilt, and the final happiness of the pair from whom our passions and reason are equally interested.[9]

For Johnson, Shakespeare's 'production' of 'many' 'diversified' characters takes precedence over plot and evidences the 'boundless invention' and realness through which the play engages the spectators' 'passions and reason'. If the aesthetic judgements here obscure the historical specificity and relevance of the play's subject, they aptly underscore one of *The Tempest*'s characterising features, the profusion of characters who wash up, or have washed up, separately on its shores: the European castaway Prospero and his daughter; his European rivals and their attendants; the Neapolitan Prince Ferdinand; the drunkards Stephano and Trinculo; the boatswain, shipmaster, and mariners sequestered for most of the play in those 'still-vexed Bermoothes'; and the spirit Ariel. Add to that Caliban, the only character actually born on the island, the testy goddesses, Iris, Juno, and Ceres, whom Prospero invokes for a masque, and the figures – Caliban's mother Sycorax, and Alonso's daughter Claribel and her new husband, the King of Tunis – who appear in the play's backstories, and *The Tempest*'s dramatic landscape seems to be remarkably overcrowded.

Given this panoply, one of the most striking choices that Shakespeare makes in structuring the play is *not* to focus on, or even to stage, Prospero's first meeting with Caliban or Ariel – that game-changing 'colonial encounter' between European selves and native others, a paradigm that critics have derived from this very play and that postcolonial rewritings, such as Aimé Césaire's *Une Tempête* (1969), have used the play to critique.[10] These histories appear only in narrative, indeed within a layering of narratives, which together diminish the importance and singularity of any given encounter, reminding us that Prospero has not been the first, any more than he will be the last, to be marooned on the island. Even then, the accounts of these beginnings function not to anchor the play but to anchor the arguments that the involved characters offer retrospectively to stake out their relative claims to power. Prospero does not mention his first meeting with either Ariel or Caliban when he informs Miranda how he and she came to be on the island. Rather, he brings that past up initially – and reports doing so 'once a month' (1.2.262) – in order to rebuff Ariel's accusation that he has reneged on his promise to release Ariel from service: 'Thou best know'st / What torment I did find thee in … / It was mine art, when I arrived and heard thee, that made gape / Thy pine and let thee out' (1.2.286–87, 291–93). Caliban recalls the time when Prospero 'cam'st first' and 'strok'st me and made much of me' in order to fend off Prospero's repeated threats of punishment ('For this be sure tonight thou shalt have cramps'; 'thou shalt be pinched') (1.2.332–33, 325, 328). In turn, Prospero recasts this history ('I have used thee – / Filth as thou art – with humane care, and lodged thee / In mine own cell, till thou didst seek to violate / The honour of my child') in order to justify confining the 'poisonous slave' (1.2.345–48, 319).[11]

Embedded in these histories is a crisis that could – but does not – drive the play: a point of no return, when the status of the newly encountered islanders has changed radically from confinement to liberty or liberty to confinement, torment to gratitude or gratitude to torment. But when the play opens, not only have these transformations already occurred, at an unspecified sometime within the twelve-year span that Prospero has resided on the island; his relations with Ariel and Caliban have melded into a comfortable, if adversarial, status quo. Ariel repeatedly insists that the time for freedom has come: 'Thou did promise / To bate me a full year'; 'On the sixth hour, at which time … / You said our work should cease' (1.2.249–50; 5.1.4–5). In response, Prospero repeatedly delays that release by making it contingent on one more task or 'trick' and one more deadline: 'after two days / I will discharge thee'; 'Shortly shall all my labours end, and thou / Shalt have the air at freedom' (4.1.37; 1.2.297–98; 4.1.265–66). Even in the final scene, although Prospero promises yet again to free Ariel, yet again he does not and instead produces another 'charge' that must be completed before Ariel can 'then' be released 'to the elements' (5.1.317). Since all the revels now are ended, we might *imagine* that this time will be the clincher, but that is *not* what we see: when the drama ends, Ariel is still in service. In the epilogue, Prospero tries to highjack the position of confinement for himself, declaring that he 'must be here confined by you, / Or sent to Naples' and asking that the audience, with their 'indulgence', 'set [him] free' (5.1.322–23, 338). But if the audience's applause saves him from limbo, that freeing only amplifies Ariel's repeatedly forestalled release.

This episodic pattern helps us recognise a similar predictability within the interactions between Prospero and Caliban, which are far fewer and less contentious than still valuable readings of the play's colonialist politics might lead us to believe. We see the two together only at the beginning and the end of the play, in scenes first of contestation and then of reconciliation that are suggestively linked by being the only staged exchanges between these characters. In both cases the interaction is defined by the expectation that, amid a volley of curses and threats of punishment, the day-to-day work that Prospero will order, Caliban will do: 'make our fire, / Fetch in our wood, and serv[e] other profitable offices'; 'fetch us fuel, and be quick' (1.2.311–13, 365–66). When Caliban first speaks (from off stage), he anticipates Prospero's demands, even before hearing why Prospero calls him from the cave. Caliban's first line, 'There's wood enough within' completes Prospero's 'Thou earth, thou, speak', resolving its spondaic stresses with an iambic beat in a manner that is not necessarily contentious. In this case, as in Ariel's, Prospero creates and relies on the proposition that there is always 'other business' that must – and will – be performed (1.2.315, 366). The routine and the apparent complacency may be disrupted momentarily by the 'foul conspiracy' that Caliban orchestrates with his ragtag 'confederates', Stephano and Trinculo, against Prospero (4.1.139, 140). Yet that not only makes us question the limits of Caliban's confinement, but it also appears to be a comic prelude to a pardon, enacted in the second of the two representations of the Prospero–Caliban exchange and followed predictably by Prospero identifying new business that Caliban must and will complete: 'Go, sirrah, to my cell; / Take with you your companions. As you look / To have my pardon, trim it handsomely' (5.1.293).[12]

This is not to say that these relations are not grounded on colonial oppression and violence: we see Prospero, via Ariel, following through on his threats to punish Caliban with 'cramps' and 'pinches' (4.1.261). But, unexpectedly I think, the play takes that dynamic for granted, figuring it not as a primary source of dramatic or political crisis, of cross-cultural discovery or surprise, but as a long-sustained and apparently sustainable pattern of behaviour, already so accomplished and complete that it almost goes without saying. Instead of defining a dramatic or political crisis, the repetition of curses and threats, demands and delays, appears to be such an uncontested matter of course, in fact, that allegations of a past attempted rape (Caliban of Miranda) appear neither as a cause for action or alarm, nor as a pivot point of the plot, but as one among many accusations mutually levied and embraced not merely by Prospero but by Caliban as well to bolster their own agendas. Breaking the form and terms of their imitative discourse, Caliban actually interrupts his verbal sparring with Prospero to announce that he 'must eat [his] dinner' (1.2.330), and whether or not we take that interruption as a stage direction, it nonetheless draws attention to the ordinary basis of the day – the practicality that appears between the lines of the discursive polemics and exposes life in this strange new world as neither strange nor new.

If the impact of the presumably ground-breaking encounters between these long familiar figures is thus diffused by being treated as yesterday's news, the breaking story that puts and keeps the main plot in motion is the second wave of shipwrecks, bringing Prospero's European rivals on shore twelve years after his landing and catalysing his now expected return home. This too is a story of encounter, but one organised around a series of exchanges among discrete factions of a new castaway group, whose survival depends as much upon their interactions with each other as it does on their encounters with unfamiliar islanders. On the sidelines, Ferdinand unites romantically with the apparently native Miranda, and Trinculo and Stephano conspire with Caliban. But the main action centres rather on Alonso, his apparent loss of and eventual reunion with his only son and heir, with the 'noble Neapolitan' Gonzalo providing comfort and support to the grieving king on one side (1.2.61), and Sebastian and Antonio plotting a coup against him on the other. Although Prospero does appropriate and eclipse these stories in order to reveal and reinstate himself, their stories are not entirely his, as his move to cut short Alonso's reconciliation with Ferdinand suggests: 'There, sir, stop. / Let us not burden our remembrances with / A heaviness that's gone' (5.1.198–200). Nor are they entirely theirs, appearing as mediated by the expectations that the voyagers bring to the experience of travel as they are by Prospero's art. In giving priority to these second-wave encounters in lieu of the more expected first, the play sets the ordinary against the extraordinary, experience against expectation, cueing us to wonder whether the stories travellers tell, or want to tell, are ever based on truth.

Strange, strange, strange, strange: if there is one key word within *The Tempest*, and within its representation of second-wave encounters, it is this one. Yet strangeness surfaces here not as the essence of the island but as an artful supplement. All of the extraordinary features of the play's brave, new world – from spectacular tempests, wonder-inducing songs, and sleep-inducing music, to banquets and dances performed by 'several strange shapes' (3.3.19 SD), to a masque of goddesses, nymphs, and reapers – are illusions which Prospero has engineered, and we see him verbally ramping up their mystique. When Miranda correctly attributes the opening tempest to Prospero's 'art', for example, he recasts the event and its outcome – the shipwreck of his European 'enemies' – as an 'accident most strange', prompted supernaturally by 'bountiful Fortune' (1.2.1, 178–79).

Ironically, however, as the newly landed Europeans encounter these illusions, they locate strangeness only in their more ordinary aspects. Sebastian, for example, remarks on the 'strange drowsiness' and 'strange repose' that overtakes his company soon after their first landing (2.1.197, 211). Gonzalo is awakened by 'a humming' which he amplifies as 'a strange one' (2.1.316). When Prospero aborts the pageant he has created for Miranda and her new prince, Ferdinand declares Prospero's sudden show of 'passion' 'strange' (4.1.143). At the end of the play, when Prospero reunites all the castaways with the mariners, Alonso declares the reunion 'as strange a maze as e'er men trod', 'not natural' and growing from 'strange to stranger' by the minute (5.1.242, 227–78). Extrapolating from what he witnesses in this scene, he anticipates that the 'story' that Prospero will tell 'of [his] life' will 'take the ear strangely' (5.1.312–13). When Caliban, Stephano, and Trinculo then come forward, Alonso declares what he sees 'a strange thing as e'er I looked on' (5.1.289), but it is Prospero only who takes that 'strange thing' to refer solely to Caliban, emphasising that this 'thing of darkness' 'is as disproportioned in his manners / As in his shape' (5.1.275, 291–92). Here, what's 'strange' to Alonso – who is preoccupied rather with his drunken compatriots and where they have found 'this grand liquor' (5.1.280) – may be the discovery of two drunks, as he says, 'in this pickle' (5.1.281).

Drowsiness, noise, passion, reunions, storytelling, inebriated countrymen: these are not necessarily the stuff of strangeness. Nor are they features we would necessarily expect to define what lies 'outside one's own land' – an early denotation for 'strange'.[13] In emphasising the incongruity, the play suggests its castaways are predisposed to see the ordinary as extraordinary. The comic initial encounter of Trinculo with Caliban underscores by exaggerating just such inclinations. Trinculo comes into the exchange using the pretext of carnival displays of 'monsters' – painted 'fish' and 'dead Indian[s]' – who 'make [i.e. enrich or define] a man' to decide whether Caliban is indeed 'a man or a fish' and 'dead or alive' (2.2.24–25, 28–30, 32). Although he then recognises Caliban as 'an islander that hath lately suffered by a thunderbolt' and familiarises him as a 'strange bedfellow', as he and his compatriot Stephano then drink their way into a conspiracy leveraged by Caliban's knowledge of the island, they almost compulsively add the tag 'monster' to descriptions of his ordinary moves or aspects, declaring him 'a most delicate monster', 'a most poor, credulous monster', 'a most perfidious and drunken monster', 'a most ridiculous monster', 'a howling monster', 'a brave monster', and so on (2.2.25, 38–89, 85–86, 140, 144, 159, 174, 183). The wheel comes full circle as both ultimately, and perhaps inevitably, drop the adjectives altogether, letting the abstract codification of 'monster' stand on its essentialising own (3.2.104, 132, 148; 4.1.246, 251). This sequence cuts significantly against other instances of the term's use: for example, when Antonio fabricates 'a din to fright a monster's ear' to justify why he and Sebastian are standing over the waking king with their swords drawn (2.1.313); or when Gonzalo attributes 'monstrous shapes' to the fabricated 'islanders' who bring in a banquet, at Prospero's behest; or when Alonso declares 'monstrous, monstrous' a voice that he has heard (Ariel's) and that 'pronounced / the name of Prosper' along with the death of Alonso's son (3.3.31, 95, 99). If these politically pointed articulations have more cause, they do not have more ground – at least from what we see. The vocabulary of monstrosity denaturalises what might otherwise seem merely unfamiliar, if that, and, in its repetition and excess, exposes the predilections of speakers, who reshape, instead of representing, the essence of island subjects.

In fact, across *The Tempest*, expectation, derived discursively in significant part from travellers' tales, seems to set and challenge scripts of strangeness, more than do observation or experience. In dramatising the second-wave encounters, the play exposes and unsettles the textual underpinnings of the characters' reactions, leading tellingly with the bookish character, Gonzalo, who, according to Prospero, supplied that exiled duke with prized 'volumes' and who idealises the castaways' survival as a 'miracle' and the island as a place with 'everything advantageous to life' (1.2.7; 2.1.6, 50). His descriptions are not only punctured by the scepticism of Antonio and Sebastian, who see 'tawny' 'ground' where he sees 'lush and lusty' 'green' 'grass' and who, in crediting the landscape with 'an eye of green', seem to be critiquing Gonzalo's vision (2.1.53–54, 55). They are also disrupted notably by odd literary-historical detours. Gonzalo brings the 'widow Dido' into a conversation about Claribel, the new queen of Tunis, making an uneasy association, which his interlocutors question as the product of his 'miraculous harp' and which I think registers as disjunctive, even if we can mine from it some historical sense or link it intertextually to Strachey's digressive reference to 'Queen Dido', whose land he presents as approximating Virginia's in size (2.1.275, 285).[14] In addition, Gonzalo interrupts a conversation about Alonso's grief with a canned disquisition on the utopian 'commonwealth' he would implant on the island (2.1.145) – a fantasy taken, we know, from John Florio's 1603 translation of Michel de Montaigne's 'Of the

Cannibales' and leading in the present context to 'nothing', as his interlocutors stress (2.1.170).

The reference to Montaigne, an essay significantly textured by classical
pre-texts (Horace, Virgil, Plato, Aristotle), does more than underscore
the textuality of Gonzalo's 'miraculous harp[ing]'. It also draws attention
to the tendency of travellers to amplify their own credit by amplifying
their truths. Asserting that 'there is nothing' in its new world 'that is
either barbarous or savage, unless men call that barbarism which is not
common to them', Montaigne is troubled by the fact that 'subtile people' 'commonly, adorne, enlarge, yea, and Hyperbolise the matter' 'to
purchase credit to their judgement, and drawe you on to beleeve them'.[15]
On the sidelines, Sebastian and Antonio represent Gonzalo's textually
induced idealism as just this sort of enlargement and link it to material
ends, which obviously interest them. Deeming him 'a spendthrift of his
tongue' (2.1.25), the two imagine that he 'will carry the island home in
his pocket and give it his son for an apple', and 'sowing the kernels of it
in the sea, will bring forth more islands' (2.1.88–91). Where Gonzalo
antes up 'rarity' 'beyond credit', Sebastian aligns it with 'many vouched
rarities' (2.1.57–61); where Gonzalo glamorises the 'freshness and gloss'
of the company's salt-drenched garments, Antonio and Sebastian make
the pockets speak, to 'say he lies' or 'very falsely pocket up his report',
with 'pocket' here suggesting not just a suppression of but also a financial
gain from false report (2.1.62–66). We may not doubt the motives of
the 'noble Neapolitan' as much as do his underhanded peers, but if the
play sets us up to believe in the integrity of Gonzalo's character, it simultaneously prompts us to question the integrity of his textually mediated
truths and the kind of rarities and adornment that comes with them and
other travel-telling.

The play itself offers no easy truths, but rather puts its spectators in
the middle of that mediation. Amid these competing impressions of
report and credit, not only is it hard to tell fiction from fact (are the garments fresh or aren't they?), it is also difficult to gauge to what degree
and end these travellers and their forebears invest in the stories that they
revive and relay. When the new arrivals – all who, like Prospero, count
on returning home – imagine the stories they will narrate, they do so in,
and only in, response to 'strange shapes' – the pageant of 'several strange
shapes bringing in a banquet' (3.3.19 SD) – creating the impression that,
for them, to tell of travel is necessarily to tell of wonders. Their bench-
mark is an established tradition of travel lore, from and to which they
extrapolate in order to assess the truth of what they see. Yet the more

they do so – in an exchange whose insignificance to plot suggests its significance to meaning – the less clear and less relevant what they actually believe seems to be. Sebastian fictionalises the spectacle as 'a living drollery' and insists: 'Now I will believe / That there are unicorns; that in Arabia / There is one tree, the phoenix throne, one phoenix / At this hour reigning there', a remark whose sincerity is fractured by an 'if I believe this, I'll believe anything' edge (3.3.21-24).[16] Willing himself similarly to 'believe both', Antonio positions himself against 'fools at home' who condemn 'travellers' as liars and uses that expressed belief as a blanket excuse for swearing that anything without 'credit' is true: 'And what does else want credit, come to me, / And I'll be sworn 'tis true. Travellers ne'er did lie, / Though fools at home condemn 'em' (3.3.24-7). Here, what he decides he is licensed to swear not only trumps but also obscures what he actually imagines to be true, his preoccupation with material 'credit' once again all too clear. Even the idealistic Gonzalo measures the truth of what he reports by what his audience might believe: 'If in Naples / Should I report this now, would they believe me?' (3.3.27–28). His insistence that the 'monstrous shape[s]' are 'certes' 'people of the island' emerges as a discursive move that fends off, by interrupting and eclipsing, his worry (to which he does not return) about what would happen 'if I should say I saw such islanders' (3.3.29–31).

Part of the problem, for him as for us, is the possibility and expectation that travellers *do* lie, for credit or gain, in the 'now' that both he and Sebastian reference. Gonzalo distinguishes a past time, 'when we were boys', when no one believed in 'mountaineers / Dewlapped like bulls, whose throats had hanging at 'em / Wallets of flesh' or 'men / Whose heads stood in their breasts', the clichés of classical cosmographies, from a 'now', when 'we find / Each putter-out of five for one' – travellers or investors – 'will bring us / Good warrant of' such figures to verify the truth of the travel for a five-to-one return on their investment (3.3.43–49).[17] That distinction is posed as a rhetorical question ('When we were boys, *who would believe* that there were mountaineers / … which now we find / Each putter-out of five for one will bring us'), comes with a prescribed answer ('no one'), presumably marking the difference between a disbelieving past and a believing present. Gonzalo's perspective on that change is obscured, however, both by the double resonance of 'when we were boys', an indication either of a time past or a state of (naïve) boyishness and, more significantly, by his shift in focus from what used to be (or not be) believed to what is now commonly, perhaps too commonly, brought back 'in good warrant' through report. As telling replaces believing, it undoes all (including our own) ability to assess truth. The point of Gonzalo's argument is, after all, to convince the wary Alonso to eat the 'viands' left by the 'strange shapes' (3.3.41). The king, like Caliban, must eat his dinner. Ultimately, practicality trumps truth, and what remains is an unsettling implication for the now: what travellers believe may not matter as much as what their audiences will credit, and what their audiences will credit may have little to do with what anyone believes.

In cutting through the stuff of strangeness to expose these confounding cultural resonances, *The Tempest* turns travel writing on its head, asking us to recognise the discursively mediated nature of that tradition's extraordinary truths. Prospero's fantastical shows and narrative recreations of his initial encounters may make it as difficult for us, as for the other players, to see the ordinary aspects of the island world. Yet it is all too telling that the dramatic resolution depends crucially, as Johnson suggests, on a domestic marriage plot involving Ferdinand and Miranda, the only encounter we see from start to finish of a European outsider with an established, though by birth European, islander. That plot, which builds dramatic interest out of wordplay more than action, immediately naturalises the language of wonder as it moves from Ferdinand's apostrophe to Miranda ('O you wonder!') to her correction ('no wonder') to his reappropriation of the noun as verb ('A single thing, as I am now, that wonders') (1.2.427–28, 433). The domestic plot also repeatedly associates the physical bondage that Ferdinand and – in an obvious parallel – Caliban endure to metaphors of courtship, as when Ferdinand distinguishes Miranda as 'perfect and peerless' by setting her against the 'many' ladies whose harmonious 'tongues' 'that into bondage brought [his] too diligent ear' (3.1.47, 39, 41–42).[18] We are, it seems, never far from home. And what is most dramatically interesting and surprising about the love plot – like the other second-wave encounters that eclipse the singularity of the first – is not how (predictably) it unfolds but that it unfolds predictably in this 'brave new world', giving the lie to more sensational stories that might bring five for one.

'A True Reportory': Telling the 'Truth'

What happens if we, then, turn to the 'true reportory' and read Strachey's 'travailous history' with an eye to Shakespeare's play? What happens, that is, if we imagine that the drama asks us to rethink the extraordinary aspects of its source? Like *The Tempest*, the letter begins with the spectacle of 'a dreadful storm', which Strachey amplifies as 'a hell of darkness', full of 'horror' – its winds 'as mad as fury and rage could make them' – 'overmaster[ing]' and amazing everyone's senses, to the point that the company 'could not apprehend in our imaginations any possibility of greater violence'.[19] In addition, Strachey introduces Bermuda as a place 'called commonly the Devil's Islands and feared and avoided of all sea travelers alive above any other place in the world'.[20] He also details a number of violent encounters with New World Indians – for example, of 'certain Indians' of 'barbarous disposition' who 'seized' an Englishman, Humphrey Blunt, 'led him up into the woods and sacrificed him', or of others, 'who were ever our deadliest enemies', who 'would assault and charge with their bows and arrows, in which manner they killed many of our men'.[21] Yet Strachey is not Prospero any more than Prospero is Shakespeare, and, in the main, the letter does not produce a new world so deadly that it defies apprehension and instills inordinate fear. If we follow Shakespeare's cues, we can see in Strachey a multivocal narrative that not only breaks through such expectations to bring its story home, exposing the tensions among the voyagers – rather than between them and the New World – as their biggest threat; it also takes on the breaking of expectation as work that travellers must do.

Like travel literature generally, Strachey's letter is filled with intertextual references to other texts, from the classical odes of Horace to sixteenth-century 'histories' of the East and West Indies as well as of the Virginia Colony – among them Richard Eden's *Decades of the New World* (1555) and Gates's *True Declaration of Virginia* (1610), which Strachey quotes in the final pages of his letter, substituting Gates's voice for his own. But if he draws on certain well-respected texts to support and augment his account, he places his own authority and experience above the impressions fostered in a more common, if not more influential, discourse, of the sort spread by voyagers themselves. Most notably, in his description of the storm and consequent shipwreck in Bermuda, which *The Tempest* clearly invokes, Strachey interrupts his 'narration' of events in order to debunk two sensational truths and expose their ordinary undersides.[22] As he tells of his company witnessing – 'with much wonder and carefulness' – 'a sparkling blaze', he takes aim at the 'many constructions' that 'superstitious seamen' make of the 'sea fire' – Greeks taking it 'for an evil sign of great tempest', Italians calling it 'a sacred body', and Spaniards assigning it 'an authentic and miraculous legend'.[23] He then sets his company's practicality above these sailors' mystifications: declaring the phenomenon 'usual in storms', he credits his men with laying 'other foundations of safety or ruin than in the rising and falling of it', something that they would only take as a 'miracle' if it could (as it cannot) 'miraculously' light their way.[24] In his account of Bermuda, Strachey pauses again 'to deliver the world from a foul and general error': the common belief that the islands have been 'given over to devils and wicked spirits'.[25] In order to make his case that Bermuda is 'as habitable and commodious as most countries of the same climate and situation', with a heads-up to his reader ('Your Ladyship') he includes a 'brief description' of the island's lucrative natural resources – much like Eden's 'briefe description of Afrike' in his account of Guinea voyages, but without the mythological figures (Blemines, Anthropophagi, Troglodytica) that Eden recycles from classical texts.[26]

In clearing the decks of these kinds of fictions, Strachey sets his 'experience' explicitly against expectation and presents his text as 'Truth'.[27] There is a mixed message in his attendant argument that 'men ought not to deny everything which is not subject to their own sense', which recasts the problem of men believing 'foul and general error' as a problem of men believing only in what they see.[28] But if Strachey here is struggling with the problem of verifying experience textually, he is also registering his awareness that both scepticism and superstition stand in the way of experience, and the reader and the voyager in the way of 'Truth'.

But what exactly is the 'Truth' that Strachey wants to tell? As in *The Tempest*, it is the contention among the Europeans themselves, rather than their encounter with New World figures or features, that emerges as the primary focal point, the source of 'dangers and devilish disquiets' as well as of narrative and historical tension.[29] As Strachey tells it, the problem with Bermuda is not that its conditions are life-threatening but that they are advantageous – so advantageous that a faction of the party does not want to go on, fearing that the 'fish, flesh, [and] fowl which here ... at ease and pleasure might be enjoyed' would not be so 'in Virginia'.[30] Indeed, when famine strikes Jamestown, the governor sends men back to Bermuda to gather 'six months' provision of flesh and fish'.[31] The result is a growing disagreement between those who, like Strachey, would and those who would not remain loyal to the interim governor, Gates, the latter arguing, as Strachey records, that 'it was no breach of honesty, conscience, nor religion to decline from the obedience of the governor or refuse to go any further led by his authority (except when it so pleased themselves), since the authority cease when the wreck was committed.'[32] The crisis culminates in a 'conspiracy' of 'confederates', who raid the company's storehouse of arms and supplies under the lead of 'a gentleman amongst them, Henry Paine'.³³ Ultimately Gates, in his first imposition of martial law, condemns Paine to death for his continued insolence and insistence that 'the governor had no authority' – 'evil language' ('let the governor ... kiss, etc.') which Strachey deems too 'unreverent' to record before 'the modest ear'.³⁴

When Prospero denounces the 'foul conspiracy / Of the beast Caliban and his confederates', *The Tempest* is likely creating a loose parallel between the native Caliban and the English Paine, with the alliteration between 'Caliban' 'conspiracy' and 'confederates' simultaneously taking some of the emphasis from Prospero's 'beast' (4.1.139–40). But however the lines play out in Shakespeare, as the suggestive elision of these strange bedfellows resonates retrospectively in Strachey, it underscores the fact that the challenge to authority here is internal not external. Indeed, in the account of Bermuda, there is no mention of Indians: instead, sailors 'villainously' kill each other, and 'savages' appear only figuratively, in Strachey's mention of an initial worry that some voyagers would be left behind – 'given up like savages' – when the main company proceeded to Virginia.³⁵ Moreover, the outing and condemning of Paine provides the narrative foreground for a parallel story of Jamestown, where the Bermuda refugees discover a shocking 'desolation and misery'.³⁶ Strachey blames the colony's decline on a dissenting underclass of 'mariners', a 'shameless people' who steal provisions, carry on black market trade with the Indians, and deny aid to 'our poor people in want', looking rather to make a 'four or five to one' return on their investments – the kind of return, we might notice, the putters-out referenced in *The Tempest* expect from their tales.³⁷

On the sidelines of the Jamestown episodes, the letter does point to general and specific 'practices of villainy' effected by the Indians, bringing a 'daily' danger to the colony and proving their 'barbarous disposition'.³⁸ This emphasis is notably tempered, though, by Strachey's larger preoccupation with the internal problems. For example, acknowledging that 'the Indians killed as fast without, if our men stirred but beyond the bounds of their blockhouses, as famine and pestilence did within', he amplifies as unspeakable 'the many more particularities of their sufferances (brought upon them by their own disorders that last year) than I have heart to report' – 'sufferances' catalysed by the colonists' 'pervasive idleness' and exacerbated by dissent.³⁹ What most troubles the relations between the Indians and the English and leads 'boldly' 'to the death and starving of many a worthy spirit', are, he says, the underhanded dealings of the mariners, who in the night overpay the Indians for their goods, with the result that 'when the truckmaster for the colony in the daytime offered trade, the Indians would laugh and scorn the same'.[40] Even so, Strachey makes clear that the colonists repeatedly look to the Indians for 'help' and sympathise with the fact that, 'at their best', the natives live 'from hand to mouth', being often too 'poor', not just unwilling or too crafty, to trade.[41] The narrative ends with a major showdown between the newly arrived and authoritarian lord governor Thomas West, Baron De La Warr, and the Indian leader ('werowance') Powhatan – with each promising catastrophic violence if the other does not meet his terms: Powhatan vows, on the one hand, to 'give in command to his people to kill us and do unto us all the mischief which they at their pleasure could and we feared' if the English venture outside Jamestown, and the lord governor, on the other, to 'suddenly' 'fire all his neighbor cornfields, town, and villages' if Powhatan does not return English captives.[42] As the letter and Strachey's time in Virginia come to an end, he admittedly cannot tell whether the governor's threats 'will work' to repair relations.[43] Still, as Strachey reports sailing back to England with Gates as well as with Powhatan's son, the Indians and English taking leave 'with all terms of kindness and friendship', the warring voices of Powhatan and La Warr (along with the narrating voice of Strachey) are eclipsed by an extended excerpt from Gates's *True Declaration of Virginia* – a text which argues vigorously for the continued support for the colony by detailing its abundant resources and blaming its troubles on the mariners, 'the scum of men', who have 'created the Indians our implacable enemies'.[44]

Despite Strachey's own insistent idealisation of Gates and the Jamestown project, the letter is, in fact, defined by competing, sometimes ordinary voices. In the domestic undersides of Bermuda and Jamestown, we hear, 'every Sunday two sermons [are] preached by our minister', while on Thursdays, 'true preachers' 'take their weekly turns', and the company is mustered daily morning and evening for 'public prayer'.[45] A cook, Thomas Powell, marries the 'maidservant of one Mistress Horton'; John Rolfe's daughter, Strachey's goddaughter, is christened 'Bermuda' and Strachey's godson, 'Bermudas'.[46] Through indirect discourse, Strachey presents the diverse voices of superstitious seaman, outspoken dissenters, governors, and Indians, marking differences within and among the factions of opponents and peers. Strachey's truths are, of course, textured by his own artful agendas – one which may have been to secure the patronage of the 'Excellent Lady' to whom he writes, sometimes identified as Lucy, Countess of Bedford, once a patron of John Donne.[47] But if *The Tempest* is any guide, it – what the editors of this volume have distinguished as 'voyage drama' – helps us see beyond the extravagant inscriptions, to understand travel and travel stories as a dynamic negotiation of experience and expectation, with multiple players and multiple plots competing for terrain, if not also for credit, testing the terms they have brought with them.

If *The Tempest* is any guide: we tend to mine Shakespeare's 'sources' for information, looking for points where historical facts can clarify dramatic uncertainties, or departures from those facts can expose dramatic inventions. Yet dramatic texts have as much to bring to the historical texts that they invoke as historical texts have to bring to drama. Here, as *The Tempest* takes that challenge on, it places imagination and mediation at the heart of travellers' tales and ordinary tensions and contentions at the heart of extraordinary worlds. And in the end, what we 'see better' than a 'true reportory' may alone convey is that the primary object of travel stories may not always be the truth.[48]

Notes

1 William Shakespeare, *The Tempest*, ed. Stephen Orgel (Oxford University Press, 1987), 1.2.14, 51. All further quotations from *The Tempest* will be cited by act, scene, and line numbers within the text.

2 William Shakespeare, *Othello*, ed. Michael Neill (Oxford University Press, 2006), 1.3.139.

3 William Strachey, 'A True Reportory of the Wreck and Redemption of Sir Thomas Gates, Knight', in *A Voyage to Virginia in 1609: Two Narratives*, ed. Louis B. Wright (1964; Charlottesville, VA: University of Virginia Press, 2013), 6.

4 *'The Tempest' and Its Travels*, ed. Peter Hulme and William H. Sherman (Philadelphia: University of Pennsylvania Press, 2000), surveys these possibilities; see especially, 73–145. For challenges to the link between the play and Strachey's letter, see Alden T. Vaughan, 'William Strachey's "True Reportory" and Shakespeare: A Closer Look at the Evidence', *Shakespeare Quarterly* 59 (2008), 245–73. Compare Peter Hulme, *Colonial Encounters: Europe and the Native Caribbean, 1492–1797* (London: Methuen, 1986), 89–134, at 92–94.

5 Strachey, 'A True Reportory', 67; the title added to the published letter puts emphasis on the 'redemption of Sir Thomas Gates'. On Strachey's history, see Hobson Woodward, *A Brave Vessel: The True Tale of the Castaways Who Rescued Jamestown* (New York: Penguin, 2009).

6 Strachey, 'A True Reportory', 100.

7 Ibid., 3.

8 Elizabeth Spiller, 'Shakespeare and the Making of Early Modern Science: Resituating Prospero's Art', *South Central Review* 26, nos. 1 and 2 (2009), 24–41, at 24.

9   Samuel Johnson, 'General Observations on the Plays of Shakespeare', in *The Works of Samuel Johnson, LL.D: A New edition, in Twelve Volumes. With an essay on his Life and Genius, by Arthur Murphy, Esq.* (London: Luke Hensard and Sons, 1810), vol. II, 197.

10 In *Colonial Encounters,* Hulme uses *The Tempest* to set the terms of colonial discourse analysis. See also Roberto Fernández Retamar, *Caliban and Other Essays,* trans. Edward Baker (Minneapolis, MN: University of Minnesota Press, 1989), an influential postcolonial appropriation of the play.

11 See Orgel's note to 1.2.350–61, which the Oxford edition assigns to Miranda, as do the Signet and Riverside editions.

12 Compare Francis Barker and Peter Hulme, 'Nymphs and Reapers Heavily Vanish: The Discursive Con-texts of *The Tempest*', in *Alternative Shakespeares* (London: Routledge, 1985), 191–205, at 201–04; and Hulme, *Colonial Encounters,* 118–22.

13 *OED online,* accessed 1 Sept. 2015.

14 Critics have tried to normalise the reference by supplementing Gonzalo's terms, arguing for the proximity of Tunis and Carthage, geographically, historically, and politically (e.g., Hulme, *Colonial Encounters,* 111–12; Orgel, note to 2.3.82). Strachey describes the colony's 'ground' as 'half an acre (or so much as Queen Dido might buy of King Iarbas)', 'A True Reportory', 79.

15 *The Essayes, Or, Morall, Politike and Militarie Discourses: of Le: Michaell de Montaigne, Knight,* trans. John Florio (London: Val. Sims for Edward Blount, 1603), I. xxx ('Of the Caniballes'), 101.

16 See the editor's note to 3.3.21.

17 The 'putter-out of five' was, as Orgel explains, 'either the traveller, who invests his money at the rate of five to one' in his venture as a means of insuring and recovering his expenses (giving one to an insurer in order to reap fivefold benefits 'if he returned with proof that he had reached his destination'), or the insurer, 'who pays at that rate and reports the traveller's tales'. See the note to 3.3.48. On 'venturing', see Anthony Parr, '"For his Travailes let the *Globe* witnesse": Venturing on the Stage in Early Modern England', Chapter 1 in this volume.

18 Compare Michael Neill, '"Noises, / Sounds, and sweet airs": The Burden of Shakespeare's *Tempest*', *Shakespeare Quarterly* 59, no. 1 (2008), 36–59, at 39–43.

19 Strachey, 'A True Reportory', 6, 7, 4, 6. On the intertextual resonances within the representation of this 'formula' storm, see Barbara Mowat, '"Knowing I loved my books": Reading *The Tempest* Intertextually', in *'The Tempest' and Its Travels,* ed. Hulme and Sherman, 27–36, at 30–32. See also Gwilym Jones, *Shakespeare's Storms* (Manchester University Press, 2015).

20 Strachey, 'A True Reportory', 16.

21 Ibid., 88–89, 93.

22 Ibid., 16. It may be that Shakespeare borrows directly from Strachey's description of the storm words such as 'tempest', 'glut', 'roar', and even 'amazement' to represent his characters' reactions to that phenomenon, as Woodward argues in *A Brave Vessel,* 57–59. Compare Hulme, *Colonial Encounters,* 94–101.

23 Strachey, 'A True Reportory', 13.
24 Ibid., 13.
25 Ibid., 16.
26 Ibid.; Eden's account was published in Richard Hakluyt, *The Principal Navigations, Voyages, Traffiques & Discoveries of the English Nation*, 3 vols. (London: George Bishop, Ralph Newberie, and Robert Barker, 1599), vol. II, part 2, 10–11. See my discussion in *Speaking of the Moor: From* Alcazar *to* Othello (Philadelphia: University of Pennsylvania Press, 2008), 57–58.
27 Strachey, 'A True Reportory', 16.
28 Ibid.
29 Ibid., 45.
30 Ibid., 41.
31 Ibid., 87.
32 Ibid., 44.
33 Ibid., 47.
34 Ibid., 48.
35 Ibid., 54, 50.
36 Ibid., 64.
37 Ibid., 72–73.
38 Ibid., 89.
39 Ibid., 64, 67.
40 Ibid., 73.
41 Ibid., 64, 75, 71.
42 Ibid., 93, 92, 94.
43 Ibid., 94.
44 Ibid., 94, 97.
45 Ibid., 53, 80, 53.
46 Ibid., 54.
47 Woodward, *A Brave Vessel*, 446.
48 William Shakespeare, *King Lear*, in *The Norton Shakespeare*, ed. Stephen Greenblatt et al. (London: W. W. Norton, 1997). 1.1.156. Many thanks to the 2015 community of the Middlebury Bread Loaf School of English, who helped inspire this work. I have gained too from conversations with Claudia Johnson and Gwyneth Lewis, and from the comments of the volume editors.

CHAPTER 10

Travelling Characters in Early Modern Drama

David McInnis

University of Melbourne

Early modern plays offering mercantile, religious, and colonial perspectives on travel have received a steady stream of critical attention, but considerably less attention has been given to the figure of the stage traveller whose peregrinations are governed by desire alone.[1] Although lampooned in satirical drama by Ben Jonson, travelling characters occur in a number of early modern plays, often in the context of a debate about the merits of voyaging. Anthony Parr, for example, draws attention to how '[t]he individual tourist, long a target of "character" writing, is repeatedly a figure of ridicule on the English stage, and his (or occasionally her) absurdities must often have been taken as supporting the case against travel as frivolous and degrading'.[2] In this chapter, I offer a complement to the critical censure of such idle voyagers by considering instances where travellers derive pleasure from their wanderings, whether because they are able to witness the marvels they had previously read about in books, because they value the transformative potential of venturing beyond their native soil, or because they simply revel in the opportunity to immerse themselves in exotica. The connection between reading, writing, and travelling is particularly important in this regard, for it potentially subverts the intuitive expectation that travels are only recorded for profitable, utilitarian purposes and that any other use leads to trouble.[3]

This chapter focuses on lesser-studied examples of travelling characters, beginning with travellers who read in Thomas Dekker's *Old Fortunatus* (1599), before considering whether playgoers' experiences of such stage-travellers as Mirabell in John Fletcher's *The Wild-Goose Chase* (1621), and Springlove, Meriel, and Rachel in Brome's *A Jovial Crew* (1641) can be seen as a comparable inspiration to travel. The travelling-character (as opposed to simply the 'foreigner') is a recurrent

I would like to thank Claire Jowitt for feedback on a draft of this chapter, and my fellow panelists and chair (Rachel Willie, Maria Shmygol, and Daniel Carey) at the Society for Renaissance Studies conference in Southampton (July, 2014), where I delivered an earlier version of this paper.

'type' in journeying plays, and this characterological approach enables
consideration of the role and value of staged travel for early modern
playgoers. This, in turn, affords insights into what binds together the
generically disparate plays referred to as journeying plays: the travelling
or displaced protagonist may be of more central importance than the
nature of their story.[4]

Although I am aware of the unfashionability of characterological studies in an apparently post-theory context, the fact that early moderns
so consistently evaluate the moral 'character' of characters who travel
encourages me to revisit a critical approach that has largely fallen by the
wayside.[5] In part, what makes travelling characters so interesting is the
destabilising influence they exert on Aristotelian notions of character
as 'good or fine' (having moral purpose) and exhibiting 'consistency' –
travellers being frequently neither 'good' nor 'constant'.[6] Andrew
Hadfield has observed how Roger Ascham's invective against Italianised
Englishmen expresses a widespread concern that 'travelers to Italy bring
back vices that undermine stability, having tasted excessive and damag-
ing freedom abroad':[7] travel was a potentially corruptive pursuit for
Englishmen at a time when the English nation state was barely nascent.
Accordingly, texts offering advice on travel tend to depict early modern
English travellers as 'characteristically' inconstant and culturally amorphous (so much so that Jonson's traveller in *Cynthia's Revels* (1600) is
actually called 'Amorphous').[8] Despite this, and somewhat surprisingly, in
early modern drama the virtues of the travelling character are frequently
espoused. Accordingly, I want to revisit and offer an alternative to Sara
Warneke's suggestion that '[t]ravelers, particularly educational travelers,
were not only the comic relief of early modern English drama and popular literature, they were also darkly threatening Machiavellian Italianates,
moral degenerates, cultural renegades and habitual liars.'[9] Notably
absent from Warneke's list are the characters whose pleasurable travels
potentially form a point of identification or affinity for the playgoer at
a public theatre who might yearn to see beyond his or her immediate
surroundings.

Rather than pursuing any specific individual playwright's method of
character-construction, I want to think about the relationship between
'character' and playgoer. This relationship has previously been emphasised by Ruth Lunney, who draws attention to the implicit bond
between player and playgoer and identifies 'character' as the precise
nexus of that affiliation when she argues for 'a significant shift in audience and reader response' to character in pre- and post-Marlovian drama,

'from an attention to ethical concerns to an interest in individual psychology'.[10] Whereas the older morality plays led audiences to ask ethical questions (*should* a character pursue a certain course of action?), after Marlowe the interest lay instead in *why* a character pursued that action.[11] As I will argue in this chapter, both the ethics and motivations of travelling characters come under scrutiny on the early modern stage, but a conspicuous number of stage-travellers escape censure for their supposedly subversive acts and are instead positively celebrated within the context of the play world.[12] In other words, they seem to offer a model for emulation or endorsement by the playgoer at least as often as they are depicted in negative terms, and where they are censured it is typically for something other than their wanderlust. Hence although early modern journeying plays were written primarily for entertainment, and the veracity of travel writing more generally is notoriously unreliable (hence travellers may proverbially lie with authority),[13] I want to make a claim for the stage's contribution to the history of travel in another sense.[14] In terms of the presentation of 'character', journeying plays are almost uniquely qualified to help shape the popular imaginary by offering a proxy for playgoers' desires. 'Character' is an intensely dramatic concept,[15] and the way the stage presents the recurring type of the travelling character should be seen not as a mere parasitic reflector of broader discourses of travel, but as actively determining or affecting those discourses in the public arena.

Reads pages and leaves

Peregrine Joyless in Richard Brome's *The Antipodes* (1638) is a key example of the wanderlust-afflicted character type. His father's description of Peregrine's illness attributes the affliction to his obsessive reading of John Mandeville's fantastic *Travels* and other accounts of exotica:

> In tender years he always loved to read
> Reports of travels and of voyages.
> And when young boys like him would tire themselves
> With sports and pastimes, and restore their spirits
> Again by meat and sleep, he would whole days
> And nights (sometimes by stealth) be on such books
> As might convey his fancy round the world.[16]

By reading '[r]eports of travels and voyages', Peregrine has become utterly absorbed in a world of fictional travels, to the point that he has not even consummated his marriage of three years. What is significant

here is that 'books ... might convey his fancy round the world' *and* spur
him on in his desire for actual travel.[17] We learn that:

> When he grew up towards twenty,
> His mind was all on fire to be abroad.
> Nothing but travel still was all his aim;
> There was no voyage or foreign expedition
> Be said to be in hand, but he made suit
> To be made one in it. (1.1.138–43)

As Claire Jowitt has shown, plays such as *The Antipodes* frequently
'engage with humanist debates about the respective merits of action and
contemplation' in the realm of travel and travel writing.[18] These debates
typically turn on the utility of reading as compared with first-hand experience (a version of the more famous tension between reliance on antiquarian forms of knowledge and the first principles approach of Francis
Bacon and others). Journeying plays undoubtedly engage with such
epistemological questions about 'the ideal relationship between reading
and action in relation to travel', but a lesser studied aspect of such plays'
interests in reading and travelling centres on the extent to which lived
experience offers gratification or pleasure, rather than confirmation of
second-hand knowledge.[19]

Julie Sanders has noted that what plays such as Brome's 'invariably tell
us most about ... are not the locations of travel, the exotic far-off lands,
actual or fictional, to which their characters journey, but the fantasies
of those doing the travelling and therefore of the theatre audience that
shares the experience'.[20] Implicit here is a sense of the playgoer's potential
identification with the 'fantasies' of the character aspiring to travel; an
eminently sensible supposition, yet one that is often overshadowed by
the ridiculous depictions of stage-travellers such as Sir Politic Would-Be
in Jonson's *Volpone* (1606). I see a similarity between Brome's Peregrine
and Marlowe's Faustus, who journeys 'to prove cosmography', and to
see first-hand what he has read about, for the simple reason that doing
so is enjoyable. Faustus 'long[s] to see the monuments / And situation
of bright splendent Rome', and Mephistopheles guides him through the
city of seven hills, noting the 'flowing Tiber's stream,' 'the bridge called
Ponte Angelo,' and 'the gates and high pyramides / That Julius Caesar
brought from Africa'.[21] Early modern travellers did have such foreknowl-
edge of the sights they would see: the Swiss tourist Thomas Platter, for
example, visited St Paul's in London in 1599 and noted: '[o]n descent
I observed that there are two choirs or churches in St. Paul's, one above

the other; and in the choir, I saw an uncommonly imposing monument to Christopher Hatton, which Camden describes.'[22] Although conservative humanists like Roger Ascham expressed concern over the experience (rather than knowledge) of foreign lands,[23] the anticipation of witnessing at first hand what they had read about in books was for Faustus and Peregrine a distinctly pleasurable forerunner of modern tourism.[24]

In the paradigm set up for Brome's Peregrine, it is not travelling that causes dementia, but blockage of the ability to act on *desires* to travel.[25] The conditioning and indulgence of desire (rather than knowledge) is important here, and Brome's favoured medium (the theatre) was well placed to endorse proto-tourism precisely because it was equally receptive, in a Horatian manner, to the acquisition of both pleasure and knowledge. In his censure of stage plays, the anti-theatricalist Stephen Gosson was keenly attuned to what he perceived as the dangerous pleasures underpinning both travel and theatre, objecting that 'Tragedies and Commedies stirre up affections, and affections are naturally planted in that part of the minde that is common to us with brute beastes', before noting that '[h]e that travelleth to advance the worst part of the minde, is like unto him, that in governement of Cities, gives all the authoritie to the worste men.' Travel should be undertaken to improve the mind and benefit the country, not for pleasure. Gosson continues the travel metaphor, likening the playgoer to a horseman who lacks control: 'But the Poetes that write playes, and they that present them upon the Stage, studie to make our affections over-flow, whereby they draw the bridle from that parte of the mind, that should ever be curbed, from running our heade.'[26] Journeying plays must have been particularly vexing for Gosson, it seems. The stimulation but ultimate prevention of Peregrine's affections is recognised by Brome as being problematic: Peregrine reads, seeks to travel, but is thwarted. Travel (whether real or imagined) is distinctly therapeutic in Brome's play. As an aspirant traveller, Peregrine is arguably a proxy for playgoer desires, rather than the fulfilment of them, but the mechanism for satisfying Peregrine's cravings is theatrical (a staged voyage to the Antipodes), hence members of the playgoing public who had read about distant lands but who were unable to voyage abroad could, in theory, attempt to sate their appetite for exotica through an on-stage proxy in the form of a travelling character like Faustus or an aspirant traveller like Peregrine.

Possibly the most celebrated travelling character in early modern drama is Old Fortunatus. The German legend of Fortunatus – the Cypriot whom Lady Fortune supplies with an inexhaustible purse, and whose theft of a magical wishing cap provides him with instantaneous transportation – was popular on London stages in the 1590s. A lost Fortunatus play (or two-part play) appears in the diary of the Rose playhouse manager Philip Henslowe as an old play returning to the Admiral's repertory in the spring season of 1596, and probably existed as early as 1594.[27] In 1599, Dekker was paid for a new play on the subject, *Old Fortunatus*,[28] which was promptly altered for performance at Richmond Palace that Christmas, and appeared in print in 1600.[29] A version of Dekker's play enjoyed an afterlife on the continent too. A German Fortunatus play, *Comœdia von Fortunato und Seinem Secekel und Wünschhütlein*, which critics agree is clearly related to Dekker's play, was published in Leipzig in 1620;[30] it was probably performed in Graz in 1608 and again in Dresden in 1626. June Schlueter argues that the German text corresponds to the public theatre version of Dekker's play, which preceded the alterations for the performance before Queen Elizabeth I.[31] It represents the stage of composition prior to the English text that was published in 1600. Since fantastical voyaging is synonymous with the name 'Fortunatus', it is reasonable to assume that the popularity of dramatised versions of the legend is indicative of a widespread appreciation of the vicarious experience of instantaneous transportation that stage plays afforded their audiences. Rather than being merely whimsical, however, these plays make a sustained and deliberate case for the virtues of pleasurable travel over the more conservative approach advocated in *ars apodemica* literature.[32]

When Dekker's Old Fortunatus dies in Act 2, he bequeaths to his sons the inexhaustible purse given to him by Lady Fortune and the magical wishing cap that he stole from an Eastern sultan. These fantastical items have facilitated his extraordinary travel in the first two acts of the play, but they are not the only travel-related objects that Fortunatus's sons inherit. Their father's dying words are the injunction, 'Peruse this booke: farwell'.[33] The 'booke' referred to is Fortunatus's diary and this is the first hint that the old man had been keeping one: but what information does it contain, and why does he want his sons to read it? What was worth passing on to his children? While Ampedo grieves, Andelocia announces: 'ile sit and read what Storie my father has written here' (2.2.327–28). A little later he reveals the book's contents: 'See, heres a Storie of all his travels; this booke shall come out with a new Addition: Ile treade after my Fathers steps; ile goe measure the world' (2.2.368–71). His use of the word 'Storie' here is telling, in that it suggests narrative or biography on his father's part, rather than the mere recording of facts and figures. His subsequent announcement that 'this booke shall come out' implies not only an intention to continue travelling after the manner of his deceased father, but also an intention to publish the travel observations in anticipation of the mode of eccentric traveller-observers such as Thomas Coryate, Fynes Moryson, or William Lithgow,[34] and the seeking of a more extensive readership than just him and his brother.[35] Its effect is immediate: it spurs Andelocia on to greater travels himself. Intriguingly, the effect is even more pronounced in the German version, whose details may have been compressed by Dekker in a bid to make room for the additional material required for the court performance of his play. Andelosia (as his name is spelled in the 1620 edition) draws his brother's attention to the book and says:

> unter dessen habe ich unsers Vatern BIBLIOTHEC gar durch gesuchet / und ein Buch gefunden / worin er alle seine Reisen die Zeit seines Lebens eingeschrieben / und finde wie er in seiner Jugendt die halbe Welt / alle Christliche Königreiche durchzogen / und da er unser Fraw Mutter schon gehabt / ist er noch in die Heidenschafft gezogen / derhalben lieber was wollen wir anfahen / laß uns unsers Vatern Fußstapffen auch nachtreten / laß uns ziehen und nach Ehren streben / wie unser Vater gethan / hastu es nicht gelesen / so liß es noch / ich weiß du wirst in eine Anmuth dadurch kommen.

> in the meantime I have searched through our dear father's library / and found a book / in which he noted down all of the travels he has done throughout his lifetime / and found out how in his youth he went through half the world / through all Christian kingdoms / and even though he had our dear mother already / he still went to heathendom / because of this what shall we embark upon / let's follow in our dear father's footsteps / let's go and strive for honours / in the way our dear father has done / did you not read it / so read it now / I know you will get into its charm.[36]

Andelosia enthuses about the pleasures of reading his father's account ('its charm') and hopes his brother will share his enthusiasm. The stimulus to travel is clear; one son, at least, wants to set off just like his father had earlier encouraged them both to do.[37]

This positive depiction of voyaging is all the more noteworthy because Dekker was demonstrably aware of the risks to one's moral character posed by travel, yet chose to offer a positive counter-example. In his 1606 pamphlet, *The Seven Deadly Sins of London*, he devotes a lengthy section to the vice of 'apishnesse', which is predicated on the fear that English character will be corrupted:

> *Apishnesse* rides in a Chariot made of nothing but cages, in which are all the strangest out-landish Birds that can be gotten: the Cages are stucke full of Parats feathers: the Coach-man is an *Italian Mownti-banck* who drives a Fawne and a Lambe.[38]

Andelocia's initial response to seeing his father returned from travels is to level abuse of precisely this kind at him (he describes his father as 'a young Ape, full of fantasticke trickes, or a painted Parrat stucke full of outlandish feathers') (2.2.25–26), but, as we have seen, Andelocia quickly becomes a convert. Moreover, none of the travelling characters are punished for their travelling fancy, only for their riotous waste of riches. When Fortune returns to claim Fortunatus's life, it is his extravagance that is lamented:

> From beggerie
> I plum'd thee like an Estrich, like that Estrich
> Thou hast eaten Metals, and abusde my giftes,
> Hast plaid the Ruffian, wasted that in ryots,
> Which as a blessing I bestowed on thee. (2.2.233–37)

Fortune appears utterly unconcerned about Fortunatus's fantastical voyages, instead noting that 'endlesse follies follow endless *wealth*' (2.2.239; my emphasis) and singling out his wastefulness rather than wanderlust as the cause of his demise ('His life hath wastefull beene, and let it waste') (2.2.254). His sons are likewise shown to be greedy and intemperate, Andelocia dying a miserable 'reprobate' who acknowledges his 'abuse' of '[r]iches and knowledge' (5.2.169, 173–74), while his ostensibly virtuous brother Ampedo is denounced by Virtue for his lack of wisdom ('The Idiots cap I once wore on my head, / Did figure him') (5.2.271–72).

Though the squandering of riches is explicitly condemned, travel is implicitly celebrated for affording ordinary men like Fortunatus and his sons (and by extension, ordinary playgoers) a glimpse of the broader world beyond their shores. Fortunatus expresses this desire succinctly, in terms that resemble Richard Hakluyt's famous censure of his countrymen for 'sluggish security':

> When in the warmth of mine owne countries armes
> We yawn'd like sluggards, when this small Horizon
> Imprison'd up my body, then mine eyes
> Worshipt these clouds as brightest; but, my boyes,
> The glistring beames which doe abroad appeare,
> (In other heavens) fire is not halfe so cleare.[39]

His sentiments are modest in one sense: this is no megalomaniac warmonger like Tamburlaine, who travels to conquer (a distinction reinforced by the fact of both elderly protagonists leaving behind weak sons to follow in their fathers' footsteps). This is a man of humble origins who simply wants to see the world, and regards remaining at home as claus-trophobic and soporific.

In a similar way, Fortunatus's son Andelocia responds to the servant Shadow's conservative belief that 'its better staying in your owne countrie' with the sharp retort, 'like a Cage-birde and see nothing?' (2.2.397–400). This outburst prompts Shadow to reply:

> Nothing? yes, you may see things enough, for what can you see abroad that is not at home? The same Sunne cals you up in the morning, and the same man in the Moone lights you to bed at night, our fields are as greene as theirs in summer, and their frosts will nip us more in winter: Our birds sing as sweetly, and our women are as faire: In other countries you shall have one drinke to you, whilst he kisse your hand, and ducke, heele poyson you. (2.2.401–07)

As Tiffany Stern notes in her recent edition of *A Jovial Crew*, Brome reworked this passage in the context of the young steward Springlove taking leave of his master Oldrents.[40] Where Andelocia resented being cooped up like a caged-bird, Springlove accuses his master of having kept him like 'a swallow in a cage' (1.1.178), prompting Oldrents to criticise his 'gadding humour' and expound at length on the merits of staying at home:

> Does not the sun as comfortably shine
> Upon my gardens as the opener fields?
> Or on my fields as others far remote?
> Are not my walks and greens as delectable
> As the highways and commons? Are the shades
> Of sycamore and bowers of eglantine
> Less pleasing than of bramble or thorn-hedges?
> Or of my groves and thickets than wild-woods?
> Are not my fountain-waters fresher than
> The troubled streams where every beast does drink?
> Do not the birds sing here as sweet and lively
> As any other where? Is not thy bed more soft,
> And rest more safe, than in a field or barn?
> Is a full table, which is called thine own,
> Less curious or wholesome than the scraps
> From others' trenchers, twice or thrice translated? (1.1.192–207)

Oldrents, like Shadow, remains unconvinced about the merits of taking '[d]iversity of air' (1.1.218). Garrett A. Sullivan, Jr., observes that Oldrents contrasts 'the lands Springlove manages and those across which he longs to roam', comparing 'exclusivity and order' with 'uncultivated nature' in such a way that 'these interlocking comparisons are not only

descriptive ... but also evaluative', establishing a clear opposition between
aristocratic notions of space and travel and 'vagabond desires'.[41] The
purpose is ostensibly to dissuade Springlove from travel, but an implication of Stern's editorial gloss is that Brome must have read Dekker, since
there are no performance records of *Old Fortunatus* from this period.
He would therefore have known the effect of basing Oldrents's arguments on the unconvincing objections of the miserly Shadow. Dekker's
play leaves no doubt that travel is exhilarating and rewarding, and that
Shadow's objections hold little authority. Springlove's response is unsur-
prising: 'I must abroad or perish' (1.1.226). In *Old Fortunatus* Shadow
(like Oldrents) remains sceptical, demanding to know 'what can you see
abroad that is not at home?' (2.2.401–02). Andelocia ignores his protes-
tations and resolves that they both shall travel to England, for no greater
purpose than personal interest.

Although *Old Fortunatus* occasionally verges on criticism of fanciful
transportation, it consistently shies away from it. For example, the play
opens with Fortunatus lost in a wandering wood or *selva oscura*, which,
like the Redcrosse Knight and Una's encounter with Error in Book 1 of
Spenser's *Faerie Queene*, ought to exemplify how to wander (to travel
idly, without purpose) is to err.[42] However, Dekker does not censure
Fortunatus for such wandering: the wood in Dekker's play is (as Joseph
Loewenstein observes) a reflection of the protagonist's distracted and
dejected mind.[43] His miserableness in this first scene, in which he is the
embodiment of perpetual motion in a confined space, forms a clear contrast with the exuberance bestowed on him by unfettered travel throughout the next two acts of the play:

> Boyes be proud, your Father hath the whole world in this compasse, I am
> all felicitie, up to the brimmes. In a minute am I come from *Babylon*, I
> have beene this halfe howre in *Famagosta*. (2.2.123–25)

Stasis entails dejection; travel produces felicity. In a similar vein, one
might expect that the means by which Fortunatus acquires his ability to
travel might come under greater scrutiny. The wishing-hat was not Lady
Fortune's gift; it was stolen ('I robd the *Souldan* of it') (2.2.297), yet at
no point does this theft attract criticism. Likewise, despite the fact that
the sultan uses the fantastical hat with temperance and restraint ('By
this I steale to every Princes court, / And heare their private councels
and prevent / All daungers which to *Babylon* are meant') (2.1.90–92),
Fortunatus is never tempted to emulate the sultan's shrewd statecraft,
preferring instead to 'cut through the ayre like a Falcon' and 'progresse ...

through the world' (2.2.128, 221). Fortunatus's indulgent use of the hat ultimately escapes censure, and stimulates a comparable wanderlust in his son once Andelocia reads about his father's escapades. Andelocia continues to travel at will, but exceeds his father's lavish spending, at one point burning 'Cynamon, Cloves, Nutmegs, Licorish and all other spices' instead of firewood to cook a banquet (3.1.434–35). It is thus the spend-thrift nature of Fortunatus and his sons' lavish lifestyle ('their ryots made them poore') (5.2.211) that attracts condemnation from Lady Fortune (and, we assume, the audience). It may or may not be coincidental that the writing of a play about the (mis)use of fabulous, inexhaustible riches coincided with a period of financial difficulty for Dekker: he was impris-oned for debt in 1598 and again in 1599.[44]

Birds of a Feather: Travelling Characters and Like-Minded Playgoers

The paradigm I am discussing, wherein pleasurable travel is prompted by a textual cue (i.e., the depiction of pleasurable travel in Fortunatus's diary), has implications for understanding how early modern playgoers might respond to the depiction of such travel in performance. As long ago as the mid-twentieth century, Louis B. Wright noted the probable attraction that an English reader felt in response to tales of travel on the printed page:

> The common man found in the narratives of travel not only a romantic literature more fascinating than fiction, but a call to personal adventure. These were stories, not of King Arthur or of fabulous knights, but of men who lived and had their being in Elizabethan England. To any apprentice might come adventures that would have dazzled even Guy of Warwick, as Captain John Smith himself had witnessed.[45]

Wright's comments could easily be applied to the stage, and it may be worth remembering in that context that Smith did in fact claim in his 1630 folio *The True Travels* that 'they have acted my fatall Tragedies upon the Stage', though regrettably the play in question is now lost.[46] In the plays of Marlowe, Dekker, and Brome we see clear examples of char-acters who are inspired to travel by the examples set forth in books. A case could be made, I think, for arguing that the theatrical examples of returned travellers function analogously to the exemplum of the printed page. It is the role of character, rather than the depiction of place, that is central to my case, however; the untravelled playgoer is not in a posi-tion to evaluate the veracity or verisimilitude (if any) of exotic locales

represented on the early modern stage, but they *are* in a position to identify with travelling characters' desires.

As Laurie Maguire and Aleksandra Thostrup, Jonathan Crewe,
Leanore Lieblein, and others have noted, the word 'character' in early
modern England primarily signified the inscription of letters or symbols
in written communication;[47] however, Lieblein in particular (drawing on
observations made by the playwright Thomas Heywood in his *Apology for
Actors*, 1612) has drawn a striking comparison between page and stage
precisely in these terms, suggesting that '[a] dramatic character, too, is a
form of writing, a transformation of materials, a synthesis, and an interpretation. However, the writing is accomplished by the actor's process
of performing a part, and the material transformed is the actor's body.'[48]
There is, in other words, a neat parallel between recording/writing about
one's travels in a book (as inspiration for travel) and travelling-characters
as 'a form of writing ... accomplished by the actor's process of performing a part' on stage, before an audience. In this final section, I want to
offer two further examples of travelling characters to support this theory,
and to help make the transition from books to plays as the prompt for
adventure: Meriel and Rachel in Brome's *A Jovial Crew*, and Mirabell in
Fletcher's *The Wild-Goose Chase*.

Although Brome's play offers social commentary on vagabondage
and aristocracy, offering an escape from the mounting political turmoil
that would culminate with the English Civil War, it explores 'liberty
and freedom' as desirable qualities of everyday life, not just within the
political context of the cavaliers.[49] Oldrents's daughters acknowledge the
advantages they have been born into, but feel constrained by the 'rules
and government' of their father's house (2.1.19); Meriel yearns for the
freedom that peregrination affords:

> absolute freedom such as the very beggars have, to feast and revel here
> today and yonder tomorrow, next day where they please, and so on still,
> the whole country or kingdom over? There's liberty! The birds of the air
> can take no more. (2.1.20–25)

Perhaps given Brome's debts to Dekker elsewhere, it should not be
surprising that there is such a prevalence of bird imagery throughout
A Jovial Crew; it is a leitmotif of *Old Fortunatus* and an obvious choice for
representing unfettered freedom of travel. Although Rachel and Meriel's
suitors try to talk the girls into domestic tourism ('Dover's Olympics or
the Cotswold Games') (2.1.95), they ultimately offer to take them 'as
far as horse and money can carry us' (2.1.100–01). Once the adventure

is agreed upon, Hilliard (one of the suitors) offers a curious twist on the bird imagery. His concern is whether the aristocrats, who have led a sheltered existence (like armchair travellers), will assimilate into the company of beggars. He says: '[i]f we light raw and tame amongst 'em – like cage-birds among a flight of wild ones – we shall never pick up a living but have our brains pecked out' (2.1.231–34). Although he is not as ardently pro-travel as the women, Hilliard ultimately recognises the limitations of having remained 'caged' so long.⁵⁰

If travel provides a desirable alternative to the restrictions and limitations produced by class in Brome's play, in Fletcher's *The Wild-Goose Chase*, 'wandering' maps onto another transgressive desire: the 'wandering eye' of the rakish wild-goose of the play's title, Mirabell. The temptations of 'Italian liberty' are championed over the dreariness of the home-culture, France, in a manner redolent of Andelocia's exchange with Shadow and Springlove's exchange with Oldrents.⁵¹ Again we have an insistence on the benefits of going abroad: 'There's no reason,' says the fellow traveller Pinac, that '[a] gentleman and a traveler should be clapped up' (1.2.81–82). Although exotica are encountered, they are sexualised man-eating 'she-cannibals' rather than genuinely Mandevillian anthropophagi (2.1.72). The 'brags of a wanderer' are sexual, not fabulous (Pinac's phrase 'clapped up' may well refer to syphilis and thus the circumscription of sexual as well as geographical liberty), and the 'freedom of a traveller' is prized by the young men (1.3.189, 1.2.71).

Like Fortunatus, the returned traveller Mirabell has a book too, in which he keeps track of his adventures; but in a world where spatial and sexual liberties are equated, his is necessarily a less savoury book of conquests, a 'debt-book' of his 'mistresses' (2.1.169). Although Mirabell takes pride in his sexual greed and 'travelled liberty', the 'inventory' causes offence (to Oriana, his betrothed, and her brother De Gard) rather than imitation, and attracts a certain censure even if this rakish character is also somewhat seductive as far as the playgoer is concerned (2.1.19, 168).⁵² Yet it is striking that despite his revulsion at Mirabell's treatment of his sister and other 'conquests', De Gard, who had earlier expressed scepticism over the benefits of young men travelling abroad (1.1.18–27), still does not think entirely ill of travel, encouraging Mirabell only to maintain a distinction between his indulgences:

> Be not too glorious foolish;
> Sum not your travels up with vanities,
> It ill becomes your expectation. (2.1.180–82)

Travel, in this formulation, has its merits, provided 'boorish behaviour' does not diminish the benefits.[53]

Certainly there are instances in which doubt is expressed over the value of foreign experience. Lillia-Bianca, another of Mirabell's potential brides, describes her ideal husband thus:

> Travelled he should be, but through himself exactly,
> For 'tis fairer to know manners well than countries. (1.3.186–87)

Although she seems to acknowledge the value of knowledge gained through travel ('Travelled he should be'), she hastens to explain that she refers to self-knowledge (knowledge 'through himself') and to assert that being well versed in the custom of one's own country ('manners') is preferable to gaining experiences abroad. This is not precisely an attack on the foreign, however, so much as a preference for the domestic; and as the play progresses, the metaphor of travel as a form of sexual as well as geographical liberty is increasingly foregrounded, such that it is difficult to disentangle objections to promiscuity from objections to wandering. As marriage becomes a virtually inevitable fate for Mirabell, he rehearses and appropriates the by now familiar arguments about travel's benefits and dangers, but transposes the questions of knowledge and freedom onto a sexual register. In what might be construed as at least a tacit acknowledgement of the efficacy of the pro-travel arguments, he turns to a rhetoric that establishes marriage as sedentary ('Lie lazy here, / Bound to a wife...?') and travel as a desirable escape:

> I'll amble all the world over,
> And run all hazards, misery, and poverty,
> So I escape the dangerous Bay of Matrimony. (5.2.2–3, 16–18)

The sexualisation of travel persists to the play's final line, when the newly betrothed Belleur (Mirabell's fellow traveller) abandons his libertinism in favour of monogamy, and anticipates the consummation of marital vows via another travel metaphor: 'No more for Italy; for the Low Countries, I' (5.6.110). Although Mirabell and his companions are genuine travellers, the greater significance of 'travel' in Fletcher's play is as metaphor for unfettered sexual indulgence. Geographical wandering itself is not the true object of scorn, and Mirabell's increasingly desperate attempts to preserve his bachelor's lifestyle are ultimately curtailed by the formal comedic resolution of marriage to Oriana.

Theatre differs from written accounts of travel in its animated representation of voyaging to distant lands; it can be seen (as in the case of Brome's

Peregrine) to offer a kind of solution for the individual whose wanderlust cannot be satisfied by reading alone, but simultaneously it is not a perfect substitute for the lived experience of travel. Through their positive representation of travelling characters and their experiences, plays might be seen to stimulate the playgoer's desire for travel at least as much as they satisfy such desires, but they do not offer this tantalising possibility with an intention to corrupt. While the spendthrift nature of Fortunatus and his sons, the libertine indulgences of Mirabell, and the transgression of class embraced by Brome's young aristocrats are variously censured by other characters or by their plays' formal resolutions, the travel that accompanies these indulgences rarely attracts criticism within the drama. When it does, in Dekker's and Brome's plays in particular, it is met with some of the most forceful defences of travel to be found in any early modern text.

Although English travellers of the early modern period were conventionally prone to corruption of identity and degeneration of (especially nationalistic) 'character', stage depictions of travelling-characters are oddly noteworthy for the relative stability of this inherently unstable 'type'. This is true regardless of where they fall on the continuum between ethical and psychological development delineated by Lunney. Old Fortunatus knowingly uses the wishing hat in a manner that contrasts with the sultan's ostensibly ethical use of it for statecraft, and his sons consequently expect him to return like 'a painted Parrat stucke full of outlandish feathers', but his outlandish (literally 'foreign') attire ultimately does not erode his moral fibre (2.2.26). Instead, his inexhaustible purse does: 'golden solutions left social problems unresolved', as William H. Sherman shrewdly observes of the play's proto-capitalist fantasy of wealth.[54] At the other extreme, in which the psychology (rather than ethics) of travel is considered, Brome's Peregrine shuns historical explorers such as Sir Francis Drake, Sir Thomas Cavendish, Sir John Hawkins, and Sir Martin Frobisher in favour of an adventurer, Mandeville, whose contribution to travel literature is decidedly more pleasurable than functional, but his simulated 'travels in th'Antipodes' are not at fault (1.3.20–31, 5.2.385). To Warneke's taxonomy of detestable and derisible travellers, then, we should add the apparently more positive example of the returned traveller whose exploits are not condemned. Doing so will help us recognise the importance of 'character' to understanding and even defining the early modern 'journeying play' by offering a clear focal point and unifying principle common to plays as generically diverse as the 'tragedy' of *Tamburlaine* (which is not especially tragic) and the 'comedy' of *Old Fortunatus* (which is not especially comic).

Notes

1 For mercantile readings, see, for example, Richard Wilson, 'Visible Bullets: *Tamburlaine the Great* and Ivan the Terrible', *English Literary History*, 62 (1995), 47–68; Crystal Bartolovich, '"Baseless Fabric": London as a "World City"', in *The Tempest' and Its Travels*, ed. Peter Hulme and William H. Sherman (London: Reaktion Books, 2000), 13–26; Joan Pong Linton, 'Inconstancy: Coming to Indians Through *Troilus and Cressida*', in *The Romance of the New World: Gender and the Literary Formations of English Colonialism* (Cambridge University Press, 2006), 131–54; or Edward M. Test, '*The Tempest* and the Newfoundland Cod Fishery', in *Global Traffic: Discourses and Practices of Trade in English Literature and Culture from 1550 to 1700*, ed. Barbara Sebek and Stephen Deng (New York: Palgrave Macmillan, 2008), 201–20. Readings that foreground questions of religion and religious difference include Barbara Fuchs, 'Faithless Empires: Pirates, Renegadoes, and the English Nation', *English Literary History* 67 (2000), 45–69; Daniel Vitkus, *Turning Turk: English Theater and the Multicultural Mediterranean, 1570–1630* (New York: Palgrave, 2003); and numerous others. For readings of race and colonisation, see, for example, Stephen Greenblatt, *Marvelous Possessions: The Wonder of the New World* (Oxford: Clarendon Press, 1991); Emily C. Bartels, *Spectacles of Strangeness: Imperialism, Alienation, and Marlowe* (Philadelphia: University of Pennsylvania Press, 1993); or Richmond Barbour, *Before Orientalism: London's Theatre of the East, 1576–1626* (Cambridge University Press, 2003).

2 Anthony Parr, '"For his Travailes let the *Globe* witnesse": Venturing on the Stage in Early Modern England', Chapter 1 in this volume.

3 For an overview of the *ars apodemica* tradition, see, for example, Daniel Carey, 'Hakluyt's Instructions: *The Principal Navigations* and Sixteenth-Century Travel Advice', *Studies in Travel Writing* 13, no. 2 (2009), 167–85; Daniel Carey, *Continental Travel and Journeys Beyond Europe in the Early Modern Period: An Overlooked Connection* (London: Hakluyt Society, 2009). Parr's chapter notes the inherent danger in the fact that '[b]ooks and plays that do not foster an understanding of the Christian path are liable to transport their auditors into the wrong kind of experience' (23).

4 On journeying plays, travel drama, and voyage drama as key terms, and how attention to lost plays stands to alter our conception of them, see the 'Introduction' to this volume.

5 On Aristotelian *ethos* in relation to character in early modern drama, see Jonathan Crewe, 'Reclaiming Character?', *Shakespeare Studies* 34 (2006), 35–40. The special issue in which Crewe's article was published explores whether the concept of character survives after theory.

6 Ibid., 38.

7 Andrew Hadfield, 'The Benefits of a Warm Study: The Resistance to Travel Before Empire', in *A Companion to the Global Renaissance: English Literature and Culture in the Era of Expansion*, ed. Jyotsna G. Singh (Chichester: Blackwell, 2009), 101–13, at 103; see also Anthony Parr, *Renaissance Mad*

Voyages: Experiments in Early Modern English Travel (Farnham: Ashgate, 2015), 124–25.

8 See Ben Jonson, *Cynthia's Revels* (Quarto Version), ed. Eric Rasmussen and Matthew Steggle, in *The Cambridge Edition of the Works of Ben Jonson*, ed. David Bevington, Martin Butler, and Ian Donaldson (Cambridge University Press, 2012), vol. I, 429–547, at 443.

9 Sara Warneke, 'Educational Travelers: Popular Imagery and Public Criticism in Early Modern England', *Journal of Popular Culture* 28, no. 3 (1994), 71.

10 Ruth Lunney, *Marlowe and the Popular Tradition: The Revels Plays Companion Library* (Manchester University Press, 2002), 126.

11 Ibid., 126.

12 It may be significant that the surviving corpus of journeying plays is almost exclusively *not* tragic; comedy is inherently tolerant of (or even encouraging of) experimentation with social norms within a 'safe' generic space that guarantees formal closure and the reconstitution of the status quo by the play's end. It is unclear whether travelling characters would have been so positively depicted in the lost 'New World's Tragedy' (Anon., 1595), 'Conquest of the West Indies' (John Day, William Haughton, and Wentworth Smith, 1601), or 'The Plantation of Virginia' (Anon., 1623), for instance. On the surprisingly positive depiction of genuine travellers on stage, see Daniel Vitkus, 'Rogue Cosmopolitans on the Early Modern Stage: John Ward, Thomas Stukeley, and the Sherley Brothers', Chapter 7 in this volume.

13 R. W. Dent, *Proverbial Language in English Drama Exclusive of Shakespeare, 1495–1616* (Berkeley, CA: University of California Press, 1984), T476*.

14 On the critical neglect of stage travel in discussions of the history of travel, see Daniel Vitkus, 'Labor and Travel on the Early Modern Stage: Representing the Travail of Travel in Dekker's *Old Fortunatus* and Shakespeare's *Pericles*', in *Working Subjects in Early Modern English Drama*, ed. Michelle M. Dowd and Natasha Korda (Farnham: Ashgate, 2011), 225–42. A rare and still significant exception to the neglect identified by Vitkus is Samuel C. Chew's *The Crescent and the Rose: Islam and England During the Renaissance* (New York: Oxford University Press, 1937).

15 In *Character & Person* (Oxford University Press, 2014), John Frow takes 'fictional character as the starting point from which to examine the spectrum of modalities along which persons exist', because 'fictional characters have a more clearly modal existence than real people do (they are more clearly constructs of the imagination), and in that sense they are exemplary of the way a mode of reality is ascribed to persons of all sorts' (vi). He connects fictional 'character' to real-life personhood by observing that 'characters and persons are at once ontologically discontinuous … and logically interdependent', suggesting that we should 'understand persons not as ontological givens but as constructs, which are in part made out of the same materials as fictional characters' (vii). The construction of character in drama therefore has implications for the 'construction' of the playgoers who witness such plays, and

journeying plays offer a particularly complex and fascinating example of this phenomenon on account of the notoriously malleable identity of the stage traveller in early modern England, prone as it is to acts of self-fashioning and affectation.

16 Richard Brome, *The Antipodes*, 1.1.131–37, in *Three Renaissance Travel Plays: The Revels Plays Companion Library*, ed. Anthony Parr (Manchester University Press, 1995). All further quotations refer to this edition and will be cited by act, scene, and line numbers in the text.

17 See David McInnis, 'Therapeutic Travel in Richard Brome's *The Antipodes*', *Studies in English Literature, 1500–1900* 52, no. 2 (2012), 447–69.

18 Claire Jowitt, 'Hakluyt's Legacy: Armchair Travel in English Renaissance Drama', in *Richard Hakluyt and Travel Writing in Early Modern Europe*, ed. Daniel Carey and Claire Jowitt (Farnham: Ashgate, 2012), 295–306, at 297–98.

19 Ibid., 306.

20 Julie Sanders, 'The Politics of Escapism: Fantasies of Travel and Power in Richard Brome's *The Antipodes* and Ben Jonson's *The Alchemist*', *Writing and Fantasy*, ed. Ceri Sullivan and Barbara White (London: Longman, 1999), 137–50, at 137. Sanders concentrates on 'the potency of fantasies of travel, their complicity in the colonial desires for power and possession, and the politics of fantasies of this nature in the period' (138), and has more to say about the social critiques embedded in utopian fantasy than about the analogue between reading, playgoing, and sightseeing that interests me.

21 Christopher Marlowe, *Doctor Faustus*, 3.1.49–50 and 34–45; references are to the B-text in *Doctor Faustus,* A- and B-texts (1604, 1616): *The Revels Plays*, ed. David Bevington and Eric Rasmussen (Manchester University Press, rpt. 1995). See also my *Mind-Travelling and Voyage Drama*, 67–69.

22 Clare Williams, *Thomas Platter's Travels in England 1599* (London: Jonathan Cape, 1937), 176.

23 See Hadfield, 'The Benefits of a Warm Study', 103.

24 For more on the secularisation of travel and the rise of sight-seeing, see Parr, *Renaissance Mad Voyages*, 108.

25 Cf. Lisa Jardine and Anthony Grafton's article, 'How Gabriel Harvey Read His Livy', which emphasises the Renaissance investment in active / purposeful reading and – in the context of Philip Sidney's 1580 letter to Edward Denny – the possibility that 'aspiring men of action' with too much time on their hands (owing to Queen Elizabeth's resistance to military engagement) ought to read and study as an 'approved, character-forming way of relieving boredom' (*Past and Present* 129 (1990), 30–78, at 39). Such relief, they hasten to qualify, is predicated on the notion of envisaging 'action as the *outcome* of reading – not simply reading as active, but reading as trigger for action' (40). Their argument is made in the context of Gabriel Harvey as an 'armchair politician' (39).

26 Stephen Gosson, *Playes Confuted in Five Actions* (London: Thomas Gosson, 1582), sigs. F$^{r–v}$.

27 See *Henslowe's Diary*, ed. R. A. Foakes. 2nd edn (Cambridge University Press, 2002), 34–37.

28 Ibid., 126–27.

29 After Henslowe paid Dekker in full for *Old Fortunatus*, he paid him a further 20s the very next day for unspecified alterations, and followed this with a payment of 40s on 12 December 1599 'for the eande of fortewnatus for the corte' (Foakes, ed. *Henslowe's Diary*, 127–28). The precise nature and extent of Dekker's alterations are uncertain, but seem to involve (at least) the prologue and epilogue which explicitly address the queen, and probably a substantial enlargement of the subplot involving the supernatural characters Virtue, Vice, and Fortune.

30 For a modern edition, see *Engelische Comedien und Tragedien* [...] *Gedruckt im Jahr M. DC. XX.* See *Spieltexte der Wanderbühne*, ed. Manfred Brauneck (Berlin: Walter de Gruyter, 1970).

31 June Schlueter, 'New Light on Dekker's *Fortunati*', *Medieval and Renaissance Drama in England* 26 (2013), 120–35.

32 On the nature and characteristics of the instructions for travellers genre, see Carey, *Continental Travel*.

33 Thomas Dekker, *Old Fortunatus*, 2.2.313 in *The Dramatic Works of Thomas Dekker*, vol. I, ed. Fredson Bowers (Cambridge University Press, rpt. 1970). All further quotations from *Old Fortunatus* are from this edition and will be cited by act, scene, and line numbers within the text.

34 See Hadfield, 'The Benefits of a Warm Study', 102, for a discussion of this kind of quasi-celebrity travel writing.

35 *OED*, 'to come out' s.v. 'come, v. 12' (available from 1573).

36 *Von Fortunato*, Act 3, p. 148, ll. 11–21 in *Spieltexte der Wanderbühne*; translation provided by Elena Benthaus.

37 See Dekker, *Old Fortunatus*, 2.2.172–89.

38 Thomas Dekker, *The Seven Deadly Sins of London* (London: Printed by E[dward] A[llde] and S. Stafford] for Nathaniel Butter, 1606), 32. On the English anxiety over imitation and identity, see Nandini Das, '"Apes of Imitation": Imitation and Identity in Sir Thomas Roe's Embassy to India', in *A Companion*, ed. Singh 114–28, at 116–18, which discusses this passage from Dekker.

39 Richard Hakluyt, 'To the Right Honorable Sir Francis Walsingham', *The Principall Navigations, Voiages and Discoveries of the English Nation Made by Sea or Over Land* (London: George Bishop and Ralph Newberie, 1589), sig. *2; Dekker, *Old Fortunatus*, 2.2.164–69.

40 See Richard Brome, *A Jovial Crew*, in *Arden Early Modern Drama*, ed. Tiffany Stern (London: Bloomsbury Arden Shakespeare, 2014), 1.1.190–207n. All further quotations from *A Jovial Crew* refer to this edition and will be cited by act, scene, and line numbers within the text.

41 Garrett A. Sullivan, Jr., *The Drama of Landscape: Land, Property, and Social Relations on the Early Modern Stage* (Stanford, CA: Stanford University Press, 1998), 162–63.

42 Edmund Spenser, *The Faerie Queene*, ed. Thomas P. Roche, Jr. (London: Penguin, rpt. 1987), 1.1.13.

43 Joseph Loewenstein, *Responsive Readings: Versions of Echo in Pastoral, Epic, and the Jonsonian Masque* (New Haven, CT: Yale University Press, 1984), 135.

44 His second wife Elizabeth's renouncing of the administration of his estate in 1632 also suggests he died in debt; see John Twyning, 'Dekker, Thomas (*c.*1572–1632)', *Oxford Dictionary of National Biography* (Oxford University Press, 2004; online edn, Jan 2008) [www.oxforddnb.com/view/article/7428].

45 Louis B. Wright, *Middle-Class Culture in Elizabethan England* (London: Methuen, 1964), 547–48.

46 John Smith, *The True Travels, Adventures, and Observations of Captaine John Smith, In Europe, Asia, Africa, and America, from Anno Domini 1593 to 1629* (London: Printed by I[ohn]. H[aviland]. for Thomas Slater, and are to bee sold [by Michael Spark], 1630), sig. A2^{r-v}.

47 Laurie Maguire and Aleksandra Thostrup, 'Marlowe and Character', in *Christopher Marlowe in Context*, ed. Emily C. Bartels and Emma Smith (Cambridge University Press, 2013), 40; Crewe, 'Reclaiming Character?', 36; Leanore Lieblein, 'Embodied Intersubjectivity and the Creation of Early Modern Character', in *Shakespeare and Character: Theory, History, Performance, and Theatrical Persons*, ed. Paul Yachnin and Jessica Slights (Basingstoke: Palgrave Macmillan, 2009), 119.

48 Lieblein, 'Embodied Intersubjectivity', 121.

49 Stern, ed. *Jovial Crew*, 19.

50 The name *Peregrine*, of course (as it appears in Brome's *Antipodes* but also as the veteran traveller in Jonson's *Volpone*), suggests a falcon famed for its movements, and the ill-fated sea captain of *Eastward Ho* has a similarly avian name: *Seagull*.

51 John Fletcher, *The Wild-Goose Chase*, 1.2.86 in *Three Seventeenth-Century Plays on Women and Performance: The Revels Plays Companion Library*, ed. Hero Chalmers, Julie Sanders, and Sophie Tomlinson (Manchester University Press, rpt. 2012). All further quotations from *The Wild-Goose Chase* are from Sophie Tomlinson's edition in that volume and will be cited by act, scene, and line numbers within the text.

52 Mirabell's 'fair return' at the start of the play brings a 'general joy' (1.3.61–62), and his boasts of past conquests ('I have done a thousand more', 2.1.6) resemble the litany of abuses proudly claimed by Aaron and Barabas (Shakespeare, *Titus Andronicus*, ed. Jonathan Bate [London: Routledge/Arden, 1995], 5.1.124; Marlowe, *The Jew of Malta*, ed. James R. Siemon [London: A&C Black / New Mermaids, rpt. 2001], 2.3.176–203).

53 Tomlinson, ed., *Wild-Goose Chase*, 2.1.181–82n.

54 William H. Sherman, '"Gold is the strength, the sinnewes of the world": Thomas Dekker's *Old Fortunatus* and England's Golden Age', *Medieval and Renaissance Drama in England* 6 (1993), 85–102, at 96.

'Constant Changelings', Theatrical Form, and Migration: Stage Travel in the Early 1620s

Clare McManus

University of Roehampton

At the heart of this essay, as at the heart of travel drama, lie questions of identification and recognition. To ask what travel drama is, to question its relationship to generic categorisation, and to ask how an early modern audience might have recognised it when they saw it leads quickly to the related issue of how we too, as modern readers, audiences, and critics, know a travel drama when we see one. In addressing these questions, this essay reconfigures the relationship between early modern English travel drama and genre, reshaping the category of 'stage travel' by attending to theatrical form rather than to source or content. Early modern plays of travel and encounter have conventionally been analysed as responses to actual journeys, or their documentation, or for their incorporation of journeying into dramatic narrative.[1] In contrast, what follows attends instead to theatrical form and, in doing so, proposes a new relationship between travel drama and the fluid generic categories of early modern English theatre. Specifically, this essay takes as its focus a group of plays printed and performed in close proximity in the early 1620s – the early years of the Palatinate crisis – and the shared structures, tropes, and figures that circulate between these plays and which are saturated with the associations of stage travel. Hence, this new understanding of stage travel illuminates the mobility, the migration, of the 'parts' of early modern theatre and offers a redefinition not only of stage travel but of early modern dramaturgy itself.[2]

Under the pressure of the Palatinate crisis that gripped the European continent and dominated courtly and parliamentary debate, English theatre of the early 1620s was preoccupied with the tropes and structures of stage travel, and a range of genres were permeated by its associated theatrical scenarios.[3] A small group of plays performed and printed in the years 1621–22 demonstrate shared structural and aesthetic qualities that suggest a new phase of stage travel and to some extent reshape this category, which for my purposes contains both early modern travel and voyage drama.[4] William Rowley and Thomas Middleton's *The Changeling* was first performed on 7 May 1622 at the Phoenix by the Lady Elizabeth's Men, a performance which can be set against the context of two plays that might conventionally fit the categories of travel plays or voyage dramas and which were, in different ways, its near neighbours.[5] *The Island Princess*, John Fletcher's tragicomedy of imperial and confessional conflict in Maluku, was staged by the King's Men at Whitehall for James I on 26 December 1621 while William Shakespeare's tragedy *Othello* was printed for the first time in quarto only months later in 1622.[6] Barring perhaps only Middleton's *A Game at Chess* (1624), *The Changeling* is one of the most topical plays in the canon, as its connections to the Overbury affair and Frances Howard's notorious virginity test suggest: many interpretations link it to its political moment and, in particular, to the crises of the Bohemian succession and Thirty Years War, and to the planned Spanish Match.[7] Though written around twenty years apart, Fletcher's and Shakespeare's plays, too, contribute to the debates swirling around the Palatinate crisis.[8] Fletcher's eponymous protagonist, Quisara, has been seen as a figure for the imperilled Elizabeth Stuart, while the decision to print *Othello* almost two decades after its first performance is informed by the theatrical fashion for plays about 'Moors', island settings, conversion, or apostasy, and a fiercely political interest in martyrdom, all of which tie this old play closely to its new circumstance.[9]

My interest in examining a set of plays performed or printed in such close proximity does not lie in a focus on the relationship between theatre and a moment of crisis per se.[10] The points of contact between *The Changeling*, *The Island Princess*, and *Othello* indicate a broader phenomenon, namely the permeation of the tropes and structures of stage travel into early 1620s theatre under the pressure of European catastrophe. Hence, what follows will attend to what such moments of political crisis reveal about theatrical dramaturgy and the means by which the aesthetic construction of a closely related subset of plays itself becomes politicised: specifically, I will attend to the circulation between this small group of play texts of aesthetic tropes and structures that gather political resonances through repetition and transformation under the pressure of crisis. It may be surprising to find *The Changeling*, which has been variously categorised as revenge drama, high tragedy, and even tragicomedy, considered next to plays explicitly concerned with travel, but – fittingly for a theatrical period of generic experimentation – reading Rowley and

Middleton's text alongside those of Fletcher and Shakespeare reveals that this group shares tropes of voyaging and its consequences, and brings the migration of these theatrical units and their relationship to stage travel into view. This approach has particular consequences for our understanding of stage travel and its place in the dramaturgy of the 1620s.

The interconnections between printings and performances of *The Island Princess*, *Othello*, and *The Changeling* in 1621–22 highlight *The Changeling*'s place in the circulation or migration of theatrical elements. Put most broadly, it echoes several other play texts, including Christopher Marlowe's *Doctor Faustus* (printed 1604 and 1616), Shakespeare's *Twelfth Night* (1600–01), Ben Jonson's *Hymenaei* (1606), and Middleton's own *Hengist, King of Kent* (1616–20).[11] Clearly, then, the conversation between *The Changeling*, *Othello*, and *The Island Princess* differs from the kind of playwrighterly collaboration on individual plays that has long preoccupied critics of *The Changeling*:[12] the circle of influence is expanded to include Fletcher, Middleton, Rowley, and, in his print afterlife, Shakespeare, as the focus shifts to account for the migration between these three play texts of shared theatrical tropes, scenarios, and structural components – part of what Janet Clare calls 'stage traffic'.[13] This is partly a question of scale, of looking not to the play text but to smaller theatrical units shared between texts. Indeed, William N. West argues against the primacy of the play as the fundamental unit of early modern theatre, proposing that we should instead understand plays 'as networks of traceable elements of action, the form and pressures of which have left their mark in more fixed media like scripts and texts'.[14] In considering the movement of such materials between plays, the architectural concept of the 'adaptive reuse of structures inherited from earlier builders' invoked by Mary Malcolm Gaylord as a more general literary model is useful to explain the way such theatrical elements are taken up and reconstituted to construct discrete new plays – a testament to West's call for 'understanding theatre as made out of other performances'.[15] In the case of *The Changeling*, such elements are tropes and scenarios that have become associated with stage travel, in other words 'theatregrams' set in dialogue with each other in their 1620s moment and recognisable to a theatregoing audience.[16] Flexible and supple in the face of generic circumstance, mobile theatregrams of travel import aesthetic and political information from elsewhere. In *The Changeling*, these theatregrams are the trope of the erotic disruption caused by the arrival of a desirable man from the sea and that of the desirable heretical woman who seduces a Christian traveller to apostasy. In tracing the migration of these tropes between plays, we can identify the exchange, trade, and mobility that both preoccupies and constitutes stage travel.

This focus on an early 1620s model of dramaturgy that uses and reuses theatregrams in a flexible, efficient, and above all dialogical way of constructing plays from a stock of shared resources can pinpoint an aesthetic response to the wider political context, cutting across usual definitions of repertory, company allegiances, and a focus on either stage or page to allow for a redefinition of stage travel itself. My chosen group of plays is, of course, artificial and could be expanded almost indefinitely: the mobile tropes under scrutiny here do not come to rest in this constructed group of play texts but continue migrating into, for instance, Fletcher and Philip Massinger's *The Sea Voyage*, licensed a little over a month after *The Changeling* in June 1622.[17] However, my choice of plays reveals points of contact that might be obscured by looking only at print or performance rather than at early modern theatrical culture in the round, available to both audiences and readers. Setting *The Changeling* against its close counterparts makes it possible to identify the crystallisation of certain theatrical and structural qualities of stage travel in the early 1620s, recognising its sheer reach on the early modern stage and raising questions of its slippery relationship to genre.

The editors of this volume redefine the category of 'the travel play' by opposing the textual transmission of sources to playwrighterly imagination; however, the investigation of stage travel needs also to account for the problematic relationship of 'the travel play' as conventionally defined (marked here in scare quotes) to genre itself. As a category, the 'travel play' is both capacious and ambiguous. In an earlier anthology, working with conventional definitions, Anthony Parr calls 'the travel play' 'an offshoot of [the] vigorous, confused and fluid [early modern] project' of travel writing, which sets out 'to describe the variousness of the world and its inhabitants'.[18] In this iteration, 'the travel play' cuts across and troubles the generic categories of early modern drama, and pinning down its generic specifics is tricky. Scholarship does not often offer a clear generic definition, categorising it primarily by its content rather than its dramatic and theatrical generic characteristics: to quote David McInnis, English voyage dramas (used interchangeably with 'travel plays') 'incorporate scenes of travel, deploy genuinely exotic settings which are not mere foils for London, or are in some way concerned with the motivations and consequences of travel' – the 'travel play' has often been identified straightforwardly by an interest in travel itself, or its staging.[19] Unsurprisingly, given the importance of the cultural categories involved, most critics have focused on the dynamics of encounter and the representative strategies used to depict plays' different ethnic or religious constituencies (e.g., Jean-Pierre Maquerlot and Michèle Willems; Parr), they have excavated important new subcategories for stage travel such as the 'Turk play' and 'conversion play' (e.g., Daniel Vitkus), the 'Persian play' (Jane Grogan), or mercantile drama (Jonathan Gil Harris), and, as they have done so, they have prioritised culture, religion, or what Jonathan Burton and Ania Loomba call the 'protracted and erratic' history of race.[20] Hence, the pressing questions of colonialism, imperialism, encounter, exchange, religion, gender, trade, and economics that have concerned scholars for the past three decades have overshadowed questions of the theatrical genre and structure of stage travel.[21]

As Lucy Munro observes, it may be helpful to think of 'stage travel' not in terms of a generic category to which plays belong but as a mode in which they participate.[22] In this model, the stage travel mode can be identified through the migrating tropes and scenarios which have, over time, become associated with the performance of travel, and the mode is created by the circulation of these units in different generic circumstances – domestic tragedy (*Othello*), tragicomedy (*The Island Princess*), and a hybrid of tragedy and tragicomedy (*The Changeling*). In this sense, the travel mode itself moves through and inflects different genres, self-reflexively connecting the theme of travel and the formal deployment of associated migrating tropes and scenarios. If, then, the categories of voyage drama and the travel play are to be more than the imposition of present-day concerns onto a varied body of dramatic material, it is important to identify the distinctive aesthetic or structural features that might recognisably belong to stage travel for early seventeenth-century theatregoers. The memory and experience of stage travel permeates other genres and plays which, like *The Changeling*, do not immediately strike us as examples of travel plays and voyage dramas, but which nonetheless reconfigure tropes which were by then imbued with the concepts and consequences of travel.[23] Looking to the issues of theatrical genre, mode, and structure in the staging of travel allows us to begin to trace this all-important mobility in the theatre of the 1620s.

This chapter takes *The Changeling* as a test case for the exploration of circulating traces of stage travel and the meanings that accrue around shared theatregrams and scenarios as they themselves travel between plays and genres: like the returned traveller, these tropes are both changed by their movement between plays and transform the play into which they are assimilated. In particular, *The Changeling* bears the traces of a set of migrating tropes, repeated and reformulated within a distinctively 1620s dramaturgy, which evoke stage travel in distinct generic circumstances to represent Europe to England to particular political effect. In this way, it is possible to identify migrating features of stage travel and their distinctive connections to the crisis years of the early 1620s – in other words, to identify a politicised aesthetics and the contribution of the techniques of the staging of travel to an early 1620s dramaturgy.

The Changeling and Stage Travel

Rather than thinking of *The Changeling* only as thematically related to the crisis of the Bohemian succession and the Thirty Years War (as *A Game at Chess* without the allegory), if we attend instead to its theatricality and dramatic structure within a tightly circumscribed repertory from 1621 to 1622, the play reveals the migration of aesthetic tropes of stage travel to be both a symptom of and response to the pressures of a political moment. In the circulation and rearticulation of particular tropes and scenarios of stage travel, *The Changeling*'s aesthetics connect it to its political moment just as much as any thematic content or topical allusion. Middleton and Rowley redeploy at least two stage travel scenarios. First, like Ferdinand in *The Tempest* (1611), a desirable seafaring man lands in an exotic society, causing erotic shockwaves that destabilise settled bonds.[24] Second, in a scenario common to other 1620s plays such as Massinger's *The Renegado* (1624), an exotic, heretical ruling woman – here, Donusa, niece to the Ottoman Sultan – seduces a Christian man.[25] In *The Changeling* and *The Island Princess*, this seduction aims to draw a Christian servant to the murder of an inconvenient suitor in favour of a more desirable lover and it fails when the servant outwits his mistress. With this second scenario comes both the attendant penetration of an eroticised foreign space associated with the body of the exotic woman and the structural component of *peripeteia*, or the 'turn', both now imbued with associations of 'Otherness' and travel. Prior to the 1620s, *peripeteia* is well established as central to stage encounter; consider, for instance, the firing of Benwash's house and the harbour at Tunis in Robert Daborne's *A Christian Turned Turk* (1612) or the defeat of the Great Turk in John Day, William Rowley and George Wilkins's *The Travels of the Three English Brothers* (1607).[26] By 1621–22, *peripeteia* produces a fertile overlap between tragedy and stage travel, both in *The Changeling*'s own generic experimentation and in the association in stage travel of Aristotelian tragic *peripeteia* with the reversals of fortune suffered by the intemperate heretic whose hyperemotive response becomes a convention of the opposition between heresy and Christian temperance. As I will discuss, the specifics of these reframed tropes of travel show how they become mobile sites for a theatrical response to political upheaval and the politicised representation of Europe to England. *The Changeling*, then, is a site of exchange and transmission, its dialogue with stage travel magnified by the political context of European crisis and English response. In a moment when England looked with equal fear and enthusiasm towards Europe, fearful of Counter-Reformation infiltration and vocal in the call for war in support of the Palatinate, travel and the encounter with the foreign Other become fraught ideas.[27] The deeply felt danger of the insinuating Other is reflected in aesthetic representation and theatrical form.

The hybrid form of *The Changeling* has long inspired generic speculation. The title figure has many incarnations, from Antonio ('*The Changeling*' of the 1653 dramatis personae) to Beatrice, but the play too is a generic changeling. As Gordon McMullan writes, *The Changeling* 'represents a paradigmatic Jacobean revenge play ... yet it ... both parod[ies] the idea of revenge and ... foreground[s] the increasingly hybrid nature of the genre', reaching a resolution which is at least partly tragicomic.[28] Indeed, *The Changeling* concludes in a flurry of generic transgression generated by ideas of change and transformation. Raymond J. Pentzell identifies the collision of the asylum and citadel plots in the final scene, and Alsemero's concluding catalogue of 'changes' given over the bodies of Beatrice and De Flores, as prime instances of *The Changeling*'s generic drift:

> ALSEMERO What an opacous body had that moon
> That last changed on us! Here's beauty changed
> To ugly whoredom; here, servant-obedience
> To a master-sin: imperious murder!
> I, a supposèd husband, changed embraces
> With wantonness, but that was paid before.
> [*to Tomazo*] Your change is come too: from an ignorant wrath
> To knowing friendship.

Then comes a last, comically unsettling question directed at the feigned asylum inmates Antonio and Franciscus: 'Are there any more on's?'.[29] In its jarring change in tone, this question makes a sudden turn from tragic summary to the self-conscious tragicomic requirement to tie up all loose plot ends. In this way, Alsemero's bathetic tonal shift sums up the accentuated, discomforting generic swerve required of this final scene.

Tragic and tragicomic though it certainly is, *The Changeling* also invokes well-used tropes of stage travel and romance in an opening scene set between the 'temple' and the harbour (1.1.1): it begins, in fact, as an attenuated voyage drama or travel play. Its first scene presents us with a familiar scenario: a man travelling to oppose Turkish heresy on a Mediterranean island is distracted from his martial duties by a beautiful woman, to fatal effect. If this sounds like *Othello*, Michael Neill's analysis of the verbal, structural, and thematic convergences between the two plays makes it clear that this is no coincidence:

> [I]n both the details of its execution and its larger metaphoric structure [*The Changeling*] often appears to be a self-conscious rewriting of the earlier tragedy, adapting and recombining elements of its model.[30]

While the points of contact between the two plays run throughout *The Changeling*, it is in 1.1 that the presence of travel tropes and structures is most striking. Alsemero's excursion to Malta – perhaps to share in its defence against the Turks – may, like Othello's redundant Cyprus mission, be a thwarted imperial voyage to a battle that does not long concern the play.[31] Equally, from the servants who declare themselves 'safer on land' (1.1.57), to Jasperino's language of venturous trade and privateering as he approaches Diaphanta (itself reworking *Othello* 1.2.49–50)[32] – 'I meant to be a venturer in this voyage. Yonder's another vessel; I'll board her: if she be lawful prize, down goes her topsail' (1.1.89–92) – and Beatrice's imagining of the impending loss of her virginity as a traveller's adieu – 'Can such friends divide, never to meet again, / Without a solemn farewell?' (1.1.200–01) – the opening scene is saturated with the discourses of stage travel.

These connections run deep. Of *The Changeling*'s fourteen scenes, only the first escapes the claustrophobic interiority of the citadel and the asylum. Encounter is the primal stuff of stage travel and Alsemero, the man who lands from the sea, relates his first encounter with Beatrice at a temple located close to the shore, a meeting with a long history in epic, romance, and stage encounter. Alsemero's initial sighting of Beatrice likens her to Venus, the '*dea certe*' Aeneas meets on landing at Dido's Carthage,[33] or, since Alsemero must also compete with a deformed servant with a sexual interest in the daughter of the household, to Ferdinand's 'goddess / On whom these airs attend'.[34] In this, too, *The Changeling* echoes *Othello*'s deployment of romance. In a common romance trope, Shakespeare's lovers are separated by a sea voyage and 'the warlike Moor, Othello' arrives belatedly on Cyprus to worship

Desdemona as his own island goddess (2.1.28), an implicit comparison drawn via the parallels to the hymn to Venus in Spenser's *Faerie Queene* IV.x.44.[35] The first scene of *The Changeling* offers its characters a licence which endangers them as much as does Cassio's freedom in his 'bold show of courtesy' to Emilia and Desdemona at the Cyprus docks (2.1.100). For Beatrice, the scene is an exposition of the erotic shockwaves that the man who arrives from the sea sends through the society into which he sets down, and, indeed, the trope's next resting place clarifies the disruption caused by female desire. Fletcher and Massinger's *The Sea Voyage* was licensed just over a month after *The Changeling* and its iteration of the trope of the maritime adventurer, in this case the shipwrecked Albert, who has swum from the barren island seeking succour, exceeds both *The Tempest* and *The Changeling*. *The Sea Voyage* multiplies the women who are taken for 'goddesses' (2.2.81) and makes them not dutiful daughters to an island mage or commander of the citadel but sexually frustrated members of an Amazonian 'commonwealth' (2.2.17) on the edge of rebellion that must be righted by the restoration of established marriage bonds. Though Alsemero's landing is altogether less traumatic than that of Aeneas, Ferdinand, or Albert, his disruptive effect is evident from the start and his own turn from the direct route of epic to the wandering, digressive teleology of romance is made clear in Beatrice's words, 'I am beholden to this gentleman, / Who left his own way to keep me company' (1.1.160–01).[36] Moreover, his effect on Beatrice is immediate: her subsequent fall into a 'giddy turning' of desire is that of the heretical woman of stage travel and is mapped out in this opening scene in a schematic representation of the established contours of this theatrical mode (1.1.159).

The discourses of stage travel are carried through *The Changeling* in the structural component of the dumbshow,[37] and in the language of 'venture' which both De Flores and Beatrice take up: Beatrice laments that 'There's no venturing / Into [Alsemero's] bed', and De Flores forces Beatrice into unwilling sex with the words 'Thou'lt love anon / What thou so fears't and faint'st to venture on' (4.1.11–12, 3.4.173–74). The discourse of erotic venturing echoes its layering of eros and mercantilism elsewhere: in *The Island Princess*, when Armusia rejects Quisara's demand that he convert to Islam, he asks, 'Is this the venture / The trial that you talked of?' (4.5.43–44). *The Changeling*, then, has the bones of a voyage drama or travel play put to the service of fleshy tragedy and worldly tragicomedy, and its opening scene locates the structures of travel within this fluid generic context. It sets the scene for the continued reappearance of the mode of stage travel and its tropes and, as I shall suggest, for their politicised use to expound the alluring threat of continental European heresy to England.

In their migration between genres, mobile theatregrams, tropes, and scenarios are part of what West sees as 'a series of forms changing into something else while still remaining recognizable': the state of change is a defining characteristic – to invoke my title, theatregrams are 'constant changelings', gathering new valences in fresh generic or historical circumstances.[38] In the heat of the Palatinate crisis, Thomas Scott uses this phrase in his polemical anti-Spanish and anti-Catholic tract *The Belgicke Pismire* (1622) to refer to the unreformed and unreformable 'sluggard' who does not see the imminent danger to his soul and yet who too, analogously, is in a state of constant change: 'Hee is a resolute waverer, a constant changeling: *vult & non vult.*'[39] This intensely politicised conception of religious faith and affiliation is embedded in *The Changeling*. In its theology, Beatrice is inevitably damned as a reprobate whose fate hangs 'Beneath the stars, upon yon meteor' (5.3.154): 'Was my creation in the womb so cursed[?]', she asks (3.4.168). In 1622, of course, Scott refers not to theatrical changelings (be that a circulating scenario or a heroine who, as I will examine below, turns constantly) but to the continual changeability of religious and national changelings, those who, in anti-Catholic propaganda, possessed the dangerous ability to transform themselves and infiltrate England but who are themselves always damned. Such are the Jesuit infiltrators of Middleton's *A Game at Chess*, who, in 'great princes' services' act as 'counsellors of state' and 'secretaries', but who really serve 'in notes of intelligence … / To th' Father General'; they are the English Catholics who, in Scott's earlier pamphlet *Vox Populi*, 'should worke so far into the body of the State … that with the helpe of the Jesuites, they would undermine them with meere wit (without gunpowder)'.[40] This is what Mark Hutchings calls 'the English Protestant fear of danger lurking within – whether of English Catholics or Spanish emissaries … subversive agents in the service of Rome'.[41] Beatrice, a Spanish aristocrat often understood as a figure for the Infanta María, the woman around whom the controversy of the Spanish Match centred, is above all a changeling, even to herself.[42] Her transformation from virtue to murderousness, though conventional of the fallen woman, is one which involves her in the same discourses of infiltration, deception, disguise, and eventual revelation that circulated in the heated anti-Catholic discourse of the early 1620s – her constant turning, examined below, renders her a version of the woman of stage travel who is both constantly Othered and internalised to Europe. All theatregrams take on new valences in altered circumstances, but the changeability of *The Changeling*'s basic components is echoed in its protagonist's constant, seemingly unstoppable changeability: theatrical form underlines the fear of the internal Other.

While John Stachniewski's Calvinist interpretation of the play rejects change in favour of the discovery of Beatrice's true, already fallen identity, proposing a model of revelation rather than transformation, the paradoxical state of constant transformation evoked by Scott and the structural transformations that Beatrice undergoes throughout the play suggest that the heretical condition of incessant mutability is itself a constant that denies genuine change and hence refuses the non-elect any possibility of escape.[43] Read in the religiopolitical and gendered terms of the time, this condition of constant transformation connects the heretic, the ruling woman, and the player in the protean space of theatre. Spanish, Catholic, and variable of affection, Beatrice is the changeable, heretical foreign woman, a common figure of 1620s stage travel, and, as I will discuss, fully embodied in Fletcher's Quisara. The travel mode, so often presided over by a bewhored Fortune,[44] both requires and increasingly interrogates the figure of the heretical, changeable woman: hence Beatrice's lament that Alsemero, 'the man was meant me', should come 'so near his time, and miss it!' both echoes Fortune's fickleness and begins her own ongoing transformations (1.1.85–86). In a neat discursive double bind, even Beatrice's famous cry, 'This fellow has undone me endlessly' (4.1.1), uttered after she is coerced into sex with De Flores, is further evidence of her changeability: as Judith Haber points out, 'to be "undone" is literally to be unperfected, deprived of closure, made forever "endless"'.[45] In the representation of Quisara and Beatrice, *The Island Princess* and *The Changeling* share the figure of the changeable foreign woman and her attendant mobile desire, inherent even in Quisara's name, which echoes the Spanish 'quisiera' (the conditional of 'to desire, to love'). Beatrice's 'giddy turning' and 'change' of 'saint' on meeting Alsemero and her rape by De Flores offers a dark counterpart to Quisara's more sustained, though incomplete, royal control over her own body (1.1.158–59).[46] Both characters are unconstant, their erotic attentions transferred between three male characters, and each seeks to have one of these men murder another to avoid an unwished for marriage. Indeed, while *Othello*, too, is based around the sexual competition between three men (also two elite and one servant), in dramatising a female protagonist whose desire is fixed upon one object – her husband – its interest in mobile female desire lies in the realm of male fantasy and fear. Such fickleness is, of course, fundamental to the kind of misogynist discourse that the depiction of the slandered Desdemona interrogates, but in *The Changeling* and *The Island Princess*, female desire is imagined as a stylised hyper-changeability that connects Beatrice to the figure of the ruling heretical woman increasingly common to early modern stage travel.

'[T]urn and turn, and yet go on / And turn again' (*Othello* 4.1.223–24): Stage Travel and the Heretical Woman

From its opening scene, the ideas and consequences of travel permeate *The Changeling* in the redeployment of the trope of the heretical seductress, a part played by the Spanish and Catholic Beatrice. This is manifested in three ways, each deriving from their increasingly common use in stage travel: first, in the structural technique of *peripeteia*, second in the spatial figuration of eroticised space, in which the body of the alluring heretic is mirrored in the play's architectural imagination, and third in the importation of the scenario of the heretical woman who is outwitted in her attempts to seduce a man to murder, a repeated scenario in the early 1620s.

Into the generic fluidity of *The Changeling*, Rowley and Middleton import *peripeteia*, a structural device common to tragedy and, increasingly, to stage travel, consisting of a sudden reversal of fortune. Neill's important study of *The Renegado* (1624) identifies *peripeteia* as an inherently politicised dramatic structure that relates the 'turn' of Massinger's *peripeteia* to that of apostasy and conversion, offering a way into the play's religio-political context and illuminating the way that such a structural 'turn' others and racialises the heretic.[47] Neill's focus is on Massinger, but, as noted above, *peripeteia* had become central to stage travel and encounter. Both the mobility and the cumulative politicisation of this structural device become clear by comparing two near-identical scenes: the conventional use of the trope with which Massinger concludes *The Renegado* in the defeat of the heretical Viceroy of Tunis, Asambeg (5.8), who rants like the intemperate 'Turk', and the short but pivotal scene 2.5 of *The Island Princess*, in which the accumulated travel conventions of *peripeteia* are revealed. Just as Asambeg is foiled by the Venetian Vitelli, 2.5 finds the Governor of Ternate – a character previously without any religious association – outwitted by the Christian Armusia; like Asambeg three years later, his fulminations are the conventional capitulation speech of the Eastern tyrant.[48] Significantly, the Governor then vanishes, returning at the start of 4.1 to infiltrate the Tidorean court disguised '*like a Moor priest*' (4.1.0 SD). Fletcher, then, shows us a character of previously indeterminate religious affiliation in the throes of *peripeteia*: his response marks him with the trope of the intemperate heretic, the figure Grogan calls the 'raging Turk'.[49] Indeed, the Governor's depiction in 2.5 signals a shift from the secular romance of Acts 1 and 2 into the open religious conflict of the final acts. The 'raging Turk' clearly emerges from the discursive representation of encounters with Turkish and North African cultures, shaped and disseminated by the depiction of Turkish excess (as in the Turk's 'inhumane and more than barbarous crueltie' at the siege of Malta in 1565 in Richard Knolles's *The Generall Historie of the Turkes*),[50] or William Painter's depiction of the luxurious tyranny of Mohamet, conqueror of Constantinople, in the tale of 'Hyrenee the Fair Greeke'.[51] However, the figure is also shaped by the adaptive reuse of *peripeteia*, which, over time, becomes associated with the representation of the Other of travel and with stage travel. In the case of the Governor, structure produces character: his transformation into the 'raging Turk' is precipitated by the associations of structure as much as by the discourse of encounter. By the 1620s, then, these moments of *peripeteia* take on an Eastern valance, invoking a geographically vague but religiously quite specific 'Easternness': they act as structural markers of 'Moorishness', heresy, and the Other of stage travel.

Such structures of reversal pervade *The Changeling* in both the citadel and the asylum plot, and Beatrice's condition of constant, heretical transformation itself becomes structural in the repeated *peripeteia* at the play's heart. In a play in which '[c]hange is insistently linked with love and religion from the beginning', Beatrice turns throughout.[52] From her change of saint on meeting Alsemero, to her outwitting by De Flores (3.4), her manipulation of Alsemero's virginity test (4.2), the bed-trick and the fire that kills Diaphanta (5.1), to the final confrontation with Alsemero, and her death at De Flores's hands (5.3), Beatrice undergoes a cumulative sequence of reversals that she cannot eventually control. She turns from the outset, her pleasurable awareness of her own 'giddy turning' in 1.1 is a marker of Scott's state of constant transformation, the hallmark of the heretic, the Catholic, the Spanish, or the infiltrator. Beatrice, like Quisara and the exotic female heretics of stage travel, internalises *peripeteia* in her own turning. Attempting to entrap Quisara as she plots to engage him to murder the virtuous Armusia, Pinheiro exclaims 'She turns, for millions!' (3.1.239), identifying her as a heretical apostata or 'turner' while also invoking the sexualised turning of Cleopatra, the

'Triple-turned whore' of *Antony and Cleopatra*,[53] just as Othello – the real 'turner' of Shakespeare's play – defames Desdemona by claiming that she 'can turn, and turn, and yet go on / And turn again'. Beatrice is thus aligned with Quisara's mobile affections and the slandered Desdemona. Just as Quisara reacts to successive waves of seductive Portuguese arrivals, for Beatrice the entrance of the maritime adventurer Alsemero sparks a chain of seemingly fickle erotic changes in the elite woman. The result, when combined with the *peripeteia* associated with the Eastern Other, is to easternise Beatrice. It is no coincidence that, when De Flores prevents the discovery of the bed-trick, Beatrice declares, 'The east is not more beauteous than his service' (5.1.71).[54] Like Quisara, the exotic Muslim woman, Beatrice's heresy is both Catholicism and 'Moorishness'. Beatrice's Spanish blood (in the predominant English shorthand of the day, which Barbara Fuchs defines as the 'frequent racialization of Spain in the period – a facet of the Black Legend that insisted on Spain's miscegenated nature, its Jewish and Moorish blood') connects her to 'the Moor' and to Islam.[55] Spanish and Malukan characters, then, are drawn together in their divergence from English Protestantism, and the imported resonances of stage travel combine to produce Beatrice as the figure of the heretical, easternised, and hence changeable woman.

As Beatrice's 'giddy turning' suggests, her heresy is imagined both structurally and spatially: she is brought closer to the figure of the exotic woman of stage travel through the eroticisation of the interiorised space associated with the body of that figure. Critics have long observed the eroticised interiority of *The Changeling*'s spatial imaginary and the clear analogy between possession of the citadel and sexual possession of Beatrice.[56] As Vermandero says of the citadel, 'within are secrets' (1.1.169), and they are exploited both by the upstart servant, as when De Flores leads Piraquo through 'ways and straits' so tight that he must hang his arms upon the wall (2.2.161, 3.1.10 SD), or by the woman whose body the space represents, as when Beatrice's exploration of Alsemero's 'physician's closet' reveals the medicalised secrets of the feminine corporeal interior (4.1.20, 4.1.17–53). This, of course, is the same closet where, later, De Flores will murder her in a grim parody of sexual climax. Less often noted is that what Neill calls the 'castellated body', the sexualised mapping of interior space to police the female body, migrates into *The Changeling* through its dialogue with the stage travel with which that trope has gradually become associated.[57] In an earlier deployment of the trope, *Othello* stages an equivalent voyeuristic progression into the Cypriot citadel, the marital bedchamber, and, eventually, the curtained

bed. In stark contrast to Beatrice and Quisara, the elite women of citadel and palace, respectively, Desdemona's outsider status in the Cypriot
citadel means that she never controls this masculine, martial space.
A rather different dynamic is clear in *The Island Princess* where Quisara
does control her own space: its third act dramatises the penetration into
the eroticised interior and Pinheiro's progression past gatekeepers, 'my
great lady's followers: / Her riddle-founders and her fortune-tellers', to
reach Quisara's bed chamber is reminiscent of Guyon's progress through
Spenser's Bower of Bliss (3.1.107–08).[58] The princess's control is broken
only by Armusia, who gains access by half-seducing Quisara's waiting-
woman, Panura. The trope occurs to great effect in the spectacle staged
by Hippolyta in 3.2 of Fletcher and Massinger's *Custom of the Country*
(1619) and, as noted above, recurs in *The Renegado* in Vitelli's seduction
by Donusa (2.4).[59] When *The Changeling* abandons the light and air
of the harbour to turn inwards upon itself in a claustrophobic internal
progression to the heart of the citadel and the intertwined acts of murder
and rape staged there, it participates in the circulation of a trope of interior progression characteristic of *Othello* and *The Island Princess*, and of
religious and erotic encounter with the foreign, ruling woman.

Deep inside the eroticised interior that represents her own corporeality, and where she is marked as a heretical 'turner', 2.2 and later 3.4 find
Beatrice enacting the stage travel scenario of the heretical woman who
attempts to seduce a servant to murder an unwanted future husband in
favour of a more desirable partner. Thus *The Changeling* directly reworks
the central encounter between Quisara and Pinheiro in *The Island
Princess* 3.1: the tragicomic trajectory of that play depends on this scene
and is achieved when Pinheiro, whose constancy is a striking alteration
from Fletcher's sources, explicitly diverts the play from tragedy to tragicomedy by declaring that his 'honest' nature will not change (3.1.24).
Hence, the turn to tragicomedy paradoxically requires Pinheiro's constancy: like Jonson's good traveller who 'came back untouched', Pinheiro
preserves his 'honest' nature.[60] For regular theatregoers in 1621–22,
generic expectation and innovation would undoubtedly be at issue in
this playing and replaying of a scenario to distinct generic purposes. Each
iteration of the scenario is the pivot on which the generic trajectory of
tragedy or tragicomedy turns: considered together, they seem consciously
to invoke generic and narrative alternatives. *The Island Princess* 3.1, then,
is the moment when Pinheiro's self-conscious retention of his masculine
Christian constancy prevents disintegration into tragedy, the precise fate
that awaits Beatrice and De Flores. Hence Beatrice's failed attempt to

manipulate De Flores, her bafflement at his rejection of her class-based
and economic power over him, and her degradation at his hands, is
informed for a knowledgeable audience by Pinheiro's more benevolent –
if imperialist – treatment of Quisara in the earlier play.

The scenes resemble each other remarkably closely. While both share
an economic image, Pinheiro speaking of Quisara in terms of a wager –
'She turns, for millions!' (3.1.239) – and Beatrice trying to buy De
Flores's silence, both men also respond in blood: De Flores's 'O my
blood! / Methinks I feel her in mine arms already' (2.2.148–49) is a
heightened version of Pinheiro's insight that a weaker man might fall
to Quisara's beauty, 'Some bloods would bound now, / And run a-tilt'
(3.1.239). Indeed, De Flores requires in full the sexual payment from
Beatrice that Pinheiro insists on in the attenuated form of Quisara's kiss
(4.2.83–88). Furthermore, each man manipulates the rhetoric of 'service',
one of Christopher Ricks's 'keywords' for *The Changeling*.[61] Pinheiro,
who 'scorn[s]' his 'able youth should plough for others / Or [his] ambition serve for pay', is rewarded by Quisara's kiss and the words 'My servant, if you please. I seal it thus, sir' (3.1.221–22, 265).

The contrasting generic trajectories of this replayed scenario stem,
somewhat counter-intuitively, from the absence of religious conflict
in *The Changeling*. The encounter between De Flores and Beatrice in
Alicante is not that between Muslim woman and Christian man found
in Fletcher's Maluku, but one between compatriots and co-religionists.
Rowley and Middleton's transplantation of the travel trope from the
theatre of encounter into a homogeneous society means that *The
Changeling*'s heretical woman cannot be converted by the equally heretical De Flores. Such a transposition is made explicit when Vermandero
discovers that Alsemero, at first a seeming foreigner, is in fact a compatriot – indeed, the son of a family friend: Vermandero's surprised
comment, 'A Vàlencìan? / That's native' (1.1.170–71), makes clear the
transplanting of the travel trope onto home soil. *The Changeling*, then, is
a self-contained version of voyage drama or the travel play, in which the
structure of such plays turns in on itself to suggest internal enemies and
in which the tropes of stage travel are focused on internal division within
the nation, body politic, or self. In this iteration of stage travel, De
Flores is the feared inside man, the traitor within so vividly imagined in
Middleton's *A Game at Chess*. Hence this fear is not only tied to the resonant English fear of Spanish infiltration but is also a structural redirec-
tion of the tropes of stage travel towards a new destination – home. Stage
travel, in this iteration, is now peculiarly self-contained, dealing not with

the encounter between nations or faiths but with internal encounters and divisions.

This internal trajectory, however, has far-reaching gendered consequences for Beatrice. Alsemero's approach to Beatrice, imbued with the tropes and discourses of travel, necessarily estranges and exoticises her, positioning her as the foreign woman encountered on a foreign shore. Much has been made of Beatrice as a marker of feared Spanish queenship in the years leading up to the Spanish Match and the ongoing, though ultimately futile, negotiations for the marriage of Prince Charles and the Infanta María.[62] Internal to Europe but estranged from an English audience because of her Spanishness, Beatrice is further estranged even from her own nation through the importation of travel tropes which render her the exotic, seductive but heretical woman – this hyperchangeable foreign woman of stage travel is also made a foreigner to her own father, to her compatriots, nation, bloodline, and – most pressingly – to herself. Her resonant words to her father at her death clarify this process:

> BEATRICE O come not near me, sir. I shall defile you.
> I am that of your blood was taken from you
> For your better health. (5.3.149–51)

Beatrice's tainted blood is a potent image of the anti-Hispanic discourse of miscegenated Spanish blood, contaminated – it was believed – because 'Moorish', and both she and it must be expelled. Brought close to her Muslim counterpart in the replaying of a travel scenario set within the structural and spatial dynamics of stage travel, Beatrice is an eloquent intensification of the image of the foreign heretical woman – she is what happens when that image is redirected not towards exotic travel but towards Europe.

***

The Changeling is a play about the consequences of travel, both achieved and thwarted: it opens by invoking the scenarios and tropes of stage travel, and Beatrice becomes a murderous Dido, her hand forced by the caprice of fortune. A mode rather than a genre, stage travel demonstrates particular shared scenarios and tropes that have accumulated meaning over time and that migrate beyond plays concerned explicitly with travel, mutating flexibly in their new generic circumstances. The workings of repertory mean that the plays into which these tropes move are permeated with the discourses of stage travel: tracing the migration of these tropes into a range of generic circumstances identifies the aesthetic mediation of political crisis within the self-reflexive theatrical culture of the early 1620s. Specific scenarios mediate and comment upon England's relationship with Europe in 1621–22 in anti-Spanish discourses of

Counter-Reformation Catholic heresy. In the case of *The Changeling*, this work is done by the tropes of the heretical woman and the erotic intervention of the maritime adventurer: that woman's potential to degrade men into religious and sexual apostasy is a loaded trope in the years of the Palatinate crisis. Through its underpinning structures of stage travel, *The Changeling* participates in the fraught representation of Europe and imperial encounter and aligns the Catholic, Spanish Beatrice with her heretical Muslim counterparts as Rowley and Middleton's hybrid tragedy is infiltrated by the tropes of tragicomic travel. Hence, *The Changeling*, one of the most topically political plays in the canon, is even more profoundly politicised in its structures and aesthetics by the tropes and scenarios of travel that migrate through both it and the theatre of the early 1620s.

Notes

1 I would like to thank Ian Haywood, Lucy Munro, and the members of the Theater Without Borders International Working Group for comments on these materials, especially Melissa Walter and Melinda Gough. Peter Holland's "'Travelling hopefully': The Dramatic Form of Journeys in English Renaissance Drama' (in *Travel and Drama in Shakespeare's Time*, ed. Jean-Pierre Maquerlot and Michèle Willems (Cambridge University Press, 1996), 160–78) is an exception in its focus on dramatic form, and this essay builds on his attention to the formal qualities of stage travel.

2 For studies of this approach to the dramatic 'part' or fragment from the angle of, respectively, documentary evidence, performance, and editorial approach, see Tiffany Stern, *Documents of Performance in Early Modern England* (Cambridge University Press, 2009); William N. West, 'Intertheatricality', in *Oxford Twenty-First Century Approaches to Literature: Early Modern Theatricality*, ed. Henry S. Turner (Oxford University Press, 2013), 151–72; Sonia Massai, 'Editing Shakespeare in Parts', *Shakespeare Quarterly* 68, no. 1 (2017), 56–79.

3 For details of the Palatinate crisis, see Robert Zaller, *Parliament of 1621: A Study in Constitutional Crisis* (Berkeley, CA: University of California Press, 1971); Peter H. Wilson, *Europe's Tragedy: A History of the Thirty Years War* (London: Allen Lane, 2009), 269–361.

4 For the categories of 'travel drama' and 'voyage drama', see Claire Jowitt and David McInnis, 'Introduction: Understanding the Journeying Play', in this volume.

5 N. W. Bawcutt, ed., *The Control and Censorship of Caroline Drama: The Records of Sir Henry Herbert, Master of the Revels, 1623–73* (Oxford: Clarendon Press, 1996), 136.

6 John Fletcher, *The Island Princess*, ed. Clare McManus (London: Arden Early Modern Drama, 2013), 15, 82–83. All further quotations from *The Island Princess* refer to this edition and will be cited by act, scene, and line number in the text.

7 See, for example, Cristina Malcolmson, '"As Tame as the Ladies": Politics and Gender in *The Changeling*', *English Literary Renaissance* 20 (1990), 320–39; Lisa Hopkins, 'Beguiling the Master of the Mystery: Form and Power in *The Changeling*', *Medieval and Renaissance Drama in England* 9 (1997), 149–61; A. A. Bromham and Zara Bruzzi, *The Changeling and the Years of Crisis, 1619–24: A Hieroglyph of Britain* (London: Pinter Press, 1993).

8 Suzanne Gossett and Gordon McMullan date *Othello* as 1601–03: *The Norton Shakespeare*, 3rd edn, ed. Stephen Greenblatt et al. (New York: W. W. Norton, 2015), A35.

9 McManus, *Island Princess*, 25–26. Zachary Lesser discusses the contribution of *Othello*'s publication to debates over England's relationship to war in Europe in *Renaissance Drama and the Politics of Publication: Readings in the English Book Trade* (Cambridge University Press, 2004), 166, 202–16.

10 Jerzy Limon has explored the 'political function' of the 1623–24 theatrical season: *Dangerous Matter: English Drama and Politics in 1623/34* (Cambridge University Press, 1986), 14–19, 131. Paul Salzman analyses the critiques of Jacobean policy towards the Palatinate found in cultural works of 1621: *Literary Culture in Jacobean England: Reading 1621* (Basingstoke: Palgrave Macmillan, 2002).

11 Hopkins, 'Beguiling the Master', 156.

12 See David Nicol, *Middleton and Rowley: Forms of Collaboration in the Jacobean Playhouse* (University of Toronto Press, 2012).

13 '[T]he matter and practice of plays were trafficked amongst playwrights and amongst communities of spectators … histories, narrative patterns, and dramatic scenarios were circulated on the stage... Dramaturgy passed from one play to another': *Shakespeare's Stage Traffic: Imitation, Borrowing and Competition in Renaissance Theatre* (Cambridge University Press, 2014), 1.

14 West, 'Intertheatricality', 154.

15 'Cervantes's Other Fiction', in *The Cambridge Companion to Cervantes*, ed. Anthony J. Cascardi (Cambridge University Press, 2002), 100–30, at 102; West, 'Intertheatricality', 154.

16 Louise George Clubb writes of 'the interchange and transformation of units, figures, relationships, actions, *topoi*, and framing patterns, gradually building a combinatory of theatergrams that were at once streamlined structures for svelte play making and elements of high specific density, weighty with significance from previous incarnations': *Italian Drama in Shakespeare's Time* (New Haven, CT: Yale University Press, 1989), 6.

17 John Fletcher and Philip Massinger, *The Sea Voyage*, in *Three Renaissance Travel Plays*, ed. Anthony Parr (Manchester University Press, 2000), 135–216. All further quotations from *The Sea Voyage* refer to this edition and will be cited by act, scene, and line numbers in the text. Cyrus Hoy, 'Introduction', John Fletcher and Philip Massinger, *The Sea-Voyage*, ed. Fredson Bowers in *The Dramatic Works in the Beaumont and Fletcher Canon*, gen. ed. Fredson Bowers (Cambridge University Press, 1994), vol. IX, 1–94, at 3.

18 Parr, 'Introduction', *Three Renaissance Travel Plays*, 1–54, at 4.

19 David McInnis, 'Lost Plays from Early Modern England: Voyage Drama, A Case Study', *Literature Compass* 8/8 (2011), 534–42, at 535.

20 Jean-Pierre Maquerlot and Michèle Willems, ed., *Travel and Drama in Shakespeare's Time* (Cambridge University Press, 1996); Daniel Vitkus, ed., *Three Turk Plays from Early Modern England* (New York: Columbia University Press, 2000) and *Turning Turk: English Theater and the Multicultural Mediterranean, 1570–1630* (Basingstoke: Palgrave Macmillan, 2003), 107–62; Jane Grogan, *The Persian Empire in English Writing, 1549–1622* (Basingstoke: Palgrave Macmillan, 2014); Jonathan Gil Harris, *Sick Economies: Drama, Mercantilism, and Disease in Shakespeare's England* (Philadelphia: University of Pennsylvania Press, 2004); Jonathan Burton and Ania Loomba, ed., *Race in Early Modern England: A Documentary Companion* (Basingstoke: Palgrave Macmillan, 2007), 1.

21 In addition to Holland, 'Travelling hopefully', see also Jonathan Burton, *Traffic and Turning: Islam and English Drama, 1579–1624* (Newark, DE: University of Delaware Press, 2005), 18, 29–30; Richmond Barbour *Before Orientalism: London's Theatre of the East, 1576–1626* (Cambridge University Press, 2003), 37–38.

22 Lucy Munro, 'The Travels of Massinger's *Believe as You List*', unpublished conference paper (British Shakespeare Association Conference panel, 'Dramatising the Early Modern Local and Global: The Archive and the Travel Play', 2009).

23 Excluding masques and entertainments, there were roughly ten plays of travel or encounter in the 1580s, thirty-two in the 1590s, twenty-two in the 1600s, nine in the 1610s, seventeen in the 1620s, nine in the 1630s, and five in the 1640s. See *DEEP: Database of Early English Playbooks* [http://deep.sas.upenn.edu/]; *Lost Plays Database* [http://lostplays.folger.edu]; Burton, *Traffic and Turning*, 257–58; Grogan, *The Persian Empire*; Linda McJannet, 'Bringing in a Persian', *Medieval and Renaissance Drama in England* 12 (1999), 236–67. These figures do not include revivals, which complicate the picture: e.g., *Othello* alone was revived in 1610 (at Oxford and the Globe), 1612–13, 1629, and 1636 (Andrew Gurr, *The Shakespeare Company 1594–1642* (Cambridge University Press, 2004), 283).

24 William Shakespeare, *The Tempest*, ed. William H. Sherman, in *Norton Shakespeare*, ed. Greenblatt et al., 3205–66 (1.2.373 SD-500).

25 Philip Massinger, *The Renegado*, ed. Michael Neill (London: Arden Early Modern Drama, 2010), 2.4.

26 Robert Daborne, *A Christian Turned Turk*, in *Three Turk Plays*, ed. Daniel Vitkus (New York: Columbia University Press, 2000), 149–239 (scene 11); John Day, William Rowley, and George Wilkins, *The Travels of the Three English Brothers*, in *Three Renaissance Travel Plays*, ed. Parr, 2.1–10.

27 Limon, *Dangerous Matter*, 13, 51.

28 Gordon McMullan, '*The Changeling* and the Dynamics of Ugliness', in *The Cambridge Companion to English Renaissance Tragedy*, ed. Emma Smith and

Garrett A. Sullivan, Jr. (Cambridge University Press, 2010), 222–35, at 222, 228.
29 Rowley and Middleton, *The Changeling*, 5.3.196–203. All references, unless noted, are to William Rowley and Thomas Middleton, *The Changeling*, ed. Douglas Bruster, in *Thomas Middleton: The Collected Works*, ed. Gary Taylor and John Lavagnino (Oxford: Clarendon Press, 2007), 1632–78, and will be cited by act, scene, and line numbers within the text. Raymond J. Pentzell, '*The Changeling*: Notes on Mannerism in Dramatic Form', *Comparative Drama* 9, no. 1 (1975), 3–28, at 3–4.
30 Michael Neill, *Issues of Death: Mortality and Identity in English Renaissance Tragedy* (Oxford: Clarendon Press, 1997), 169.
31 In the play's source, 'History IV' of John Reynolds' *The Triumph of Gods Revenge* (London: 1621), Alsemero 'resolves to see *Malta* that inexpugnable Rampier of *Mars*, the glorie of Christendome, and the terrour of Turkie, to see if he could gaine any place of command and honour either in that Iland; or in their Gallies' (Book 1, 108).
32 All references are from Shakespeare, *The Tragedy of Othello, the Moor of Venice: Quarto*, ed. Clare McManus in *Norton Shakespeare*, ed. Greenblatt et al. (Digital edition, 2016). Further quotations will be cited by act, scene, and line numbers in the text.
33 Virgil, *Aeneid*, trans. H. Ruston Fairclough (London: William Heinemann, 1916), Book I, 328.
34 Shakespeare, *The Tempest*, 1.2.420–21.
35 Patrick Spottiswoode proposes Spenser as a source for the Folio's 2.1.67–73 or the Quarto's 2.1.66–73 (where it is assigned to the Second Gentleman): '*Othello*: Three Notes for Dr Ralph to Query', in *Shakespeare in the Light*, ed. Paul Menzer (Newark, DE: University of Delaware Press, forthcoming).
36 See David Quint, 'The Boat of Romance and Renaissance Epic', in *Romance: Generic Transformation from Chrétien de Troyes to Cervantes*, ed. Kevin Brownlee and Marina Scordilis Brownlee (London: University Press of New England, 1985), 178–202, 179, 187.
37 Holland points out that the dumbshow is common to stage travel: '"Travelling hopefully"', 165. Rowley and Middleton, *The Changeling*, 4.1.0 SD. The dumbshow achieves remarkable complexity in the tableau of the Sherley brothers, separated by oceans but brought together by Fame's '*perspective glass*': Day, Rowley, Wilkins, *The Travels of the Three English Brothers*, Epilogue 13 SD.
38 West, 'Intertheatricality', 171.
39 Thomas Scott, *The Belgike Pismire* (London: 1622), 10.
40 Thomas Middleton, *A Game at Chess*, ed. Gary Taylor, in *Thomas Middleton: The Collected Works*, ed. Taylor and Lavagnino, 1830–1885: 1.1.55–59; Scott, *Vox Populi* (London: 1620), B2, cited by Malcolmson, '"As Tame as the Ladies"', 332.
41 Mark Hutchings, 'De Flores Between the Acts', *Studies in Theatre and Performance* 31, no. 1 (2011), 95–111, at 109.

42 Malcolmson, "'As Tame as the Ladies'", 333–34.
43 John Stachniewski, 'Calvinist Psychology in Middleton's Tragedies', in *Three Jacobean Revenge Tragedies*, ed. R. V. Holdsworth (Basingstoke: Macmillan, 1990), 226–46, at 229.
44 E.g., *The Island Princess*, 5.5.64 and *A Christian Turned Turk*, 1.1.1–9.
45 Judith Haber, *Desire and Dramatic Form in Early Modern England* (Cambridge University Press, 2009), 89.
46 De Flores's coercion of Beatrice into sex is clearly a rape in current terms. There is debate, however, over the early modern concept: see Frances E. Dolan, 'Re-reading Rape in *The Changeling*', *Journal for Early Modern Cultural Studies* 11, no. 1 (2011), 4–29.
47 Michael Neill, 'Turn and Counterturn: Merchanting, Apostasy and Tragicomic Form in Massinger's *The Renegado*', in *Early Modern Tragicomedy*, ed. Subha Mukherji and Raphael Lyne (Cambridge: D. S. Brewer, 2007), 154–74, at 155–56.
48 See Massinger, *The Renegado*, 5.8.32–39 and Fletcher, *The Island Princess*, 2.5.17–27. Though confessional differences may seem to divide Armusia from English audiences, Shankar Raman outlines a fissured set of identities for Fletcher's Portuguese protagonists, arguing that Armusia at one point represents a Catholic Portuguese colonist and at others an English Protestant hero competing against the Portuguese for control of the 'Moluccas': Raman, 'Imaginary Islands: Staging the East', *Renaissance Drama* 26 (1995), 131–61. See also McManus, *The Island Princess*, 24–30. For the confessional politics of *The Renegado*, see Neill, *The Renegado*, 33–54, and Claire Jowitt, 'Massinger's *The Renegado* (1624) and the Spanish Marriage', *Cahiers Élisabéthains* 65 (2004), 45–53, at 50–51.
49 Grogan, *The Persian Empire*, 135.
50 Richard Knolles, *The Generall Historie of the Turkes* (London: 1603), 803.
51 William Painter, *The First Tome of the Palace of Pleasure* (London: 1575), 'The. xl. Novell'. See also the analysis of George Peele's lost 'The Turkish Mahomet and Hiren the Fair Greek' (1589?) in the *Lost Plays Database* [http://lostplays.folger.edu].
52 Bromham and Bruzzi, *The Changeling*, 11.
53 Shakespeare, *Antony and Cleopatra*, ed. Virginia Mason Vaughan, in *Norton Shakespeare*, ed. Greenblatt et al., 2775–2864, 4.12.13.
54 The 1653 text has 'East'.
55 Barbara Fuchs, *Poetics of Piracy: Emulating Spain in English Literature* (Philadelphia: University of Pennsylvania Press, 2013), 64.
56 See, for example, Thomas L. Berger, 'The Petrarchan Fortress of *The Changeling*', *Renaissance Papers* (1969), 37–46.
57 Neill, *Issues of Death*, 175–80.
58 Edmund Spenser, *The Faerie Queene*, ed. A. C. Hamilton et al. (Harlow: Longman, 2007), 2nd edn, Book II, Canto 12.

59 John Fletcher and Philip Massinger, *The Custom of the Country*, ed. Cyrus Hoy, in *The Dramatic Works in the Beaumont and Fletcher Canon*, gen. ed. Fredson Bowers (Cambridge University Press, 1992), vol. VIII, 633–758.

60 Ben Jonson, 'Epigram 128: To William Rowe', line 14, in *Epigrams*, ed. Colin Burrow, *The Cambridge Edition of the Works of Ben Jonson*, David Bevington, Martin Butler, and Ian Donaldson, gen. ed. (Cambridge University Press, 2012), vol. V, 187.

61 Christopher Ricks, 'The Moral and Poetic Structure of *The Changeling*', *Essays in Criticism* 10, no. 3 (1960), 290–306, at 290.

62 For Fuchs, 'the play presents a Spanish marriage as a hopelessly disingenuous move, given the predatory, immoral nature of the bride, as figured in Beatrice-Joanna' (*Poetics of Piracy*, 69).

CHAPTER 12

The Uses of Cultural Encounter in Sir William Davenant's Caroline-to-Restoration Voyage Drama

Claire Jowitt
University of East Anglia

During a literary career that stretched from the mid-1620s to the Restoration, William Davenant (1606–68) repeatedly returned to the genre of voyage drama to enact and re-enact moments of encounter between groups and individuals from a range of different cultures.[1] How 'voyage drama' should be defined and categorised has been dealt with elsewhere in this volume,[2] but, for Davenant, the 'meme' or more properly – since for the most part this chapter focuses on performed and printed drama – the 'theatregram' of encounters between cultures was clearly an important device.[3] I use the term 'voyage drama' flexibly for all Davenant's publicly performed works, including masques and operas that depict cross-cultural encounters, either directly or indirectly (all of which were later printed), and for his dramatic epyllion, or little epic, 'Madagascar' (published, with other poems, in 1638).[4] This chapter seeks to answer the key question of *why* he chose persistently to employ the 'moment of encounter' dramatic trope. Of course it can be seen as a particularly charged meme at this time in history since English desires for an overseas empire and activities to secure it both intensified significantly, but I argue that there is something *qualitatively* meaningful in Davenant's use of it. Indeed, the full significance of Davenant's use of the encounter theatregram cannot be understood in an isolated case study but needs to be understood as a developing technique that he returned to and refined over a number of decades. As such, the meaning and significance of each instance that he uses the theatregram are interdependent on all the other instances. Not only does Davenant's lengthy career provide an opportunity to quantify the ways he used his favoured topos, but its malleable and flexible nature also made it an ideal vehicle to respond to the series of major political upheavals and regime changes he lived through. Other dramatists – William Shakespeare in *The Tempest* (*c.*1611) of course, but also Christopher Marlowe, Thomas Heywood, Ben Jonson, Philip Massinger, John Fletcher, George Chapman, John Marston, and many others – explored similar themes about encounter in their work,[5] but this does not mean that Davenant was simply *à la mode* or that he used the trope in merely conventional or imitative ways. In fact, this theatre-gram offered him the opportunity to compare attitudes, institutions, and systems from different cultures, and to critique his home society either explicitly or through the use of allegory, or other distancing rhetorical strategies. In short, over his career the topos became an increasingly powerful agent of meaning, and this essay seeks to explore a new critical trajectory in Davenant scholarship: how he redirected and turned in upon itself one of the most charged tropes of expansionist colonial discourse and thus questioned the very nature of English 'civility' itself.

The full extent and complexity of Davenant's depiction of moments of cultural encounter, as well as their intertextual references, have been both under-explored and under-appreciated by critics. Scholarship often focuses on Davenant's texts about travel in isolation or small groups, and reads them in relation to discrete political periods in his career. Later works such as *The Cruelty of the Spaniards in Peru* (1658) and *The History of Sir Francis Drake* (1659) have attracted most attention, with discussion focusing on innovative theatrical and performance techniques of these mixed-form entertainments (part drama, part opera), and the ways a notorious royalist negotiated and intervened in Interregnum political debates (producing propaganda for Oliver Cromwell's foreign policy in support of the 'western design').[6] Davenant's and John Dryden's Restoration rewritings of Shakespeare plays – especially *The Tempest, or the Enchanted Island* (1667), which was one of the most frequently performed plays of Charles II's reign – have also been discussed regularly.[7] The individual input of the two collaborators to the revision, and the play's relationships with its *c.*1611 original text, have been chief concerns.[8] Davenant's interest in cross-cultural encounter exceeds these familiar instances: the typographical style of the last masque produced in the Caroline era, *Salmacida Spolia* (1640), with its scenic descriptions and division into entries rather than acts, was the model for *The Siege of Rhodes* (1656, published 1659), and for *Peru* and *Drake*, and all three were revived, and revised or enlarged in Restoration performances or publications.[9] Davenant's masque *The Temple of Love* (1635) and poem 'Madagascar' also provide important models for the way the interplay between 'civil' and 'primitive' cultures in moments of encounter could be used. In 1656 Davenant wrote to John Thurloe, Cromwell's Secretary of State, to persuade him to support public performances in London, suggesting that 'some use may be made' of 'the Spaniards' barbarous conquests in the West Indies' as well as 'the several cruelties' inflicted upon the English in the New World.[10] In the light of Davenant's aesthetic theories concerning the didactic potential of these moments of cultural encounter, this essay examines their ideological and political co-ordinates. In so doing, the chapter examines the ways that continuities and changes in Davenant's use of the 'encounter' theatregram reveal his targets for support, critique, and reform, both at home and abroad, and the ways he developed the topos.

Oblique Encounter: Caroline Voyage Drama

From early in his writing career Davenant engaged with ideas concerning moments of cultural encounter. In his Caroline plays he approached the trope obliquely. In *Newes from Plymouth* (1635) set in the 'wind-bound' port, for instance, Davenant wrote satirically of the dismal failure of a group of seamen to travel and thus encounter any other culture than their own.[11] Davenant's aspirant travellers are becalmed and militarily frustrated seamen carousing and competing instead for the sexual favours of the resident women, who are the only 'prizes' and 'carracks' they encounter. 'Carrack' is the rich widow of a sea dog who 'took a prize / From the Hamburghers, and Brasile Men'; she stands in for the ship and the means of transportation between disparate regions and cultural encounters it enables.[12] The play was performed as a vacation play at the Bankside Globe (a vast outdoor theatre that attracted mixed-class audiences and operated in the long summer vacation when the indoor playhouses were closed), and its objects of satire are domestic and current: the lack of serviceableness of England's amphibious fighting men and fleet. After the dispiriting failure of the continental wars with Spain and France in the 1620s, the English fleet was a laughing stock in Europe.[13] In order to address navy weakness – indeed to provide a force to enable moments of cultural encounter to take place at all – and to secure the king an income without Parliamentary grants, the ship money levy was introduced in maritime counties in 1634, and extended to inland counties in 1635. It was an unpopular tax; the name Sir Furious Inland in *Newes from Plymouth* invokes the controversy explicitly since he provokes fights because, he claims, 'I love the King! And am bound / In conscience and good nature to kill his enemies' (2.139).[14] The launch of the first ship money fleet in 1635 and renewed naval strength was supposed to show to European rivals that English neutrality could no longer be taken for granted.[15] In *Newes from Plymouth* optimism about England's future influence on European foreign policy is eroded. The fleet waits uselessly in port and the only legitimate target for Inland's rage – the only possible king's enemy included in the play – is a Dutch captain, Bumble, whom he befriends.[16]

Likewise, even when Davenant includes characters who are described as able to actually experience cultural encounter overseas, such as Thorello in *The Fair Favourite* (1638), the focus remains on the domestic situation and is specifically directed to English courtly concerns. The estrangement of Thorello, the returning traveller, from his homeland after foreign experience, echoes the situation of the monarch in Davenant's play.[17] Performed at the Cockpit-in-court, the Royal Household's private Westminster theatre, in late 1638, the plot focuses on the marital and political difficulties of an unnamed King of Naples. It opens with a group of courtiers debating 'the excellency of travel', more specifically the apparent capacity of this fashionable activity to 'perfecteth / Your very ape', refining the creature's manners so that he 'kiss[es] his hairy hand, most Monsieur like' on receipt of a present.[18] The sarcasm is aimed at the experienced traveller Thorello, and the hostility of the remark reveals just how troubling travel and cultural encounter were for conservative elements of the court. They make it impossible to distinguish ape from human, thus connecting with other disturbing early modern issues: where exactly the border between ape and human falls, and whether it was fixed or unstable.[19] Thorello is described as becoming a stranger to his own country because of his foreign encounters: 'thou art a right traveller, / An old acquaintance in every town / Abroad, and a new stranger still at home', comments the courtier Saladine (1.1.214). This position as outsider at home requires explanations to be given concerning the nature and origin of the problems facing the court: Thorello has to be reintroduced just as the audience/reader requires orientation. But this focus on the returning traveller made strange by foreign encounter also questions where 'civil' values reside, particularly as his estrangement also echoes the King's situation, since he has returned from foreign wars on the same day and is equally alienated from the court.[20] While Thorello was travelling, the King has been tricked into a dynastic marriage resulting in widespread political distrust, an unconsummated marriage, and an apparently on-going affair. His fitness to rule is questioned, and even he desires to give up his position because it makes him a 'monster' (1.1.211). In other words, the situations of both king and Thorello resonate with the strangeness of the 'very Ape', who after cultural encounter through travel is able to master a whole host of fashionable gentlemen's pursuits 'most Monsieur like', but the attainment of each marker of sophistication only compounds the unnaturalness, indeed monstrousness, of the animal's position. Cultural encounter is represented as useful, not for bringing back new information, skills, or commodities, or even for enabling proselytising – the benefits most frequently cited – but for educating the returning traveller to see his home society with fresh eyes.[21] Yet the resemblances in the situations of the king, Thorello, and ape simultaneously reveal troubling, even destabilising, qualities associated with cultural encounter. Borders between animal and human, outsider and insider, civil and uncivil, king and subject, appear indistinct and under stress.

Davenant wrote two other texts in the mid-to-late 1630s that focus on cultural encounter: the masque *The Temple of Love*, performed by Henrietta Maria and members of the court at Whitehall on Shrove Tuesday 1635, and the poem 'Madagascar'. Both focus on the 'East' as an important target of English mercantile, imperial, and/or colonial ambitions, but neither export English 'civility' in a straightforward manner. In the masque, the queen takes the role of Indamora, sovereign of the Hindu kingdom of Narsinga, whose arrival in 'this island' of England re-establishes the Temple of Chaste Love 'by the influence of her beauty' and thereby returns order to the court.[22] Though the masque engages with 'elsewhere' in its use of 'Indian' flora and fauna, as well as luxury, rare and exotic commodities, and Persian nobles and Brachmani (Brahmin) Hindu priests, all made familiar to the English by the travel accounts published by Richard Hakluyt and Samuel Purchas as part of their collections or as the cargoes of East India Company ships,[23] importantly the movement of the cultural encounters the text describes is *solely* from East to West. Put another way, the direction of traffic is only one way: all the 'Eastern' commodities and peoples described arrive in England as exotic imports, rather than being exported from England 'elsewhere'. As a result, the masque does not celebrate the export of English goods or civility through trade or expansion; instead 'India' appears superior. The political message is easy to decipher: the queen's foreignness reforms the English court, as the French princess, herself an import, is shown as a powerfully beneficial influence on court and king.

By contrast, 'Madagascar', written in first-person poetic voice, depicts cultural encounter first-hand, but here again obliqueness acts as a distancing mechanism.[24] The epyllion imagines the conquest of this strategically important island for English 'Eastern' expansion by Charles I's nephew Prince Rupert three times: first in a blood-less yielding of the Malagasy when confronted by Rupert's beauty, and then after English forces twice defeat (in single combat, then through war) an unnamed, rival colonial nation (probably the Portuguese).[25] Cultural encounters are not represented straightforwardly; English conquest of the island only takes place in the poetic voice's fervid, illness-induced dream vision (perhaps a recurrence of Davenant's 1630 life-threatening bout of syphilis?), and hence the tenor of 'Madagascar' is not easy to judge.[26] In one way, of course, its distance from the realities of cultural encounter (Rupert's beauty is enough for the Malagasy to cede their land to him immediately), or its lack of effort in representing its challenges or dangers (Rupert's ships command the seas due to his uncle's powerful, Neptune-style Trident rather than maritime superiority) is understandable. Rupert never actually embarked for Madagascar, despite support for the project from prominent courtiers including Davenant's patrons Endymion Porter and Henry Jermyn, and the earls of Essex, Warwick, Arundel, Northumberland, and Bedford. The ambiguity in tone over the glorious-ness of the expedition (English leaders appear heroic in defeating their unnamed colonial rivals through trial-by-combat, but newly successful non-elite English colonisers swiftly degenerate in the face of overabundant and sexualised nature) captures some of the complex reactions the scheme provoked. Davenant describes how wealth is 'greedily explor'd' so that, reminiscent of medieval representations of the 'Land of Cockaigne', the island appears to yield so plentifully that the language begins to convey immorality, surfeit, and even, perhaps, disgust. Madagascan pearls are so 'pond'rous' in size that their weight 'sinks weaker Divors' (perhaps drowning them?) and 'yokes a tender Ladies Neck'; the enormous jewels can only be worn where 'some well truss'd Giantesse is Queene', while the 'old Oysters' producing them 'lay gapeing there / For ev'ry new, fresh flood, a hundred yeares'. These images describe pain and frustration, and convey extraordinary size as aberration and excess; likewise, the colonial scene is depicted with class-based language of exploitation, rape, and destruction. The English swarm across the landscape in search of 'new temptations': they are 'busie ... In virgin Mines', they 'root up Corall Trees, where *Mermaids* lie', and 'rude dull Mariners' use rare '*Ambar-Greece*', normally used in perfumery, prosaically to make their shoe leather supple (365–408).

Davenant might, perhaps, be seen as attempting to inspire the king to support the Madagascan scheme and, specifically, to ensure that the elite heroism of the mission's leaders becomes the model for English colonial cultural encounters. But the impracticality of the bloodless yielding of land that Rupert's beauty provokes makes such a reading unlikely. Likewise, colonial rivals make 'honour' impossible to maintain as they refuse to abide by chivalric codes of combat. The range and types of behaviour access to riches encourages, as lower-class Englishmen degenerate to become uncivil in the face of overabundant nature, strike the poem's most prominent cautionary notes. The threat extends as far up the social rank as the poem's auto-fictional persona of an impecunious 'Davenant', who awakes from his dream of cultural encounter because he fears he is vulnerable to accepting bribes.[27] Perhaps, too, recounting English success as part of a dream signalled the scheme's political crosswinds, since at this time Rupert's mother Elizabeth, Dowager Queen of Bohemia, remained without her Palatine territories, and many courtiers blamed the king for a lack of decisive action in supporting his sister in reclaiming them. In other words, the Madagascar enterprise was a dangerous distraction (Elizabeth wrote to her agent in London Sir Thomas Roe about the 'Romance' in 'Ruperts head ... when he shall Don Quixotte-like conquer that famous island', and urging Roe to 'in earnest seek to put such windmills out of his head') from more pressing European territorial responsibilities.[28] The use of a dream vision serves to increase the text's functional ambiguity; on one level the poem is proleptic, anticipating and thereby enabling English colonial success, but, at the same time, the ambiguous origin and meaning of dream visions,[29] as well as the corruption that cultural encounter engenders among non-elite Englishmen, and 'Davenant', moderates the poem's apparent support of colonial expansion through chivalry. Just as Don Quixote's knightly behaviour was misplaced (and disastrous) in Cervantes's romance, outmoded knightly values prove ineffective and idealistic in subduing colonial rivals or controlling non-elite Englishmen in 'Madagascar'. Indeed, the 'romance' features of the poem, which emphasise meandering and digression, and contrast with the purposeful linearity and 'political instrumentality' associated with 'epic',[30] suggest that, even generically, the text is unsuited to its subject matter.

Cultural Encounter in Protectorate and Restoration Voyage Drama

After the experience of defeat in the English Civil War, the execution of the king in 1649, and Davenant's own imprisonment until 1652, it was not until 1653 that he began petitioning Cromwell's government to allow theatrical performances to resume, arguing in 'A Proposition for Advancement of Moralitie, by a New Way of Entertainment of the People' for 'the establishment of a moral academy where, under strict government surveillance, theatrical productions combining music, scenery and discourse would be performed for the purpose of teaching civic virtue directly to the lower classes'.[31] As a first step towards restoring drama proper, Davenant began writing generically hybrid, operatic-style theatrical performances in which the dominant themes are cultural encounter with apparently primitive and uncivil peoples, and long-range travel. In particular, in *Peru* and *Drake*, both performed at the Cockpit in Drury Lane, Davenant dramatised sixteenth-century cultural encounters between Old and New Worlds. Finally, in the year before his death, he adapted Shakespeare's play with Dryden to produce a semi-operatic version of *The Tempest* for the Duke's Theatre at Lincoln's Inn Fields. New 'primitive' characters were introduced to the play, including sisters for Miranda and Caliban; and Hippolito, a shipwrecked young man kept in isolation by Prospero, who 'never saw Woman' before; and an expanded group of shipwrecked sailors.[32] The remainder of this essay focuses on the political and ideological uses Davenant (with Dryden in *The Tempest*) makes of the repeated representation of apparently primitive and uncivil characters in these three voyage dramas. Of course 'wild men/women' had long been staple figures of travel writing. They reveal the anxiety and fascination with what Earl Miner termed 'the wild man [*sic*] through the looking glass', referring to the belief of the vulnerability of 'civil' travellers degenerating into savagery through proximity, since, as Paul Brown puts it, 'the same discourse which allows for the transformation of the savage into the civil also raises the possibility of a reverse transformation.'[33] *Peru*, *Drake*, and *The Tempest* unite in their concern to debate what it means to be 'uncivil', and who should be seen in that way, in order to reflect domestic issues. Indeed the incivility of Old World characters is not necessarily caused by proximity to 'uncivil' groups; rather, as we shall see, the incivility most frequently arrives with the colonists.

In Davenant's Commonwealth dramas the depiction of cruel, greedy, and incompetent Spanish colonists in the New World supports Cromwell's 'western design', an expansionist, anti-Spanish foreign policy capable of cutting across the Royalist–Parliamentarian divide at home.[34] In *Peru*, for instance, the drama ends anachronistically with the rescue by the English of Peruvians from Spanish abuse, notwithstanding the fact that the English were not a colonial presence in Peru in the historical period depicted. The play is divided into scenes called 'entries', and the Sixth Entry explains this historical inaccuracy concerning the English as 'discoverers': 'These imaginary English forces may seem improper, because the English had made no discovery of Peru in the time of the Spaniards' first invasion there; but yet in poetical representations of this nature, it may pass as a vision discerned by the Priest of the Sun before the matter was extant, in order to his prophecy.'[35]

In fact, there is continuity between this drama's 'vision' and that expressed by Davenant in 'Madagascar' since both include, and debase, English colonial rivals and 'imagine' English forces in regions from where they were historically or geographically absent. In the poem the forces of the rival colonial nation only arrive on the island 'the day before' because they learn of Rupert's interest: 'In envy of thy hopes they hither came' (99). In the drama Spanish conquistadors are depicted as gold-and-blood-thirsty 'beasts' torturing 'natives and English mariners' and enslaving Peruvians with uncontrolled brutality. They are also shown to be incompetent: the Spaniard 'loaden with ingots of gold and silver ... discovers a weariness and inclination to sleep, to which purpose he lies down, with his basket for his pillow', loses his booty when he is attacked and driven away by apes and a 'great baboon', played by actors in costumes (5.4; 6.42–45). Davenant's description of the Spaniard's failure is indebted to accounts of similarly sleepy Spaniards in accounts of Drake's circumnavigation (1577–80). In the version published in *The World Encompassed by Sir Francis Drake* (1628) by Drake's nephew, also called Sir Francis Drake, the English come across a sleeping Spaniard who 'had lying by him 13 barres of silver' in Tarapacá, Peru. Solicitously expressing regret at disturbing the Spaniard's rest, the narrative – somewhat ironically – represents the stealing of the silver as a humanitarian act to ensure continued peaceful sleep: 'but seeing we, against our wills, did him that injury [i.e., woke him], we freed him of his charge, which otherwise perhaps would have kept him waking, and so left him to take out (if it pleased him) the other part of his sleepe in more security.'[36] The exaggerated gentility of this apparent concern for the Spaniard's well-being reduces the sense of wrongdoing as thievery is reimagined as solicitude. Davenant's version, however, replaces Drake and his men with apes, joined by a baboon, who were earlier shown as part of the natural landscape in the First Entry ('on the boughs of other trees are seen monkeys, apes and parrots') (1.10–11). The use of such creatures to take revenge on the sleepy Spaniard thus reverses the traditional hierarchy of man over animal, as here an animal is shown to be superior to (Spanish) man. Similar to his pre-Civil War play *The Fair Favourite*, Davenant uses the 'encounter' theatregram to engage with the wider political implications of having an unstable distinction between ape and human. In *Peru*, the apes dance with the baboon prior to waking the Spaniard, and the Sixth Entry ends with the animal group 'driving him [the Spaniard] into the wood' in a manner reminiscent of the way that the Fifth Entry ended with the Spaniard 'reviving' the 'weariness' of the enslaved Peruvians 'with his truncheon' before he 'drives them [the Peruvians] again into the wood' (6.48; 5.72). The replacement of men with apes as the agent of punishment for Spanish incompetence, greed, and cruelty to Peruvians serves to further undermine and ridicule Spanish rule: even the natural world wishes to remove Spaniards from its landscape. By describing the Spanish as more 'beastly' and primitive than animals, and then depicting their reduction in status in the stage action, Davenant implies a future amity between the English, Peruvians, and the natural world once the Spanish have been ejected. In political terms, Davenant's recycling and redeployment of the relationship between ape and human in a Spanish American context re-internationalises the trope he used before the Civil War in *The Fair Favourite* for domestic political critique. Primitivism in this Commonwealth text participates in an outward-looking English colonialist discourse which imagined and justified territorial expansion into the Spanish-dominated colonial sphere, but just a year or so later, at a time of considerable internal political uncertainty, the theatregram of cultural encounter in South America became once more the vehicle for comment about domestic concerns.

In *Drake*, anti-Spanish sentiments, similar to those articulated in *Peru*, are fiercely expressed, but the issue of the characteristics that make a good leader is the text's principal focus. The issue of heroic leadership was highly topical in late 1658 and early 1659 after Cromwell's death in September 1658, and the inheritance of the role of Lord Protector by his son, Richard. By the time Davenant wrote *Drake* (it was entered in the Stationers' Register on 20 January 1659), 'reviving' the famous sixteenth-century mariner had become an established means of commenting on current policies and leaders through the invocation of, and comparison with, a glorious past of heroic action.[37] In Davenant's drama – which focuses on Drake's attack on the mule trains transporting Peruvian gold and silver from Panama on the Pacific coast to Nombre de Dios on the Atlantic seaboard for onward export to Spain – desire for gold displayed by members of different ethnic groups determines their moral worth. Spanish lust for gold is repeatedly emphasised: Drake comments, 'nothing can afflict them [the Spanish] more, / Than to deprive them of that store'.[38] In contrast to Spanish rapacity, Drake, the Peruvians, and the 'Symerons' (i.e., Cimarrons) are united in only seeking gold for what it will enable them to achieve.[39] In *Peru*, the English intend to disrupt the flow of treasure into Europe where it 'afflict[s] the peaceful world with war', and the Peruvians and Symerons support Drake's plan because of the inhumane treatment both groups have endured under Spanish control (2.94).[40]

The heroism and success of Drake's raid is accentuated in Davenant's text as historical events are redacted and rewritten. In particular, Davenant chose not to describe the failure of the raid at first attempt in January 1573, instead concentrating on Drake's second, successful, attack which took place in April. The decisive input of the French privateer Guillaume Le Testu to the mission's success is omitted; likewise, the deaths of two of Drake's brothers, and the quarrel with James Ranse (Rouse in the play) are not mentioned.[41] Instead the drama emphasises Drake's reputation and leadership skills, including his ability to manage and maximise the value and input of his compatriots and allies to the raid's success. Honour, courage, modesty, and restraint are repeatedly described as central to Drake's personal behaviour, and his glorious reputation is also significant in recruiting followers and maintaining their allegiance: when asked by Drake to join him, Rouse immediately agrees, commenting 'What man is that, loved Admiral, / Who does not hasten at your call? / He must be either deaf, or ever lame, / Who follows not your loud and leading fame' (1.74–77). Drake is shown to be insistent that the men under his command follow his honourable moral code, reining in his brother John's blood-lust when hunting, and enforcing sexual restraint on the Symerons after they capture Spanish women, despite their desire to revenge the rape of their own womenfolk (4.23–28; 5.109–14). In contrast to Richard Cromwell, who, it was said, only became 'a Colonel of Horse now fighting is over' and lost the support of the army within weeks of becoming Lord Protector,[42] Davenant's Drake is represented as an ideal commander, able to control unruly elements through personal charisma and the respect inspired by his glorious military record. Drake's heroic and active leadership and his ability to harmonise apparently discordant elements to an overall mission thus point to all that was absent from the rule of the new Lord Protector. Cultural encounters from sixteenth-century English colonial history are used opportunistically to reflect pressing domestic concerns. Indeed, the political attitude implied by Davenant's depiction of Drake may have been apparent at the time: John Evelyn reports that he 'could not resist' going to see a performance of *Drake* in May 1659 'though my heart smote me for it', commenting that 'it was prodigious that in a time of such public consternation such a vanity should be kept up, or permitted', and the House of Lords did order an investigation into Davenant's 'operas', imprisoning him briefly in August 1659 in connection with a supposed Royalist plot.[43]

The final text under discussion, Davenant and Dryden's adaptation of *The Tempest*, accentuates Shakespeare's focus on how boundaries between 'primitive' and 'civilised' peoples are under threat of collapse, by showing them *dissolving* across a wider range of characters. The intensity of the play's focus on this issue enables me to consider how and why late in his career, and after the monarch was restored, Davenant continued to use the depiction of cultural encounters in geographically remote locations to convey domestic political issues. By the mid-1660s, following the reopening of public playhouses under licence from Charles II, the renewal and augmentation of English ambitions for colonial territory and imperial power in a wider range of regions, and the resulting flare-up of rivalries and wars in Europe, plays that depicted cultural encounters between Europeans and peoples indigenous to, or already inhabiting, a desired terrain were commonplace.[44] Both *Peru* and *Drake* were restaged in the Restoration when Davenant incorporated them into his miscellany *The Playhouse To Be Let* in 1663 as Acts Four and Three respectively;[45] in 1664 Dryden and Robert Howard produced a play about the Incas, *The Indian Queen*, and due to its popularity, the following year Dryden wrote a sequel, *The Indian Emperour*. Even the fragments rescued from Drake's by-now rotting *Golden Hind* received hyperbolic treatment: in 'Ode. Sitting and Drinking in the Chair, made out of the Reliques of Sir Francis Drake's Ship' (1662), Abraham Cowley armchair-travelled around the world, drunkenly, in 'the only Universal chair' made from the salvaged timbers of the ship that had 'compass'd all the Earth'.[46] In fact Cowley's drunken maritime (over)ambitions were a harbinger. Though Charles II's accession in May 1660 was met with public celebration, the regime's popularity swiftly waned. The king's reputation for sloth, drunkenness, and lechery, the lack of a legitimate male Protestant heir, the plague of 1665–66 and the Great Fire which ended it, all eroded public enthusiasm for the regime. In particular, the disastrous Second Anglo-Dutch War, provoked by the Lord High Admiral, the Duke of York, which the nation could not afford or the navy sustain, significantly decreased popular support for the policies of the king and his coterie. The war had been sparked by the Duke of York's ambitious belief that

England could best the Dutch in a naval war in the Channel and North Sea, suggesting to his brother that the war would be self-financing through the English navy's regular seizing of East Indiamen laden with valuable goods from Asia and silver bullion for Spain.[47] In fact the king was forced to hastily conclude peace in July 1667 after the Dutch Medway raid in June when, humiliatingly, the navy was unable to prevent two English warships being captured, towed, and sailed in triumph as prizes across the North Sea to the United Provinces.

The production of Davenant and Dryden's *The Tempest*, which opened on 7 November 1667, clearly took advantage commercially of the upsurge in popular interest in material that connected maritime and colonial encounters to failures of government. It was also a direct commercial response to the production of *The Storm*, a revival of *The Sea Voyage* (1622) by John Fletcher and Philip Massinger, staged by the rival playing company, Thomas Killigrew's King's Men, which began on 25 September 1667 and played to an 'infinitely full' house according to Samuel Pepys, with the opening night attended by the king.[48] Prospero is a much diminished figure in his Restoration incarnation,[49] as repeatedly he is shown to lack authority and judgement, and both his own powers and the threats against him are reduced: indeed, his usurpers, Alonzo and Antonio, have repented prior to their arrival on the island and there is no plot against his life by Caliban and his low-plot cronies. Patriarchal authority appears under threat; as Candy Schille comments, all Prospero can do at the end of the play is recover 'the illusion of control or agency'.[50] It is Ariel who determines the outcome of events, narrowly averting tragedy when Prospero harshly and unjustly condemns Ferdinand for the murder of Hippolito, curing the youth's wound with his 'simples'.[51] Indeed, Prospero's eagerness to condemn Ferdinand, which borders on blood-thirstiness ('No pleasure now is left me but Revenge') (4.4.497), echoes that of his female counterpart in *The Storm*, the faux amazon Rosellia, who savagely seeks to execute the sons of the men she (wrongly) believes caused her husband's death and her own shipwreck, and requires restraining. Both plays unite in their concern to examine from multiple perspectives how easily civility becomes savagery, both in the socially elite figures of the main plots and the lower-class characters of the subplots.

The expanded group of sailors, who compete for control of the island and its inhabitants, as well the inclusion of the sexualised and potentially reproductive female figure of Sycorax, who can provide an heir to the island, serve to intensify the colonial dynamics of this version of the moment of cultural encounter. Caliban's culpability is reduced first by the removal of his murderous rebellion against Prospero and, more significantly, because his situation and behaviour echo those of his colonial master. As patriarchs within their family units, both men seek to dispose of female relatives to create homosocial alliances (Caliban seeks an alliance with Trincalo, and Prospero with Ferdinand, heir to the Dukedom of Savoy, and Hippolito, rightful Duke of Mantua). High and low plots share other similarities; there is no clear distinction between the play's representation of Sycorax's libidinous nature or the rapacious sexuality of Miranda and Dorinda, for instance. Repeatedly, distinctions between what and who are 'civil' or 'savage' break down. Indeed the play's conclusion does not redraw the boundary effectively since, with Hippolito, a wild man raised on an island in a cave, restored as Duke of Mantua, the savagery bred 'elsewhere' is going 'home'. On one level the restoration of Hippolito's birthright invokes, of course, the situation of the restored Charles II, and might be seen as a warning of the political naivety of inexperienced rulers. The playing of Hippolito by an actress (Moll Davis) throughout the whole performance (this is not a breeches part) acts as a further example of the ways this role, as well as the play more generally, seeks to undermine conservative orthodoxies – absolutism, patriarchy, hierarchy of birth, and the superiority of Europeans and the Christian religion over other peoples and belief systems. Prospero's failures – both patriarchal authority and colonial rule break down and are never fully re-established – and Hippolito's restoration signal what is politically at stake, as Davenant, a loyal, but never triumphant or slavish royalist meditates on the difficulties facing the new regime.

Taken together Davenant's use of the 'encounter' theatregram reveal just how versatile and nuanced it was for expressing political meaning. It was a device that appears to have offered him an infinitely adaptable means to comment on diverse figures and events, and for offering advice with lightness and humour. Uniquely in Davenant, we have a dramatist at the centre of politics *and* the heart of theatrical performance and innovation in all four regimes of the mid-seventeenth century. More importantly still, perhaps due to the turbulent politics and regime changes of the period, and the reversal of fortunes they engendered in Davenant's own life, we have a writer from this period who is unusually alert to the powerful pull that colonialist discourse in literature and drama could exert on domestic and foreign policy: by offering comment on and advice to the most powerful in English society, literature could shape history, Davenant seems to assert when using repeatedly the encounter theatregram. Dryden, for instance, is often seen as the dominant writing-partner in their Restoration collabora-tions, in part in recognition of his role in developing 'heroic drama' and his first usage of the term 'noble savage' in *The Conquest of Granada* (1672).[52] Yet Davenant's continual turn to the 'encounter' theatregram in his voyage drama can be cited as evidence to confirm Dryden's own acknowledgement of Davenant's continuing influence on his drama as in *Granada*.[53] In Davenant's use of the 'moment of cultural encounter' trope, itself a defining characteristic of voyage drama, it seems he found an infinitely malleable topos, able to carry coded and double meanings, and to self-reflexively turn readers' and audiences' gazes in upon them-selves to ask searching questions about the values, maintenance, and indeed fragility of their own English 'civility'.

Notes

1 I have benefited from discussion with audiences at the University of Portsmouth's English Department Research Seminar, the Folger Shakespeare Library's 'Work-in-Progress' Seminar, and early modern colleagues at the University of East Anglia. I am also grateful to David McInnis, Julie Sanders, Will Rossiter, and Stephen Watkins for comments on earlier drafts of this essay.

2 For a definition of 'voyage drama', see this collection's 'Introduction'.

3 On the use of the Romance term 'meme', see Helen Cooper, *The English Romance in Time: Transforming Motifs from Geoffrey of Monmouth to the Death of Shakespeare* (Oxford University Press, 2004). In drama 'theatre-grams' are the 'interchange and transformation of units, figures, relation-ships, actions, *topoi*, and framing patterns'; see Louise George Clubb, *Italian Drama in Shakespeare's Time* (New Haven, CT: Yale University Press, 1989), 6; Jacques Lezra, 'Trade in Exile', in *Transnational Mobilities in Early Modern Theater*, ed. Robert Henke and Eric Nicholson (Farnham: Ashgate, 2014), 199–216; Henke and Nicholson, 'Introduction', 1–23. For discus-sion, see also Gavin Hollis, *The Absence of America: the London Stage 1576–1642* (Oxford University Press, 2015), and Clare McManus, '"Constant Changelings", Theatrical Form, and Migration: Stage Travel in the Early 1620s', Chapter 11 in this volume.

4 Richard Kroll suggests there was 'vigorous cross-talk between the staging of plays and the idea of the masque' in the 1630s, and John Orrell argues for the influence of Caroline theatrical practices on Restoration staging. See Kroll, *Restoration Drama and "The Circle of Commerce": Tragicomedy, Politics, and Trade in the Seventeenth Century* (Cambridge University Press, 2007), 94; Orrell, *The Theatres of Inigo Jones and John Webb* (Cambridge University Press, 1985) and *The Human Stage: English Theater Design, 1567–1640* (Cambridge University Press, 1988).

5 Scholarship on early modern drama and discovery/encounter is an immense field, and it became particularly vibrant after the publication of Stephen Greenblatt's influential study of colonial appropriation, *Marvelous Possessions: The Wonder of the New World* (University of Chicago Press, 1991). Scholars have explored the work of the wide variety of playwrights who used the trope in a range of plays, but see, most recently, Hollis, *The Absence of America*, which also includes a useful survey of criticism, 1–32. As the essays in this collection by Emily C. Bartels on *The Tempest* and Clare McManus on *The Changeling* continue to show, the topic remains vigorous: Shakespeare's famous drama of discovery/encounter can be read afresh as a 'dynamic negotiation of experience and expectation' (184), while William Rowley and Thomas Middleton's play is shown as an unrecognised voyage drama containing 'migrating tropes and scenarios' (211) taken from contemporary plays about encounter, such as John Fletcher's *The Island Princess* (1621).

6 For discussion, see Janet Clare, ed., *Drama of the English Republic, 1649–60* (Manchester University Press, 2002); 'Countering Anti-Theatricality: Davenant and the Drama of the Protectorate', in *The Oxford Handbook of Literature*, ed. Laura Lunger Knoppers (Oxford University Press, 2012), 498–515; see also Susan Wiseman, *Drama and Politics in the English Civil War* (Cambridge University Press, 1998). On Davenant's theatrical innovations, see, in particular, Dawn Lewcock, *Sir William Davenant, the Court Masque, and the English Seventeenth-Century Scenic Stage, c.1605–c.1700* (New York: Cambria Press, 2008); David McInnis, *Mind-Travelling and Voyage Drama in Early Modern England* (Basingstoke: Palgrave, 2013), 147–63; Kroll, *Restoration Drama*, 93–206.

7 Samuel Pepys records having seen the play at least eight times between 1667 and 1669. The licence to establish a new playing company issued to Davenant by the king included a performance monopoly for certain plays but required that they be 'improved'. See James J. Marino, *Owning William Shakespeare: The King's Men and Their Intellectual Property* (Philadelphia: University of Pennsylvania Press, 2011), 143–60.

8 For discussion of the relative contributions of each author to writing the adaptation and its relationship with Shakespeare's *The Tempest*, see Barbara A. Murray, *Restoration Shakespeare: Viewing the Voice* (London: Associated University Presses, 2001), 74–88, 233–36. Recent work includes Cary DiPietro, 'Seeing Places: *The Tempest* and the Baroque Spectacle of the Restoration Theatre', *Shakespeare* 9, no. 2 (2013), 168–86; and John Shanahan, 'The Dryden–Davenant *Tempest*, Wonder Production, and the State of Natural Philosophy in 1667', *The Eighteenth Century* 54, no. 1 (2013), 91–118.

9 A. M. Gibbs, 'Biographical Introduction', *Sir William Davenant: The Shorter Poems and Songs from the Plays and Masques* (Oxford: Clarendon Press, 1972), xvii–xxxviii; Mary Edmond, 'Davenant, Sir William (1606–1668)', *Oxford Dictionary of National Biography* (Oxford University Press, 2004);

online edn, Oct. 2009 [www.oxforddnb.com/view/article/7197], accessed 30 July 2014; Clare, *Drama*, 181–92; on the continuities and differences in structure and style between pre-Civil War masques and Interregnum operas, see Wiseman, *Drama and Politics*, 137–64.

10 See C. H. Firth, 'Sir William Davenant and the Revival of Drama During the Protectorate', *English Historical Review* 18 (1903), 103–20.

11 For a discussion of other contemporary plays that show failing travellers, see Claire Jowitt, 'Hakluyt's Legacy: Armchair Travel in English Renaissance Drama', in *Richard Hakluyt and Travel Writing in Early Modern Europe* ed. Daniel Carey and Claire Jowitt (Farnham: Ashgate, 2012), 295–306.

12 William Davenant, *Newes from Plymouth* in *The Dramatic Works of Sir William D'Avenant*, 5 vols. (Edinburgh and London: William Paterson and H. Sotheran, 1873), 4.1.2, 120. All further quotations refer to this edition and will be cited by act, scene, and line numbers within the text.

13 See N. A. M. Rodger, *The Safeguard of the Sea: A Naval History of Britain 660–1649* (New York and London: Norton, 1999), 363.

14 For discussion of the ship money fleet, see Ian Ferrier, 'Ship Money Reconsidered', *British Tax Review* 5 (1984), 227–36. The masque *Britannia Triumphans* (1637) is Davenant's most direct response to the ship money crisis. See Todd Butler, *Imagination and Politics in Seventeenth-Century England* (Ashgate: Aldershot, 2008), 87–92.

15 Kevin Sharpe, *The Personal Rule of Charles I* (New Haven, CT: Yale University Press, 1992), 509–36; see also Sharpe, *Criticism and Compliment: The Politics of Literature in the England of Charles I* (Cambridge University Press, 1987), 54–108.

16 The ship money fleet was expected to worsen Anglo-Dutch relations. For a detailed study, see Anton Poot, 'Anglo-Dutch Relations: A Political and Diplomatic Analysis of the years 1625–1642' (unpublished PhD thesis, Royal Holloway University of London, 2013), 155–78.

17 On the relationship between Italian and English settings, see Michele Marrapodi, 'Introduction: Appropriating Italy: Towards a New Approach to Renaissance Drama', *Italian Culture in the Drama of Shakespeare and His Contemporaries* (Aldershot: Ashgate, 2007), 4; J. Bate, 'The Elizabethans in Italy', in *Travel and Drama in Shakespeare's Time*, ed. Jean-Pierre Maquerlot and Michèle Willems (Cambridge University Press, 1996), 55–74.

18 William Davenant, *The Fair Favourite*, in *The Dramatic Works*, 4.1.1, 207, 209. All further quotations refer to this edition and will be cited by act, scene, and line numbers within the text. Courtiers were accustomed to kiss their hands, a practice satirised by Touchstone and Corin in Shakespeare's *As You Like It*, ed. Alan Brissenden (Oxford: Clarendon Press, 1993), 3.2.38–60.

19 See Susan Wiseman, 'Monstrous Perfectibility: Ape–Human Transformations in Hobbes, Bulwer, Tyson', in *At the Borders of the Human: Beasts, Bodies, and Natural Philosophy in the Early Modern Period*, ed. Erica Fudge et al. (Basingstoke: Palgrave, 1999), 215–28.

20 For analysis of the political dimensions of the play, see Sharpe, *Criticism and Compliment*, 54–108.

21 On the art of travel, see Joan-Pau Rubiés, 'Instructions for Travellers: Teaching the Eye to See', *History and Anthropology* 9 (1996), 139–90; Daniel Carey, *Continental Travel and Journeys Beyond Europe in the Early Modern Period: An Overlooked Connection* (London: Hakluyt Society, 2009).

22 William Davenant, *The Temple of Love: A Masque*, in *The Dramatic Works*, I, 286. See Amrita Sen, 'Playing an Indian Queen: Neoplatonism, Ethnography, and *The Temple of Love*', in *Indography: Writing the 'Indian' in Early Modern England*, ed. Jonathan Gil Harris (New York: Palgrave, 2012), 209–22; Karen Britland, *Drama at the Courts of Queen Henrietta Maria* (Cambridge University Press, 2006), 131–49.

23 See James Knowles, '"The faction of the flesh": Orientalism and the Caroline Masque', in *The 1630s: Interdisciplinary Essays on Culture and Politics in the Caroline Era*, ed. Ian Atherton and Julie Sanders (Manchester University Press, 2006), 111–37.

24 In 1635 Walter Hamond, an East India Company surgeon on the *Jonas* or *Jonah*, spent four months on Madagascar, probably joining the Courteen Association on return. Hamond advocated English colonisation of the island, and his pamphlet *A Paradox. Proving, That the Inhabitants of the Isle called Madagascar, Or St. Laurence, (In Temporal things) are the happiest People in the World* was published in 1640. See Louis B. Wright, 'The Noble Savage of Madagascar in 1640', *Journal of the History of Ideas* 4, no. 1 (1943), 112–18. In 1646 Richard Boothby, an East India Company merchant, also published a pamphlet about the island, *A Briefe Discovery or Description Of the most Famous Island of Madagascar or St Laurence*. Boothby briefed the Privy Council, and Rupert, at the behest of Porter, while the project was still under discussion and is probably the main source of Davenant's information.

25 Sir William Davenant, 'Madagascar', in *The Shorter Poems*, 5–21. All further quotations refer to this edition and will be cited by line numbers within the text.

26 For a fuller discussion, see Claire Jowitt, '"To sleep, perchance to Dream": The Politics of Travel in the 1630s', *Yearbook of English Studies* 44 (2014), 249–64.

27 On the difficulties of Davenant's financial situation, see J. P. Feil, 'Davenant Exonerated', *Modern Language Review* 58 (1963), 335–42.

28 Ethel Bruce Sainsbury, *A Calendar of the Court Minutes Etc. of the East India Company, 1635–1639* (Oxford: Clarendon Press, 1907), 244–45; quoted by Gibbs, *Sir William Davenant*, 343. See Marlin E. Blaine, 'Epic, Romance and History in Davenant's "Madagascar"', *Studies in Philology*, 95 (1998), 293–319; Sharpe, *Criticism and Compliment*, 96–97.

29 See Peter Holland, '"The Interpretation of Dreams" in the Renaissance', in *Reading Dreams: The Interpretation of Dreams from Chaucer to Shakespeare*, ed. Peter Brown (Oxford University Press, 1999), 125–46; *Reading the Early*

Modern Dream: The Terrors of the Night, ed. Katherine Hodgkin et al. (New York and London: Routledge, 2008); Carole Levin, *Dreaming the English Renaissance: Politics and Desire in Court and Culture* (New York: Palgrave Macmillan, 2008).

30 Barbara Fuchs, *Romance: The New Critical Idiom* (New York: Routledge, 2004), 66; see also Colin Burrow, *Epic Romance: Homer to Milton* (Oxford: Clarendon Press, 1993).

31 James R. Jacob and Timothy Raylor, 'Opera and Obedience: Thomas Hobbes and "A Proposition for Advancement of Morality" by Sir William Davenant', *Seventeenth Century* 6, no. 2 (1991), 205–50, at 205.

32 William Davenant, *The Tempest*, in *The Dramatic Works*, 5.395–521, at 418.

33 Earl Miner, 'The Wild Man Through the Looking Glass', in *The Wild Man Within: An Image in Western Thought from the Renaissance to Romanticism*, ed. Edward Dudley and Maximillian E. Novak (University of Pittsburgh Press, 1972), 87–114; Paul Brown, '"This thing of darkness I acknowledge mine": *The Tempest* and the Discourse of Colonialism', in *Political Shakespeare: Essays in Cultural Materialism*, ed. Alan Sinfield and Jonathan Dollimore (Manchester University Press, 1985), 48–71.

34 On the Western Design, see David Armitage, 'The Cromwellian Protectorate and the Languages of Empire', *Historical Journal* 35, no. 3 (1992), 531–55; Wiseman, *Drama and Politics*, 147–51.

35 William Davenant, *The Cruelty of the Spaniards in Peru*, in Clare, *Drama*, 6.7–11. All further quotations refer to this edition and will be cited by scene and line numbers within the text.

36 Sir Francis Drake, *The World Encompassed by Sir Francis Drake* (London, 1628), 54–55. See Claire Jowitt, *The Culture of Piracy, 1580–1630: English Literature and Seaborne Crime* (Farnham: Ashgate, 2010), 47–78.

37 See, in particular, W. T. Jewkes, 'Sir Francis Drake Revived: From Letters to Legend,' in *Sir Francis Drake and the Famous Voyage, 1577–1580: Essays Commemorating the Quadricentennial of Drake's Circumnavigation of the Earth*, ed. Norman J. W. Thrower (Berkeley, CA: University of California Press, 1984), 112; Mark Netzloff, 'Francis Drake's Ghost: Piracy, Cultural Memory, and Spectral Nationhood', in *Pirates? The Politics of Plunder 1550–1650*, ed. Claire Jowitt (Basingstoke: Palgrave, 2006), 137–50; Marco Nievergelt, 'Francis Drake: Merchant, Knight and Pilgrim', *Renaissance Studies* 23 (2009), 53–70; Bruce Wathen, *Sir Francis Drake: The Construction of a Hero* (Woodbridge, Suffolk: Boydell and Brewer, 2009).

38 Davenant, *The History of Sir Francis Drake*, in Clare, *Drama*, 2.91–92. All further quotations refer to this edition and will be cited by scene and line numbers within the text. On heroic action, see Laura Brown, *English Dramatic Form, 1660–1760* (New Haven, CT: Yale University Press, 1981), 3–27.

39 Cimarrons were armed groups of escaped black slaves, specific to this region, who, having fled to the mountains, established free black colonies called *palenques*. Spanish authorities feared the alliance of cimarrons with, in particular, French and English pirates. The leader of the Nombre de Dios or

Panama cimarrons, with whom Drake was allied, was Pedro Mandinga. See Ruth Pike, 'Black Rebels: The Cimarrons of Sixteenth-Century Panama', *The Americas* 64, no. 2 (2007), 243–66.

40 For discussion of the reasons behind Peruvian and Symeron hostility to the Spanish, see, in particular, 5.152–57.

41 The first attack on the *trajin* en route between Panama and Nombre de Dios ended in failure since the ambush was discovered and the trains carrying the most valuable cargo turned back to Panama. The second raid, undertaken in consort with Le Testu, seized large quantities of treasure, carrying off the gold and burying the silver. See Philip Nichols, *Sir Francis Drake Revived: Calling Upon this Dull or Effeminate Age, to Folowe his Noble Steps for Golde & Silver* (London: E. A. for Nicholas Bourne, 1626), 61–65; 82–83; see also Harry Kelsey, *Sir Francis Drake: The Queen's Pirate* (New Haven, CT: Yale University Press, 1998), 40–67.

42 Peter Gaunt, 'Cromwell, Richard (1626–1712)', *Oxford Dictionary of National Biography* (Oxford University Press, 2004); online edn, Oct 2009 [www .oxforddnb.com/view/article/6768?docPos=1], accessed 12 August 2014.

43 See Lewcock, *Sir William Davenant*, 108.

44 See Bridget Orr, *Empire on the English Stage: 1660–1714* (Cambridge University Press, 2001).

45 Framing by a meta-theatrical first act, where lowly playhouse workers discuss their situation prior to watching a medley of comic, heroic, and operatic material alters, of course, the tenor of *Peru* and *Drake* in performance and print.

46 The *Golden Hind,* after eighty years as a tourist attraction and banqueting house, was broken up, and some planks were made into a chair and presented by John Davis of Deptford to the Bodleian Library. See Abraham Cowley, 'Upon the Chair made out of Sir Francis Drake's Ship' and 'Drake's Chair Lands in Oxford' [http://cowley.lib.virginia.edu/works/drakeshipode .htm; http://cowley.lib.virginia.edu/small/drake.htm].

47 See J. R. Jones, *The Anglo-Dutch Wars of the Seventeenth Century* (London: Longmans, 1996).

48 John Fletcher and Philip Massinger, *The Sea Voyage*, 'Introduction' by Cyrus Hoy, in *The Dramatic Works in the Beaumont and Fletcher Canon*, ed. Fredson Bowers, 10 vols. (Cambridge University Press, 1994), vol. IX, 7.

49 Prospero's appearance in *The Tempest* was not the first time Davenant used the name; in *Love and Honour* (1634), another 'Prospero' has to be schooled from savagery to civility in his mistreatment of women as the spoils of war.

50 Candy B. K. Schille, '"Man Hungry": Reconsidering Threats to Colonial and Patriarchal Order in Dryden and Davenant's *The Tempest*', *Texas Studies in Literature and Language* 48, no. 4 (2006), 273–90, at 288; Gavin Foster reads the play as a response to the Medway crisis, but sees the apparently harmonious conclusion as expressing support for the monarchy in 'Ignoring *The Tempest*: Pepys, Dryden, and the Politics of Spectating in 1667', *Huntington Library Quarterly* 63, nos. 1–2 (2000), 5–22; see also Kroll, *Restoration Drama*, 199–206.

51 Davenant and Dryden, *The Tempest*, in *The Dramatic Works*, 5.5.1, 506. All further quotations refer to this edition and will be cited by act, scene, and line numbers within the text. For discussion, see Heidi Hutner, *Colonial Women: Race and Culture in Stuart Drama* (New York: Oxford University Press, 2001), 45–64.

52 See Eugene M. Waith, *Ideas of Greatness: Heroic Drama in England* (London: Routledge, 1971); John Douglas Canfield, *Heroes and States: On the Ideology of Restoration Tragedy* (Lexington, KY: University Press of Kentucky, 2000).

53 Dryden praised Davenant for introducing 'examples of moral virtue' in his Interregnum drama. See Hollis, *The Absence of America*, 215–25, at 217.

Bibliography

Adams, Percy G., *Travel Literature and the Evolution of the Novel*. Lexington, KY: University Press of Kentucky, 1983.

Adrian, John M., *Local Negotiations of English Nationhood, 1570–1680*. Basingstoke: Palgrave Macmillan, 2011.

Agnew, Jean-Christophe, *Worlds Apart: The Market and the Theater in Anglo-American Thought, 1550–1750*. Cambridge University Press, 1986.

Akhimie, Patricia, 'Strange Episode: Race in Stage History', *Shakespeare Bulletin* 27, no. 3 (2009), 363–76.

Andrews, Kenneth R., *Trade, Plunder and Settlement: Maritime Enterprise and the Genesis of the British Empire, 1480–1630*. Cambridge University Press, 1984.

Ships, Money, and Politics: Seafaring and Naval Enterprise in the Reign of Charles I. Cambridge University Press, 1991.

Barbour, Richmond, *Before Orientalism: London's Theatre of the East, 1576–1626*. Cambridge University Press, 2003.

(ed.), *The Third Voyage Journals: Writing and Performance in the London East India Company, 1607–1610*. New York: Palgrave Macmillan, 2009.

Barker, Francis and Peter Hulme, 'Nymphs and Reapers Heavily Vanish: The Discursive Con-texts of *The Tempest*', in Francis Barker, Peter Hulme, and John Drakakis (ed.), *Alternative Shakespeares*. London: Routledge, 1985. 191–205.

Barker, Roberta and David Nicol, 'Does Beatrice Joanna Have a Subtext? *The Changeling* on the London Stage', *Early Modern Literary Studies* 10, no. 1 (May, 2004), 3.1–43. http://extra.shu.ac.uk/emls/10-1/barknico.htm

Bartels, Emily C., *Spectacles of Strangeness: Imperialism, Alienation, and Marlowe*. Philadelphia: University of Pennsylvania Press, 1993.

Bevington, David, Martin Butler, and Ian Donaldson (ed.), *The Cambridge Edition of the Works of Ben Jonson*. Cambridge University Press, 2012.

Birdwood, George (ed.), *The First Letter Book of the East India Company, 1600–1619*. London: Bernard Quaritch, 1893.

Blackmore, Josiah, 'The Shipwrecked Swimmer: Camões's Maritime Subject', *Modern Philology* 109, no. 3 (2012), 312–25.

The Inner Ship: Maritime Literary Culture in Early Modern Iberia. University of Chicago Press, forthcoming.

Blanton, Casey, *Travel Writing: The Self and the Word*. London: Routledge, 2002.

Boas, Frederick S., *Shakespeare and the Universities, and Other Studies in Elizabethan Drama*. Oxford: Basil Blackwell, 1923.

Boutcher, Warren, 'Marginal Commentaries: The Cultural Transmission of Montaigne's *Essais* in Shakespeare's England', in Pierre Kapitaniak (ed.), *Shakespeare et Montaigne: vers un nouvel humanisme*. Paris: Société Française Shakespeare, 2003. 13–27.

Brayshay, Mark, *Land Travel and Communications in Tudor and Stuart England: Achieving a Joined-up Realm*. Liverpool University Press, 2014.

Brayton, Dan, 'Angling in the Lake of Darkness: Possession, Dispossession, and the Politics of Discovery in *King Lear*', *English Literary History* 70, no. 2 (Summer 2003), 399–426.

Britland, Karen, *Drama at the Courts of Queen Henrietta Maria*. Cambridge University Press, 2006.

Brown, Paul, '"This thing of darkness I acknowledge mine": *The Tempest* and the Discourse of Colonialism', in Jonathan Dollimore and Alan Sinfield (ed.), *Political Shakespeare: Essays in Cultural Materialism*. Manchester University Press, 1985. 48–71.

Buisseret, David, *Monarchs, Ministers and Maps: The Emergence of Cartography as a Tool of Government in Early Modern Europe*. University of Chicago Press, 1992.

Burke, Peter and Roy Porter, *Languages and Jargons: Contributions to a Social History of Language*. Cambridge: Polity Press, 1995.

Burrow, Colin, *Epic Romance: Homer to Milton*. Oxford: Clarendon Press, 1993.

Burton, Jonathan, *Traffic and Turning: Islam and English Drama, 1579–1624*. Newark, DE: University of Delaware Press, 2005.

Butler, Martin, *The Stuart Court Masque and Political Culture*. Cambridge University Press, 2008.

Campbell, Mary B., *The Witness and the Other World: Exotic European Travel Writing, 400–1600*. Ithaca, NY: Cornell University Press, 1988.

Carey, Daniel, 'Hakluyt's Instructions: *The Principal Navigations* and Sixteenth-Century Travel Advice', *Studies in Travel Writing* 13, no. 2 (2009), 167–85.
  Continental Travel and Journeys Beyond Europe in the Early Modern Period: An Overlooked Connection. London: Hakluyt Society, 2009.
  'Truth, Lies and Travel Writing', in Carl Thompson (ed.) *The Routledge Companion to Travel Writing*. London: Routledge, 2016. 3–14.

Cartelli, Thomas, 'Prospero in Africa: *The Tempest* as Colonialist Text and Pretext', *Repositioning Shakespeare: National Formations, Postcolonial Appropriations*. London: Routledge, 1999.

Cartwright, Kent, *Theatre and Humanism: English Drama in the Sixteenth Century*. Cambridge University Press, 1999.

Certeau, Michel de, *L'invention du quotidien, vol. I: Arts de faire*. Paris: Gallimard, 1990.

Cheney, Patrick, *Marlowe's Counterfeit Profession: Ovid, Spenser, Counter-Nationhood*. University of Toronto Press, 1997.

Chew, Samuel C., *The Crescent and the Rose: Islam and England During the Renaissance*. New York: Oxford University Press, 1937.

Clare, Janet (ed.), *Drama of the English Republic, 1649–60*. Manchester University Press, 2002.

Clubb, Louise George, *Italian Drama in Shakespeare's Time*. New Haven, CT: Yale University Press, 1989.

Cohen, Ralph A., 'The Function of Setting in Eastward Ho', *Renaissance Papers* (1973), 85–96.

Coleman, David, 'Purchasing Purgatory: Economic Theology, Archipelagic Colonialism, and *Any Thing for a Quiet Life* (1621)', in David Coleman (ed.), *Region, Religion, and English Renaissance Literature*. Burlington, VT: Ashgate, 2013. 87–103.

Conley, Tom, 'The Essays and the New World', in Ulrich Langer (ed.), *The Cambridge Companion to Montaigne*. Cambridge University Press, 2005. 74–95.

Damish, Hubert, *L'Origine de la perspective*. Paris: Flammarion, 1987.

Dillon, Janette, *Language and Stage in Medieval and Renaissance England*. Cambridge University Press, 1998.

Dimmock, Matthew, *New Turkes: Dramatizing Islam and the Ottomans in Early Modern England*. London: Routledge, 2005.

Mythologies of the Prophet Muhammad in Early Modern English Culture. Cambridge University Press, 2013.

Duval, Edwin M., 'Lessons of the New World: Design and Meaning in Montaigne's "Des Cannibales" (I:31) and "Des Coches" (III:6)', *Yale French Studies* 64 (1983), 95–112.

Edelman, Charles (ed.), *The Stukeley Plays*. Manchester University Press, 2005.

Evans, G. Blakemore, 'The Authenticity of Keeling's Journal Entries on "Hamlet" and "Richard II"', *Notes & Queries* 196 (1951), 313–15.

'The Authenticity of the Keeling Journal Entries Reasserted', *Notes & Queries* 197 (1952), 127–28.

Fleming, Juliet, 'The French Garden: An Introduction to Women's French', *English Literary History* 56, no. 1 (1989), 19–51.

Forker, Charles, 'Shakespearean Imitation in Act 5 of *Anything for a Quiet Life*', *Papers on Language and Literature* 7 (1971), 75–80.

Foster, William, 'Forged Shakespeariana', *Notes & Queries* 145 (1900), 41–42.

'J. P. Collier's Fabrications', *Notes & Queries* 195 (1950), 414–15.

Fuchs, Barbara, *Mimesis and Empire: The New World, Islam, and European Identities*. Cambridge University Press, 2001.

Fury, Cheryl A., *Tides in the Affairs of Men: The Social History of Elizabethan Seamen, 1580–1603*. Westport, CT: Greenwood Press, 2002.

(ed.), *The Social History of English Seamen: 1485–1649*. Woodbridge: Boydell Press, 2012.

Gal, Ofer and Yi Zheng (ed.), *Motion and Knowledge in the Changing Early Modern World: Orbits, Routes and Vessels*. Dordrecht: Springer, 2014.

Games, Alison, *The Web of Empire: English Cosmopolitans in an Age of Expansion, 1560–1660*. Oxford University Press, 2009.

Gillies, John, *Shakespeare and the Geography of Difference*. Cambridge University Press, 1994.

Gillies, John and Virginia Mason Vaughan, *Playing the Globe: Genre and Geography in English Renaissance Drama*. Madison, NJ: Fairleigh Dickinson University Press, 1998.

Gordon, Andrew and Bernhard Klein (ed.), *Literature, Mapping, and the Politics of Space in Early Modern Britain*. Cambridge University Press, 2001.

Greenblatt, Stephen, *Marvellous Possessions: The Wonder of the New World*. Oxford: Clarendon Press, 1991.

Grogan, Jane, *The Persian Empire in English Writing, 1549–1622*. Basingstoke: Palgrave Macmillan, 2014.

Gunthio, Ambrose, 'A Running Commentary on the Hamlet of 1603', *European Magazine*, New Series, 1, no. 4 (Dec. 1825), 339–47.

Hadfield, Andrew, *Literature, Travel, and Colonial Writing in the English Renaissance, 1545–1625*. Oxford University Press, 1998.

(ed.), *Amazons, Savages and Machiavels: Travel and Colonial Writing in English, 1550–1630*. Oxford University Press, 2001.

'The Benefits of a Warm Study: The Resistance to Travel Before Empire', in Jyotsna G. Singh (ed.), *A Companion to the Global Renaissance: English Literature and Culture in the Era of Expansion*. Chichester: Blackwell, 2009. 101–13.

Hair, P. E. H., '*Hamlet* in an Afro-Portuguese Setting: New Perspectives on Sierra Leone in 1607', *History in Africa* 5 (1978), 21–42.

Africa Encountered: European Contacts and Evidence 1450–1700. Variorum Collected Studies Series. Aldershot: Ashgate, 1997.

Hamlin, William, 'Florio's Montaigne and the Tyranny of "Custome": Appropriation, Ideology, and Early English Readership of the *Essayes*', *Renaissance Quarterly* 63, no. 2 (2010), 491–544.

Hampton, Timothy, 'The Subject of America: History and Alterity in Montaigne's "Des Coches"', in Elizabeth Fowler and Roland Greene (ed.), *The Project of Prose in Early Modern Europe and the New World*. Cambridge University Press, 1997. 80–103.

Harris, Jonathan Gil, *Sick Economies: Drama, Mercantilism, and Disease in Shakespeare's England*. Philadelphia: University of Pennsylvania Press, 2003.

Marvellous Repossessions: The Tempest, Globalization, and the Waking Dream of Paradise. Vancouver: Ronsdale Press, 2012.

Harvey, P. D. A., *Maps in Tudor England*. London: British Library, 1993.

Hebb, David D., *Piracy and the English Government, 1616–1642*. Brookfield, VT: Ashgate, 1994.

Helgerson, Richard, *Forms of Nationhood: The Elizabethan Writing of England*. University of Chicago Press, 1992.

Self-Crowned Laureates: Spenser, Jonson, Milton, and the Literary System. Berkeley, CA: University of California Press, 1993.

Hoenselaars, A. J., *Images of Englishmen and Foreigners in the Drama of Shakespeare and His Contemporaries*. Rutherford, NJ: Fairleigh Dickinson University Press, 1992.

Holderness, Graham, *Tales from Shakespeare: Creative Collisions*. Cambridge University Press, 2014.

Holland, Peter, '"Travelling hopefully": The Dramatic Form of Journeys in English Renaissance Drama', in Jean-Pierre Maquerlot and Michèle Willems (ed.), *Travel and Drama in Shakespeare's Time*. Cambridge University Press, 1996. 160–78.

Hollis, Gavin Russell, 'Stage Directions: Shakespeare's Use of the Map', unpublished MPhil dissertation, Shakespeare Institute. 2000.

The Absence of America: the London Stage 1576–1642. Oxford University Press, 2015.

Horden, Peregrine and Nicholas Purcell, *The Corrupting Sea: A Study of Mediterranean History*. Oxford: Blackwell, 2000.

Houston, Chloë, '"Thou glorious kingdome, thou chiefe of Empires": Persia in Early Seventeenth-Century Travel Literature', *Studies in Travel Writing* 13, no. 2 (2009), 141–52.

Howard, Jean, 'Introduction: English Cosmopolitanism and the Early Modern Moment', *Shakespeare Studies* 35 (2007), 19–23.

Theater of a City: The Places of London Comedy, 1598–1642. Philadelphia: University of Pennsylvania Press, 2007.

Hsy, Jonathan Horng, *Trading Tongues: Merchants, Multilingualism, and Medieval Literature*. Columbus, OH: Ohio State University Press, 2013.

Hulme, Peter, *Colonial Encounters: Europe and the Native Caribbean, 1492–1791*. London: Methuen, 1986.

'Patagonian Cases: Travel Writing, Fiction, History', in Jan Borm (ed.), *Seuils & traverses: Enjeux de l'écriture du voyage*, vol. II, Brest: Centre de recherche bretonne et celtique, 2002. 223–37.

Hulme, Peter and William H. Sherman (ed.), *'The Tempest' and Its Travels*. London: Reaktion Books, 2000.

Hutner, Heidi, *Colonial Women: Race and Culture in Stuart Drama*. Oxford University Press, 2001.

Ingram, Anders, *Turkish History in Early Modern England*. London: Palgrave, 2015.

Ingram, Jill, 'Economies of Obligation in *Eastward Ho*', *Ben Jonson Journal* 11 (2004), 21–40.

Jacobson, Miriam, *Barbarous Antiquity: Reorienting the Past in the Poetry of Early Modern England*. Philadelphia: University of Pennsylvania Press, 2014.

Jenner, Mark, 'Circulation and Disorder: London Streets and Hackney Coaches, *c*.1640–*c*.1740', in Tim Hitchcock and Heather Shore (ed.), *The Streets of London from the Great Fire to the Great Stink*. London: Rivers Oram Press, 2003. 40–53.

Jones, Gwilym, *Shakespeare's Storms*. Manchester University Press, 2015.

Jowitt, Claire, *Voyage Drama and Gender Politics, 1589–1642: Real and Imagined Worlds*. Manchester University Press, 2003.

The Culture of Piracy, 1580–1630: English Literature and Seaborne Crime. Farnham: Ashgate, 2010.

'Hakluyt's Legacy: Armchair Travel in English Renaissance Drama', in Daniel Carey and Claire Jowitt (ed.), *Richard Hakluyt and Travel Writing in Early Modern Europe*. Farnham: Ashgate, 2012. 295–306.

Kermode, Lloyd E., 'Experiencing the Space and Place of Early Modern Theatre', *Journal of Medieval and Early Modern Studies* 43, no. 1 (Winter 2013), 1–24.

Kliman, Bernice, 'At Sea About *Hamlet* at Sea: A Detective Story', *Shakespeare Quarterly* 62, no. 2 (2011), 180–204.

Kroll, Richard, *Restoration Drama and "The Circle of Commerce": Tragicomedy, Politics, and Trade in the Seventeenth Century*. Cambridge University Press, 2007.

Lee, Sir Sidney, *A Life of William Shakespeare*. London: Smith, Elder 1898.

Lockey, Brian, *Early Modern Catholics, Royalists, and Cosmopolitans: English Transnationalism and the Christian Commonwealth*. Farnham: Ashgate, 2015.

Loomba, Ania, 'Shakespearean Transformations', in John Joughin (ed.), *Shakespeare and National Culture*. Manchester University Press, 1997. 109–41.

Loxley, James, Anna Groundwater, and Julie Sanders (ed.), *Ben Jonson's Walk to Scotland: An Annotated Edition of the 'Foot Voyage'*. Cambridge University Press, 2014.

Lupton, Julia Reinhardt, 'Creature Caliban', *Shakespeare Quarterly* 51 (2000), 1–23.

MacLean, Gerald, *Looking East: English Writing and the Ottoman Empire Before 1800*. Basingstoke: Palgrave Macmillan, 2007.

Maquerlot, Jean-Pierre and Michèle Willems (ed.), *Travel and Drama in Shakespeare's Time*. Cambridge University Press, 1996.

Marin, Louis, *Utopics: Spatial Play*, Robert A. Vollrath (trans.). London: Macmillan, 1984.

Markham, Clements R. (ed.), *The Voyages of Sir James Lancaster, Kt., to the East Indies*. London: Hakluyt Society, 1877.

Markley, Robert, *The Far East and the English Imagination, 1600–1730*. Cambridge University Press, 2006.

Matar, Nabil, *Islam in Britain 1558–1685*. Cambridge University Press, 1998.
  Turks, Moors and Englishmen in the Age of Discovery. New York: Columbia University Press, 1999.
  Britain and Barbary 1589–1689. Gainesville, FL: University of Florida Press, 2005.

Matei-Chesnoiu, Monica, *Re-imagining Western European Geography in English Renaissance Drama*. Basingstoke: Palgrave Macmillan, 2012.

Matvejevic, Predrag, *Mediterranean: A Cultural Landscape*, Michael Henry Heim (trans.). Berkeley, CA: University of California Press, 1999.

McInnis, David, 'Lost Plays from Early Modern England: Voyage Drama, A Case Study', *Literature Compass* 8, no. 8 (2011), 534–42.
  Mind-Travelling and Voyage Drama in Early Modern England. Basingstoke: Palgrave Macmillan, 2013.

McInnis, David and Matthew Steggle (ed.), *Lost Plays in Shakespeare's England*. Basingstoke: Palgrave Macmillan, 2014.

McJannet, Linda, *The Sultan Speaks: Dialogue in English Plays and Histories About the Ottoman Turks*. New York: Palgrave Macmillan, 2006.

McMullan, Gordon, '*The Changeling* and the Dynamics of Ugliness', in Emma Smith and Garrett A. Sullivan, Jr. (ed.), *The Cambridge Companion to English Renaissance Tragedy*. Cambridge University Press, 2010. 222–35.

McRae, Andrew, *Literature and Domestic Travel in Early Modern England.* Cambridge University Press, 2009.

Mendieta, Eduardo, 'From Imperial to Dialogical Cosmopolitanism', *Ethics & Global Politics* 2, no. 3 (2009), 241–58.

Mentz, Steve, 'Toward a Blue Cultural Studies: The Sea, Maritime Culture, and Early Modern English Literature', *Literature Compass* 6 (2009), 997–1013.

At the Bottom of Shakespeare's Ocean. London: Bloomsbury, 2009.

'Half-fish, half-flesh: Dolphins, Humans, and the Early Modern Ocean', in Jean Feerick and Vin Nardizzi (ed.), *The Indistinct Human in Renaissance Literature.* London: Palgrave, 2012. 29–46.

Merritt, Julia F., *The Social World of Early Modern Westminster: Abbey, Court, and Community 1525–1640.* Manchester University Press, 2005.

Miner, Earl, 'The Wild Man Through the Looking Glass', in Edward Dudley and Maximillian E. Novak (ed.), *The Wild Man Within: An Image in Western Thought from the Renaissance to Romanticism.* University of Pittsburgh Press, 1972. 87–114.

Montgomery, Marianne, *Europe's Languages on England's Stages: 1590–1620.* Burlington, VT: Ashgate, 2012.

Murray, Barbara A., *Restoration Shakespeare: Viewing the Voice.* London: Associated University Presses, 2001.

Neill, Michael, *Issues of Death: Mortality and Identity in English Renaissance Tragedy.* Oxford: Clarendon Press, 1997.

'Turn and Counterturn: Merchanting, Apostasy and Tragicomic Form in Massinger's *The Renegado*', in Subha Mukherji and Raphael Lyne (ed.), *Early Modern Tragicomedy.* Cambridge: D. S. Brewer, 2007. 154–74.

Netzloff, Mark, *England's Internal Colonies: Class, Capital, and the Literature of Early Modern English Colonialism.* New York: Palgrave, 2003.

Nuti, Lucia, 'The Perspective Plan in the Sixteenth Century: The Invention of a Representational Language', *Art Bulletin* 76, no. 1 (March 1994), 105–28.

Orgel, Stephen, *The Illusion of Power: Political Theatre in the English Renaissance.* Berkeley, CA: University of California Press, 1975.

Orr, Bridget, *Empire on the English Stage: 1660–1714.* Cambridge University Press, 2001.

Orrell, John, *The Theatres of Inigo Jones and John Webb.* Cambridge University Press, 1985.

The Human Stage: English Theat Design, 1567–1640. Cambridge University Press, 1988.

Ostovich, Helen et al. (ed.), *The Mysterious and the Foreign in Early Modern England.* Newark, DE: University of Delaware Press, 2008.

Parente, James A., *Religious Drama and the Humanist Tradition.* Leiden: E. J. Brill, 1987.

Parr, Anthony (ed.), *Three Renaissance Travel Plays.* Manchester University Press, 1995.

Parr, Anthony, 'Foreign Relations in Jacobean England: The Sherley Brothers and the "Voyage of Persia"', in Jean-Pierre Maquerlot and Michèle Willems (ed.), *Travel and Drama in Shakespeare's Time.* Cambridge University Press, 1996. 14–31.

'"Going to Constantinople": English Wager-Journeys to the Ottoman World in the Early Modern Period', *Studies in Travel Writing* 16, no. 4 (2012), 349–61.

Renaissance Mad Voyages: Experiments in Early Modern English Travel. Farnham: Ashgate, 2015.

Race, Sydney, 'J. P. Collier's Fabrications', *Notes & Queries* 195 (1950), 345–46.

'The Authenticity of Keeling's Journal Entries on "Hamlet" and "Richard II"', *Notes & Queries* 196 (1951), 513–15.

'The Authenticity of the Keeling Journal Entries', *Notes & Queries* 197 (1952), 181–82.

Ray, Sid, 'Marlow(e)'s Africa: Postcolonial Queenship in Conrad's *Heart of Darkness* and Marlowe's *Dido, Queen of Carthage*', *Conradiana* 38, no. 2 (2006), 143–61.

Rubiés, Joan-Pau, 'Instructions for Travellers: Teaching the Eye to See', *History and Anthropology* 9 (1996), 139–90.

Rundall, Thomas (ed.), *Narrative of Voyages Towards the North-West, in Search of a Passage to Cathay and India, 1496–1631*, Hakluyt Society first series, 5. London: Hakluyt Society, 1849.

Sacks, David Harris, 'Richard Hakluyt and His Publics, c.1580–1620', in Bronwen Wilson and Paul Yachnin (ed.), *Making Publics in Early Modern Europe: People, Things, Forms of Knowledge*. New York: Routledge, 2010. 159–76.

Sager, Jenny, *The Aesthetics of Spectacle in Early Modern Drama*. Houndmills: Palgrave Macmillan, 2013.

Samson, Alexander (ed.), *The Spanish Match*. Aldershot: Ashgate, 2006.

Sanders, Julie, *The Cultural Geography of Early Modern Drama, 1620–1650*. Cambridge University Press, 2011.

'Geographies of Performance in the Early Modern Midlands', in Susan Bennett and Mary Polito (ed.), *Performing Environments: Site-Specificity in Medieval and Early Modern English Drama*. Basingstoke: Palgrave Macmillan, 2014. 119–37.

Scammell, G. V., 'Manning the English Merchant Service in the Sixteenth Century', *The Mariner's Mirror* 56, no. 2 (1970), 131–54.

Scanlan, Thomas, *Colonial Writing and the New World, 1583–1671: Allegories of Desire*. Cambridge University Press, 1999.

Schleck, Julia, *Telling True Tales of Islamic Lands: Forms of Meditation in English Travel Writing, 1575–1630*. Cranbury, NJ: Associated University Presses, 2011.

Scott, Hamish, 'Travel and Communications', in Hamish Scott (ed.), *The Oxford Handbook of Early Modern European History, 1350–1750. Volume I: Peoples & Place*. Oxford University Press, 2015. 165–91.

Seaton, Ethel, 'Marlowe's Map', *Essays and Studies by Members of the English Association* 10 (1924), 13–35.

Sebek, Barbara and Stephen Deng (ed.), *Global Traffic: Discourses and Practices of Trade in English Literature and Culture from 1550 to 1700*. New York: Palgrave Macmillan, 2008.

Sell, Jonathan P., *Rhetoric and Wonder in English Travel Writing, 1560–1613*. Aldershot: Ashgate, 2006.

Semler, L. E., 'Marlovian Therapy: The Chastisement of Ovid in *Hero and Leander*', *English Literary Renaissance* 35, no. 2 (2005), 159–86.

Shickman, Alan, 'The "Perspective Glass" in Shakespeare's *Richard II*', *Studies in English Literature 1500–1900* 18, no. 2 (April 1978), 217–28.

Short, John Rennie, *Making Space: Revisioning the World, 1475–1600*. Syracuse, NY: University of Syracuse Press, 2004.

Singh, Jyotsna G. (ed.), *A Companion to the Global Renaissance: English Literature and Culture in the Era of Expansion*. Oxford: Wiley-Blackwell, 2009.

Skura, Meredith Anne, 'Discourse and the Individual: The Case of Colonialism in *The Tempest*', *Shakespeare Quarterly* 40 (1989), 42–74.

Smith, Bruce R., 'Taking the Measure of Global Space', *Journal of Medieval and Early Modern Studies* 43, no. 1 (Winter 2013), 25–48.

Smith, D. K., *The Cartographic Imagination in Early Modern England*. Aldershot: Ashgate, 2008.

Smith, Grady (trans. and ed.), *Travel Abroad: Frulovisi's 'Peregrinatio'*. Tempe, AZ: Arizona Centre for Medieval and Renaissance Studies, 2003.

Spiller, Elizabeth, 'Shakespeare and the Making of Early Modern Science: Resituating Prospero's Art', *South Central Review* 26, nos. 1 and 2 (2009), 24–41.

Stachniewski, John, 'Calvinist Psychology in Middleton's Tragedies', in R. V. Holdsworth (ed.), *Three Jacobean Revenge Tragedies*. Basingstoke: Macmillan, 1990. 226–47.

Stanivukovic, Goran (ed.), *Remapping the Mediterranean World in Early Modern English Writings*. London: Palgrave Macmillan, 2007.

   Knights in Arms: Prose Romance, Masculinity, and Eastern Mediterranean Trade in Early Modern England, 1565–1655. University of Toronto Press, 2016.

Starobinski, Jean, *Montaigne in Motion*, Arthur Goldhammer (trans.). University of Chicago Press, 1985.

Sullivan, Jr., Garrett A., *The Drama of Landscape: Land, Property, and Social Relations on the Early Modern Stage*. Stanford, CA: Stanford University Press, 1999.

Suranyi, Anna, *The Genius of the English Nation: Travel Writing and National Identity in Early Modern England*. Newark, DE: University of Delaware Press, 2008.

Taylor, Gary, '*Hamlet* in Africa, 1607', in Ivo Kamps and Jyotsna Singh (ed.), *Travel Knowledge: European 'Discoveries' in the Early Modern Period*. New York: Palgrave, 2001. 223–48.

Tazon, Juan E., *The Life and Times of Thomas Stukeley, 1525–1578*. Burlington, VT: Ashgate, 2003.

Thomson, Janice E., *Mercenaries, Pirates, and Sovereigns: State-building and Extraterritorial Violence in Early Modern Europe*. Princeton University Press, 1994.

Traub, Valerie, 'The Nature of Norms in Early Modern England: Anatomy, Cartography, *King Lear*', *South Central Review* 26, nos. 1–2 (2009), 42–81.

Tribble, Evelyn, 'Distributing Cognition in the Globe', *Shakespeare Quarterly* 56, no. 2 (2005), 135–55.

Turner, Henry S., *The English Renaissance Stage: Geometry, Poetics, and the Practical Spatial Arts, 1580–1630*. Oxford University Press, 2006.

Van Den Abbeele, Georges, *Travel as Metaphor from Montaigne to Rousseau.* Minneapolis, MN: University of Minnesota Press, 1991.

Vaughan, Alden T., 'William Strachey's "True Reportory" and Shakespeare: A Closer Look at the Evidence', *Shakespeare Quarterly* 59 (2008), 245–73.

Vitkus, Daniel, *Turking Turk: English Theater and the Multicultural Mediterranean,1570–1630.* New York: Palgrave, 2003.

'Poisoned Figs, or "The Traveller's Religion": Travel, Trade and Conversion in Early Modern English Culture', in Goran Stanivukovic (ed.), *Remapping the Mediterranean World in Early Modern English Writings.* New York: Palgrave, 2007. 41–58.

'Labour and Travel on the Early Modern Stage: Representing the Travail of Travel in Dekker's *Old Fortunatus* and Shakespeare's *Pericles*', in Michelle M. Dowd and Natasha Korda (ed.), *Working Subjects in Early Modern Drama.* London: Routledge, 2016. 225–42.

Walker, Greg, *Plays of Persuasion: Drama and Politics at the Court of Henry VIII.* Cambridge University Press, 1991.

West, William N., 'Intertheatricality', in Henry S. Turner (ed.), *Oxford Twenty-First Century Approaches to Literature: Early Modern Theatricality.* Oxford University Press, 2013. 151–172.

Williams, Clare (ed. and trans.), *Thomas Platter's Travels in England 1599.* London: Jonathan Cape, 1937.

Wilson, Peter Lamborn, *Pirate Utopias: Moorish Corsairs and European Renegadoes*, 2nd edn. New York: Autonomedia, 2003.

Wilson, Richard, 'Visible Bullets: *Tamburlaine the Great* and Ivan the Terrible', in D. Grantley and P. Roberts (ed.), *Christopher Marlowe and English Renaissance Culture.* Aldershot: Scolar, 1996. 51–69.

Woodward, David, *The History of Cartography, vol. III. Cartography in the European Renaissance*, part 2. University of Chicago Press, 2007.

Woodward, Hobson, *A Brave Vessel: The True Tale of the Castaways Who Rescued Jamestown.* New York: Penguin, 2009.

Youngs, Tim, *Cambridge Introduction to Travel Writing.* Cambridge University Press, 2013.

Zwierlein, Anne-Julia, 'Shipwrecks in the City: Commercial Risk as Romance in Early Modern City Comedy', in Dieter Mehl, Angela Stock, and Anne-Julia Zwierlein (ed.), *Plotting Early Modern London: New Essays on Jacobean City Comedy.* Aldershot: Ashgate, 2004: 75–94.

Index